AMERICA INVULNERABLE

THE QUEST FOR ABSOLUTE SECURITY
FROM 1812 TO STAR WARS

BY

JAMES CHACE

AND

CALEB CARR

SUMMIT BOOKS

NEW YORK   LONDON   TORONTO   SYDNEY   TOKYO

Copyright © 1988 by Swain Enterprises and Caleb Carr

All rights reserved
including the right of reproduction
in whole or in part in any form.
Published by SUMMIT BOOKS
A Division of Simon & Schuster Inc.
Simon & Schuster Building
Rockefeller Center
1230 Avenue of the Americas
New York, NY 10020
SUMMIT BOOKS and colophon are trademarks of Simon & Schuster Inc.

Designed by Irving Perkins Associates
Manufactured in the United States of America

1   3   5   7   9   10   8   6   4   2

Library of Congress Cataloging in Publication Data
Chace, James.

America invulnerable: the quest for absolute security from 1812
to Star Wars/by James Chace and Caleb Carr.
p. cm.
Bibliography: p.
Includes index.
ISBN 0-671-61778-8
1. United States—National security.   I. Carr, Caleb.
II. Title.
UA23.C45   1988   87-31686
355'.033073—dc19   CIP

THIS BOOK IS DEDICATED TO
NICHOLAS X. RIZOPOULOS

ACKNOWLEDGMENTS

We have dedicated this book to Nicholas X. Rizopoulos, in gratitude for his wise counsel and extraordinary editorial skills, and in appreciation of his profound understanding of the effect of history on policy.

Robert Dallek, Paul M. Kennedy and Walter LaFeber have read the entire manuscript, and we are deeply grateful for their comments and suggestions.

Arthur Samuelson and James Silberman have encouraged this project from the outset; their editorial guidance has been of signal importance to its success.

F. Joseph Spieler's enthusiasm for this work sustained us both during its conception and its execution.

Our special thanks to the John Simon Guggenheim Foundation for its financial assistance.

The staffs of the New York Society Library, the Economics and Public Affairs Division of the New York Public Library, Yale University's Sterling Library, the Seeley G. Mudd Library at Princeton University, the Franklin D. Roosevelt Library at Hyde Park, and the Military and Diplomatic History departments of the National Archives all rendered invaluable assistance in making it possible for us to do the needed research.

Our particular thanks go to Janis Kreslins and the rest of the staff at the Council on Foreign Relations Library, Martha Crawley at the U.S. Navy's Operational Archives, Dr. Richard Sommers and David Keough at the U.S. Army's Military History Institute, Linda Hanson at the Lyndon Baines Johnson Library and Dennis Bilger at the Harry S. Truman Library.

Susan Chace has shown us patience beyond measure, as well as consideration and understanding for our travails. This book is her gift to us.

CONTENTS

PROLOGUE

AS Henry Adams once observed, "Of all historical problems, the nature of a national character is the most difficult and the most important." Fundamental to the understanding of any nation's character is an exploration of how its people have chosen to define their country's territorial integrity and provide for the security of the state and its institutions. Throughout history, leaders of empires and republics alike have been called on to respond to threats from abroad. In maintaining the integrity of their borders and their governments, these leaders established patterns of behavior that eventually became national characteristics, and determined in no small degree how each of their countries would interact with other members of the world community in generations to come.

In the United States, the leadership both in the Congress and the executive has shown itself especially sensitive to the possibility of external threat. Although there is a tendency today to think of "national security" as a modern concept—quite possibly because the National Security Council is a comparatively recent creation (formed under Harry Truman in 1947), and because its rise to

eminence as an arm of foreign-policy making has been rapid and
often dramatic—the principle of national security is modern only
in its terminology. Long before there were White House advisers
packed into basement offices, security issues exercised a powerful
influence over American behavior in international affairs. Indeed,
national security was the realm of foreign policy that most concerned the Founding Fathers. We are and have always been a nation preoccupied with security. But because of the special way in
which we have defined that security, our preoccupation has often
taken a violent form that Americans themselves have been hard
put to understand.

Since the earliest days of the republic, the United States has
sought to ensure the political and territorial integrity of the nation
without the assistance of other powers. Though willing to cooperate with other nations of the world in economic matters, the United
States has been singularly unwilling to allow outside involvement
in questions of national safety. This solitary—or unilateral—approach to security affairs has carried with it an implicitly absolute
goal: not to permit America's security to be undermined by the
behavior of other powers. Such an approach also brought with it a
strong disposition to respond militarily to any perceived threat, for
the nation that chooses to treat any danger—actual or potential—
as less than vital runs the risk of seeing other powers seize geographic or political positions of perilous influence. Because of this
danger, Americans have never shied away from employing force
unilaterally—either in defense of their own borders or in foreign
regions viewed as vital—as a way of grappling with perceived
threats to the security of the nation.

Americans have, of course, gone to war for a variety of specific
reasons—to expand their territory for economic gain, in response
to affronts to their national honor and territorial integrity, to secure their nation's role as the guardian of freedom and the pro-
moter of democratic values. But the overarching response to
America's need for safety and well-being has been the use of unilateral action as the surest method of achieving national security.
This is not to say that all American statesmen have seen absolute
security as an immediately attainable goal; most have been forced
by the realities of world politics to accept it only as an ultimate end.
But for over two centuries the aspiration toward an eventual condition of absolute security has been viewed as central to an effective
American foreign policy.

That military action should so often have accompanied this aspiration is not surprising. Statesmen have only two basic tools at their disposal when pursuing the national interest—diplomatic negotiation and military force. But negotiation—and this point has never been lost on America's leaders—implies compromise. Absolute security, on the other hand, cannot be negotiated; it can only be won. This is especially true when the nation that seeks it acts in solitude.

Solitude—not isolation. The American reluctance, and often refusal, to use diplomatic means before resorting to military force as a way of ensuring national security cannot be seen as isolationism, when the alternative path chosen required both declared wars with rival powers and intervention in the affairs of other states. Despite popular conceptions to the contrary, then, the United States has never been truly isolationist. Even in the period between the two world wars, America was only isolationist toward Europe; in the Western Hemisphere, the United States was openly interventionist; and in the Far East, Washington played an active role. True, most American leaders have fully appreciated the large measure of safety from external threats—what has been called "free security"—that America's geographical position offered. As Thomas Jefferson himself said, the fact that the United States was "separated by nature and a wide ocean from the exterminating havoc of one quarter of the globe" was, and has remained, a blessing to the cause of American security. But no American leader, including Jefferson, has ever been prepared to see the nation's safety rely on that blessing alone. Military interventions—not only in the Western Hemisphere but in all parts of the world—have also been seen as necessary in order to safeguard the American people.

This principle was first driven home with dramatic force in 1812, when a new breed of American nationalists—men whose zeal, unlike that of the Founding Fathers, had not been tempered by experience—spurred the country into open hostilities with Great Britain in order to remove even the possibility of future British interference on the borders of the United States. The War of 1812 saw military stalemates and later the destruction of America's new capital—but rather than prompting doubt over the need to pursue absolute security unilaterally, the burning of Washington only heightened the sense of urgency that surrounded that quest. During subsequent generations, this urgency grew as American power and world interests increased, and inspired ever more extensive attempts to secure the United States against any and all foreign threats.

For example, our activist and even aggressive foreign policy in the mid- to late nineteenth century centered on our continued anxiety over British intervention in the Western Hemisphere following the War of 1812. But that policy did not disappear when the British threat evaporated in the 1890s. At the turn of the nineteenth century, with the domestic American economy increasingly dependent on foreign markets, the search for security against such rising naval powers as Germany and Japan led to the creation of a world-class fleet, while fears of strategic and economic dislocation meant sending that fleet to remote parts of the world in order to gain overseas bases.

Then, in the years just before World War I, radical ideologies of the left and right gravely affected America's perception of security. The rise of imperial German militarism represented a clear danger to the nation; and the threats of socialism, communism and anarchism, while not purely territorial, were nonetheless viewed as perils that could undermine the strength and even the physical safety of the United States by promoting internal dissent and civil strife. These threats were countered by American presidents, most notably Woodrow Wilson, by exporting American liberal democracy— under the protection of U.S. troops—to Latin America, Europe and Asia.

Traditional territorial fears thus merged with ideological threats in determining America's international behavior, and during the Second World War and the Cold War that followed it, these anxieties prompted the creation of interventionist policies unprecedented in their global scope. In our own time, the legacy of the Cold War—the need for a universal response to both physical and ideological threats—has not only led American forces into remote regions such as Vietnam and Lebanon, but has finally provoked a defense program that takes our two-century-old quest for absolute security into a new realm—outer space.

During the course of this quest, Americans have on occasion also found it in their interest to follow George Washington's advice to "safely trust to temporary alliances for extraordinary emergencies." Some of our most important and extensive military endeavors—particularly during the two world wars—have resulted from this practice. But these undertakings have been the exceptions rather than the rule in America's efforts to attain national security. Following more consistently Washington's directive to "steer clear of permanent alliances with any portion of the foreign world," the United States has far more often sent its troops abroad without real allies; and although many of these activities have become obscured by their smaller scale and their often confused motives, they are of equal importance in trying to trace out an American security tradition.

Thus James Polk's conquest of California in 1846, sparked primarily by perceptions of foreign threat, merits a place alongside the more celebrated American campaigns in Texas and Mexico, which were prompted by a much broader range of interests; Woodrow Wilson's Siberian expedition of 1918 deserves attention as the purest and most extensive embodiment of that troubled president's fear of radical ideologies; and America's annexation of the Philippines and subsequent expansion of her strategic interests in the Pacific during the early twentieth century—all undertaken in the name of national security—led to an almost inevitable reckoning with Japan and ultimately to American entry into World War II. By focusing on such episodes, we can see a pattern of behavior in America's efforts to secure the nation from both territorial and ideological threats.

That pattern has consisted of quick and forceful American responses not only to *actual* dangers but also to *perceived* threats. It is important to bear in mind, when analyzing these responses, that while there was sometimes an adequate basis for military action in America's search for absolute security, there often was not. But, above all, in the overwhelming majority of cases American leaders *believed* the dangers to be real. It is of less importance in this respect to say that in the 1840s Great Britain had no desire to impose its designs on California or Oregon to the point of war than it is to try to understand why President Polk saw the British as willing and able to do so. Only by grasping how American leaders saw the world around them at the time that they were forced—or *felt* they were forced—to take action can we begin to understand America's remarkably consistent perception of her security. And only by understanding both the causes and the expression of that perception can we hope to alter it.

Such an alteration is clearly called for. Since the time of the Revolution, there have also been American leaders who have warned us that the goal of absolute security was, in Alexander Hamilton's words, a "deceitful dream," one based on false confi-

dence in American moral exceptionalism and geographical remoteness and on exaggerated fears that the United States, because
of its democratic government and its wealth of natural resources,
had been targeted for attack by foreign powers. Senator Thomas
Hart Benton, during the Polk presidency, dismissed fear of Great
Britain as "a cry of wolf where there was no wolf"; Woodrow Wilson's secretary of state, Robert Lansing, warned that Wilson's consistent refusal to confront complex political realities openly and his
subsequent retreat into the utopian dream of a League of Nations
represented "a plaything of the President's mind which he takes to
bed with him" and that would sow the seeds of future conflict; and
Franklin D. Roosevelt's secretary of war, Henry Stimson—having
learned the hard lessons of America's failure to balance goals with
capabilities in the Pacific during the 1920s and 1930s—urged a
policy of realistic accommodation, rather than confrontation, with
the Soviet Union following the conclusion of World War II.

This dissenting strain in the story of America's quest for absolute
security has also arisen from the perception of threat. But these
warnings have largely gone unheeded. To explore the nature of
this failure is essential to any understanding of how America has
defined and pursued her national security. In the nuclear age especially, to ignore such voices of reason could ultimately endanger
not only the integrity but even the very existence of the republic.

I

THE BURNING OF WASHINGTON—
ABSOLUTE VULNERABILITY

1811–1815

ON August 3, 1814, a force of 5,000 British soldiers, sailors and marines embarked from Bermuda for the mid-Atlantic coast of the United States. Among them were 3,800 seasoned infantrymen, veterans of the Peninsular campaign against Napoleon—"Wellington's Invincibles." For five years they had fought alongside other British units and native guerrillas on the plains and in the mountains of Spain, costing Bonaparte 50,000 men a year and contributing significantly to the emperor's first abdication. Now, together with the smaller contingents of sailors and marines, they were turning their attention to another enemy, one whose experience in organized warfare was far more limited—and whose determination the redcoated foot soldiers had good reason to doubt.

The commander of this force, General Robert Ross, was a handsome and immensely brave officer known for preferring the front line of battle to the safety of his headquarters—in the Peninsula, he had had two horses shot out from under him. Graced with personal charm and an easy Irish smile, Ross was nonetheless a strict disciplinarian and an accomplished student of Wellingtonian strategy, which he had studied firsthand in the Duke's service. But on this latest campaign, the general would have little opportunity to use it. His orders from London were ambiguous in their language, specific in their meaning: Ross was to "effect a diversion on the coasts of the United States of America in favor of the army employed in the defence of Upper and Lower Canada."

For just over two years, the United States and Great Britain had been at war in North America. Up to this point, however, the main fighting had occurred on the western frontiers and in the north. Both sides had dramatic victories to their credit, but the war remained a stalemate in 1814. It was because of this deadlock that British troops were now moving up the Atlantic coast. General Ross and his naval co-commander, Vice-Admiral Sir Alexander Cochrane, had set out on a mission that they hoped would so demoralize and distract the Americans that an important victory might be won in the areas of established conflict to the north. As Cochrane had written before leaving for America, "I have it very much at heart to give them a complete drubbing before the peace is made." Moving into the Chesapeake Bay and then the Patuxent River in eastern Maryland, Cochrane's first move was to rendezvous with a man who knew a good deal about "drubbing" Americans.

Rear-Admiral Sir George Cockburn had, during the spring and summer of 1814, become something of a nightmare to Americans living in the Chesapeake area. Brash, confident and possessed of a genius for destruction, Cockburn had taken the lighter ships of Cochrane's North American squadron—responsible for blockading the trade of the United States—and embarked on an amphibious campaign of raiding farms, stealing tobacco crops, burning towns, terrorizing civilians and, when he could find them, crushing the local militia. He carried out these acts with a gallant zest that only further infuriated the civil population; as Theodore Roosevelt later observed in his classic study of the war's naval operations, "The government of the United States was, in fact, supported by the people in its war policy very largely on account of these excesses." But Cockburn's schemes had yet to reach their outlandish apex.

After meeting with Cochrane in the Patuxent east of the new American capital of Washington, Cockburn convinced his senior officer as well as General Ross that the time was ripe for a decisive move against the American interior. Ross's men debarked from

Cochrane's ships at Benedict, Maryland, on August 19 and made ready to march alongside Cockburn's sailors. American observers of these movements, reporting back to their capital, could give no definite indication as to what direction the British march might take. Unaware of their enemy's specific intentions, Washingtonians went about their affairs in the style that had already become characteristic of their city.

Though it had not reached the grandiose dimensions envisioned by its designer, Pierre L'Enfant, the Washington of 1814 made up in spirit what it lacked in size. Paris might have been more sophisticated, and London more commercial, but the American capital— despite its extreme climate, primitive roads and shortage of housing—was nonetheless socially lively and intellectually refreshing. European ministers and plenipotentiaries found the ladies of Washington charming and the endless rounds of parties diverting —if sometimes spiced by rough-edged courtesy. Since the reserved and philosophical James Madison had become president in 1809, Washington society had been presided over by his wife, who did not share her husband's subdued social manner. Dolley Madison, tireless in her vivacity, had given an air of celebration to a city that was, like the First Lady herself, uniquely American, an intriguing blend of courtly manners and native ingenuousness. By day, the business of the nation was conducted with gusto; by night, the celebration of a still-young nation was carried on in like spirit.

In fact, so preoccupied with the affairs of its statesmen and the parties of its hostesses was Washington that in the two years the United States had been at war, no defenses had been constructed anywhere within or outside the city.

When news of the British landing in the Patuxent reached Washington, the city responded in typical fashion. Everywhere there was activity, yet almost none of it was directed to any purpose. Militia and regulars were called out, but no one was able to find their commander, General William Winder. Winder, a competent bureaucrat but a cautious and irresolute field commander, was in fact not absent from the city, but simply locked away in his office, trying to sort out the administrative problems involved in creating a new force with which to protect a district that had no plans for its own defense. In his efforts to organize an effective command, Winder initially received little assistance from either government officials or civilians, most of whom refused to believe that the British were contemplating an attack on Washington—Baltimore, perhaps, or

Annapolis, but not the capital. Winder himself was somewhat skeptical, as were his superiors, most notably Secretary of War John Armstrong. A capable but cripplingly egotistical man, Armstrong summed up popular sentiment about the invasion best when he stated incredulously, "They certainly will not come here; what the devil would they do here?"

Only Madison himself was initially willing to accept the idea that the British might be making for Washington. Physically slight and personally unimposing, dressed invariably in drab black, "Little Jemmy" (as Washington Irving had labeled him) nonetheless possessed a prodigious intellect, one that left its powerful imprint on the Constitutional Convention and *The Federalist Papers*. Thomas Jefferson had said of his fellow Virginian, "I do not know in the world a man of purer integrity, more dispassionate, disinterested, and devoted to genuine Republicanism; nor would I in the whole scope of America and Europe point out an abler head." But Madison's great mind could not disguise the idiosyncrasies of his character. Since childhood he had been a hypochondriac who showed little interest in managing his family's large Virginia plantation. Instead, the young Madison retreated into a world of books and study, a solitary existence that left him with a lifelong inability to relate to those around him except on the most private level; even in aristocratic Virginia, such was a severe handicap for an aspiring politician. But his deep insight, especially into the issues of religious freedom and centralized government, outweighed his personal peculiarities and propelled him to national fame—and that same insight, in the summer of 1814, allowed him to interpret British movements in eastern Maryland with greater accuracy than the politicians and soldiers around him.

Ross's and Cockburn's actions following the landing near Benedict indicated, to Madison, "the most inveterate spirits against the Southern States," an antipathy that "may be expected to shew itself against every object within the reach of vindictive enterprize. Among these the seat of Government cannot fail to be a favorite one." The president expressed such thoughts repeatedly to Secretary of War Armstrong, who—having failed to receive actual command of the Washington defenses because some members of the administration considered him politically and militarily unreliable—seemed more than ready to let the city shift for itself. Masking extreme bitterness behind a condescending and sometimes blasé attitude, the secretary offered no constructive advice during this period of gravest danger.

As American soldiers began to drill in a square across from the White House, definite indication of British intentions still had not reached the capital. Finally, in a move typical of his pragmatic, hardworking farmer's background, Secretary of State James Monroe (a colonel during the Revolution) took thirty dragoons and headed east to himself scout for the British main force. Monroe drove his dragoons to the point of exhaustion, but never caught more than a fleeting glimpse of Ross and Cockburn. In light of Cockburn's previous activities in the area, the British began to take on the dimensions of a phantom menace, and as the presumed advances on Baltimore and Annapolis failed to materialize, it seemed hourly to grow more likely that their goal was the unspeakable: an assault on Washington. The city began to panic.

By early evening on Sunday, August 21, a stream of evacuees were leaving the capital, heading into Virginia over the long bridge that spanned the Potomac. Those who stayed behind searched desperately for places to hide their jewels and other valuables. General Winder finally organized enough men—about two thousand, including a regiment of cavalry and twenty pieces of artillery—to move southeast. Making camp at the Wood Yard, some twelve miles from Washington, he actually had an opportunity to launch a surprise attack against Ross, who was nearby and unaware of his opponent's movements. But Winder let the opportunity slip, deciding that the British were not yet strong enough to represent a real threat. His time, he believed, would be better spent gathering his defensive forces. In a matter of days, Ross's weathered veterans of the Peninsula would demonstrate the cost of such wariness.

Even as the possibility of a British assault on Washington became clearer, and even as Winder dashed about the countryside along the Eastern Branch of the Potomac, trying to determine where the enemy could most advantageously be met, there remained disbelief in many corners of both the government and the civilian population. The idea was too extreme, even to have been hatched by the hated Admiral Cockburn, and the motives behind it were too obscure. Washington had no military importance; why would the British commit a significant number of men to an expedition that could be little more than punitive? Such reasoning, while it might have soothed frayed nerves in the capital, did little to deter Ross

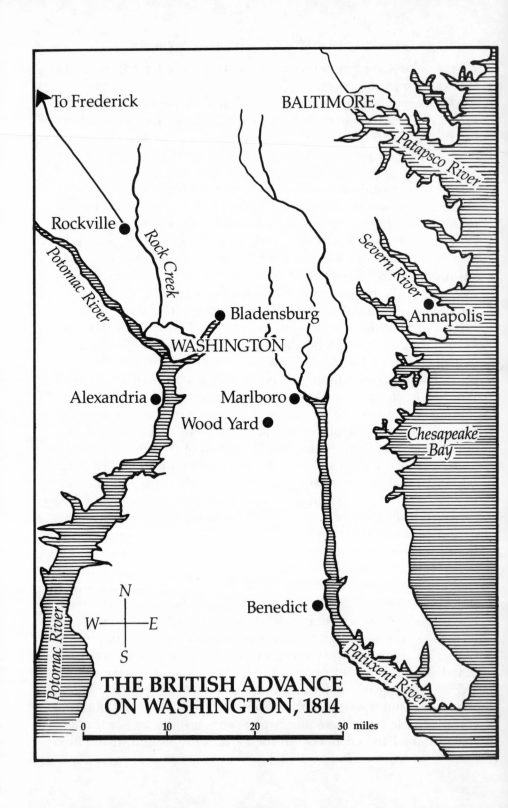

To Frederick

BALTIMORE

Patapsco River

Rockville

Rock Creek

Potomac River

Severn River

Bladensburg

WASHINGTON

Annapolis

Alexandria

Marlboro

Wood Yard

Chesapeake Bay

N

W   E

S

Benedict

Patuxent River

Potomac River

**THE BRITISH ADVANCE
ON WASHINGTON, 1814**

0   10   20   30 miles

and Cockburn. On Monday, an official dispatch arrived for Madison from Monroe, who was still in the field with his thirty dragoons: "The enemy are in full march for Washington. Have the materials prepared to destroy the bridges. You had better remove the records."

On Tuesday, as Madison reviewed the American troops at the Wood Yard, General Winder informed the commander in chief of his belief that British numbers were inadequate for any move on Washington. But Madison knew that such opinions meant little. As the president wrote to Dolley, "The reports as to the enemy have varied every hour." The most recent dispatches had indicated "that they are not very strong, and are without cavalry and artillery, and of course that they are not in a condition to strike at Washington." Secretary Armstrong dismissed the idea of an attack on the capital yet again, stating that "they can have no such intention. They are foraging, I suppose." Madison, after personally interrogating two British deserters, reasserted that the British might be planning an assault on the city. Even if they were not yet in sufficient force to do so, argued the president, "their temerity may be greater than their strength." That afternoon he returned to the capital to provide a steadying hand in the confused process of preparation and evacuation.

On the following morning, Winder moved his force—now brought up to almost six thousand by the addition of militia and regulars from Maryland—in a ragged line toward Bladensburg, a village northeast of Washington on the Eastern Branch. Here the Americans prepared to meet Ross's advance units. Madison and many of the members of his cabinet, believing their place to be with the army at such a decisive hour, left the city to join Winder —and were almost captured by the British in doing so. When they did reach the American troops, they quickly realized that it might be wisest to leave "military movements now to the military functionaries who were responsible for them"—for the fighting was already under way.

It was not much of a battle, and it did not take much time. Even before early afternoon, the disjointed American line—numerically superior but inexperienced and badly uncoordinated—was breaking under the steady attack of the British. Madison, grasping the severity of the predicament, began the trip back to Washington and sent his aide, Charles Carroll, ahead to urge the First Lady to leave the city. But Dolley would not go. In part, her refusal was motivated by a desire to see her husband safe; in part, it reflected the extraordinary attitude of many Washingtonians. "Mr. Carroll," she wrote, "has come to hasten my departure and is in a very bad humor because I insist on waiting until the large picture of General Washington is secured, and it requires to be unscrewed from the [dining room] wall."

By three o'clock, the American forces at Bladensburg were in full flight. Terrorized by the flash and scream of Ross's Congreve rockets—weapons of little destructive power but quite effective psychologically—they fled across open fields to the safety of nearby woodlands and hills with a speed that inspired newspapermen and poets to dub the encounter "The Bladensburg Races." Ross, whose notes on the campaign reflected a sobriety that often bordered on the humorous, observed that, "The rapid flight of the enemy, and his knowledge of the country, precluded the possibility of taking many prisoners."

No one was more stunned by the severity of the defeat than the American commander in chief. Madison, like many of the Founding Fathers, had always shared Thomas Jefferson's confidence that in a contest between American freemen fighting for the liberty of their soil and paid professional soldiers from the Old World (in this case Englishmen drawn from social strata that had often aroused scorn even in their former commander, the Duke of Wellington), the Americans would emerge triumphant. But the tremendous determination of Ross's redcoats—fighting without the benefit of significant cavalry or artillery units and in the face of superior numbers—and the unabashed panic of the American troops allowed the president to witness firsthand the unreliability of this theory; his subsequent personal confusion, bringing with it doubt and philosophical gloom, was grimly reflected in the terror-stricken movements of those citizens and officials who had yet to abandon the now defenseless capital.

Pausing only briefly at the deserted White House (Dolley had finally agreed to depart), Madison next proceeded across the Potomac into rural Virginia, where he had arranged to seek refuge. Attorney General Richard Rush and others had joined the president's party, though the First Lady's own search for safety caused their continued separation. After a day of unprecedented confusion and activity, night did at last descend on Washington and its environs. Night—but not darkness.

Ross and Cockburn had entered Washington at six o'clock to

find part of the city in flames—the retreating Americans had set fire to the Navy Yard, so that its valuable ships and military stores would not fall into British hands. By the light of this spectacular blaze, the remaining residents could clearly see that Ross and Cockburn had no intention of occupying Washington. Detachments of British soldiers and sailors moved swiftly to key points throughout the city, and paid less attention to private houses or civilians than to official buildings and government property. As the first fires were lit inside the new halls of democracy, British intentions were made plain even to the unbelieving. The American capital was to be an example and a warning to the rest of the nation.

First to be looted was the Capitol, which, with its heavy limestone walls, proved somewhat difficult to burn. Not so the White House, in which Cockburn toasted the name of King George with presidential wine and took one of Dolley Madison's seat cushions as a ribald keepsake. Throughout the night of the twenty-fourth and into the next day, the admiral reveled in the sacking of the city, personally overseeing the demolition of several buildings. These included the offices of the *National Intelligencer,* where he ordered the entire supply of typeset to be smashed. "Be sure that all the C's are destroyed," Cockburn called to his men triumphantly. "So that the rascals can't abuse my name any more!" The *Intelligencer* would later retaliate by painting a portrait of the admiral's behavior that was both vindictive and revealing: "Cockburn was quite a mountebank in the city, exhibiting in the streets a gross levity of manner, displaying sundry articles of trifling value of which he had robbed the President's house, and repeating many of the coarse jests and vulgar slang of the *Federal Republican* [an anti-Madison publication] respecting the chief magistrate and others, in a strain of eloquence which could only have been acquired by a constant perusal of that disgrace to the country."

In contrast, General Ross had little taste for the task before him, and followed his orders with characteristic restraint and detachment. "Judging it of consequence," he wrote, "to complete the destruction with the least possible delay, so that the army might retire without loss of time, the following were set on fire and totally consumed." He proceeded to list the Capitol—both Senate and House wings—the large building shared by the Departments of War and State, the dockyards and other public structures. Only the patent office was saved, through the ingenuity of its director in exploiting Ross's personal respect for the work of creative minds.

The general had already expressed regret over the burning of the Library of Congress, and it proved easy to convince him that the designs in the patent office were private, not public, property. Further and general orders were given by both Ross and Cockburn to limit damage to all civilian homes and possessions. Indeed, the two commanders behaved with remarkable gallantry toward the civilian population, Cockburn even threatening to execute one of his own sailors after a local prostitute claimed she had been assaulted by an Englishman. (The woman subsequently proved too hysterical to identify her attacker.) Though some British troops were unable to resist the temptation to loot, crimes of that nature were generally carried out by Washington's sizable indigent population, who were safe amidst the confusion of a burning city.

From their vantage point in the hills of Virginia, President Madison and his party watched the night sky above Washington first leap with the flames and explosions of the Navy Yard, and then turn a glowing red with the destruction of the official buildings. Winder's force, the only formal American military command in the area, was now in complete disarray. There was nothing for the president and his advisers to do but bear witness to this blazing, dramatic demonstration of the reach of British power—a humiliating testament to the true extent of American vulnerability to threats from abroad.

It was a signal moment in U.S. history. Americans had come, during and after the Revolution, to view their geographical remoteness as a blessing and a safeguard, a sign that Providence favored their new experiment in government. "Our detached and distant situation," Washington had stated in his Farewell Address, "invites and enables us to pursue a different course." British and French harassment of U.S. frontiers and trade during the 1790s and the early nineteenth century had steeled American resolve to reinforce the security offered by the seas more than it had prompted any overriding doubt of the existence of that security. The practical result of this process was the policy of "armed neutrality" (although that specific phrase was often denied by American leaders), which involved the creation of the Navy Department, the fitting for sea of battle-worthy frigates and the revival of the Marine Corps. But the burning of Washington gave grim proof that while the United States might be favored by Providence, its protection by less ethereal forces was far from assured. The country was in deep and mortal peril.

On the night of Thursday, August 25, having completed their mission of destruction and diversion, General Ross and Admiral Cockburn withdrew from Washington. Behind them they left the charred ruins of America's houses of government. After an abortive move toward Baltimore, which resulted in little other than the loss of General Ross to American sniper fire, the British moved back to the eastern coast, where they embarked for Jamaica. Slowly, the Americans who had evacuated the capital began to return, horrified by what they found.

Despite Ross's and Cockburn's efforts to control outrages against private property by both their own soldiers and civilian looters, there had been much damage done. Yet this did not compare to the loss of America's new official buildings. Perhaps the most poignant moment occurred when the First Family returned to the White House, the scene of so many of Washington society's most festive galas; Dolley Madison found only the exterior walls of the building intact. The president's palace, like the country itself, had been violated and disgraced, and the resultant sense of shame took on truly national significance. Even the rugged Americans of the frontier, who had previously had little use for the dandifications of their capital, took the burning of Washington as a grievous insult. Together with the rest of the country, they resolved to secure their nation against any such threats and calamities in the future.

Some forty years before the disaster of Washington's destruction, America's Founding Fathers had first grappled with the question of how best to safeguard the thirteen struggling colonies against not only the oppressions of the British Crown, but the grasping ambitions of other European powers and assaults by marauding Indian tribes as well. National security was an area of special interest to the nation's first leaders, and with a characteristic blend of Enlightenment erudition and American idealism, they set out to formulate a program that would offer the United States a real measure of political and territorial safety without involving it in the complex diplomatic maneuverings of Europe.

The security system that most profoundly—if negatively—affected the Founding Fathers in their search for such a program was the European balance of power, which had its roots in the Italian Renaissance. But the Italian system, like the men who created it, was far more cabalistic than its European inheritor. Deceit and treachery, when employed in the service of a prince, were seen as necessary and even virtuous. Security during the Italian Renaissance therefore depended almost exclusively on the maneuverings of individual statesmen, and finally degenerated into the intense factional competition and regional warfare that characterized Italian history during much of the early modern period.

The European balance of power, as it emerged in the seventeenth and eighteenth centuries, was scarcely more successful at preventing bloodshed than the Italian system had been. But it did at least establish the notion that security was both a relative commodity and a collective concern of the new nation-states. By its terms, one country could increase its own security only at the expense of another's. When the relative security (and insecurity) of each European power reached an appropriate level, the system ideally would balance out. In short, lengthy, large-scale warfare of the kind that had plagued Europe in the late Middle Ages could be curtailed only through the organized diligence of attentive rulers; as Frederick the Great wrote, "When the policy and prudence of the princes of Europe lose sight of the maintenance of a just balance among the dominant powers, the constitution of the whole body politic resents it." But for all its occasionally beneficial effects, the balance of power was an essentially cynical system. By ascribing amoral, or at the very least selfish, motives to each participating nation, and by presuming that the ambitions of each could only be checked by those of the others, it condemned its members to a relative security that was fraught with suspicion and anxiety.

It was this aspect of the balance of power that disturbed America's first leaders. Viewing Europe from the remove of a new continent, the Founding Fathers generally regarded the European security system as one that managed and exploited human weakness without promoting virtue. The constructive lessons of the balance of power—that security is relative and can be achieved only by working together—were seen as less important than its vices. Nonetheless, these were men of the eighteenth century, who understood the practical usefulness of the balance if confined to Europe. Indeed, a Europe ruled by the balance of power was less likely to menace the New World. The greatest danger was that the European security system would become dominated by a single great power that would then seek control over the Western Hemisphere.

In response to the possibility that the European balance of power would break down, the Founding Fathers were determined not to tie American security to the actions or fate of any one power. (The alliance with France during the American Revolution, the single exception to this rule, was a source of deep concern to many American leaders because of its political and military provisions.) Rather, the Founding Fathers aspired to a security that would be unaffected by the behavior of other powers, and thus be absolute. Such security, though hardly possible given the fragility of the new republic, was nonetheless confirmed as the ultimate goal of American foreign policy. And the American determination to avoid formal alliances—resting on the Founding Fathers' conviction that alliances implied danger as surely as did enmities—became the cornerstone of the new American diplomacy.

"The nation," said the departing President Washington in 1796, "which indulges toward another an habitual hatred or an habitual fondness is in some degree a slave." Any "passionate attachment of one nation for another produces a variety of evils," leading "to concessions to the favorite nation of privileges denied to others, which is apt doubly to injure the nation making the concessions by unnecessarily parting with what ought to have been retained." Only by acting alone, according to Washington, could these pitfalls be avoided, and the result of such determinedly solitary behavior would someday be nothing less than absolute safety from foreign threats: "If we remain one people, under an efficient government, the period is not far off when we may defy material injury from external annoyance."

Thomas Jefferson's emphasis on the geographical blessings of the new nation provided a foundation for this nascent American idea of security. Jefferson saw the United States as "possessing a chosen country, with room enough for our descendants to the hundredth and thousandth generation." Under such circumstances, invulnerability did not seem an unreasonable aspiration. But even the blessings of geography would fail if they were not accompanied by moral vision. Following the lead of the eighteenth century French *philosophes*, Jefferson envisaged an American foreign policy that rested for its success on moral principle rather than diplomatic complexity.

The pursuit of absolute security through exploitation of geographic advantage and moral superiority was a theme also echoed by Jefferson's great antagonist (and close friend), John Adams. Serving as one of the American representatives in Paris in 1781, Adams informed the French foreign minister that "the dignity of

North America does not consist in diplomatic ceremonies or any of the subtleties of etiquette; it consists solely in reason, justice, truth, the right of mankind and the interests of the nations of Europe." The American interpretation of the European balance of power as politically expedient, then, was finally to prove less determinant in American affairs than the moral imperative that called on American statesmen to exploit the blessings of geography and liberal democracy and reject for all time the cynicism of the Old World.

Not all the Founding Fathers, however, were so convinced that the American experiment was either unique or sufficiently protected by nature to allow ultimate dissociation from the affairs of Europe. Alexander Hamilton's worldly mind rejected the "idle theories which have amused us with promises of an exception from the imperfection, weaknesses and evils incident to society in every shape." He asked, "Is it not time to awaken from the deceitful dream of a golden age and to adopt as a practical maxim for the direction of our political conduct that we, as well as the other inhabitants of the globe, are yet remote from the happy empire of perfect wisdom and perfect virtue?" But Hamilton's warnings were largely disregarded: the new American foreign policy was, above all, the work of Jefferson and Adams, and Jefferson and Adams, each in his own way, were confirmed disciples of American exceptionalism.

That exceptionalism was to play a key role in defining American national security. The Founding Fathers believed that the special nature of American democracy, combined with the fact that it had taken hold on a continent of almost incalculable wealth, made the United States an irresistible target for aggression and subversion from abroad. This sense of targeting obviously had its roots in the colonial experience; many early American settlers had been refugees from the wars, oppressions and religious persecutions of Europe. By the time revolutionary agitation began, the belief that democracy, far from a spreading influence in the world, was in fact on the defensive had many distinguished adherents, none more eloquent than Thomas Paine. "Freedom," wrote Paine in *Common Sense*, "hath been hunted around the globe. Asia and Africa have long expelled her, Europe regards her like a stranger, and England hath given her warning to depart." This left America with the sole hope of becoming "an asylum for mankind." Paine, like most Americans, did not believe that the dynasties of Europe would allow this to happen without a struggle. What he could not know, but what Adams and Jefferson would discover, was that this struggle would not end with the war for independence.

Following the signing of the Treaty of Paris in 1783, it quickly became apparent that the desires of European powers to seize and exploit portions of the rich American continent would continue after the end of revolutionary hostilities. Neither President Washington, nor Vice President Adams, nor Secretary of State Jefferson allowed themselves any illusions as to what this meant for the new nation. While geography and moral virtue alone might favor the United States in future struggles against foreign aggression, they could not guarantee success. Another element was required: the continuous and forceful determination of American citizens to respond to threats from abroad. "No facts," Adams had written to Benjamin Franklin in 1780, "are believed but decisive military conquests; no arguments are seriously attended in Europe but force."

Even Jefferson, by the time of his own presidency, had come to believe that the vulnerability of the new nation might require greater interaction with foreign powers than he had originally envisioned for America, perhaps to the point of temporary alliances. For that reason he was prepared in 1802 "to marry ourselves to the British fleet and nation" the day "that France takes possession of New Orleans." But, in the words of Henry Adams in his history of the Jefferson administration: "Such an alliance, offensive and defensive, with England, contradicted every principle established by President Washington in power or professed by Jefferson in opposition" and was "an act such as the Republicans of 1798 would have charged as a crime."

Given such diplomatic constraints, in the period between 1783 and 1812 Americans fought hard and successfully to ensure the nation's security on their own. The territorial integrity of the United States was preserved against designs by Great Britain, France and Spain, as well as against the hostile actions of Indian tribes. Abroad, American commercial interests were safeguarded in a war with the Barbary pirates. And at several points, opportunities for actual expansion were seized, sometimes covertly, as in the case of West Florida in 1810, where American-born settlers were encouraged to rise up against their Spanish rulers, and sometimes openly, as in the case of Jefferson's Louisiana Purchase in 1803.

Fearful that Napoleonic France—which he described as "a tor-

rent which has for some time been bearing down all before it"—
would establish itself as the dominant power on the North American continent, Jefferson was determined to enhance American security by gaining control of the Mississippi River and its adjacent
territories, as well as the port of New Orleans. As it happened,
Bonaparte, his power in the Western Hemisphere weakened by
the loss of Haiti, agreed to part with the expansive Louisiana Territory for $15 million; and the United States gained not only vast
room for exploration and settlement, but a greatly increased measure of safety from foreign threats.

Thus while the continental wars that convulsed Europe during
the closing years of the eighteenth century and the first decade of
the nineteenth could not help but have deep implications for the
United States, American leaders consistently sought—and were
required by the American people to seek—policies that would safeguard the territory of the new nation without aligning it to either
side in the European conflict. And with success in this endeavor
came a newly invigorated American nationalism, fiercely independent in nature and having as one of its principal goals the elimi-
nation of any and all threats to the remarkable social and political
experiment that was under way within the borders of the United
States.

No group better exemplified this dynamic American spirit than
the "Young Republicans," or "war hawks," that dominated the
House of Representatives during the Twelfth Congress of 1811.
Theirs were the voices of a new generation, a postrevolutionary
generation, and the lessons of prudence and compromise that
years of hard struggle had taught to older men such as Jefferson
and Adams had not yet made their mark on this new collection of
zealots. For the most part they represented the states of the frontier, such as Kentucky and Tennessee, although some came from
the agrarian South. These regions had suffered much (though not
most) from the harassment of the British and the French during
the years following the Treaty of Paris. And although the French
withdrawal from Haiti and Louisiana had effectively eliminated
any reason for war with France, calls for a righteous war against
the British Empire grew steadily louder on the frontier throughout
the first decade of the nineteenth century. With the assumption of
legislative power by the war hawks, these cries reached a crescendo.

There were four general areas of contention between the United

States and Great Britain when the Twelfth Congress was called into session in 1811. First, and most insulting to Americans, was the policy of impressment, by way of which British seamen sailing on American vessels—and there were many during this period— were forced onto British ships to serve in the war against France. Since no laws governing expatriation yet existed, the British could easily claim to be within their rights. But in characteristically high-handed fashion, they used this legal loophole to press into service any man on an American ship whose voice was even slightly tinged with an accent native to some part of the British Isles. Impressment therefore resulted in the effective kidnapping of American nationals.

The second American grievance concerned British harassment of American commerce, both in North America—where British traders and merchants had repeatedly clashed with Americans on the Mississippi River and on the eastern section of the Canadian-American border—and at sea. The third affront to American sovereignty, also commercial in nature, was the closing of European ports to American ships by the British and the concurrent British policy of preventing European trade with various American harbors, especially New York. Known as the orders in council, this practice was justified by the British on the grounds that American commerce aided the cause of Napoleonic France, Great Britain's longtime enemy (the British were and would always remain quick to block the trade of neutrals when it was destined for ports unfriendly to the crown). Finally, the United States held Great Britain responsible for many of the Indian attacks on American frontier settlements that hampered American expansion into the great continental wilderness.

These grievances had varying degrees of substance, but all shared one quality in equal strength: they were long-standing. None could have been called, in 1812, the sort of precipitous outrage that might spark a declaration of war (indeed, the orders in council were suspended shortly before the American declaration of hostilities, although this was not known in Washington). Why, then, did the United States pick that year to fight?

There were many Americans who had consistently resisted any pressure for war with Great Britain, especially among the Federalists of the Northeast. Their influence had been vital in preventing hostilities prior to 1812. Traditionally Anglophile by reason of heritage and commercial connection, their opposition to any declaration of hostilities was reinforced by concern over the growing power of the western states. A war with Britain, in the opinion of such eminent Federalist representatives as Josiah Quincy of Massachusetts, would only add new states to the western bloc, states that would eventually drown out the collective voice of the Northeast in Congress. It is the conventional wisdom that time and continued British abuses eventually overwhelmed the opposition of such men, and that war then became inevitable. The Federalists waited for either a shift in British policy or the downfall of the Republican party to return their party to national leadership, but they waited in vain. The British, preoccupied with the struggle against Napoleon, had no ear for American complaints, even when uttered by sympathetic voices; and the Republicans, far from losing ground, only reaped the political benefits of Britain's aggressive behavior.

Much of this view of the causes of the War of 1812 is undeniably accurate. Yet it does not fully explain the American desire for conquest and expansion that surfaced during the legislative debates of 1811–12, a ferment that arose in no small part because of the quest for absolute security. In the House of Representatives, as well as in newspapers and private correspondence, that passion was most clearly stated by the new leaders of the American frontier.

"Young politicians with their pin-feathers yet unshed, the shell still sticking upon them—perfectly unfledged, though they fluttered and cackled on the floor." Such was the pronouncement of Josiah Quincy on the Young Republicans of the West and the South. Yet despite their youth (none was older than thirty-six, and most a good deal younger) and relative inexperience, these war hawks of the Twelfth Congress were a brilliant and formidable collection, bound and determined to push their country into a war they were confident—indeed, overconfident—of winning.

Their leader was Henry Clay, who was elected Speaker in a demonstration of the power of this new faction of the House. Later in his life Clay would become famous as the "Great Pacificator," the man who resolved not one but three crises that threatened to divide the union, prompting Abraham Lincoln to deem him "my beau ideal of a statesman." But in 1811 Clay was not so eventempered. The master of the famed Ashland plantation in Kentucky was also an inveterate gambler and carouser, with a face and bearing that beguiled women and frustrated portraitists. The most arresting of the war hawks, Clay possessed an oratorical style that

could shift from lividly aroused to eloquently composed with neither warning nor effort. In a passionate speech before the House
on December 31, he argued for raising new military forces, convinced that war with Great Britain was inevitable: "What are we to
gain by war, has been emphatically asked? What are we not to lose
by peace? commerce, character, a nation's best treasure, honor!"
As the winter months wore on, the nation listened with ever-
growing interest to this parliamentary master.

Clay was ably supported by a group who were also renowned in
later life, not least among them John C. Calhoun of South Carolina. Calhoun, somber and socially restrained in comparison to
Clay, was nonetheless the Speaker's match when it came to arguing
in favor of war and against diplomatic contacts with Great Britain.
In February of 1812 he wrote to Dr. James MacBride of Charles-
ton: "Heretofore, the conductors of our affairs, have attempted to
avoid and remove difficulties by a sort of political management;
. . . by commercial arrangiments [sic] and negotiations. This might
suit an inconsiderable nation, . . . [but] Experience has proved it
improper for us. Its effects have been distrust at home and contempt abroad. We have said, we will change; we will defend ourselves by force. I hope Congress will stick to this salutory resolve."

Still more future luminaries fought hard to force President Madison into declaring war against the British: there was Richard M.
Johnson of Kentucky, a future vice-president; Peter B. Porter of
New York, chairman of the Foreign Affairs Committee; and Felix
Grundy, Tennessee's foremost criminal lawyer. Together these
men sent waves of shock and excitement through the House, and
subsequently through the entire nation, with their skilled and im-
passioned pleas for revitalization of the American character, which
they believed had been tarnished by long years of submission to
foreign harassment. Indeed, amidst the brilliance of such speakers
it was possible to lose sight of precisely what their goal was in
favoring a war with Great Britain.

The men who urged commencement of formal hostilities with
the greatest vehemence did not envisage such a conflict as simply a
way to redress long-standing grievances—they saw it as an opportunity to completely eradicate the British presence in North America. Their goal was not to establish mutually acceptable peace terms
that would offer the United States respect and relative security, but
to eliminate future British threats altogether. More than any other
single issue, this notion that the country could, through conquest,

be made secure against the designs of a powerful, longtime antagonist pushed a decisive number of Representatives who had been
hesitant or opposed to war into voting approval for President Madison's War Message, which was delivered to the House on June 1,
1812.

The call for an end to British jurisdiction over any part of North
America—including Canada, which the war hawks hoped to seize
—was repeated again and again in the statements and speeches of
noted frontiersmen during the term of the Twelfth Congress. Andrew Jackson, writing in March 1812 of the reasons why America
should fight, first listed the well-established grievances that Madison would also include in his Message: impressment, trade violations, blockades and incitement of Indians on the frontier. But the
Tennessean then went on to say that the United States should seek
"security against future aggressions, by the conquest of all the British dominions upon the continent of North America." Richard
Johnson expressed a widespread sentiment when he said, "I shall
never die contented until I see her [Great Britain's] expulsion from
North America, and her territories incorporated within the United
States." And Felix Grundy, who was so vociferous in his calls for
an open declaration of hostilities that the House opposition often
referred to the war fever as "Grundyism," declared that, "We shall
drive the British from our continent." For all of these men—and
they were fully representative of their states and constituencies—a
war for the just settlement of grievances was not enough. Future
security was also required, and future security meant the complete
removal of the agent of threat.

But in the summer of 1814 it would take an irrepressible British
admiral and a brave veteran of the Peninsula just three days to
create a profound crisis in the American conception of national
security and the means by which it was to be attained.

The War of 1812 settled none of the established points of contention between the United States and Great Britain. The Treaty
of Ghent, signed in December of 1814 (though not ratified by the
Senate until February 1815), did little more than end the fighting
and establish Canadian-American borders along the lines of
the status quo antebellum. True, it did create a basis for future
negotiations, some of which would settle the more serious of the
Anglo-American differences. But the reasons for which each of
the opposing nations had fought—the Americans for the eradica-

tion of the British presence and an end to London's strident commercial and naval practices, the British for the assertion of their predominance as a great power—remained virtually unchanged by a long and fairly costly conflict. The importance of the war, then, lies less in its outcome than in its legacy.

The most far-reaching results of the War of 1812 were the aggravation of antipathy between the United States and Great Britain and an elaboration by Americans of their concept of national security to embrace not only the British threat but *all* potential dangers. These effects were interrelated. The burning of Washington, as well as accompanying British victories on the western frontier and the Canadian border, had taught the war hawks of 1812 a lesson that the Founding Fathers had been forced to accept early on—invulnerability was not yet within reach. And with this awakening came the complementary realization that the absence of invulnerability implied vulnerability. The British march on Washington had at first seemed an insignificant (if not incomprehensible) threat. But in the end it had proved—not least in terms of psychology and morale—to be vital. The lesson appeared to be that a nation that allowed itself to view *any* designs on its integrity as insignificant could not hope to achieve absolute security. In this way, America's traditional inclination to view herself as a target nation was dramatically heightened by the sudden awareness of an expanded range of foreign threats.

It would be difficult to overestimate the effect of this on American policymakers. The goal of absolute security did not change as a result of the War of 1812; if anything, its importance was underlined. Americans were no more willing in 1815 than they had been in 1811 to admit that their national security might be relative or dependent on diplomatic interaction with other powers. But safety, it was acknowledged, would require increased effort and greater vigilance. Geography, ideology and even force of arms had failed to guarantee security in 1812. The American nation, already quick to use force both in defense of its own borders and in foreign regions seen as vital, would have to become still quicker to fight— for the threats from abroad that had so long perplexed American leaders had proved grimly real.

Thus mindful of the dangers confronting their nation, Americans prepared to commit themselves to the enlarged task of providing for their own safety. It is perhaps only natural, given both the burning of Washington and the process of redefinition of national security, that in seeking to detect future threats from abroad after the War of 1812, Americans should have looked first and foremost to Great Britain. The year 1815 marked the beginning of a more than seventy-five-year obsession with supposed British ambitions in North America, an obsession rivaled in American history only by the twentieth-century preoccupation with Soviet communism. During the nineteenth century, Americans saw the British threat everywhere—in Mexico and Central America, in the Pacific Northwest, and, of course, on the high seas. At times, there was justification for the belief that the British intended to establish a larger presence in North America; more often there was not. But fear of British intentions was the dominant negative influence on American foreign policy during the last century. Even the campaign of westward expansion that consumed American energies and resources during that same period was affected to no small degree by that deep anxiety, an anxiety initiated by the experience of the Revolution and dramatically deepened by the humiliations suffered during the War of 1812.

When James Madison returned to the city of Washington following the departure of General Ross and Admiral Cockburn, the citizens of the American capital greeted him in a fashion that was no doubt mortifying. Still hampered, as president, by a limited ability to effectively manage those around him, Madison certainly did not possess the temperament to handle a mob; yet this was exactly what faced him in the smoldering ruins of Washington. Blamed for the unpreparedness of the city, vilified for his flight into Virginia, the president only narrowly escaped bodily injury at the hands of the enraged citizens of the capital. His reputation would not recover during his lifetime. The responsibility for the disaster, responsibility that by rights belonged to every American who had cried out for war and voted its declaration, was placed squarely on a man who during his long career had done far more than most of his countrymen to ensure liberty and democracy in America.

If it was to take years to remove the unfair tarnish from the name of James Madison, the nation itself was redeemed with relative speed. On February 16, 1815—nearly two months after the signing of the Treaty of Ghent—Congressman George M. Troup of Georgia rose to address the House of Representatives, inspired by news that had only recently reached Washington: Andrew Jackson had won a great victory at New Orleans on January 8. Troup, chairman of the Military Affairs Committee, had spared no effort since 1812 to prosecute the war against Great Britain, working hard to raise troops through enlistment and conscription bills. Later in his life, he would argue for a standing peacetime army fixed at no fewer than ten thousand men—and the Battle of New Orleans would supply him with ample rationale for such a stand.

The circumstances of Jackson's victory were no less remarkable for their having occurred after the signing of the peace treaty. Jackson—who had despised the British ever since his youth, when he had refused to polish the boots of an English officer during the Revolution and had received a scarring saber gash across the head in return—had driven his militiamen hard to build a formidable series of earthworks amidst the swamps of the Mississippi delta; Britain's General Sir Edward Pakenham, in one of the most colossal blunders in military history, had sent 5,300 men against Jackson's fortifications; the ragged but battle-worthy Americans had poured a murderous rain of artillery and musket fire down on the English, inflicting casualties of 2,036 killed; when the firing had stopped, fewer than a dozen Americans lay dead. Two and a half years of war had at last produced a great victory, and in its rhetoric Troup's speech reflected the national public reaction to Jackson's triumph:

"That regular troops, the best disciplined and most veteran of Europe, should be beaten by undisciplined militia with the disproportionate loss of an hundred to one [the severity of British losses was not yet known] is, to use the language of the commanding General, almost incredible. . . . Europe [has] seen that to be formidable on the ocean we need *but will it*. Europe will see that to be invincible on the land it is only necessary that we judiciously employ the means which God and nature have placed at our disposal. The men of Europe, bred in camps, trained to war—with all the science and all the experience of modern war are not a match for the men of America taken from the closet, the bar, the counting house and the plough."

Whatever its oratorical shortcomings, Troup's speech was reprinted and widely read throughout the nation, and understandably so. All the central elements of American national security—the favorable comparison of American militia to European professional soldiers, the beneficent influence of God and nature and above all the notion that absolute security was a matter of *"will"*—

were contained in the address. The memory of the burning of Washington remained in the public mind, without question; but it was soon overshadowed by the glory of Jackson at New Orleans. The capital's public buildings, like the national spirit, were eventually rebuilt, in forms that outshone their forerunners—but the knowledge that foreign nations might at any time try to strike at the very heart of the republic never vanished.

I I

GENERAL JACKSON AND
MISTER ADAMS

1816–1823

THE fort stood on Prospect Bluff, overlooking and controlling one of the most fertile sections of the Apalachicola Valley in the Spanish province of West Florida. Its walls were prodigious, and its armaments some of the best that British money could buy—for it had been a British officer who had overseen its construction, during the War of 1812, with the object of using Creek and Seminole warriors as well as runaway slaves to harass the southern border of the United States and perhaps even assault New Orleans. Major Edward Nicholls had been an extraordinary man, who, for reasons perhaps known to himself but baffling to the London government, seemed to have felt that he held the powers of a plenipotentiary. In his dealings with the Creek and Seminole tribes he made exaggerated promises in the name of Great Britain, although these had meant little when, in the spring of 1814, he was chased from westernmost Florida to the Apalachicola by Andrew Jackson. Nicholls escaped to build his mighty fort on Prospect Bluff, but his Creek allies were first crushed by Jackson at Horseshoe Bend and

41

then forced by the general to accept the humiliating Treaty of Fort Jackson, by which they lost many of their best lands.

Andrew Jackson had been especially ruthless during this campaign, as he so often was when dealing with the problem of America's frontiers. Looking at the generally crude maps of North America that were available in 1815, the general could see a body of land just south of the United States whose outline all too closely resembled a massive, threatening pistol—the Spanish Floridas. The butt of this pistol was the peninsula of East Florida, a largely swampy region with a long and strategic coastline. The trigger guard—the valley of the Apalachicola River in West Florida—was made up of some of the best farmland in the Southeast. So too was the pistol's barrel, a long strip of land that cut under the Alabama and Mississippi territories and above New Orleans to nuzzle menacingly against the most coveted commercial artery in all of North America, the Mississippi.

Jackson knew that without these provinces—filled as they were with hostile Indians, runaway slaves, foreign adventurers and duplicitous Spanish officials—there could be no real territorial security for the United States, and certainly no safe process of westward expansion. He also knew that Spain, though bound by Pinckney's Treaty of 1795 to forcibly restrain the Florida tribes from attacking American borders and settlers, had in fact neither the will nor the troops to enforce such a policy. In addition, the Spanish governors of Florida had for decades allowed runaway American slaves to live as either free farmers or members of the Creek and Seminole tribes inside Florida; for an established slaveowner such as Jackson, the danger was clear. The situation played on nearly every one of Jackson's deep personal hatreds, not merely of the British, but of hostile Indian tribes, of Spanish impotence, of anything that might threaten his country. Following the conclusion of the Fort Jackson Treaty, the general promptly marched—with neither presidential nor congressional authorization—on the provincial capital of Pensacola in West Florida, using the presence of Nicholls and his officers as justification for an overt act of aggression. At Pensacola he delivered a stinging message to the Spanish governor:

"The power of Spain is competent, she must assume the nutral [sic] character she is bound to the United States for and restrain the Tomahawk and Scalping Knife, or the head which excites their use, shall feel the sharpness of their edge. I know that head. I am well advised of the influence which has heretofore furnished and excited the use of these savage implements. It is not on the heads of helpless women and children that retaliation will be made, but on the head which countenanced and excited the barbarity. He is the responsible person, and not the poor savage whom he makes his instrument of execution. An Eye for an Eye, Toothe for Toothe and Scalp for Scalp."

As Jackson returned to Louisiana to prepare for the British assault on New Orleans, Major Nicholls, aware of Jackson's threats, began to drill a force of runaway blacks and Indians at the Prospect Bluff fort. Following the news of the Treaty of Ghent, however, Nicholls was forced to return to England, where he and the alliances he had signed with the Indian tribes were disavowed—though never in writing—by the Government. The major took one of the Seminole chiefs, the Prophet Francis, back to England with him, and the Indian was received in a manner that belied the official disavowal of Nicholls. Francis was given a brigadier general's scarlet uniform and visited the Prince Regent, then returned to Florida full of hope that English assistance—which could not be officially continued after the conclusion of the peace—would at least be covertly maintained. It was an opinion shared by many Americans, not least General Jackson.

Meanwhile, the Prospect Bluff fort was left in the hands of a garrison of over three hundred men, primarily ex-slaves. Some one thousand free blacks and renegade Indians farmed and lived under the protection of what came to be known as the "Negro Fort," and when American settlers and traders drifted too close to the area, the results were often grim. The fort soon became a magnet, drawing slaves from all over the southern states and territories. The Spanish did little to prevent the predatory activities of the blacks and Indians and even less to expel the British officers and traders who made those actions possible. The truth was that Florida was open country, Spanish in name only; indeed, with the rapid power shifts in Madrid itself during the previous decade—from Ferdinand VII to Joseph Bonaparte to the "Junta Central" and back to the tyrannical Ferdinand—it was virtually impossible to determine what Spanish rule really meant. But certain facts were nonetheless clear to Americans—so long as Florida remained outside their authority, their southern border would be exposed, their southern citizens prey to Indian attacks and their slaves likely to grow ever more restive. As the months of 1815 wore on, with murders and reprisals committed all along the borderlands, the

Negro Fort became an intolerable symbol of this condition to Andrew Jackson and to many citizens of the United States.

Early in 1816 Jackson sent another threatening message to the Spanish governor of West Florida: "In your answer, you will be pleased to state whether that fort has been built by the Government of Spain, and whether those negroes who garrison it are considered as the subjects of His Catholic Majesty, and, if not by His Catholic Majesty, by whom, and under whose orders, it has been erected." The governor could do no more than try to assure Jackson that he was merely waiting for the right moment to deal with the problem of the fort, but Jackson's emissary informed the general on his return that the Spanish forces were completely inadequate to control the blacks. Jackson's mind, ever intolerant of an issue's gray areas, became set.

He ordered General Edmund P. Gaines, military commander in Georgia, to cross into Florida and attack any hostile Indians he could find. Should an attack on the Negro Fort prove incidental to this justifiable task, Jackson (and the nation) could have no complaint. Gaines, who was at the time overseeing the construction of Fort Scott at the headwaters of the Apalachicola just inside the U.S. border, decided to bring supplies for the fort and his campaign up the Apalachicola, and in July sent a small fleet of gunboats and supply barges to the mouth of the river. The commander of this expedition, the efficient and resourceful Sailingmaster Jairus Loomis, was instructed to join forces upriver with a contingent of U.S. soldiers and friendly Creeks under Colonel Duncan L. Clinch. That rendezvous was destined to take place at the Negro Fort.

Sailingmaster Loomis, moving cautiously but steadily up the Apalachicola, sent out a scouting party in a small boat on July 15, 1816. The boat was fired on by unseen enemies. Two days later, another scouting party spotted a black man on the banks of the river. They called to him, and instantly a heavy volley of musket fire rang out from the trees. Three sailors and one officer fell dead. One man was captured, tarred and burned alive. The dead were stripped and scalped. According to a survivor, blacks from the Negro Fort were responsible. Loomis pressed on.

Farther north, Colonel Clinch managed to capture one runaway slave who had a fresh white scalp in his belt; under questioning, the man told of the raid on Loomis's boat. The blacks had committed an act that the colonel was sure would be read as justification for an attack on the Negro Fort. He picked up his pace, arriving at

Prospect Bluff to find that Loomis's boats were already there—and that a scene of immense confusion was well under way.

Almost nothing is known of the commander of the garrison of the Negro Fort, other than that his name was Garçon and that he was once a slave who belonged to a Frenchman. What is known is that when Major Nicholls abandoned the fort, he left it brimming over with arms, including 4 long twenty-four-pounder cannon, 4 long six-pounders, smaller pieces of artillery (among them a brass howitzer), 2,500 muskets, 500 carbines, 500 swords, 400 pistols, 300 quarter casks of rifle powder and 763 barrels of common powder. Garçon's men would have been better off without most of it. Despite all of Nicholls's efforts, they did not have the training to use artillery effectively, and merely fired round after round at Loomis and Clinch in a kind of crazed frenzy, without doing any damage. Loomis kept his boats out of range, and Colonel Clinch did likewise with his men. In a further act of defiance, Garçon hoisted the Union Jack and the red flag of death, designed to strike fear into Clinch's Creeks. This, too, had no effect. The Americans had come to do a job, and on the night of July 26, they set about it.

Across the river from the fort, Clinch's men dug earthworks and Loomis brought his gunboats within range. After receiving an abusive reply to his demand for surrender, Clinch ordered his batteries to open fire on the twenty-seventh; it was for Loomis, however, to devise the killing blow. His boats fired eight balls at the fort's strong walls, but all eight shots bounced off harmlessly. Then Loomis ordered a ball heated red-hot in the cook's galley while he elevated one of his guns so that the shot would be sent within the confines of the fort. The shot was loaded, Loomis fired and, incredibly, the ball ripped into the fort's main magazine, igniting Garçon's deadly stockpile. Only three defenders ultimately survived the blast. Loomis's crews and Clinch's men, stunned by the spectacle of pieces of human bodies literally raining through the air around them, took possession of Prospect Bluff slowly and without any great celebration. Garçon had survived the explosion, along with one of his allies, a renegade Choctaw chief. Both were given, along with many of the arms that had not been destroyed, to Clinch's Creeks, who quickly executed them. The next day, a force of Seminoles arrived to relieve the fort, but, surveying the scene, retreated to the Suwannee River in East Florida. The blacks who had lived under the fort's protection soon joined them there, and together they prepared for the inevitable next attack of the much hated and equally feared agents of General Jackson.

Few stories better illustrate the situation in the Floridas in 1816 than the destruction of the Negro Fort. The Spanish empire that supposedly ruled the provinces had played no part in the drama. The blacks and Indians owed what resistance they had been able to muster to British agents, who may have lacked the official approval of their government but who nonetheless played a key part in opposing the designs of the United States. Andrew Jackson had heightened his reputation as a merciless conquerer who made and lived by his own laws, acting with complete autonomy and reading his orders as commander of the Division of the South in their broadest possible sense; it was not the last time that he would do so. Above all, the fighting on both sides had been savage, only increasing the bitterness that was so rife among Indians, blacks and American settlers alike.

Confusion, violence and intrigue—within eighteen months these conditions thrust the Floridas to the very forefront of America's foreign relations.

In June of 1817, John Quincy Adams was in London, preparing to quit his post as minister to the Court of St. James and return to Washington to become James Monroe's secretary of state. The favorite son of John and Abigail Adams, John Quincy first became a public servant in 1781, at the age of fourteen, when he served as secretary to the American minister in St. Petersburg. Since that time he had been minister to the Hague, minister to Prussia, a senator from Massachusetts, minister to Russia, the head of the American delegation at Ghent and finally the American representative in Great Britain. After so many years abroad, Adams had formulated a personal political credo that was pointedly independent and nationalistic. Espousing union at home and a firmly nonaligned stance abroad, he had become America's most renowned diplomat, a force to be reckoned with in any European capital. Now he was preparing to put his beliefs to a global test—as secretary of state he would do all he could to make the United States, as he had once written to his mother, "A nation, coextensive with the North American continent, destined by God and nature to be the most populous and powerful people ever combined under one social compact."

Adams was, of course, familiar with the Florida question. A con-

firmed continentalist—his support of Jefferson's Louisiana Purchase had caused him to be ostracized by his Federalist colleagues
at home, who viewed westward expansion as a threat to the power
of the Northeast—Adams knew that the nation could not safely
push toward the Pacific with the dreaded pistol still on its flank.
When the United States had taken a portion of West Florida in
1810 and increased its control over New Orleans, Adams had argued the legality of the move by demonstrating that the area was
in fact part of the Louisiana region sold to America by Napoleon.
He hoped that the steady decline of Spanish authority might make
the peaceful acquisition of the rest of the provinces possible; but
whether peaceful or forceful, the takeover was necessary.

This stance was also becoming increasingly clear to the more
reasonable of Spain's ministers (a rare commodity under Ferdinand VII), most notably the foreign minster, José Garcia de Leon
y Pizarro. By 1817 both Washington and Madrid had generally
accepted the notion that Spain might release the Floridas if she
could get a satisfactory arrangement of the boundary between her
remaining North American possessions—Mexico, Texas and California—and the western territories of the United States. The principal problem was that Spain was known to favor the Mississippi
as that boundary. This, to Adams as to most Americans, was unacceptable. On June 7, Adams met with Lord Castlereagh—the
British foreign secretary whose mastery of balance-of-power
diplomacy had guided the shaping of post-Napoleonic Europe at
the Congress of Vienna—in London to discuss the issue. Adams's
diary entry on the meeting is revealing:

"We had some further conversation upon the state of relations
between the United States and Spain, and examined the ground
upon a map. He asked, if the Floridas were ceded to the United
States, what objection would they have to the Mississippi for a
boundary. I showed him the whole range of territory marked upon
his own map, 'Louisiana,' and said that would be the objection; but
that if Spain would but for one moment be rational with us, we
could easily come to accommodations with her. He said, smiling,
that he must admit Spain was not the easiest of parties to concede,
and he might say the same of the United States. I answered, in the
same tone, that there could be no better judge of stubbornness and
compliance than a party so very easy and accommodating as Great
Britain."

The caustic exchange was typical of Adams. The man who

would, during his years at the State Department, create a sophisticated American foreign service and code of diplomatic conduct
was nonetheless capable of extraordinary bluntness, fits of intoler-
ance and sarcastic comments that often gave offense. Above all, his
absolute faith in the righteousness of the American system and his
subsequent devotion to the security of his country caused him to
suspect nearly every European power of having designs on North
America. As a young man, he had witnessed both the Revolution
and his father's struggle to win a satisfactory peace from the British; these events had left him indelibly marked by Anglophobia,
without, however, sparking any compensating sympathy toward
other European powers. His first major diplomatic posting had
been to Holland, where he had observed the subversive work of
agents of revolutionary France and acquired a permanent distrust
of that nation and of all radical movements. From his years in
Prussia and Russia he took an unswerving aversion to tyrannical
autocracy. America was, to Adams, truly the last best hope of mankind, and only by keeping her clear of foreign influence could the
great experiment succeed. "Of all the dangers which encompass
the liberties of a republican State," he wrote, "the intrusion of
foreign influence into the administration of their affairs, is the
most alarming, and requires the opposition of the severest caution."

    The life he lived was no less exacting than this political philoso-
phy. Generally up before dawn (at Ghent he was often rising at the
time that his fellow commissioner, Henry Clay, was just returning
from a party or breaking up an all-night card game), he was a
compulsive reader and writer who nonetheless always took time
out for rigorous physical exercise—as president he would become
famous for swimming in the Potomac wearing nothing but a bath
cap and goggles. Adams managed to fit two or three days into
every one, just as his lifetime would include careers enough for
several men; yet his personality contained more than a trace of
paradox. He adored the theater, yet distrusted those associated
with it; was intrigued by women, yet disliked their frivolity; loved
his children, but was a harsh taskmaster to them. Perhaps the best
single description was recorded by his own grandson, Henry
Adams, who, in his third person autobiography, described the
aging John Quincy Adams's intervention when the young boy one
day refused to go to school:

    "He [Henry] was in a fair way to win, and was holding his own, with sufficient energy, at the bottom of the long staircase which led up to the door of the President's library, when the door opened, and the old man slowly came down. Putting on his hat, he took the boy's hand without a word, and walked with him, paralyzed by awe, up the road to the town. After the first moments of consternation at this interference in a domestic dispute, the boy reflected that an old gentleman close on eighty would never trouble himself to walk near a mile on a hot summer morning over a shadeless road to take a boy to school, and that it would be strange if a lad imbued with the passion of freedom could not find a corner to dodge around . . . ; but the old man did not stop, and the boy saw all his strategical points turned, one after another, until he found himself seated inside the school, and obviously the centre of curious if not malevolent criticism. Not till then did the President release his hand and depart. The point was that this act, contrary to the inalienable rights of boys, and nullifying the social compact, ought to have made him dislike the grandfather for life. He could not recall that it had this effect even for a moment."

James Monroe chose Adams over Henry Clay to be secretary of state in 1817 for many reasons: Adams was a New Englander (and thus balanced Monroe's southern and western ties), he was America's foremost diplomat, and he would likely prove far more trustworthy than the ever-maneuvering Clay. But in addition, that same sense of judicious relentlessness that young Henry Adams would recognize two generations later had no doubt made a deep impression on Monroe. Behind Adams's cool Massachusetts eyes and wryly pursed mouth the president could detect a complex mind whose mastery of international relations and the machinery of American security knew no equal—in the hard bargaining that was to come, Adams would prove invaluable.

For some time before Adams took over at the State Department, Great Britain had been offering to mediate between the United States and Spain. Adams's meeting with Castlereagh had given him a good idea of the motivation behind these offers—"his plan of bounding us by the Mississippi was exactly what I should have expected from a British mediator." Yet the fact remained that when Adams returned to Washington, the Spanish government, through its wily representative, Don Luis de Onís, was still insisting on a line at the Mississippi and the Americans were still insisting that this would negate the Louisiana Purchase and that the inability of Spain to control the Indians in her territories constituted a violation of Pinckney's Treaty. Neither party wished to go to war over the issue, yet it seemed daily more unlikely that negotiations would provide an answer. In addition, the United States was known to be considering a move against Amelia Island, off the coast of the Florida-Georgia border. Also nominally Spanish, the island was in fact controlled by privateers who had done a good business in smuggling and preying on commercial vessels, including those of the United States. Spain's inability to stop such behavior was another source of American outrage, and Don Luis de Onís's assertions of the integrity of Spanish domains only made the American cabinet—including John Calhoun at War, William Crawford at Treasury and William Wirt as attorney general—steadily more annoyed.

But as was so often the case in Florida, it was murder that was finally to force the train of significant events into motion.

In the spring of 1817, the War Department received an alarming message from one of its agents on the Georgia-Florida border. Apparently the Red Stick Creeks (so called because of their large red war clubs) had killed a white woman, one Mrs. Garrett, and her two children in their home and had "commenced their Red Stick dancings again." In response to the widely reported killings, General Gaines called the local Seminole chiefs to a conference, where he berated them in no uncertain or polite terms. The Indians, who kept a running account of how many of their people had been killed by whites and who viewed retaliatory murders as a businesslike way of settling the score and defending their integrity, explained that the killings were retribution for the recent murder of several of their own. Gaines, astounded, went on to accuse the chiefs of harboring fugitive slaves, indeed, of themselves making slaves of the runaways. The Indians told him that this was true; but slavery in a Seminole tribe merely meant the paying of tribute to a chief—slaves were allowed to farm their own fields and live fairly independently, and it was therefore natural that blacks from America would be drawn to Florida. The longtime friendship and interbreeding between blacks and Seminoles, the chiefs maintained, was not the business of the white general; controlling the murderous American settlers was.

By fall the situation was deteriorating. Settlers were demanding revenge for the murder of Mrs. Garrett and her children, while one Seminole chief whose lands extended across the Georgia border informed General Gaines that he would resist any American attempts to control those regions, and that the whites must stop cutting wood there. Gaines called the chief to another conference, but the man refused to attend. Gaines dispatched a party of 250 men to bring him in by force. At the chief's village of Fowltown, the American expedition discovered something far more damning than even murdered whites—British uniforms, as well as other circumstantial evidence indicating that British agents were again prowling the borders.

Nothing could have been worse for the Seminoles. For months rumors had been flying among the Americans that the Indians had a new set of British mentors, led by Alexander Arbuthnot, an eloquent, burly Scottish trader with a great white beard and a tendency to view the local tribes as savages in need of his benevolent protection and enlightenment. Arbuthnot traded heavily with the tribes, and his trade did not end at blankets, pots and rum; firearms and powder often made his schooners float low in the waters off the coasts of Florida. In addition, Captain George Woodbine and Lieutenant Robert Christie Armbrister, professional adventurers and former cohorts of the infamous Nicholls, were thought to have taken over the task of training Indians and runaway slaves to fight the Americans. The finding of British uniforms in a Seminole village near the Georgia border thus alarmed General Gaines—he ordered Fowltown burned, and in executing this order, the Americans killed two Seminole warriors and one woman. The tally of deaths was again unbalanced.

On November 30, an American lieutenant, R. W. Scott, was taking a small party of American women, children and soldiers—most of them ill—by boat up the Apalachicola. The boat was ambushed by Indians. Thirty-four soldiers, along with six women and four children, were killed. Lieutenant Scott himself, or so the rumor spread, was tortured to death. Several days later, another group of boats taking supplies up to Fort Scott was attacked, and only managed to get away after fierce fighting. The raids were in evident retaliation for the events at Fowltown.

Washington, faced with the outrage of its southern citizens, could not let such events go by without response, and that response would have to go further than another series of conferences; as General Gaines wrote to the War Department on December 4, "The poisonous cup of barbarism cannot be taken from the lips of the savage by the mild voice of reason alone; the strong mandate of justice must be resorted to and enforced." Nor would mere reprisal raids suffice; sentiment was growing for a move against the Indians in Florida on a scale larger than any that had yet been seen. Some, among them General Andrew Jackson, worried little about justifying such a move to the world. He wrote to Calhoun on December 16, 1817, that, "Spain is bound by treaties to keep the Indians, within her territory, at peace with us; having failed to do this, necessity will justify the measure, after giving her due notice, to follow the marauders and punish them in their retreat." Such a plan would require a significant number of men, for, as Gaines told Calhoun, "The Seminole Indians, however strange and absurd it may appear to those who understand little of their real character and extreme ignorance, entertain a notion that they cannot be beaten by our troops." Monroe and his cabinet were by now prepared to think in such terms—on December 16, Calhoun sent a dispatch to Gaines:

"On receipt of this letter, should the Seminole Indians still refuse to make reparations for the outrages and depredations on the citizens of the United States, it is the wish of the President that you consider yourself at liberty to march across the Florida line and attack them within its limits, should it be found necessary, unless they should shelter themselves under a Spanish post. In the last event, you will immediately notify this department."

But General Gaines was not to be the agent of the attack. New troubles flared up on Amelia Island in December, and on the 26th he was sent to subdue the various privateers. As if by fate, Andrew Jackson was ordered to the Florida border to take command personally of the Seminole expedition. In Memphis, he began to collect his volunteers for a long forced march to the border; and in Florida, the news that Jackson was himself to lead the next American assault spurred the hostile tribes into rituals of anger—and of fear. They believed they knew the character of the man who had so often punished them, and they prepared for a harsh campaign with no quarter asked and none given. Events would prove their assessments to be chillingly accurate.

For Andrew Jackson, although he may have preferred the military to the political life, was nothing if not a judge—and an exacting one, as well. True, he had, like Henry Clay, enjoyed the wild youth of a gambling duelist, creating a reputation in his native Carolinas that followed him when he emigrated to Tennessee. Yet Jackson, admitted to the North Carolina bar at twenty despite the lack of any extensive education, was on the side of hard-line conservatism when it came to the law. He worked for the moneyed interests of Nashville in his early lawyering days, and used his profits to acquire both land and slaves. By the age of thirty-one, he was a justice of the Supreme Court of Tennessee, one with a reputation for meting out harsh punishments. "I have an opinion of my own on all subjects," he later said, "and when that opinion is formed I pursue it *publickly,* regardless of who goes with me." But Jackson's opinions all too often resembled confirmed prejudices. His own belief in his interpretation of facts seldom if ever allowed him to consider seriously the views and doubts of either his colleagues or his constituents. Jackson in politics was much like Jackson in war—he was certain he understood the people around him, their faults and their virtues, and he acted in their interests as he saw fit, brooking no opposition.

By 1817, as he prepared for the Seminole campaign, Jackson's name and his image had taken on many of the heroic attributes that would stay with him: his passionate devotion to his wife Rachel, who had not been officially divorced when they were first married and whose good name Jackson was ever ready to defend; his gaunt body, wracked by the pain of chronic dysentery; his home at the Hermitage, the only place on earth, so he said, where he ever found peace; the drawn, determined face, housing a pair of remarkably piercing eyes and surmounted by a bold shock of white hair. Largely because of New Orleans, Jackson's place among America's heroes seemed assured at the time of the Florida crisis. But in the fields and swamps of those southern provinces, he would bring himself dangerously close to disgrace and disavowal, and would be saved from those ignominies chiefly through the efforts of John Quincy Adams, a man who knew nothing of frontier life or of Indian wars—and who would later become one of the general's bitterest political enemies.

On December 19, John Quincy Adams officially opened his negotiations with the Spanish minister, Don Luis de Onís, on the questions of the Floridas *and* the western boundary of the United States. The Spaniard began with what appeared to be a concession. Rather than sticking on the Mississippi, he might be willing to settle for a boundary along the lines of what had been, between 1763 and 1803, the border between Spanish and French possessions. This line ran from the area of the Mermentau and Calcasieu rivers in Western Louisiana north to the valley of the Missouri. But in exchange for such a concession, the Spanish would have to ask the United States for a firm promise not to recognize any of the new Latin American states that had gained independence from Spain during the first two decades of the century.

Onís's offer was foolish on many levels. The United States, which had already spoken of the Colorado River in Texas as a possible boundary, might have been willing to draw back from that extreme position; but the line the Spaniard had suggested would have deprived the United States of much of the Louisiana Purchase, as well as cut off communications with its key commercial holdings in Oregon—effectively, it was no better a boundary than the Mississippi. And although the American government had no intention of recognizing the new Latin American states until her own affairs with Spain had been agreeably settled, no president, least of all James Monroe, was likely to be willing to let the king of Spain dictate the foreign policy of the United States. In January, Adams informed Onís of all this, and ended on a rather ominous note: "I urged that if we should not come to an early conclusion of the Florida negotiation, Spain would not have the possession of Florida to give us."

Late in the month, Onís again asserted that Spanish demands for a border in the western Louisiana region were wholly defensible, given that the Americans expected to get the Floridas in return. The negotiations became deadlocked, and Adams knew that it would take a dramatic event to get them moving again. What he could not have known was that two days earlier, along the Apalachicola at the Georgia border, General Jackson had ordered all available livestock in the area slaughtered, issued to each of his men a three-day ration of meat and one day of corn and entered Florida.

Jackson had inherited Gaines's original orders concerning Florida—and almost immediately questioned them. In a secret note to President Monroe on January 6, 1818, the general made it clear that Spanish posts must be considered proper targets for attack if the administration wished to avoid "defeat and massacre." "Permit me to remark," he said, "that the arms of the United States must be carried to any point within the limits of East Florida, where an enemy is permitted or disgrace attends." In addition, Jackson saw the punitive nature of Gaines's mission as inadequate: "The Executive Government have ordered (and, as I conceive, very properly)

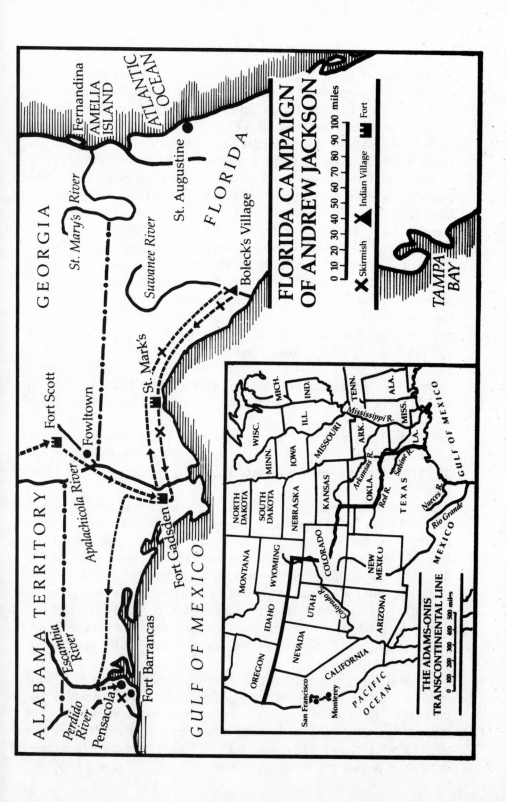

FLORIDA CAMPAIGN
OF ANDREW JACKSON

0 10 20 30 40 50 60 70 80 90 100 miles

✗ Skirmish   ▲ Indian Village   ⬛ Fort

GEORGIA

ALABAMA TERRITORY

FLORIDA

ATLANTIC OCEAN

GULF OF MEXICO

TAMPA BAY

Fernandina
AMELIA ISLAND
St. Mary's River
Suwanee River
St. Augustine
Boleck's Village

Fort Scott
Fowltown
Apalachicola River
St. Mark's
Fort Gadsden
Escambia River
Perdido River
Pensacola
Fort Barrancas

THE ADAMS-ONIS
TRANSCONTINENTAL LINE

0 100 200 300 400 500 miles

WISC.
MICH.
MINN.
IOWA
ILL.
IND.
NORTH DAKOTA
SOUTH DAKOTA
NEBRASKA
KANSAS
MISSOURI
ARK.
OKLA.
TENN.
ALA.
MISS.
LA.
TEXAS
MEXICO
MONTANA
WYOMING
COLORADO
NEW MEXICO
IDAHO
UTAH
ARIZONA
OREGON
NEVADA
CALIFORNIA
Mississippi R.
Arkansas R.
Red R.
Sabine R.
Nueces R.
Rio Grande
Colorado R.
GULF OF MEXICO
PACIFIC OCEAN
San Francisco
Monterey

Amelia Island to be taken possession of; this order ought to be carried into execution at all hazards, and, simultaneously, the whole of East Florida seized and held as an indemnity for the outrages of Spain upon the property of our citizens; This done, it puts all opposition down, secures for our citizens a complete indemnity, and saves us from a war with Great Britain, or some Continental Powers combined with Spain; this can be done without implicating the Government; let it be signified to me through any channel . . . that the possession of the Floridas is desirable to the United States, and in sixty days it will be accomplished."

In the months to come, this extraordinary message was to be the focus of widespread debate within the Monroe administration and in Congress as to whether or not Jackson actually had presidential approval when he invaded Florida. Monroe, who was ill at the time the note reached Washington, claimed that he passed it along to Secretary of War Calhoun and Treasury Secretary Crawford and did not himself read it, much less approve it. Jackson maintained that he had received (through channels he could not precisely identify) an unofficial but definite green light. Time has shown that Monroe's claims were well-founded, and Jackson's impossible to prove—but in March of 1818 such considerations were academic. Jackson had seen his duty, even if his superiors could not, and as always he did not intend to let anyone or anything prevent him from maintaining his sacred trust—the security of the United States.

Rainy weather and a lack of supplies made the general's march to the Florida border a difficult one. When he crossed into Spanish territory he was gambling that he could reach Prospect Bluff before his men's meager rations ran out. He completed this task a day behind schedule, arriving at Fort Gadsden (the former Negro Fort, renamed after the army engineer who rebuilt it) on March 15 with two thousand hungry men. After resupplying, Jackson began to push east, toward the Spanish fort of St. Mark's and, beyond that, the Suwannee River and the main concentration of Seminoles and blacks.

On March 25 he wrote to Calhoun that he had received a communication from the governor of West Florida in Pensacola. Apparently a force of Seminoles were in the area of St. Mark's and intended to take arms from—and refuge in—the fort. "Under this condition," Jackson told the secretary of war, "should I be able, I shall take possession of the garrison as a depot for my supplies, should it be found in the hands of the Spaniards, they having supplied the Indians; but if in the hands of the enemy I will possess it, for the benefit of the United States, as a necessary position for me to hold, to give peace and security to this frontier, and put a final end to Indian warfare in the South." With typical self-assurance, Jackson thus swept away the possibility of any future participation by his own government in the Florida campaign.

On April 1 Jackson, now well within those regions of Florida controlled by the Seminoles, was joined by additional American units and a force of friendly Cowetas. Thus reinforced, the general's progress toward St. Mark's became easy, and on April 2 he occupied the village of the Mekasukian chief Kenhagee, known to the whites as "King Hatchy." In the town the Americans were grimly reminded of why they had entered Florida: "In the council houses . . . more than fifty fresh scalps were found; and in the centre of the public square, the old Red Stick's standard, a red pole, was erected, crowned with the scalps, recognized by the hair, as torn from the heads of the unfortunate companions of Scott." If Jackson had entertained any thoughts of caution before this discovery, they were now dissolved completely, and he moved quickly on to St. Mark's.

On April 6 he took possession of the fort. The Spanish commandant put up no resistance, and was shipped, along with his garrison, to Pensacola on the following day. But the main force of the enemy was still to the east. "Success," Jackson wrote to Calhoun, "depends on the rapidity of my movements; tomorrow I shall march for the Suwanee river, the destroying of the establishments on which will, in my opinion, put a final close to this savage war."

The Seminoles in the Suwannee area were led by a chief of great distinction, called Bolecks or Bolicks or, more commonly, "Bowlegs." Military leadership, however, was left up to Bowlegs's head slave, a runaway black named Nero, and to Lieutenant Robert Armbrister, late of the British army. Armbrister had been wounded at Waterloo, served under Admiral Sir George Cockburn on the island of St. Helena during Napoleon's imprisonment, and subsequently been involved in a duel that made a trip to the West Indies necessary. Here he had met the infamous Nicholls, as well as the trader Arbuthnot. Arbuthnot, too, was in close contact with Bowlegs at the time of Jackson's invasion; in fact, when the Americans took St. Mark's the Scotsman was in the area, and sent a warning east to the Seminoles. Hearing that Jackson now had some

3,300 white troops and 1,500 friendly Creeks, Bowlegs decided to retreat from the Suwannee, as did Armbrister, who had been drilling the Seminoles and blacks. Nero was left to cover this movement, with a rear guard made up almost exclusively of fugitive slaves.

As Jackson moved toward the Suwannee, an American captain who had remained in the St. Mark's area, Issac McKeever, engaged in a bit of subterfuge that was to net a prized quarry. Flying a Union Jack on his boat, McKeever lured aboard not only Arbuthnot, but the Prophet Francis and the Red Stick chief Homollimico, as well. The ethics of the capture were indeed shady; but McKeever, like his commander, was willing to leave such considerations to Washington politicians. The war in Florida was savage—if undeclared—and there was no time for weighing ethics.

On April 16 Jackson was making his approach to Bowlegs's village. Forming his lines of attack and taking the center column himself, Jackson rushed the blacks who had remained behind to cover their comrades' retreat. It was not the crushing defeat the general had wanted. Only nine blacks and two Indians were killed, although the others were forced to disperse widely. Jackson took possession of the village, and that night his pickets made yet another illustrious capture—Armbrister, found wandering in the swamps. After destroying the village, Jackson turned back toward St. Mark's on the twenty-first.

From Armbrister the general learned of Arbuthnot's warning to Bowlegs, and on the basis of this a special court was convened in St. Mark's under General Gaines to try the two English citizens and the two captured Indian chiefs. The result of the trial was preordained. "On the commencement of my operations," Jackson told Calhoun, "I was strongly impressed with the belief that this Indian war had been excited by some unprincipled foreign or private agents." It was apparent that the Tennessee judge intended once again to write and execute his own law. Despite the fact that much of the evidence against the four accused men was circumstantial, and that Gaines's board of twelve officers recommended a sentence of fifty lashes and a year's confinement for Armbrister, all four men were executed. Said Jackson: "So long as the Indians within the territory of Spain are exposed to the delusions of false prophets, and poison of foreign intrigue; so long as they can receive ammunition, munitions of war, &c. from pretended traders, and Spanish commandants, it will be impossible to restrain their outrages." At St. Mark's the false prophets and foreign intriguers had been justly punished; it was now the turn of the Spanish commandants.

On May 24 Jackson occupied the fort of St. Michael's, overlooking Pensacola. The governor of West Florida, Don José Masot, retreated quickly to Fort Barancas, another six miles away, and Jackson pursued him there. Masot fired off his cannons in a gesture of defense, but then quickly surrendered, well aware of who he was dealing with. Along with all his officers, Masot was shipped to Havana, and Jackson appointed one of his own colonels governor of West Florida. As if to confirm his conquest, the general also announced that American revenue laws would henceforward be in effect in the province.

Jackson, for once, seemed to have exhausted even his own capacity for creating a furor. By attacking St. Mark's and Pensacola —not to mention appointing an American officer governor of a Spanish province—the general had deeply offended the integrity of Spain and insulted the person (or so it would later be said) of Ferdinand VII. By executing Arbuthnot and Armbrister, he had given good cause to those in Great Britain who favored yet another war with the United States. Through his uncompromising and brutal treatment of the Florida Indians and their chiefs, he had fanned the already strong anti-American sentiments of those peoples, and ensured that their hatred would burn violently for another generation. At the end of the month, weary, sick and longing for the company of his wife, the general returned to Tennessee.

Don Luis de Onís was stunned. Indeed, much of official Washington was stunned, but no one more so than the Spanish minister. The details of Jackson's invasion reached the capital in early June, and Onís quickly fired off a note to the Monroe administration. "How is it possible," he protested, "to believe that, at the very moment of a negotiation for settling and terminating amicably all the pending differences between the two nations . . . the troops of the United States should invade the Spanish provinces, insult the commanders and officers of their garrisons, and forcibly seize on the military posts and places in those provinces? . . . General Jackson has omitted nothing that characterizes a haughty conqueror."

While Onís's indignation was overstated, considering Spanish toleration of Indian violence and British agents in the Floridas, his remarks on Jackson's methods went straight to the heart of the matter. Most Americans would have agreed, before the invasion, that acquiring the Floridas was necessary. But to acquire them through a congressionally unauthorized invasion that had seen the execution of British subjects by a military court smacked of a martial spirit that made many in the country uneasy, among them President Monroe and almost every member of his cabinet. Calhoun, deeply offended that Jackson had simply ignored the directives of the War Department, demanded that the general be disavowed and punished; Crawford, a powerful politician with presidential aspirations, saw an opportunity to discredit Jackson and thus weaken a future candidate for the executive; and Monroe himself saw no way to justify the action to a confused electorate. Only one member of the cabinet stepped forward to defend the invasion of Florida—John Quincy Adams. On July 15, the day the cabinet first took up the issue, he wrote in his diary:

"The President and all the members of the Cabinet, except myself, are of [the] opinion that Jackson acted not only without, but against, his instructions; that he has committed war upon Spain, which cannot be justified, and in which, if not disavowed by the Administration, they will be abandoned by the country. My opinion is that there was no real, though an apparent, violation of his instructions; that his proceedings were justified by the necessity of the case, and by the misconduct of the Spanish commanding officers in Florida. The question is embarrassing and complicated, not only as involving that of an actual war with Spain, but that of the Executive power to authorize hostilities without a declaration from Congress."

Adams was aware of one issue above all: if the United States should disavow Jackson and his invasion, its position in the negotiations for a boundary treaty with Spain would be so weakened that the ambitious terms he had begun to envision—including a western border that would stretch, in the north, all the way to the Pacific Coast—would be impossible to obtain. Yet there was no middle ground in the issue; Jackson and his invasion must either be abandoned or supported.

The Spanish government, sensing American disunity, put forward a set of dramatic demands. Not only must Pensacola be returned and indemnities paid for damages to Spanish possessions, but the honor of Spain required "the lawful punishment of the general and the officers of this republic by whom they [the crimes against Spain] were committed." Monroe and Adams did compose a letter to Don Luis de Onís saying that they would be happy to restore Spanish authority in Florida as soon as Spanish troops were in sufficient numbers to control the Indians. In addition, a very tactful letter to General Jackson from the president explained why Pensacola could not be kept without congressional authorization. But these moves did not satisfy Spain, and a break in the treaty negotiations seemed likely.

Despite this danger, Adams maintained his position on disavowal, demonstrating that by July of 1818 he had become aware of how intimately connected Jackson's invasion of Florida and the larger issue of overall American security had become. In his dealings with Great Britain and Russia, both of which had asserted their power over various parts of the Oregon Territory, the secretary had already defended the claims of the United States on the Columbia River, where the United States had important fur and trading interests; he now saw that by forcing Spain to accept a border that would run westward somewhere in the area of the 42nd parallel, he might actually create a territorial link between the Louisiana Purchase and those vital western commercial holdings. Over time the United States, as the only contending power with such a link, could expect its influence—and its borders—to expand along the Pacific Coast. The advantage of this situation was clear—it would provide the United States, in time, with a western border that was unarguable, and above all, defensible. None of this, however, could even be dreamed of if Spain were allowed to use Jackson's invasion of Florida as an excuse to procrastinate and protest.

Adams's first concrete offer of a western boundary, made to Onís at this time, included a definite line to the Pacific—and once again, the Spanish minister was shocked. "So you are trying to dispossess us also of the whole Pacific Coast which belongs to us, and which Juan de Fuca took possession of in the King's name up to 56 degrees!"

"Nonsense," Adams said, with that blend of irascibility and righteousness so characteristic of him. "The English pretend the Columbia River is theirs. The Russians have possessions north of it which you have never disputed, and we have more right than anybody else to the River Columbia. We have establishments on its banks, and we need it to keep open our communications with the interior." Onís knew that Adams was substantially correct. "Here are their views, clear enough," he told his superiors, "and the truth is they are less exaggerated than their real ones." But the government of Spain was not yet prepared to give in; Madrid would wait and see what advantages might be won by the domestic American political crisis brought on by Jackson's invasion.

While Adams was wrangling with Onís, he had to serve double duty defending Jackson in the cabinet. In a July 20 meeting, still faced with the opposition of the president and his fellow officers, Adams cited passages from various experts on international law in his attempt to avoid disavowing the general. He acknowledged that the case was a difficult one: "But, if the question was dubious, it was better to err on the side of vigor than of weakness—on the side of our own officer, who had rendered the most eminent services to the nation, than on the side of our bitterest enemies, and against him." Outside the cabinet, pressure for disavowal was also growing. Henry Clay, ever eager to attack the administration and advance his own political fortunes, began to express doubts about the Florida campaign. But for the moment, Clay did not state his opinions openly—it remained to be seen whether or not any significant public support for disavowal could actually be drummed up.

Adams continued to hold fast in the cabinet. On July 21, he listed three additional reasons why disavowal would be dangerous: "1. It is weakness, and a confession of weakness. 2. The disclaimer of power in the Executive is of dangerous example and of evil consequences. 3. There is injustice to the officer in disavowing him, when in principle he is strictly justifiable." Adams's efforts, if they did not prompt cabinet approval, did at least succeed in delaying disavowal; and in the interim, the secretary continued to exchange treaty proposals with Onís.

By autumn there was talk of a congressional investigation into Jackson's invasion, following a new Spanish demand, this one from Pizarro, that the general be punished. On October 24, Onís made another boundary offer, once again sticking in all important respects to his previous line that excluded much of the Louisiana Purchase. Monroe was at a loss as to what course to pursue, and in his confusion and impatience he turned to the simplest solution, force. He instructed his cabinet to let it be known that he was considering asking Congress, when it reconvened, for authorization to annex the Floridas through a formal invasion. Such a move would require widespread public support, and toward the summer's end various members of the administration began to go about the arduous political process of getting it.

Another war in the Floridas seemed a very real possibility, but Spain still felt secure enough with the ethics of her position to delay any significant concessions to the Americans in the boundary negotiations. Then, too, it was known in Madrid that there had been tremendous public outcry in England over the executions of Arbuthnot and Armbrister—should war come, Ferdinand VII might very well be able to count on assistance from London. The position of the United States, ethically, politically and militarily, was perilous indeed.

It was for Adams to suddenly and dramatically turn the tables on his foreign and domestic opponents. In November, he composed a document whose significance was almost as great as that of the Monroe Doctrine five years later—and whose effects were resounding.

The Spanish government's demand that Jackson be punished had been addressed to the American minister in Madrid, George W. Erving, who had forwarded it to Washington. Adams's reply, therefore, was also addressed to Erving, who was instructed to deliver a copy of the note to the court of Ferdinand VII. In addition, copies were sent to other American ministers in European capitals, including and especially to Richard Rush in London. And before it even arrived in those destinations, the note was made available to Congress and to the American press. Dated November 28, 1818, the "Instructions to Erving" were the fruit of weeks of concerted effort—of personally collecting data, of drafting and redrafting—on the part of the secretary of state. Adams's purpose was threefold—to deal another, perhaps mortal blow to the idea of disavowing Jackson and his invasion; to demonstrate that it was Spain and not the United States whose position in Florida was indefensible; and to make it clear to Great Britain that the United States would actively respond to any British meddling in the affairs of North America. It was an ambitious undertaking, even for an intellect such as Adams's—the extent of his success was all the more remarkable.

The secretary of state began by painstakingly reviewing the course of events in Florida since the arrival of Major Nicholls in 1814, immediately assuming a tone of impatient moral indignation

and demonstrating that Spain, in violation of her treaty obligations, had allowed the Floridas to become a haven for marauders
of all nationalities. He then stated that "the President will neither
inflict punishment, nor pass a censure upon General Jackson, for
that conduct, the motives for which were founded in the purest
patriotism; of the necessity for which he had the most immediate
and effectual means of forming a judgement; and the vindication
of which is written in every page of the law of nations, as well as in
the first law of nature—self-defence."

Defense formed the cornerstone of Adams's arguments. For
both at home and abroad, criticism of the invasion had been based
on the assumption that it had been an *offensive* war—not so, said
Adams. Jackson had invaded Florida and occupied Spanish possessions "in the course of his pursuit" of the enemy, and such had
long been recognized by experts on international law as legitimate
grounds for entering the territory of another power. The Spanish
military authorities in Florida had protested that they had not been
party to the depredations of the Indians and the blacks, but simply
had not had the necessary troops to control them. On this point
Adams took a particularly tough line, stating that such excuses
might serve to "exculpate, individually, those officers; but it must
carry demonstration irresistible to the Spanish Government, that
the right of the United States can as little compound with impotence as with perfidy, and that Spain must immediately make her
election, either to place a force in Florida adequate at once to the
protection of her territory, and to the fulfilment of her engagements, or cede to the United States a province, of which she retains
nothing but the nominal possession, but which is, in fact, a derelict,
open to the occupancy of every enemy, civilized or savage, of the
United States, and serving no other earthly purpose than as a post
of annoyance to them."

As for "His Majesty's profound indignation" at having his territory invaded, Adams pointed out that Nicholls had, far more
boldly and with far less reason, also invaded Florida—"Where was
His Majesty's profound indignation at that?" Always careful to
mention the interference of the British, Adams steadily built to a
crescendo of invective against "the savage, servile, exterminating
war against the United States," turning finally to the execution of
Arbuthnot and Armbrister, whom the Spanish government had
referred to as "subjects of a Power in amity with the King." Showing that the pair had been closely involved with the Indian tribes,

and then listing some of the Indians' more atrocious behavior, the secretary asked: "Has mercy a voice to plead for the perpetrators and instigators of deeds like these?"

Having so dispensed with Spain, Adams saved his strongest warnings for Great Britain, a nation that "yet engages the alliance and cooperation of savages in war. . . . From the period of our established independence to this day, *all* the Indian wars with which we have been afflicted have been distinctly traceable to the instigation of English traders or agents. Always disavowed, yet always felt; more than once detected, but never before punished; two of them, offenders of the deepest dye . . . have fallen, *flagrante delicto*, into the hands of an American general; and the punishment inflicted upon them has fixed them on high, as an example awful in its exhibition, but, we trust, auspicious in its results, of that which awaits unauthorized pretenders of European agency to stimulate and interpose in wars between the United States and the Indians within their control."

After finishing with a demand that Spain pay indemnities to the United States for the cost of Jackson's invasion and punish her officers in Florida for their misconduct—a demand calculated to put an end to similar Spanish protestations rather than to produce any actual monies or punishments—Adams stated, "with the frankness and candor that become us," that should Spain not change her behavior, "the United States will be reluctantly compelled to rely for the protection of their borders on themselves alone."

The document, quite simply, leveled all opposition to the Monroe administration and the United States. Richard Rush wrote from London to say that the British foreign secretary, Lord Castlereagh, was now resolved to avoid any conflict with the United States, even though English public sentiment was such that war might have been declared had the government "BUT HELD UP A FINGER." (The capitals are Rush's.) John Adams Smith, John Quincy's nephew and a member of the London legation, reported that "There has scarcely been a pistol flashed since the great gun from Washington to Madrid." Similar reports came in from all over Europe. In the bold and independent style that was to become his trademark, Adams had preempted the interference of Great Britain and Europe generally in the affairs of North America.

In Madrid, the note was the death knell of Spanish procrastination. Florida was going to be lost, and all that could be gained were the most favorable terms possible in the west—but *some* settlement had to be made, before the Americans acted on their own indignation and seized Texas along with Florida. New instructions were issued to Don Luis de Onís, empowering him to get what he could but to definitely sign an accord as quickly as possible.

And at home, the vindication of Andrew Jackson was complete. Largely as a result of Adams's Instructions to Erving, both the House and Senate investigations of the invasion of Florida were aborted. Early in 1819, in a demonstration of his heightened popularity, the general embarked on a triumphant tour of the Northeast—while the secretary of state turned his attention back to the boundaries of the United States.

On February 22, 1819, the Transcontinental Treaty between Spain and the United States was finally signed. The culmination of weeks of hard bargaining—Don Luis de Onís had proved, to the end, a stubborn and tenacious negotiator—the treaty realized all of Adams's most desired goals. King Ferdinand transferred possession of all territories in the Floridas that were in his possession to the United States, in exchange for a sum of five million dollars. This money was to be used to pay off outstanding claims that American citizens had against Spain for the depredations of recent decades. As for the western border, it established unchallenged American control over all of the vaguely defined regions that had been bought from Napoleon, and included a line to the Pacific along the 42nd parallel. It was the most significant treaty that had yet—or perhaps has ever—been signed by the United States. Adams himself was fully aware of the vast import of his accomplishment:

"It was near one in the morning when I closed the day with ejaculations of fervent gratitude to the Giver of all good. It was, perhaps, the most important day of my life. . . . The acquisition of the Floridas has long been an object of earnest desire to this country. The acknowledgment of a definite line of boundary to the South Sea [the Pacific] forms a great epocha in our history. . . . I record the first assertion of this claim for the United States as my own."

It took two years for the treaty finally to be ratified in Madrid and Washington, but by February of 1821 the way was open for Americans to safely pursue the westward expansion that had been the most cherished dream of continentalists since Jefferson. As

Jackson told Monroe, "With the Floridas in our possession, our fortifications completed, Orleans, the great emporium of the West, is secure. The Floridas in the possession of a foreign power, you can be invaded, your fortifications turned, the Mississippi reached and the lower country reduced. From Texas an invading enemy will never attempt such an enterprise; if he does, notwithstanding all that has been said and asserted on the floor of Congress on this subject, I will vouch that the invader will pay for his temerity." In addition, with the Florida and boundary issues settled, the United States could finally turn its attention to the question of Spain's newly independent Latin American colonies, a question that had long badgered President Monroe and his secretary of state.

Surveying the Latin American political scene during the last years of the eighteenth century and the opening decades of the nineteenth, few American leaders perceived a group of enlightened provinces working toward emancipation and freedom. In South America, the social structures of the various states ranged from peacefully stratified to actively oppressive; in Central America, they were far worse. Violent factionalism and brutal power struggles were the order of the day throughout Latin America, and even Jefferson despaired of the region's prospects for democracy, stating that, "History . . . furnishes no example of a priest-ridden people maintaining a free civil government."

But the United States could not afford to view the affairs of Latin America with detachment. Jefferson also believed that it was the destiny of the United States to control, perhaps even rule, the "whole northern, if not the southern continent," and continentalism was a belief that crossed party lines in the early years of the republic. Its most basic requirement was American predominance in much of the Western Hemisphere. Thus, when Spain's Latin American colonies began to agitate for independence in the last years of the 1790s, their efforts were greeted with notable coolness in Washington. Any American aid that was even discussed rested on one condition: that the United States should be the sole power to actively support the rebellions of the provinces. Alexander Hamilton said in 1798 that the United States would back the efforts of the United Provinces of the Río de la Plata (Argentina) only if all other nations, especially the British, were forbidden to provide any more substantial assistance than ships. Jefferson and Madison were more rhetorically enthusiastic, but no more substantively helpful. From the beginning, then, Latin American leaders were disappointed and angered by American reluctance to assist them in their struggles for independence.

Things had not greatly changed by the time of the Monroe administration. James Monroe himself, like his more illustrious predecessors, was personally sympathetic to the Latin American cause, but knew that any attempt to recognize the new republics might provoke a misunderstanding with Spain that would jeopardize the negotiations on Florida and the western boundary of the United States. And John Quincy Adams was neither politically nor philosophically sympathetic toward the Latin Americans. In 1821 he wrote: "They have not the first elements of good or free government. Arbitrary power, military and ecclesiastical, was stamped upon their education, upon their habits, upon all their institutions. Civil dissension was infused into all their seminal principles. War and mutual destruction was in every member of their organization, moral, political, and physical. I had little expectation of any beneficial result to this country from any future connection with them, political or commercial."

There were, of course, politicians in Washington willing to argue these points with Adams, most notably Henry Clay. "Will gentlemen contend," Clay asked in the House in 1820, "because these people are not like us in all particulars, they are therefore unfit for freedom?" Clay's arguments, as was so often the case when he entered the realm of foreign policy, were primarily a method of attacking the administration and assuaging his ego, still bruised after Monroe's failure to appoint him secretary of state in 1817; yet the fact remained that after the signing of the Transcontinental Treaty, the United States had no reason to hold up recognition of the Latin republics. During the course of 1822, this process was carried out.

But not without uneasiness. Following the failure of the United States to immediately and actively take up their respective causes, the Latin Americans had sought help from other powers, and received most of it from Great Britain. In 1806 the renowned South American revolutionary, Francisco de Miranda, had been militarily assisted by none other than Admiral Alexander Cochrane, who would later command the British fleet that sailed into the Chesapeake in 1814; and José de San Martín, perhaps the most accomplished South American military leader, had been transported to Buenos Aires in 1812 by a British frigate. Such actions had aroused apprehension in the United States, and certainly caused Anglophobes such as Monroe and Adams to view their new southern neighbors with no little skepticism. A conviction that the British intended to use the Latin American rebellions to expand their commercial—and perhaps even their territorial—empire had generally taken hold of American statesmen by 1822, and official recognition of the new Latin republics did little to counteract it.

That the Monroe Doctrine of 1823 was largely the work of John Quincy Adams has long been recognized, as has the fact that domestic politics (1824 was a national election year) played a key role in the desire of various politicians to take a bold stand against the assumed ambitions of the Holy Alliance of Russia, Prussia and Austria, and of Europe generally. But seen in the light of Adams's long and painstaking attempts to ensure the security of the United States, the doctrine must also be viewed as the logical outgrowth of the nation's desire to act unilaterally to obtain the utmost security not only in North America, but throughout the hemisphere.

British Foreign Secretary George Canning's dramatic suggestion in August 1823 that Great Britain and the United States join to prevent any European continental power from taking advantage of Spain's distress in the New World made comparatively little impression on the American secretary of state. Since at least May of 1818, Adams had been arguing in the cabinet that "no proposal should be made to Great Britain for concerted measures with her to promote the independence of South America. First, because it would be a departure from neutrality. Secondly, because Great Britain, though she will readily acquiesce in the South American Independence, will cautiously avoid having the appearance of supporting it; and thirdly, because she would at once decline our overture, and make it an engine to injure us with other European powers." As always, Adams's suspicions concerning British behavior were strong—and events in 1823 were to bear most of them out.

True, Canning's offer seemed a radical shift away from Castlereagh's traditional emphasis on the Concert of Europe and toward a "New World" diplomacy. But when the American minister in London, Richard Rush, investigated the matter further, he found Canning unwilling to join the United States in a general policy of recognition for the Latin American states—Adams's second point of 1818 was therefore accurate. And although he would not pledge recognition, Canning did wish to base any joint Anglo-American policy on a renunciation by both countries of further expansion in the Western Hemisphere. To Adams, who believed in the overriding importance of America's policy of westward expansion largely for reasons of national security, such renunciation represented a clear danger.

The secretary's belief that London would use any overture between Britain and America to "injure" the United States with the European powers may have been somewhat overstated, but to a man who had served at the Court of St. James's and observed firsthand how the British pursued their role as a world power, it was thoroughly understandable. And Canning's own maneuverings (following his initial offer to Rush and Adams's apparent reluctance to accept) gave good grounds for such suspicion. As summer turned to fall in 1823 and French power in Spain became paramount, Canning decided to turn from a policy of Anglo-American cooperation to one of warning France directly of the consequences of any European incursion into the Western Hemisphere. After this approach proved successful, Canning had little use for any American connection—and vice versa. Adams was now assured that European expansion in the New World would be thwarted, yet he had made no pledge that America would not seek to enlarge her own borders.

But it was Adams's first point—that a concerted policy would be a departure from neutrality—that was perhaps the most significant. On the surface, it seemed simply to reflect his desire to assure Spain that the United States would do nothing in regard to Latin America that might jeopardize the Florida and boundary negotiations; yet it went much deeper than that. For Adams's own concept of neutrality was hardly a passive one. "The principle of neutrality to all foreign wars," he told Clay in 1821, "was, in my opinion, fundamental to the continuance of our liberties and of our Union." Adams was quick to see that the Latin American colonies were becoming a factor in European politics—Spain's desire to reassert her authority over them, and her anxious attempts to get the support of other powers, were quickly translated by the Holy Alliance into an opportunity to espouse its reactionary principles. Great Britain, already at odds with the alliance, would have to find a way to respond to this shift in the European balance of power. Thus Canning's offer was not only self-serving—in that it would protect U.S. interests to the extent that they coincided with British interests

—but, in Adams's opinion, a dangerous trap, a way to be both drawn *into* European politics and *away* from the crucial process of continental expansion. The secretary was determined to reject it.

As was so often the case, Adams was virtually alone in his opinions. Monroe himself was initially undecided on Canning's offer, and sought the counsel of his party's twin sages, Jefferson and Madison. The two former presidents both favored acceptance of the proposal, and Monroe was impressed by their reasoning—the United States could use the power of Great Britain to gain advantage for itself. Calhoun, for a variety of reasons—not least that he believed accepting the offer would discredit Adams and improve his own chances of becoming president—was also leaning in Canning's direction. In the face of this opposition, Adams once again employed the unilateral style that had served him so well in 1818.

The secretary of state knew that the time was ripe to act on the question of Europe's future role in the hemisphere—the Spanish negotiations were finished, Latin American recognition had been accomplished, and Britain was jockeying for a position of influence with the new southern republics. But Adams passionately believed the United States must act alone and in its own interests. On October 16, he met with the Russian minister, Baron de Tuyll von Seroosken, who delivered a formal note stating that the Russian government would not receive any representatives of any Latin American states. The czar, said Tuyll, was happy to see that the United States, despite its policy of recognizing the new republics, had maintained neutrality in the Latin American wars of independence. Adams replied that the United States would remain neutral so long as the European powers did; Washington had no desire to hamper any rapprochement that might be effected between Madrid and her colonies. But should Europe abandon neutrality, the United States would also have to reconsider its own position. Later in the month, Tuyll suggested that he and Adams make their conversations public, as a method of formally defining the positions of the two powers. Adams declined to do so, telling Tuyll that it would be more appropriate for the administration to state its views in the president's upcoming annual message to Congress—which became known, finally, as the Monroe Doctrine.

As he pursued his latest goal, then, Adams was once more fending off statesmen—both foreign and American, both inside and outside the cabinet—who wished to align the policy of the United States with that of other powers. Just as, in 1818, he had defended

General Jackson and negotiated with Don Luis de Onís in the face of considerable opposition, so now he fought hard to keep the United States independent and nonaligned. His reasoning, as always, derived from his conception of American security, and only incidentally concerned the question of Latin America.

For a broad range of security issues faced Adams in 1823. In the Pacific Northwest, Great Britain, Russia and the United States were contesting the precise borders of their territories and the limits of their various commercial activities. Adams was anxious to assert the right of the United States to all territories at least as far north as the Columbia River and if possible as far as the 49th parallel. In addition, the issue of the Spanish southwest had been reopened with the independence of Mexico in 1821, and several European powers were thought to be looking at the rich coastal province of California with greedy eyes. In the Caribbean, Cuba had become a key concern. Adams knew that America would probably meet overpowering resistance, particularly from Great Britain, if she moved to annex the island, but he was concerned nonetheless that Cuba remain out of the hands of any power that might once again try to threaten New Orleans and the Mississippi. He therefore wished to ensure a "hands-off" policy, keeping Cuba Spanish even though it meant failing to support any Cuban independence movement. All of these continental considerations weighed heavily on Adams's mind as he argued that a unilateral statement of American policy be embodied in the president's message to Congress. Using the threat of the Holy Alliance and the independence of the Latin American colonies as dramatic and timely subjects around which to build nationalistic arguments, a broad and fundamental statement of the vital interests of the United States might be made.

But were the new Latin republics actually in danger of invasion by the Holy Allies, whether in support of Spain or on their own behalf? Certainly, Austria had little interest in an invasion, and the Russians, without the French fleet, could not even contemplate one. The third Holy ally, Prussia, was by no means a power that could consider such a gambit on her own. For their part, the French were deeply divided over the issue, with their prime minister committed to a policy of fighting Ferdinand VII's republican enemies in Spain only; he had no intention of allowing that commitment to spread to the Latin American colonies. These facts were basically known to American policymakers in Washington, and were the cause of much speculation—but to Adams, they were largely beside the point. Thwarting the real or imaginary designs of the Holy Alliance in Latin America was only a part of his plan. His chief concern remained what it had always been—to provide for security.

In attempting to reach this goal, the secretary relied, in 1823 as he had in 1818, on the strength of his considered arguments and the eloquence of his pen.

The Monroe Doctrine itself, announced to Congress on December 2, 1823, contained three basic points. All of them had been modified by the president, but all of them remained, at heart, the work of John Quincy Adams.

The first and most famous passage of the doctrine has come to be known as the "Non-Colonization Principle," and can be summed up by the assertion that "the American Continents, by the free and independent condition which they have assumed and maintain, are henceforth not to be considered as subjects for colonization by any European power." The second point, a reaffirmation of American neutrality in the wars of Europe, echoed the language of Washington's Farewell Address: "It is only when our rights are invaded, or seriously menaced, that we resent injuries, or make preparations for our defense." Finally, the doctrine linked all territories in the hemisphere that were not already the distinct possession of a major power (such as Canada or the West Indies) to the national interest of the United States: "We could not view any interposition for the purpose of oppressing them, or controuling [sic] in any other manner, their destiny, by any European power, in any other light, than as a manifestation of an unfriendly disposition towards the United States."

This triple thrust was aimed at *all* would-be interlopers. Just as Adams's Instructions to Erving had explicitly addressed themselves to Spanish-American affairs but implicitly challenged the policies of Great Britain in North America, so the Monroe Doctrine, by answering the supposed threat of the Holy Alliance, warned Britain that her attempts to gain influence in the Western Hemisphere would be met by a determined American response. That such a warning was necessary was soon demonstrated by Canning himself, whom Adams would later call "an implacable, rancorous enemy of the United States." In 1824 Great Britain recognized the Latin

American states, and Canning proclaimed that "The deed is done; the nail is driven, Spanish America is free; and if we do not mismanage our affairs badly, *she is English.*"

The Monroe Doctrine, though a bold statement made at a time when the United States did not have the strength to back up its words, was surely no bluff. Monroe and Adams understood only too well what war with a foreign power over the integrity of American claims might mean. Monroe, after all, had participated in the Revolution, had been secretary of state during the War of 1812, and presided over the invasion of Florida in 1818. Adams, in his own distinguished career, had served in wartime diplomatic posts. It is hardly likely that when these men—or a man such as Andrew Jackson—talked of again risking war with European powers during the 1820s, they were bluffing. Their dedication to American security was absolute, and their willingness to take bold risks on its behalf unquestionable. The force behind the daring statements made by the United States in 1823 may not have consisted of overpowering naval and military strength, but its strength of determination was very real indeed. It had been demonstrated with signal clarity in Florida and Washington in 1818, when a Tennessee soldier and a New England diplomat joined forces to eliminate what they believed to be a pressing threat to the nation.

That alliance was to prove short-lived. In 1828, Andrew Jackson and the incumbent president, John Quincy Adams, ran against each other in one of the most distasteful elections in American history. Jackson's supporters leveled charges of corruption, all unfounded and unproved, at Adams's administration, and personal invectives abounded. But Adams himself refused to answer such charges, maintaining that to do so would degrade both himself and the office of the presidency. This stance may well have cost him the election. When Jackson—whose reputation owed so much to the 1818 efforts of the then secretary of state—arrived in Washington for that most raucous of inaugurations, he found that the former president had slipped out of the city the night before. There would be no traditional transfer of power, and rarely another word exchanged, between Andrew Jackson and John Quincy Adams.

I I I

MANIFEST DESTINY AS NATIONAL SECURITY

1842–1849

AT latitude 12 degrees, 15 minutes south, longitude 77 degrees, 37 minutes west—just off the South American coast near Callao, Peru—Commodore Thomas ap Catesby Jones signaled to the commanders of the American sloops of war *Cyane* and *Dale* to join him on board the frigate *United States*. All three ships, which made up the overworked main force of the United States Pacific Squadron, had hurriedly sailed out of Callao some twenty-four hours earlier, on the afternoon of September 7, 1842. Commodore Jones, a resolute and occasionally daring officer who had served his nation for the better part of four decades before assuming command in the Pacific, had been in a state of controlled agitation ever since his departure, and the meeting on board the *United States* had been called so that he might share the source of his excitement with his officers.

"Gentlemen," the commodore began, "I lay before you a letter from Mr. John Parrott, the United States consul at Mazatlan . . . which contains the manifesto of the Mexican Government . . . in relation to the difficulties pending between the United States and the Government of Mexico—from which it is quite probable that the United States and Mexico are now at war."

This news, while it did cause excitement among the officers assembled, was not wholly unexpected. The "difficulties" between the United States and Mexico to which Commodore Jones alluded were long-standing. Since Mexico had established her independence from Spain in 1821 she had been wracked by civil dissent, and American citizens and businessmen living within her territories had endured the sorts of hardships, losses and occasional outrages that often accompany extended internal power struggles. These Americans had filed claims against the Mexican government, claims that—much to Washington's annoyance—had never been paid. Mexico's grievances were no less severe: Texas's war of independence in 1836 had been mainly fought by volunteers from the United States (although Washington had subsequently declined to admit Texas into the Union). The mutual animosities thus produced had gone through varying stages of tension between 1836 and 1842, and war between the two countries had more than once been a very real possibility. But the present crisis was far more threatening than any to date, as Commodore Jones indicated in his next statement:

"I also lay before you a newspaper . . . asserting, on what the New Orleans editor considers *'authentic'* information, that Mexico has ceded the Californias to Great Britain for seven millions of dollars!"

This news was far more momentous than even a declaration of war. The atmosphere of distrust that had existed for so many years between Mexico and the United States had been consistently worsened by the specter of the British Empire. In the minds of many Americans—among them Commodore Jones—there was no doubt that England would use hostilities between the United States and Mexico as an excuse to expand her presence in North America. California was not only the most likely but, as far as the United States was concerned, the most dangerous spot for such aggression. Mexico exercised little authority over her distant Pacific province; internal feuding and a constant turnover of governors had become the hallmarks of Californian affairs. Although the full extent of the region's wealth was not yet even guessed at (for Mexican settlements in California rarely extended beyond the coast, and inland exploration had been limited), the strategic advantages of the port of Monterey and the bay of San Francisco were obvious.

By holding them, a naval power such as England or France could not only increase her commercial might, but also thwart the American dream of an expansive Pacific boundary that had been born with John Quincy Adams's Transcontinental Treaty. Commodore Jones's final piece of intelligence touched on precisely this danger—

"In corroboration of the reported cession of the Californias to Great Britain, I have to inform you that the whole of Her Britannic Majesty's [Pacific] naval force, under Rear Admiral Richard Thomas, (filled with extra provisions,) has suddenly and with utmost secrecy of purpose left the coast of Chile and Peru, under sealed orders, *just sent out from England,* and, as I have good reason to believe, is now on its way to Panama, where it will be re-enforced by troops, &c., from the West Indies, destined for the occupation of California."

The extent of the crisis was now clear. If the transfer of authority in California from Mexico to any other power was a danger to the United States, the threat was especially acute in the case of Great Britain. Since 1818, the British had been joint administrators, along with the United States, of the vast Oregon Territory. This arrangement had frequently been a source of diplomatic irritation between the two powers, centering, as it did, around the future and ultimate division of the region. To the American way of thinking, it was only logical that Great Britain would seek to bolster her Oregon claims by expanding her presence on the Pacific. In addition, Britain had lent huge sums of money to finance Mexico's various republican and dictatorial governments during the 1820s and 1830s, and by 1842 this debt had risen to well over fifty million dollars. Americans were quick to believe that the British held sway in Mexico City, and that the Mexicans might well choose to pay their debt with something other than money. But the single most disturbing aspect of the situation was that by taking California, the British would not only end American hopes for a Pacific boundary, but would extend a huge cordon of influence around the United States, stretching from Canada and Oregon to the Gulf of Mexico. The decrepit state of Californian affairs only strengthened such fears. One French official, sent in 1841 to determine whether or not his country should try to secure the province, had written that California would ultimately end up in the hands of "whatever nation chooses to send there a man-of-war and 200 men." To Commodore Jones, the sudden and secret movements of the English fleet in the Pacific were proof positive that Great Britain meant to be that nation.

The officers of the Pacific Squadron knew that they had been placed in a position of immense responsibility. Commodore Jones, like most American commanders stationed in distant posts, had never received anything more than general directives from Washington. The last of these was dated December 10, 1841, and called for "the greatest vigilance and activity," especially regarding California. Jones understood that in a crisis such as the one he now faced, he would be expected to divine the wishes of the Washington government, and to rely on his own initiative in interpreting them, since specific orders would take months to reach him. In other words, it was now up to the commodore and his officers to create and carry out the Pacific policy of the United States.

As the true extent of this obligation began to sink in on the small group of men on board the *United States*, Jones took soundings. His subordinates all agreed that war had quite probably been declared, and that they were therefore justified in removing the Pacific Squadron from the coasts of Peru and Chile and heading toward the California coast. Next came a more momentous question, one that they were careful to make a written record of— "Under what circumstances, if any, would it be proper for us to anticipate Great Britain in her contemplated military occupation of California?" Their unanimous answer was also recorded:

"In case the United States and Mexico are at war, it would be our bounden duty to possess ourselves of every point and port in California which we could take and defend. . . . [W]e should consider the military occupation of the Californias by any European Power, but more particularly by our great commercial rival, England, and especially at this particular juncture, as a measure so decidedly hostile to the true interest of the United States as not only to warrant but to make it our duty to forestall the design of Admiral Thomas if possible, by supplanting the Mexican flag with that of the United States, at Monterey, San Francisco and any other tenable points within the territory said to have been recently ceded by secret treaty to Great Britain."

This line of reasoning had become characteristically American —supposed British designs were to be countered with actual assaults on a third party's (in this case Mexico's) territory in the name of American security. Jones and his officers all signed their statement of purpose, confident of their government's approval; the

Dale was dispatched to Panama to inform Washington of the squadron's plans and to receive news of the war; and the *United States* and the *Cyane* sailed immediately for the coast of California, anchoring in the harbor of Monterey on October 19, 1842.

Monterey was at the time California's foremost port, the bay of San Francisco being virtually deserted save for the tiny village of Yerba Buena. Protected by a dilapidated "castle," Monterey was home to a mixed bag of merchants and frontiersmen, Mexicans and foreigners. The presence of the two American ships of war caused an anxious stillness to fall over the environs, and Commodore Jones was at first disturbed that no "American or neutral resident, from whom I might obtain disinterested information" appeared. Eventually, two Mexican officers did board the *United States,* in a state of great nervousness: "such was their reserve that nothing satisfactory, or even coherent, could be extracted from them, except that they had never heard of any difficulties between Mexico and the United States, and knew nothing of war." Jones considered their statements a ruse: "Every thing that I could see or hear seemed to strengthen the impressions under which I entered the port, and none more so than that no American citizen came on board, although I knew that there ought to have been several of my countrymen in Monterey. The time for *action* had now arrived."

The captain of the *United States* was sent "on shore, under a flag of truce, to demand a surrender of California to the forces under my command." The Mexicans were given eighteen hours in which to make their decision. With no hope of a successful resistance, the Mexican authorities sent two commissioners to Jones that same night at 11:30 P.M., rousing the commodore from his bed to ask for the terms of surrender.

Accompanying the Mexicans as interpreter was Thomas O. Larkin, a shrewd New England merchant who had gambled his future on a move to California some years earlier and was now Monterey's most prominent American citizen. Commodore Jones was instantly suspicious of the good-natured and eminently reasonable Larkin. Why had he not come on board earlier? The commodore's suspicions were further aroused when Larkin began to ask disturbing questions about the war. Who had declared it? When? Over what incident? Larkin said that there were comparatively recent papers and letters from Mexico in Monterey that indicated a state of peaceful relations between the two countries—did Commodore

Jones have any more recent or reliable information? Jones responded by requesting that Larkin bring him all such papers, and was perplexed when Larkin returned the next morning without them, saying that they were in fact ashore but that he had been unable to obtain them. Jones's suspicions grew; he decided first to occupy the port, then to examine the papers, if indeed they existed.

On the following morning, a force of 150 American seamen and marines rowed ashore and marched to the castle of Monterey, their bands playing "Yankee Doodle" and "The Star-Spangled Banner." Having been sternly warned by Jones not to behave in anything less than an exemplary manner, and to "especially avoid that eternal disgrace which would be attached to our names and our country's name, by indignity offered to a single female, even let her standing be however low it may," the Americans occupied the town without incident. Jones issued a proclamation to the citizens of the province, declaring that, "Although I come in arms, as the representative of a powerful nation, upon whom the Central Government of Mexico has waged war, I come not to spread desolation among California's peaceful inhabitants. Those stars and stripes, infallible emblems of civil liberty . . . now float triumphantly before you, and, henceforth and forever, will give protection and security."

The afternoon and night of October 20 passed calmly in Monterey, the American occupation force setting about the business of improving the town's defenses. But on the twenty-first Commodore Jones, who until that point had good reason to be satisfied with his own judgment and the performance of his men, received a sharp jolt—the papers and letters Larkin had spoken of were found.

Consisting of official and private correspondence, these papers confirmed that as late as August 22 there had been no declaration of war by either the United States or Mexico. In addition, they indicated that Mexico was dispatching a new governor to California, who was ordered to recruit fresh troops for the militia and otherwise do his best to reassert Mexican authority over the province. The rumors of an English occupation were false. Not only did the Mexican government deny them, but at least one Mexican newspaper had gone so far as to cite the Monroe Doctrine in warning against any new European colonization schemes.

Commodore Jones was in a precarious situation, and he knew it.

"The motives and only justifiable grounds for demanding a surrender of the territory were thus suddenly removed, or at least rendered so doubtful as to make it my duty to restore things as I had found them with the least possible delay." That same afternoon the American troops returned to their ships, and a salute was fired to the Mexican flag as it was restored to its place above the castle of Monterey. The withdrawal was conducted with remarkable geniality on both sides, Jones and the Mexican officials exchanging cordial and ceremonious assurances of friendship. As suddenly as they had appeared, the American forces vanished from California.

Although the new provincial governor, who was far to the south, had some harsh words for both Commodore Jones and the United States government, no more serious repercussions ever materialized from the Pacific Squadron's occupation of Monterey. Jones himself was relieved of command in the Pacific in deference to the pride of the Mexican government, but he suffered no greater punishment; and Americans who, like Larkin, had decided to settle and to ply their trade in California were not penalized for the commodore's mistake. A general air of unreality surrounded both the occupation and its aftermath, but one aspect of the experience remained very real indeed—Jones had reflected the extreme anxiety of American leaders regarding California. If the situation in the province were ever again to become uncertain, the governments of both Great Britain and Mexico had little doubt that the United States would resort to another quick exercise of military force in order to seize California.

Given their extremely unstable internal situation, there was little the Mexicans would be able to do about it. The British, on the other hand, were not so hampered. Following the Jones incident, they decided to appoint a vice-consul for the Monterey region in order to keep a closer eye on the influx of American settlers, to monitor the deterioration of Mexican control and to watch for opportunities to expand Britain's influence. This move was by no means intended as a prelude to conquest. But the British government, in 1842 as in 1814, was not averse to harrying the expansionist efforts of the United States in North America. And for Americans, in 1842 as in 1814, any British activities on the continent that they believed must become theirs were cause for suspicion and alarm. Commodore Jones's bold blunder may have closed peacefully enough—but it was a virtual certainty that a future crisis would break out at Monterey.

. . .

Andrew Jackson's eight years in the White House had altered nearly every aspect of American domestic politics. A newly expanded and boisterous range of voters had turned the nation into a disorderly political arena, one in which Whigs and Democrats alike competed for votes with money, slander, whiskey and partisan newspapers. Such conduct prompted more than one observer to charge that the evolution of the American political system during Jackson's two terms spelled the end of the uniquely refined and balanced governmental system that had been created by the Founding Fathers; to others, however, Old Hickory had simply brought true democracy—in all its vulgar splendor—to the United States. Perhaps the only unarguable thing about the Jacksonian era was that it reflected to an exceptional degree the character of the man in the White House.

And, just as an obsession with national security had been a cornerstone of that character before the presidential years, so it became a central concern of the national government after Jackson's election in 1828. Jackson's concept of security continued to rest primarily on a deep distrust of the British. Although that distrust could often assume the same near-paranoid dimensions it had displayed in 1812 and 1818, it was—as it had always been—more than paranoia. His understanding of the dynamics of the British Empire—of that empire's own pursuit of security—was generally accurate. As most clearly demonstrated in the 1830s and 1840s by Lord Palmerston, and later by Benjamin Disraeli, British security in the nineteenth century depended above all on Britain's reserving the right to become actively interested—and sometimes involved—in the internal affairs of any nation or region that might at a given moment affect the commercial predominance of the empire. Jackson saw this clearly. The general's great mistake, however, was in going on to assume that the intent behind such behavior was conquest rather than commerce.

It was a characteristic exaggeration. True, the British were meddlesome in world affairs; but unlike the imperial Romans, their meddling did not reflect a need to annex steadily greater territories in order to predominate. Rather, it expressed a persistent determination to satisfy the requirements of mercantile capitalism. Britain's most significant imperial holdings had been secured—if not actually incorporated into the empire—before Jackson's presidency, and future annexations would be attempted, as a rule, only in regions where violent confrontation with another power was unlikely or impossible.

But security is largely a matter of perception. Jackson based his opinions not on speculation but on the historical record, and in the case of Great Britain that record seemed to indicate that attempts at further imperial annexations could be expected. Perceiving conquest to be the continuing goal of the British Empire, Jackson popularized that view as only the founder of the party of the Democracy could. After leaving office, he continued to exercise a powerful influence over American affairs. His wife Rachel was long dead, leaving Old Hickory's mind only too free to concentrate on matters of state. From the remove of the Hermitage he wrote voluminous letters to government officials and issued invitations to Democratic party leaders that amounted to summonses, rarely missing an opportunity to warn anyone who would listen (and they were many) of the unending British threat.

By the time Jackson's disciple Martin Van Buren left the White House in 1841, the American preoccupation with British designs on North America had reached proportions unknown since the War of 1812; and when the Anglo-American dispute over the boundary between Maine and Canada turned violent at the beginning of John Tyler's administration, there were those on both sides —and especially in the press—who would have been happy to see the two powers go to war. The Webster-Ashburton Treaty of 1842 defused that crisis, but the resentment lingered. An eventual clash seemed almost fated—especially in light of the rising power of the expansionist movement in the United States.

Although the term "Manifest Destiny" was not coined until late in 1845, when *New York Morning News* editor John L. O'Sullivan triumphantly proclaimed the irresistible march of American civilization to his readers and to the world, the ideas behind the catchphrase predated O'Sullivan's florid proclamation by many years. By 1843, when Democrats and Whigs were beginning to gear up for the national election of the following year, American expansionism had split into several schools, of which Jackson and his security-minded followers were but one. Each of these schools reflected a different section of the country and a different attitude toward the federal government, and all found expression in the great foreign policy debate of the day—the annexation of Texas.

"*Re*-annexation," it was often called, for many Democrats believed that John Quincy Adams, by negotiating a boundary with

Spain in 1819 that did not include Texas, had given away territory that had technically been included in the Louisiana Purchase. But whether "annexation" or "re-annexation," the Texas issue brought the regional forces of the United States into sharper conflict than they had been at any time since the Federalist-Republican debate during the War of 1812–1815. Following Texas's successful bid for independence in 1836, Texan leaders had quickly applied to the United States for admission to the Union, a move that Jackson himself had discouraged and Van Buren flatly rejected, fearing the sectional controversy that would break out. For Texas was slave country. Slavery had been tolerated in the Mexican republic, and the Texans, having built their economy on the institution, saw no reason to abandon it when they became independent. But during the 1830s the antislavery movement in the United States grew ever more powerful, and even slaveowners such as Jackson—and the Whig leader, Henry Clay—could see the danger in admitting a huge slave state such as Texas. Clay's Missouri Compromise of 1820 had fixed the slavery line at 36 degrees, 30 minutes—and nearly all of Texas was south of that line. Until such time as compensating, nonslave territories could be annexed to pacify the North, the admission of Texas would have to be delayed.

Many influential American statesmen, however, were actively opposed to such delay. First among these was Senator John C. Calhoun, leader of the Southern Democrats. Appointed to head the State Department by John Tyler in 1844, Calhoun was eager to use the issue of Texas to test Washington's determination to stand by the economically troubled South; the immensely handsome young nationalist of 1812 had by this time evolved into a haggard, bitter sectionalist. The agricultural power of his beloved South was declining along with the overworked soil that generations of slaves had tilled for irresponsible masters; in addition, tariffs, imposed by the federal government at various junctures to protect American industries (especially those of the manufacturing states of the North) from foreign competition, had hit the southern states hard during the 1830s by restricting their access to European goods and markets; and finally, increasing numbers of abolitionists —American and foreign—were vehemently calling for an end to the South's "peculiar institution." In the face of these adversities, Calhoun decided that if the Union would not look after the interests of the South, the South would have to fend for itself.

Texas gave him the chance to force a showdown. By admitting

Texas as all-slave, the federal government would add a state (or states) of great wealth to the southern bloc, and bring fresh lands into the Union that could be worked by impoverished southern farmers. If Washington refused Texas yet again, it would be a sign that no special effort was going to be made to aid the failing fortunes of the South. As the governor of South Carolina wrote to Calhoun in the spring of 1844, "If the Union is to break, there could not be a better pretext."

It was not surprising, then, that Calhoun's first move on taking over the State Department was to frame and sign a treaty of annexation with Texas on April 12, 1844. The treaty guaranteed U.S. naval and military protection to Texas, and assured the Texan government that all its "property" laws would be respected—an indirect assurance on the slavery issue. Calhoun knew that expansionism alone would not persuade the antislavery groups in the House and Senate to support his treaty, and in the face of their opposition he sought support for the document by bringing up an issue that had rarely failed to arouse alarm in all sections of the United States—the threat of British interference.

In much the same fashion as they had gained influence in Mexico through substantial loans, the British had secured a prominent position in Texas by doling out millions of dollars to her inept leaders. In addition, having freed their own slaves some years earlier, the British, in 1844, were busily espousing the cause of worldwide emancipation. These two aspects of British behavior gave Calhoun just enough room to circulate rumors that the British, in exchange for a Texan pledge of emancipation, intended to guarantee Texan independence against both Mexico and the United States and to offer yet another huge loan. Instead of an American state, Texas would become a dangerous British client.

The logic was specious and Calhoun's charges against the British government unsubstantiated, but the South rallied behind Calhoun, particularly after he wrote a challenging note to the British foreign secretary, Lord Aberdeen, spelling out the beneficial effects of slavery on the Negro character. Many senators and congressmen rose to oppose Calhoun's annexation plan, including the great spokesmen of the Whig party, Henry Clay and John Quincy Adams. Adams had left the White House in 1828 to find his greatest political happiness in the House of Representatives, where, possessed by profound guilt over the institution of slavery and his own failure to combat it during his presidency, his warmth for expansionism was steadily outshone by an abolitionist fire. His record on the issues of American security and America's boundaries, however, served him well during the Texas debate, and his eloquently outraged opposition to all such schemes as Calhoun's did much to harry the work of the Southern faction.

But the most powerful congressional opposition to the South's self-serving expansionism came not from the Whigs but from Calhoun's fellow Democrat and slave-owner, Senator Thomas Hart Benton of Missouri. The intimidatingly huge and hyperbolic Benton was an authority on the history of political thought—classical, English and American—despite having been expelled as a young man from the University of North Carolina for stealing. The youthful Benton had confessed to the crime and subsequently exiled himself to the western frontier, where his life had become continually and sometimes grotesquely entwined with that of Andrew Jackson. During the War of 1812 the two nearly killed each other in an "affair of honor," but when they found themselves occupying adjacent seats in the Senate in 1823 they became reconciled. The same frontier code that had almost caused their deaths was crucial in maintaining one of the era's most powerful political alliances. How much that code was exaggerated, in Benton's case, by the early humiliation of expulsion for stealing is a matter for speculation. What is undeniable is that his pride in his own name, the name of his family (he was blindly loyal to his often troubled relatives) and the name of his country deeply influenced his political conduct—and his stand on the issue of American expansion and the annexation of Texas.

Texas, on becoming independent, had claimed for its southern boundary the Rio Grande. As a Mexican department, however, it had always been bounded by the Nueces, a river many miles north of the Rio Grande. The intervening territory had been a major source of humiliation for the Mexicans, who, having first lost Texas, saw no reason to accept the additional insult of having non-Texan territory stolen from them. Calhoun, in his treaty of annexation, had consented to the Texan claims to the Rio Grande–Nueces region—and Benton, who despised Calhoun for his deviousness, had made this the focal point of his criticism of the treaty.

Benton, too, wanted Texas. He profoundly believed in the American mission to expand and spread civilization. But he also had a passion for history, and history told him that Texas had no claims south of the Nueces. In addition, Calhoun's warning of British meddling was, to Benton, "a rumor of imaginary design," nothing more than a "cry of wolf where there was no wolf." To back up these claims, Benton produced statements by Lord Aberdeen denying any British intention of either tampering with Texan slavery or attempting to use loans to put Texas in a compromising position. Benton knew Calhoun's real purpose in accepting the Texan claims—to hurry the issue of annexation and bring on a test of the Union. He angrily and publicly condemned the annexationist forces for "throwing the question into our elections, perverting it from its national basis, making it sectional and partisan, prostituting it to unworthy purposes, running the question at men, and making it the means of disturbing the peace and harmony of the nation." Largely through his effective denunciations, Calhoun's treaty was defeated in the Senate on June 8, 1844.

Benton then proposed a compromise in order to annex Texas. It included a renunciation of the Texan boundary claims, negotiations with Mexico and the division of Texas into both slave and nonslave states. His bill, however, was quickly shelved. Calhoun's slavery fanatics as well as the antislavery senators of the North combined forces to defeat the voice of moderation, despite Benton's prophetic charge that the annexation of all-Texas (including the Rio Grande–Nueces region) as all-slave was "an open preparation for . . . a dissolution of the Union."

The defeat of both Calhoun's treaty and Benton's bill, and the refusal of the antislavery Whigs to come up with a Texas formula of their own (some, like Adams, simply continued to denounce slavery and some, like Henry Clay, tried as much as possible to avoid the subject of annexation altogether), did not remove the issue of expansion into that vast southern region from American politics; indeed, they only thrust that issue to the very forefront of national affairs. But despite the formidable talents of men like Calhoun, Benton, Adams and Clay, none of them found a way out of the deadlock. For although they were all Andrew Jackson's contemporaries, none of them shared the general's single-minded devotion to the cause of American national security. Characteristically, when an issue or an action—regardless of its moral persuasiveness—had been clearly defined by the government and popularly perceived as vital to America's security needs, domestic dissent evaporated.

Texas was not in itself a security issue—Jackson himself had said so after the conquest of the Floridas, and Benton had demonstrated the same by persuasively arguing that the British threat was an illusion and that one river, be it the Rio Grande, the Nueces or even the Red, was as good a boundary as another. But so long as Texas was the center of the debate on expansionism, other legitimate security goals—most notably an expanded Pacific boundary —could not be pursued.

This had long been clear to Andrew Jackson. In 1836, he had tried to convince Texan leaders to conquer California, telling them that such a move would silence the opposition of security-conscious antislavers to annexation. But a subsequent Texan military expedition to California had been a humiliating failure, and by 1844 Jackson was too old and feeble to devise a way of annexing Texas, silencing the abolitionists and moving on to the far more critical question of the Pacific boundary.

But such a way did exist—and one of Jackson's most trusted political lieutenants was destined to be its inventor. From the time of his election through the eight stormy years of his administration and beyond, the general had been aided in his various political battles by a young congressman (and later governor) from his own state of Tennessee, a man who had studied and understood, perhaps better than anyone, Jackson's concepts of national security— and who would emerge from obscurity in 1844 to become the nation's first dark horse presidential candidate, one who richly deserved the nickname he was given during the hard-fought campaign: "Young Hickory."

"Who is James K. Polk?" The question became the slogan of the Whig party during the 1844 presidential contest, and it has continued to confound historians in the generations since Polk's death. A more deliberately secretive man has never occupied the White House; Polk may have shared many of Jackson's political convictions, but their personalities were profoundly opposed. Another of the North Carolina-to-Tennessee émigrés, Polk had been a sickly child, of little help and a constant worry to his farmer father. Early in his adolescence he had endured the excruciating pain of a frontier operation to remove gallstones, the supposed source of his frequent illnesses; but the surgery, while it did afford the boy greater periods of comparative health, left him far from vigorous. His suffering and deep sense of his own physical weakness—and of the disappointment and concern he caused his parents—left their marks. Young Polk's only consolation became long hours of cloistered study.

At the same University of North Carolina that had expelled Thomas Hart Benton for stealing, Polk became a legend for his punctuality, his scholarship and his often grim reserve. But the trials of his physical condition were not yet over; during the War of 1812, Polk was turned down for military service because of poor health. In the wake of this humiliation, the young man's already strong admiration for Jackson—who had known Polk's family in Tennessee—rose to immoderate levels. Jackson, of course, was everything Polk could never be—vigorous, straightforward, ever ready to thrash his opponents physically. But Polk did not waste his energies on envy. Graduating first in his class in both mathematics and the classics, he went on to practice law back in Tennessee in the office of Felix Grundy, the famous criminal lawyer and war hawk. He also employed his prodigious mental powers in the service of the Tennessee Democratic machine and eventually went to Washington as a congressman, one whose seemingly endless hours of work and study were happily employed in bolstering Jackson's dynamic concept of popular government. Going on to become Speaker of the House and then governor of his home state, Polk nonetheless remained an enigma, even to those who worked closely with him. His passion for secrecy, his unwillingness to delegate responsibility to subordinates and a managerial acumen that too often bordered on duplicity became early trademarks of his professional style; and as the years advanced, he grew to rely on such weapons ever more heavily.

In appearance he was short and thin, but he nonetheless carried himself with remarkable fortitude. And then, too, his face and manner made it hard to disregard the man. Long hair swept back on a large skull and cut just above the shoulders framed a pair of dark, intense eyes and a tight, determined mouth. Yet out of this stony face could often come an astonishingly pleasant laugh, one that, it was remarked, made those Polk encountered—who were generally taken aback by his grim aspect—enormously grateful. He dressed simply and in black, unlike his fellow Democrat Benton, and this difference between the two was further reflected in their speeches. George Bancroft, the historian and Massachusetts Democrat who was instrumental in getting Polk the party's nomination in 1844, wrote of the Tennessean's powers as an orator— "Everyone would say of him and say justly, that his style was marked by brilliant imagery; that it was marked with profound thought; lucidity; genuine English of the best kind and the simplest, and was just the best style of language with which to address the people."

Polk had married Sarah Childress, who aroused admiration even in as keen a judge of women as Henry Clay. The union had been childless but the couple were nonetheless devoted; indeed, the lack of offspring had brought them closer than they might normally have been, the eternally seclusive Polk sharing the full range of his thoughts and feelings only with his wife. Even the diary that Polk kept during his presidency, though detailed, reveals little of the inner man, although it does demonstrate his narrowness and passion for politics. This personal obliqueness may well have obscured Polk's achievements, when it is considered that this slight and unassuming man was to spend the four years of his presidency literally working himself to death to secure for his nation expansive continental boundaries.

Whatever his personal idiosyncrasies, Polk and his agents made the deals that were necessary to gain the Democratic nomination at the drunken pandemonium that was the Baltimore convention of 1844. He placated future candidates by promising not to run for a second term; he eased the fears of the North by saying he would not abolish tariffs, and of the South by pledging to keep these at a minimum; and he recalled the spirit of Jackson by pledging to create an "Independent Treasury" to carry on the business of the nation, rather than a national bank such as the one that Jackson had destroyed and that was so hated by the nation's poorer classes. But it was in foreign policy that Polk gained the advantage in his efforts to become first a candidate and then the president—and his ideas on foreign policy began with his belief in the immediate annexation of Texas.

In April, when Polk had been hopeful of nothing more than a vice-presidential spot on the Democratic ticket, he had boldly responded to the questions of a Cincinnati party committee that was canvassing the various candidates on the issue of expansion: "Let the fixed policy of our government be, not to permit Great Britain or any other foreign power to plant a colony or hold dominion over any portion of the people or territory of either" Texas or Oregon. Early on, then, Polk had identified himself not only as the candidate of expansion into the South *and* the Northwest, but as the candidate who would most aggressively counter foreign threats to that expansion; and he had shown that he, like Jackson, had no doubt as to where those threats were likely to come from. As president, Polk would write that grasping arrogance had characterized the history of the British nation "in all their contests with other Powers for the last two hundred years."

Calhoun, on the other hand, had cited the British threat largely as a ploy. And Benton could find no just cause for war with Britain in either Texas or Oregon, where British claims to the territory above the 49th parallel were, in Benton's mind, wholly justified. Polk's opinions, then, were far broader than those of his Democratic colleagues—and reflected far more of Jackson's obsessive belief that the American nation, because of its exceptional governmental and geographic attributes, was an irresistible target for European imperialism. Following Polk's nomination, the Democrats adopted a platform that reflected the views of their candidate, including the resolution: "That our title to the whole of the territory of Oregon is clear and unquestionable; that no portion of the same ought to be ceded to England or any other power, and that the reoccupation of Oregon and the reannexation of Texas, at the earliest practicable period, are great American measures, which this convention recommends to the cordial support of the democracy of the Union." Such, too, was the growing mood of the nation.

The campaign of 1844 was a race between a demagogue and a machine, and Henry Clay's popularity very nearly defeated the Democrats. Indicative of the nature of the race was the $22,000 bet on Polk made by Francis P. Blair, editor of the *Washington Globe* and the Democrats' most powerful force in the contest between party presses, who then went on to write editorials denouncing Clay as a profligate gambler. But it was not Clay's morals that lost him the election. The Kentuckian was unclear and hesitant on the issue of expansion, and this as much as anything else gave Polk his narrow victory on December 4. The result stunned much of the country and much of the world. In London, Lord Aberdeen prepared himself and his Government for what was obviously going to be a period of heightened tension with the United States.

That tension, however, would not center on Texas (which Aberdeen was in fact prepared to concede to the United States), but on the vital question of the Pacific Coast. In the fall and winter of 1844–45, the Mexican province of California was once again thrown into domestic turmoil, which aroused concern in London.

On December 31, Aberdeen sent a note to the British minister in Mexico saying that Great Britain would look very unfavorably on any attempt by *any* nation to establish a protectorate in the troubled province. By March 1845, California's uncertain status had resulted in rumors of a British takeover—either as payment for the Mexican debt or as an outright sale. In France, a newspaper article detailing the terms of such a scheme appeared. Although both Aberdeen and Lord Palmerston (then out of power but still the authoritative voice of British belligerency) refuted the article, it received much attention in the British and American presses. With the Oregon boundary still unsettled, Washington had good reason to believe that the British might once again be scheming to improve their North American position.

Nowhere was this thinking stronger than in the Polk White House. Just before his inaugural on March 4, 1845, Polk had sat in a room with George Bancroft—who was shortly to be named secretary of the navy—and allowed himself an unusual moment of candor. "Speaking energetically," Bancroft later wrote, "he raised his hand high in the air and bringing it down with force on his thigh, he said, there are to be four great measures of my administration,—

> The settlement of the Oregon Question with Great Britain.
> The acquisition of California and a large district on the coast.
> The reduction of the Tariff to a revenue basis.
> The complete and permanent establishment of the . . . 'Independent Treasury . . .' "

Bancroft, vividly aware of the importance of the moment, was sure that Polk meant to add the annexation of Texas—technically achieved at the end of the Tyler administration but requiring Polk's support as president if it were to become a reality—to this list.

But James Polk was a meticulous man. If he had wanted Texas on his list of great measures, he would most certainly have placed it there himself. That omission, along with the emphasis on Oregon and especially on California, strongly suggests that Polk considered the Pacific boundary to be the nation's most pressing foreign policy concern. And in turn, the preeminence of the Pacific question both influenced and revealed the president's attitude toward Texas.

Polk viewed the issue of expansion as separate from that of slavery. The one was a matter of national concern; the other, for individual states to resolve. "Whatever is good or evil in the institutions of Texas," said the incoming president in his inaugural, "will remain her own whether annexed to the United States or not. None of the present states will be responsible for them any more than they are for the local institutions of each other." If this view seems unrealistic, it must be remembered that the Northern antislavery factions—as well as those who, like Thomas Hart Benton, favored compromise—were not likely to tear the nation apart if Texas were admitted as all-slave; the same could not be said of Calhoun and his followers should Polk admit a divided Texas. Then, too, Polk—like Jackson—viewed Texas largely as a stumbling block. The faster annexation could be achieved, the faster more pressing security issues could be dealt with. And with California once again in a state of internal unrest, time was not necessarily on the American side.

With this in mind, Polk's first significant act as president was to confirm and support the annexation of all-Texas as all-slave. Benton was outraged, and John Quincy Adams called it "the heaviest calamity that ever befell myself and my country." But Polk had gambled correctly, and disunion did not come. Despite the warlike rattlings of the Mexican government and the withdrawal of the Mexican ambassador, the president now felt free to turn more of his attention to the vital—and delicate—matter of the Pacific Coast.

To Polk, outright conquest of California and Oregon was out of the question. Even if the United States had possessed the military might to defeat both Mexico and Great Britain, it did not possess the moral rationale; Polk, like Benton, considered aggressive conquest an unacceptable method of behavior for America. But that did not reduce the need for a secure Pacific boundary, or the danger posed by California's troubled situation. Polk required a program that could reconcile these two conditions, and in June of 1845 he began to formulate one—being typically careful to observe the utmost secrecy.

Of the few available insights into the workings of Polk's mind, none is more revealing than the various sets of orders issued by his cabinet members to American soldiers and diplomats around the world. Polk himself was to write, near the end of his term, that "No President who performs his duty faithfully and conscientiously can have any leisure. If he entrusts the details and smaller matters to subordinates constant errors will occur." Reflecting this belief, all commands issued by his cabinet were either drafted or heavily edited by Polk; it was his way of both ensuring control and separating himself from any potentially unpopular actions. In the case of California, this tactic would be employed extensively—and with dangerous consequences.

On June 24, orders were issued by Polk through Navy Secretary George Bancroft to Commodore John Drake Sloat, then the commander of the United States Pacific Squadron. Unlike the orders given by John Tyler to Sloat's predecessor, Commodore Jones, Sloat's directive was specific (without revealing the exact or ultimate intentions of the administration) and bore the marking "Secret and Confidential." The Polk administration, said Bancroft, was earnestly seeking peace with the Mexican government, despite the fact that the latter had withdrawn its ambassador to Washington. War, however, was indeed possible should Mexico fail to recognize the Rio Grande boundary and continue to refuse payment of the long-standing claims of American citizens; and should Sloat "ascertain beyond a doubt, that the Mexican Government has declared war against us, you will at once employ the force under your command to the best advantage. The Mexican ports on the Pacific are said to be open and defenceless. If you ascertain with certainty, that Mexico has declared war against the United States, you will at once possess yourself of the port of San Francisco, and blockade or occupy such other ports as your force may permit."

This plan seemed adequate in the event of war—but war could not be counted on to break out. Should peace be maintained, residents of both Oregon and California, whatever their nationality, would somehow have to be shown the advantages first of independence and second of annexation to the United States—the same formula that had been used with such success in West Florida and later in Texas. Since the Jones incident in 1842, the American merchant Thomas O. Larkin had been appointed U.S. consul in Monterey, and Polk planned to sound him out for information as to the sympathies of the Californians. In the event of an attempted British takeover, however, the United States would need a more forceful representative than Larkin in the province. In June, such a man was dispatched.

John Charles Frémont of the U.S. Army's Topographical Engineers had already earned himself a solid reputation as an explorer and adventurer by 1845. In two expeditions to the West he had mapped much of what would become Colorado, Wyoming, Utah, Nevada, Oregon and eastern California. Fiery-eyed and daring, Frémont was a romantic figure, who in 1841 had won the heart of a seventeen-year-old beauty renowned for her deep learning—Jessie Benton, favorite daughter of the senior senator from Missouri. When Frémont began to plan a third expedition to the West, Senator Benton and President Polk himself took a somewhat surprising interest in it. Although no specific mention of California was made in the young officer's orders, it was understood that he would visit the province and, while pursuing his scientific studies of the region and trying to map a suitable route for a Pacific railroad line, would measure the temper of the populace. Frémont left St. Louis in June, picking up over fifty rugged, heavily armed frontiersmen on his way West—an odd staff, some thought, for a scientific expedition.

The first two ingredients of Polk's California plan were now in place; in the fall, a third was added in the form of Thomas O. Larkin. If anyone could be expected to understand Polk's plan to acquaint the residents of California with the virtues of true republicanism, it was the American consul in Monterey. Good-natured and gregarious, Larkin was also firmly loyal to the United States. Although there were only some eight hundred to one thousand American settlers in California (along with other foreigners and the main population of Mexican *Californios*), he felt sure that the people of the province could be persuaded that independence and then American rule were desirable—if it were done in such a way as to avoid giving offense to the sensitive pride of the *Californio* leaders. Both personally and professionally, Larkin was ideally suited to this task.

In addition, the consul was fully alert to his other, and no less important, duty—monitoring British activities in California. On July 10, 1845, he sent an alarming dispatch to Polk's secretary of state, James Buchanan. The Mexican government, said Larkin, intended once again to assert its authority in California with troops, and "There is no doubt in this Country, [that] the Troops

. . . are sent by the instigation of the English Government under the plea, that the American settlers in California want to revolutionize the Country." Larkin also noted that the British had appointed a vice-consul for the region, even though "there is no English commerce in California." On August 4 a dispatch corroborating Larkin's observations was sent to Polk from the American consul in Liverpool, who wrote that, "England has a mortgage on California." Apparently, time was not merely of the essence on the Pacific Coast—it was also running out.

President Polk took this quickly to heart. With the death of Andrew Jackson in June, Polk had become the nation's preeminent apostle of national security. Perhaps recalling Jackson's dying request that he meet the English threat with "that energy and promptness that is due to yourself, & our national character," he had also begun to talk tough to Great Britain. Late in the summer, he broke off all negotiations over the Oregon boundary. Then, on October 17, he turned to the question of British interference in California by issuing an elaborate set of orders to Larkin. These orders, though drafted in response to the British actions recorded by the consul, were to become celebrated as one of the clearest expressions of Polk's views on American security and continental expansion.

Using Secretary of State James Buchanan—whom Polk considered "in small matters without judgement, and sometimes acts like an old maid"—as his mouthpiece, the president informed Larkin that American interests "demand that you should exert the greatest vigilance in discovering and defeating any attempts which may be made by Foreign Governments to acquire a control over that Country [California]." He assured the consul that, "should California assert and maintain her independence, we shall render her all the kind offices in our power as a Sister Republic," adding that the United States should avoid the use of force, either directly or indirectly, in gaining control over the province. But then came the telling phrase—"Whilst these are the sentiments of the President, he could not view with indifference the transfer of California to Great Britain or any other European Power. The system of colonization by foreign Monarchies on the North American continent must and will be resisted by the United States."

Larkin was next informed of the specific part he was to play in Polk's plan of resistance: "On all proper occasions, you should not fail prudently to warn the Government and people of California of the danger of such an interference to their peace and prosperity —to inspire them with a jealousy of European dominion and to arouse in their bosoms that love of liberty and independence so natural to the American Continent." Should such a process lead to a desire on the part of the Californians to enter the American Union, "they would be received as brethren, whenever this can be done, without affording Mexico just cause of complaint." Larkin was to pursue these goals both openly, in his capacity as consul, and covertly. For the latter purpose, he was named a "Confidential Agent" of the administration, with an additional salary of six dollars a day.

In acting as he did, Polk cautiously laid the groundwork for a unilateralist solution to his California predicament. The Sloat orders, the dispatch of Frémont and the instructions to Larkin were not isolated actions; they were rather the start of a steady process that would build over the next nine months. But it would be unfair to say that Polk viewed unilateral action, rather than negotiation, as the single most desirable method of acquiring an expansive Pacific boundary. In November, the president dispatched Representative John Slidell of Louisiana to Mexico City to try to patch up Mexican-American differences with money. Slidell was instructed to say that should Mexico recognize the Rio Grande boundary of Texas, the American government would pay the claims of its citizens that had for so long troubled relations between the two countries. In addition, should Mexico be willing to part with its New Mexican and especially its Californian holdings, Polk would be willing to pay as much as forty million dollars.

No Mexican government, however, could have agreed to such a deal, given that nation's internal fragility and the sensitive pride of its military commanders. Polk may have known this before he made his offer. At least one American agent had written, as recently as October of 1844, that if Mexican leaders were to sell even a part of Texas or California "the chances are ten to one that their doing so would be used as an argument for shooting them." But with Anglo-American tensions rising, it is far more likely that the president was sincere in his efforts to ease the crisis with dollars. Be that as it may, unilateral action eventually became the only feasible way of obtaining California, and there is no indication that Polk viewed that with distaste.

In December 1845, Polk was to deliver his famous First Annual Message, which would later become known as the "Polk Doctrine"

or the "Polk Corollary" to the Monroe Doctrine. In it the president
reinterpreted Monroe's statements in order to stress America's
commitment to the integrity of North America, rather than to the
entire Western Hemisphere. But the previous month's instructions
to John Slidell, quite probably because they *were* confidential, much
more clearly and concisely summed up the attitude of the Polk
administration toward the future roles of both Europe and the
United States in North America. One statement to Slidell had particular relevance to coming events in California:

"To tolerate any interference on the part of European sover-
eigns with controversies in America; to permit them to apply the
worn-out dogma of the balance of power to the free states of this
continent; and above all, to suffer them to establish new Colonies
of their own, intermingled with our free Republics, would be to
make, to the same extent, a voluntary sacrifice of our independence. These truths ought everywhere, throughout the continent
of America, to be impressed on the public mind. . . . Liberty here
must be allowed to work out its natural results; and these will, ere
long, astonish the world."

That astonishment, in the case of California, would not meet
with universal approval. For by indulging his passion for secrecy
to its fullest with the orders to Commodore Sloat, the dispatch of
the Frémont expedition and the instructions to Larkin, Polk had
created a situation in which ambitious American agents inside the
borders of Mexico were given immense freedom to pursue a goal
that had never been precisely defined—it was an ideal prescription
for mishap.

On March 9, 1846, Thomas Larkin sent an urgent dispatch from
Monterey to the commander "of any American ship of war in San
Blas or Mazatlan [Mexico]." It stated that "Captain J. C. Frémont
with a party of fifty men has been within the limits of California
about two months . . . [and] has received two letters from the General and Prefecto [José Castro and Manuel Castro, influential *Californio* leaders], wherein he is ordered to leave this country, or they
will take immediate measures to compel him. . . . By tomorrow
there will be collected together nearly three hundred men with the
intention to drive out the Strangers and if required, there will be
by next week a much larger body collected. Should this force be
used against Captain Frémont, much blood will be shed. His party
though of only fifty in number have from three to six guns, rifles

and pistols each, and are very determined, both Commander and men having every confidence in each other. . . . [T]he American residents are under some apprehension of their safety hereafter."

From the moment of their arrival in California in December of 1845, Captain Frémont and his band of "explorers" and "scientists" —including the legendary Kit Carson as scout—had behaved in a high-handed fashion that had alienated much of the *Californio* community; apparently Frémont did not intend to wait for a British invasion before taking aggressive steps to bolster the American presence in the province. When Larkin had first met the captain in Monterey in January, he was given "the idea, that great plans are meditated to be carried out by certain persons."

But he had not guessed at the extent of Frémont's ambition and felt safe in asking Commandante-General José Castro to allow the captain and his party to remain in the province to carry on their scientific studies and try to locate a Pacific railroad route. This permission was neither granted nor denied, but as Frémont and his men made their intentions increasingly plain by bullying the *Californios*, insulting their women and openly encouraging American settlers to rebel against Mexican rule, rumors began to circulate that these fifty-odd frontiersmen were the advance guard of an American invasion force. Both José Castro and Manuel Castro, the prefect of Monterey, ordered Frémont to leave California on March 5, the prefect stating that should the captain refuse, "this office will take the necessary measures." Such threats stung Frémont's pride, and on that same day he withdrew to the highest point in the Gavilán Mountains, erected a log breastworks and ran up the American flag.

Larkin was amazed. This was nothing like the plan of peaceful persuasion that had been indicated by President Polk and the secretary of state. But reprimanding Frémont was not the answer. Though a somewhat rough-hewn frontier merchant, Larkin was nonetheless a perceptive diplomat; he knew that the ambitious young captain would only become truculent in response to chastisement. The consul therefore dispatched a brief and tactful note to the Gavilán camp on March 8. "It is not for me to point out your line of conduct," Larkin wrote. "You have your government instructions. . . . Your danger may remain in supposing that no uncommon means will be taken for your expulsion. . . . The result either way may cause trouble hereafter to Resident Americans." Frémont's only reply was to declare that, "I am making myself as strong as possible in the intention that if we are unjustly attacked we will fight to extremity and refuse quarter, trusting our country to avenge our death." Larkin now knew that he was involved in a situation that was becoming highly volatile, and the urgent tone of his March 9 dispatch was indeed genuine.

Frémont's illegal and disruptive behavior seems to have been aimed at inciting the American settlers in California to rebel and declare the province's independence. Such a precipitous course of action had not been indicated even in the captain's unstated orders. But Frémont, like many other adventurers, apparently felt that subsequent events—presumably an American conquest—would vindicate any excesses he might commit in preparing the way for American troops in California. To act on such an assumption when one's commander in chief was James Polk, however, was a serious miscalculation.

In response to Frémont's defiant note, Larkin quickly dispatched another carefully worded message reminding the captain of the dangers to which he was exposing American settlers, and that actions such as those he was taking would require specific government approval. Knowing that Larkin would not back him up, the captain withdrew from his Gavilán fort on the night of March 9–10. Moving north, he eventually established a base camp in the Sacramento region, where his men continued their violent excesses, including a gratuitous raid on an Indian village that Kit Carson described as "a perfect butchery." By now, Frémont realized that he might have been premature in supposing that he was to be part of a California takeover plan; and he reluctantly began to journey north toward Oregon in compliance with the orders of the Castros.

Both Frémont and Larkin were effectively out of touch with events in Washington. But Commodore John Drake Sloat, on the west coast of Mexico, was less so. At the end of March he received a new set of orders from Navy Secretary Bancroft, dated December 5 and once again marked "Secret." Relations with Mexico, said Bancroft, were improving, but the same was not and could not be said of Great Britain. The Pacific Coast was now the administration's principal concern, and Sloat was therefore to "keep all your ships in the vicinity of Oregon and Calaforria [sic]." Polk's plan of wooing the residents of California and Oregon was also to be stepped up; copies of the Texan constitution, translated into Spanish, were to be distributed in California, and five hundred copies of the president's December 2 Annual Message were to go to Oregon.

Bancroft closed, however, on a less peaceful note: "If you have any rifles or other small arms on board your ships which can be spared for the purpose, you may permit them to be exchanged with the people of that region for wheat, flour or other stores, taking all possible care that they fall into the hands of no one who is unfriendly to the United States." In April the aging, ill and altogether unenthusiastic Sloat dispatched the sloop of war *Portsmouth* to Monterey with the copies of the Texas constitution, and the schooner *Shark* to the mouth of the Columbia River, reminding the captains of those vessels: *"These orders you will keep secret."*

By the time Sloat actually dispatched the *Portsmouth* and the *Shark*, American relations with not only Great Britain but Mexico as well had become severely strained. John Slidell's diplomatic mission had been rejected by the Mexican government, and a military coup had subsequently taken place in Mexico City, headed by a general who was confident of his nation's ability to defeat the United States on the battlefield. As for the Northwest, President Polk had maintained his belligerent attitude toward the British—it was the age of the famous "Fifty-four forty or fight," a slogan that embodied the faith of many Americans in their legal title to the Oregon Territory as far north as 54 degrees, 40 minutes. Lord Aberdeen, while anxious to avoid war, was not yet ready to be as compliant as he had been in the case of Texas. Other British leaders, and especially the British press, were openly talking of war. Secretary of State Buchanan believed that Polk's policies would produce just such a result, with perhaps both Britain *and* Mexico. But the president, despite his public statements of defiance, was in fact unwilling to allow events to advance to that stage.

In October, Polk had met privately with Senator Benton, who had carefully explained to the president why American claims above the 49th parallel in Oregon were unfounded. When in the spring the Mexican situation began to deteriorate, the American minister in London was informed that if the British were to make an offer of that parallel as a boundary, it would probably be accepted. Lest this be read as a reversal of his tough stance, Polk was prepared to submit immediately any such offer to the Senate for approval, without himself passing judgment on it. The president had already decided that if there was to be war, it would be with the unmovable Mexicans rather than the more reasonable—and far stronger—British. None of this was made known to either Sloat, Larkin or Frémont. But in April yet another "Confidential Agent" of the Polk administration arrived in California, bearing letters and dispatches that would set in motion a new—and, as it turned out, final—round of covert activities.

Lieutenant Archibald Gillespie of the Marines seems to have had no greater qualification for his crucial mission to California than that he spoke Spanish. Tough and quick-witted, Gillespie was, like Frémont, fatally ambitious. On April 17 he reached Monterey and presented the State Department's October 17 orders to Larkin, urging that California be induced to come into the Union. Gillespie then moved north to search for Frémont, to whom he was to deliver a copy of the Larkin orders as well as private letters from the Benton family. On May 9, Gillespie and Frémont met in the Klamath Lakes region of the Oregon Territory, and the lieutenant delivered the various pieces of correspondence. The two men then sat by the fire in Frémont's camp and began to talk.

Neither Gillespie nor Frémont would ever reveal the precise contents of the fateful conversation. Frémont himself would later write that "Mr. Bancroft had sent Mr. Gillespie to give me warning of the new state of affairs and the designs of the President"; yet Gillespie had left New York on November 16, at a time when Polk had hopes of a negotiated settlement with Mexico. Frémont went on to say that Gillespie's intelligence "absolved me from my duty as an explorer," and confirmed "on the authority of the Secretary of the Navy that to obtain possession of California was the chief object of the President."

Precisely how Frémont extracted this meaning from his conversation with Gillespie is a mystery. Certainly, no such message was contained in the Larkin orders (which Frémont initially thought were addressed to him, unable to believe that the government would entrust so delicate a mission to a man as hesitant and incompetent as Larkin). And though the captain claimed that the letters he received from the Benton family contained such intimations, no proof of that assertion has ever surfaced—even if it had, the letters were private and carried no official authority. Certainly, Bancroft always denied having written such statements. Gillespie himself, in testifying before a subsequent Senate investigation, stated that he told Frémont nothing more than "that it was the wish of the government that we should conciliate the feelings of the people of California and encourage a friendship towards the United States."

In all probability, Frémont once more became convinced that the glorious conquest he had expected was finally to begin, and that he would be forgiven for anticipating his government's actions should his preliminary endeavors prove successful.

At any rate, the two officers moved south and back into Mexican territory, Frémont warning the American settlers in the Sacramento region that their Mexican governors intended to either expel or massacre them and that he would be happy to afford what protection he could. When a motley, drunken group of Americans in the town of Sonoma declared the independence of the "Republic of California" and raised a crude homemade banner emblazoned with a rather porcine bear, Frémont immediately lent them his support. This act, followed as it was by several instances of swaggering larceny on the part of the Bear Flaggers, caused many *Californios* who had been previously well-disposed toward the idea of peaceful annexation to the United States to change their opinions and take up arms against the arrogant invaders. Throughout the months of May and June, violence spread throughout northern California, and the greater part of these confrontations were sparked by Frémont's men, who quickly became the effective power behind the Bear Flag Republic. In short, American troops were now actively supporting a minority insurrection inside foreign territory.

What Frémont could not know was that on April 25, Mexican soldiers had attacked a contingent of American dragoons along the Rio Grande, and that on May 13 Congress had approved President Polk's indignant declaration that war had been brought on "by the act of Mexico herself." Had he been aware of these momentous events, the young captain might well have felt happily confirmed in his opinions and in his actions. In fact, the American declaration of war would bring nothing but disgrace to the daring Frémont and those who followed him in his search for glory.

Mexico's leaders were adamant in their refusals to negotiate with the United States and generally viewed the prospect of war with their northern neighbor favorably, if not with enthusiasm. In the case of Oregon, on the other hand, President Polk was able to gain peace with Great Britain through the Oregon Treaty of June 15, 1846 (establishing the 49th parallel as an official boundary), and simultaneously maintain his image as a tough talker chiefly because the British were capable of seeing reason. A war over Oregon was not, to the London government, economically justifiable, even if Polk's angry denunciations were embarrassing. But in relations with the Mexican government, the American president did not prove so lucky. Polk could have conceded the question of the Rio Grande–Nueces border region, but he did not. Nor is it likely that such a concession would have placated the incensed military regime in Mexico City. The Mexicans were confident of their warlike prowess, and were determined to resolve their inner debates with a great war against the nation that had "stolen" their territory. Thus the Mexican War was not fought to secure the nation against foreign threats, but rather to assert American predominance on the North American continent.

The acquisition of California, on the other hand, had always been viewed by Polk as vital to American security. For this reason he had tried carefully to lay the groundwork for a peaceful—and perhaps even happy—accomplishment of that end. It was hoped that in the event of war, Commodore Sloat would quickly take his ships to California and there find a native community congenially reconciled to the idea of American rule through the efforts of Larkin, Frémont and Gillespie. Yet from beginning to end, Sloat's operations deviated widely from this path.

Sloat, who had served his country during the War of 1812 and wanted nothing more than to be relieved of command and allowed to return home to die in peace, had first heard rumors of a war with Mexico in mid-May; but remembering the precipitous haste of Commodore Jones, he decided to make no move without genuine confirmation of those rumors. It was not until June 7, when he was informed of the official American blockade of Mexico's eastern coast, that the commodore finally decided to move on California as instructed.

On July 2, 1846, Sloat sailed into the same bay of Monterey that Commodore Jones had occupied almost four years earlier. The differences between the two men—Jones resolute and confident, Sloat ailing and uncertain—were reflected in their methods of conquest. Sloat waited for days before either leaving his flagship, the *Savannah*, or speaking personally to Larkin. When word reached him of Frémont's recent exploits—the captain had taken over formal command of the Bear Flag forces and was busily engaged in fighting the *Californios* throughout the north—the commodore became further confused, unable to determine what authority Frémont was acting under. Finally, Sloat decided that Frémont's actions simply confirmed the government's determination to take all of California by force. When Larkin at last came on board the *Savannah* on July 6, the commodore declared desperately, "We must take the place! I shall be blamed for doing too little or too much—I prefer the latter."

Sloat's occupation of Monterey on the following morning was in every important respect a duplicate of the Jones action. At approximately 10:00 A.M. the Marines landed and marched to the castle of Monterey; Sloat issued a proclamation that said, "[A]lthough I come in arms with a powerful force, I do not come as an enemy of California"; the American troops were warned against undisciplined behavior in precisely the same language that Jones had used; and the occupation force quickly began to reinforce Monterey's defenses. There was but one difference between the Jones action and that of Commodore Sloat—the White House in 1846 was occupied by a man who fully appreciated the importance of California to American security, and who was determined to keep the province, come what may.

Nonetheless, James Polk was not the sort of man to watch the details of a plan go awry without comment. Word of Frémont's activities soon reached Washington, and when land occupation forces were dispatched to California under General Stephen Watts Kearny late in 1846, they found many *Californios* ready to actively resist American rule, primarily out of the bitterness engendered by Frémont and his Bear Flaggers. General Kearny also found the haughty Frémont unwilling to obey all his orders. Kearny, a tough West Pointer, had just come through a bitter campaign to conquer New Mexico and was in no mood to brook the insubordination of a junior officer, even one who had powerful friends in the government.

Frémont was placed under arrest and returned to Washington to face a court-martial in November 1847. The captain was found guilty on three counts of insubordination, and when President Polk was asked to reverse the verdict, he declined to. Ironically, Frémont emerged from the trial a popular hero, a bold martyr to Washington and army politics, whereas Polk—architect of a conciliatory (if clandestine) California plan that Frémont had destroyed —was cast as the villain of the piece.

The one man who had fully understood and remained true to the substance of Polk's plan, Thomas O. Larkin, had written to Secretary of State Buchanan in January 1847 that, "It has been my object for some years to bring the Californians to look on our countrymen as their best friends. I am satisfied very many was [sic] of that way of thinking & more were becoming so . . . but proper methods were not taken to conciliate them." The ever-tactful Larkin would go no further in his condemnations; but because of the violence inspired by Frémont, the conquest of California was a protracted and messy affair. Such unpleasant behavior, however, was quickly swept aside because of the war with Mexico. By the spring of 1848, with the conclusion of a treaty of peace, James Polk had realized his greatest dream—secure continental boundaries behind which the United States could grow immeasurably strong.

The price he paid for that achievement could not have been higher. Retiring to his home in Tennessee at the conclusion of his term, the ever-frail Polk proved unable to recover from the immense exertions of his four years in office. He died on June 15, 1849, at the age of fifty-three. Unlike Jackson, Polk would have no inheritor so profoundly concerned with national security. The attention of American statesmen was increasingly focused on internal affairs after 1850, and the ardent nationalism that had allowed slaveowners such as Polk to overrule the sectionalist factions within their states grew steadily weaker as its leading voices passed from the national stage. Henry Clay outlived Polk by just three years; Thomas Hart Benton survived until 1858.

Shortly before his departure from office, Polk had authorized a confidential diplomatic mission to Spain to propose the sale of Cuba to the United States for $100 million. This offer was not made in writing, and Polk's emissary was told not to accept a written Spanish reply. Only the utmost secrecy could keep other interested powers, notably France and Great Britain, as well as American antislavery groups, from causing interference. (Cuba was the Western Hemisphere's leading importer of slaves.) Polk's offer met with a firm refusal from the Spanish, but the subject of Cuba was far from settled.

Since the time of the Founding Fathers, the lush, fertile island that lay astride the entrance to the Gulf of Mexico had been particularly attractive to American statesmen. Thomas Jefferson wrote that Cuba was "the most interesting addition which could ever be made to our system of States. The control which, with Florida Point, this island would give us over the Gulph [sic] of Mexico . . . would fill up the measure of our political well-being." Some Americans objected that Cuba, being an island, would be an inappropriate possession for a republic that had rejected colonialism; but Jefferson argued that Cuba could be defended with land forces, and that "this develops the principle which ought to limit our views. Nothing should ever be accepted which would require a navy to defend it." But even Jefferson knew that Cuba—not only an island but a wealthy Spanish colony as well—could not be had at that time without an aggressive war. He therefore preferred to postpone the question until a more propitious moment.

Fifteen years later, John Quincy Adams wrote that Cuba was "indispensable to the continuance and integrity of the Union itself"; but he, too, had preferred to delay the question until the deterioration of Spain's empire was so far advanced as to make annexation easy. Throughout the first half-century of American history, then, the annexation of Cuba was generally considered by American leaders to be so inevitable as to make a war for it superfluous.

But during the 1830s and 1840s, as the slavery question moved to the center of American affairs, Adams's enthusiasm for Cuba had changed along with his priorities regarding slavery and expansion. By the time of Polk's secret mission, there were many abolitionists who were active in their opposition to acquiring an island whose slave population very nearly equaled its freeborn. Persistent rumors that Great Britain intended to incite a slave rebellion and subsequently establish an English client state in Cuba coincided with similar claims about Texas and California, and contained about the same degree of substance. When Polk finally left office, the desire for Cuba had become mixed with both a reluctance to increase the slave territories of the United States and a very real fear that the island would end up in British hands.

During the administration of Franklin Pierce—a man who had received a generalship in the Mexican War from Polk and whose cabinet was largely made up of Polk veterans—another effort to purchase Cuba was initiated. But if Polk's move had been hampered by the question of slavery, Pierce's was aborted because of it. Under Pierce the Kansas-Nebraska Act of 1854, nullifying the Missouri Compromise of 1820 and throwing vast new territories open to slavery, was passed; and the subsequent plummet in Democratic political fortunes was shocking. Throughout the country, abolitionists were joined by moderates and even by pro-Union slaveowners of the Clay-Benton school to deal a sound beating to the

Democrats in the midterm House elections of 1854. Pierce understood the message—the days of James Polk, when expansionism overshadowed the questions of slavery and disunion, were gone. Licking his political wounds, Pierce withdrew his bid for the slave island of Cuba.

Abraham Lincoln's secretary of state, William H. Seward, hoped in 1860 that the looming American civil conflict might be avoided by initiating a foreign war to unify the nation; the most likely locale for such an adventure was Cuba. But Seward was blocked by Lincoln, largely because of Cuba's slave status. By 1861 there was no way to avoid the approaching crisis of internal security in the United States. The Civil War that would become the greatest calamity in American history would also ensure the nation's withdrawal from world affairs for the better part of two decades. Despite French efforts to establish a puppet empire in Mexico and the obvious sympathy of some British statesmen for the Confederate cause, America was far less concerned with territorial threats from abroad than with the need to reestablish federal authority over the rebellious states of the South. But when the nation finally did heal and again turned outward to attend the question of external security, it once more focused its attention on the rich island off the Florida coast. And by that time, the issue of slavery had long since been put to rest.

I V

IMPERIALISM AND INSECURITY

1890–1912

OF the nine American ships that steamed out of Hong Kong on April 25, 1898, none was a true battleship. Four were protected cruisers, armor-plated but still adorned with tall masts. Two were mere gunboats, highly vulnerable to artillery fire. One was a lowly cutter. And rounding out the roster of the United States Asiatic Squadron were a pair of colliers, useless in combat. Yet this little fleet was on its way to do battle with the land and sea forces of the Spanish empire in the Philippines—it was understandable that many British residents of Hong Kong doubted the Americans' chances for survival. "In the Hong Kong Club," wrote Commodore George Dewey, the American commander, "it was not possible to get bets, even at heavy odds, that our expedition would be a success. . . . The universal remark among our hosts was to this effect: 'A fine set of fellows, but unhappily we shall never see them again.' "

Upon arrival in Hong Kong in February, Dewey had been greeted by the news that the American battleship *Maine* had been sunk by a devastating explosion in the harbor of the Spanish port of Havana, Cuba. Dewey had further learned that many Americans, particularly newspaper editors and publishers, were saying that the explosion was an act of Spanish sabotage, carried out in cowardly retaliation for America's vociferous (though as yet nonmaterial) support of Cuba's separatist guerrillas. Then, on February 26, a confidential cable from the Navy Department had arrived in Hong Kong by way of Nagasaki, Japan, Dewey's usual base. The cable ordered the commodore to take the squadron to Hong Kong (a move that Dewey had anticipated), and to KEEP FULL OF COAL. IN THE EVENT OF DECLARATION OF WAR [against] SPAIN, YOUR DUTY WILL BE TO SEE THAT THE SPANISH SQUADRON DOES NOT LEAVE THE ASIATIC COAST, AND THEN OFFENSIVE OPERATIONS IN PHILIPPINE ISLANDS. The telegram was signed ROOSEVELT.

The signature was as portentous for Dewey as were the orders themselves. Theodore Roosevelt, the aggressive young New York aristocrat who had already made a name for himself as a civil service commissioner under Presidents Benjamin Harrison and Grover Cleveland and as the head of New York City's police department, had been named assistant secretary of the navy when William McKinley had entered the White House in 1897. Working under the more restrained head of the Navy Department, John D. Long, Roosevelt's determination to both build up American naval strength and put that strength under the command of action-minded officers had revealed itself whenever Secretary Long left the office in his assistant's charge, whether for an afternoon or for a summer's vacation. And one of Roosevelt's most unshakable goals since arriving at the Navy Department had been to get Dewey assigned to the Asiatic post—for the affable, elderly seaman with the huge mustache fit Roosevelt's image of an effective American naval officer perfectly.

Capable, unafraid to act on his own initiative, an excellent administrator and above all a man who loved a good scrapping fight, George Dewey had seen precious little action in his forty-odd years in the navy. As a boy he had, in his own words, been "full of animal spirits," and gained a reputation (one he would never quite lose) as a practical joker—as he himself put it, "I liked things to happen wherever I was." At Annapolis, "That old faculty for making things happen" resulted in "one hundred and thirteen demerit marks. Two hundred meant dismissal." As a young officer Dewey had served under the legendary David Glasgow Farragut during the

Civil War, but following that conflict he and the rest of the navy had been largely ignored by a government riddled with profiteers and a public weary of military pursuits. Theodore Roosevelt's appointment to the Navy Department in 1897 was therefore greeted by men such as Dewey with enthusiasm. That Roosevelt wanted war with Spain was known; because of this, the assistant secretary's desire that Dewey get the Asiatic Squadron was not only flattering —it held the promise of action.

The appointment had not been easy to obtain, but by the time the commodore left for Nagasaki at the end of 1897, he was virtually certain that he would see battle before he would again see the United States. Roosevelt's audacious cable only confirmed such feelings. It was not surprising, then, that when Secretary Long's official order to "Proceed at once to Philippine Islands" arrived on April 25, Dewey was more than ready to move. The squadron made full steam for the Philippines, covering the six hundred miles quickly and coming within sight of the coast of Luzon on the thirtieth.

Whether the Spanish commander had decided to defend the archipelago from the expanse of Manila Bay, or by moving into the more strategically advantageous Subic Bay, or by dispersing his ships among the smaller islands, was as yet unknown. Dewey had received news of artillery emplacements on the islands at the mouth of Manila Bay, as well as information about the movements of Spanish troops—but until he could discover the disposition of the Spanish naval forces (known to roughly equal and perhaps even outnumber his own), he would be involved in an immense gamble. Donning a white golfer's cap and maintaining a typically cool demeanor as he paced the decks of his flagship, the *Olympia*, Dewey steamed on into what might well have been disaster.

The squadron moved in column formation, blacking out at night except for small lights at each ship's stern to prevent collisions. Dewey was uncertain whether or not the Spaniards had mined the two entrances to Manila Bay, the Boca Grande and the Boca Chiqua, but such considerations would be academic if the Spanish ships were in Subic Bay, north of Manila and in a position to flank any attack on that city. Three American ships were dispatched to scout Subic, and at 3:30 P.M. on the thirtieth the ships returned to say that they had seen no Spanish vessels in the strategic inlet. Dewey, who up to this point had been alert to the grave dangers

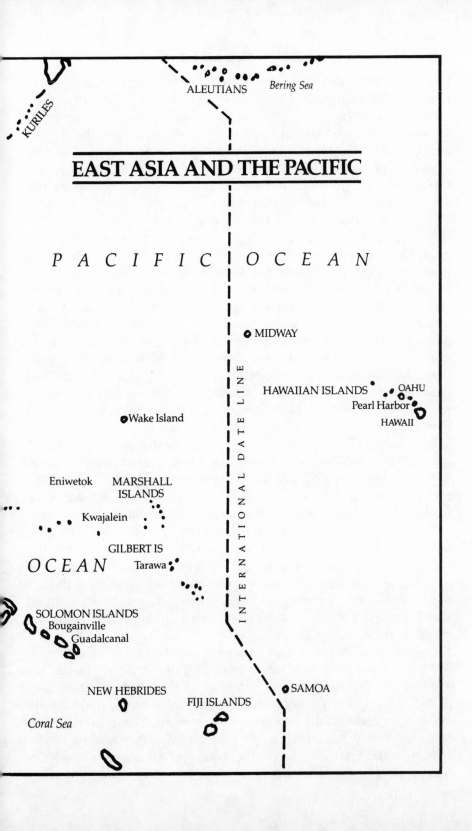

ALEUTIANS   *Bering Sea*

KURILES

EAST ASIA AND THE PACIFIC

P A C I F I C   O C E A N

◐ MIDWAY

HAWAIIAN ISLANDS • • OAHU
Pearl Harbor
HAWAII

◐ Wake Island

Eniwetok   MARSHALL
ISLANDS

Kwajalein

GILBERT IS
O C E A N   Tarawa •

SOLOMON ISLANDS
Bougainville
Guadalcanal

NEW HEBRIDES
FIJI ISLANDS
◐ SAMOA

Coral Sea

INTERNATIONAL DATE LINE

he faced, now sensed that the Spaniards were not adequately prepared for his approach. Turning to his chief of staff he said calmly, "Now we have them."

Dewey made quickly for the Boca Grande, reaching that larger mouth of Manila Bay at nightfall, still without resistance. The two key positions at the bay's entrance were the islands of El Fraile and Corregidor, both known to be protected by heavy breech-loading artillery with rifled barrels that could, in the right hands, cut most of Dewey's ships to pieces from a considerable distance. Under such circumstances, it was suggested that Dewey let another ship go in first; but the Commodore replied that he had "waited sixty years for this opportunity," and the *Olympia* took the point.

The inactivity both in and out of the water around Corregidor and El Fraile as the American ships slipped into Manila Bay under cover of darkness was somewhat unnerving, but finally, a little after midnight, the Spaniards made a move. In the words of one American seaman, "the line steamed around about four miles distant from the South side of Corregidor . . . [and] a battery of [Spanish] heavy guns opened fire. . . . It appeared to me that the rear ships were going to have a lively time of it, but for some unexplained reason, firing stopped a long time before we were out of range." That "unexplained reason" turned out to be the answering fire of four of Dewey's ships. Although none of the American guns were as big as those on El Fraile and Corregidor, the Spanish artillery crews had apparently decided that three rounds of defense were sufficient. Dewey's humble armada entered Manila Bay unscathed.

Turning south and heading toward the city of Manila and the nearby fortifications at the naval station of Cavite, Dewey sent the two colliers off to a northerly, safe position. As dawn spread over the bay and the city of Manila was passed, its fortifications offering only a few more harmless rounds, American lookouts began to make out seven Spanish warships clustered in front of Cavite. Incredibly, they were at anchor.

Commodore Dewey would later explain the extraordinary Spanish decision to moor their warships during the battle of Manila Bay as an attempt to gain the full benefits of a broadside position. But in fact, the Spanish commander, Admiral Montojo, had already conceded defeat. Neither a fool nor a coward, Montojo had been so hampered in his efforts to prepare an adequate defense of the islands by the Spanish governor-general, as well as by his seniors at home, that he had first been compelled to abandon any idea of fortifying Subic Bay and then had actually been forbidden to scatter his ships throughout the archipelago. Anchoring his most prized vessels behind the protection of rock-filled barges, Montojo awaited the Americans in the manner of a man who had divined his fate.

Aboard the *Olympia,* Dewey prepared for action with a typically generous gesture. The *Olympia*'s captain, Charles V. Gridley, was suffering from a cripplingly painful disease—in all likelihood cancer of the liver—and had actually been ordered home at the time of the American declaration of war against Spain. Gridley had asked not to be relieved at such a crucial time. "Ill as he was," Dewey wrote, "it was not in my heart to refuse the request of gallant Captain Gridley to remain in command." On the voyage to Manila, it had been apparent that Gridley did not have long to live, but at 5:40 on the morning of May 1, he relinquished the comparative comfort of the *Olympia*'s bridge to Dewey and took his post in the ship's brutally hot conning tower. When the Americans had closed to a distance of some 5,400 yards from the Spanish fleet, Dewey showed his appreciation by offering his flagship captain the day's premier honor:

"You may fire when you are ready, Gridley."

The volume of fire expended by the American warships during the next two hours was massive. Cruising in a series of narrow ellipses that edged closer and closer to the Spanish ships, the American batteries literally rained shells on their immobile Spanish victims. One American noted that "Several times our signal men reported one, or the other [of the American ships] to be on fire, notably the *Raleigh,* whose side appeared to be like a sheet of flame when seen through the smoke, caused by her rapid firing." At 7:35 Dewey received an inaccurate report that ammunition was running low and withdrew to review the situation, but by 11:15 was back in "to complete our work." The larger Spanish ships made a few attempts to run the American formation and escape the deadly bay, only to be pounded back toward Cavite by the American guns. By 12:30 Montojo, his ships either sunk, sinking, aground or ablaze, had had enough. He signaled his surrender to Dewey. The shore batteries in Manila offered some further resistance, until the commodore sent a message saying that if the firing did not cease he would bombard the city. The Spanish guns then fell silent, and the battle of Manila Bay was over.

The greatest American naval victory between the Civil and Second World Wars had taken just over half a day to complete. The Spaniards had suffered, according to Dewey, some three hundred killed and four hundred wounded. Six Americans had been slightly injured, and the only fatality proved to be Captain Gridley who, after the battle, was finally ordered home and died en route in Japan. American exhilaration over the battle knew no bounds. Dewey became an overnight hero, the exemplar of American virtue. Americans generally and their president in particular may well have been hard pressed to say where the Philippines were or, in the words of humorist Finley P. Dunne's Mr. Dooley, "whether they were islands or canned goods," but this did not lessen their admiration for the victorious commander of the Asiatic Squadron. As Roosevelt cabled the commodore following the battle, EVERY AMERICAN IS YOUR DEBTOR.

Yet certain details concerning the battle of Manila Bay, though made known only slowly, were deeply disturbing to analysts both in and out of the navy. The victory itself was revealed to be less a feat of American seamanship than an exercise in Spanish ineptitude, for Admiral Montojo had given Dewey every possible assistance during the campaign—and when the two fleets had finally joined battle, the American batteries had fired some 6,000 shots at the largely immobile enemy ships; fewer than 150 of these had found their mark. Then, too, as triumph gave way to reflection in the United States, there emerged the question of why an American victory in an unknown archipelago halfway around the world from benighted Cuba or even despised Spain should mean so much— not only to the United States, but apparently to other nations as well, most notably Great Britain, Japan and Germany, whose warships appeared in Manila Bay very soon after Dewey's victory. The British and the Japanese seemed friendly enough, but the Germans were so rude and obtrusive that Dewey actually had to fire a shot over the bow of a German torpedo launch. Was the smashing of the Spanish fleet going to involve Americans in the reviled European balar :e of power?

Such questions soon receded in the public mind as Americans turned their attention toward the naval and military contests in Cuba. But those campaigns, though generally as successful as the Philippine, would eventually raise the same uncomfortable points. It became increasingly difficult for many observers to avoid the conclusion that the American victory in the Spanish War was less a question of American skill than of Spanish political and military decrepitude. It simultaneously became harder to see how the United States might frustrate the apparently insatiable desire of other European powers to profit from Spain's decline. With an impressive devotion, Americans turned away from such complexities to the business of celebrating their victories, victories that were to be handed down to subsequent generations as legends—Manila Bay, Santiago de Cuba, San Juan Hill.

But ultimately the nagging doubts and questions returned, and a few became overriding. Had the war in actual fact proved American strength? Was America any more secure at its conclusion than at its start, or had she only multiplied the range of possible threats to her integrity? In years to come, a wide variety of politicians, academics and intellectuals would try to answer such questions— and their responses were destined to ignite debate, controversy and still more war.

Although the European powers had by no means shown themselves disinterested in the outcome of America's war to end slavery and preserve the Union from 1861 to 1865, Washington's diplomacy had succeeded in neutralizing any European interference in that conflict. Despite this, several European nations did manage to take advantage of America's Civil War more successfully in another part of the Western Hemisphere.

The troubled nation of Mexico had become even more chaotic at the end of the 1850s, when large groups of Mexican Indians, long repressed by their Spanish rulers, began to demand rights. In 1861 their leader, Benito Juárez, gained the Mexican presidency and suspended his country's international financial obligations. Mexico's principal creditors—Great Britain, France and Spain— quickly responded with a large military expedition whose ostensible mission was to make the Mexicans pay up. In reality, however, the move embodied Napoleon III's outlandish desire to place a European ruler on a New World throne, make a mockery of the Monroe Doctrine and reshape the European balance of power. By 1862 the British and Spanish had withdrawn from Mexico, but Napoleon clung tightly to his scheme, and in 1864 proclaimed the Archduke Maximilian of Austria emperor of Mexico, backing him up with French troops. President Lincoln and Secretary of State William Seward could do nothing to meet this most serious of challenges to the Monroe Doctrine, but as soon as the Civil War had ended Seward let it be known that force would not be ruled out as a method of restoring Juárez. By 1867, Seward's skillful use of threats and pressures—combined with the valiant and successful resistance of Juárez—had forced Napoleon to give in, and Maximilian was left to die before a Mexican firing squad.

The experience did much to reinforce America's long-held conviction that the powers of Europe would use any display of American weakness as an excuse to meddle in the affairs of the Western Hemisphere and so threaten the integrity of the United States. But in the years immediately following the Civil War, America was too weakened to undertake dramatic initiatives in foreign policy. Nonetheless, Secretary Seward, who continued to serve Andrew Johnson after Lincoln's assassination, did manage in 1867 to secure two key acquisitions whose significance went unrecognized—the Russian province of Alaska and the Midway Islands. Both were important in bolstering the American presence in the Pacific, where sea routes to China had become vital after the dramatic expansion of trade with that empire in 1844. The strengthening of the American commercial and residential presence in the Sandwich, or Hawaiian, Islands during this same period—culminating with the leasing of Pearl Harbor in 1887—further demonstrated the importance of the China trade.

Following Seward's departure, Americans settled into a long period of inconsequential activity in foreign affairs, contenting themselves with erecting high walls of tariff protection around the nation and exploiting the resources of the defeated South and the new states and territories of the West. And as they did so, political corruption, fed by the amazing fortunes amassed in all regions of the country and in all sectors of the economy, grew to unparalleled dimensions. The tragic influence of special interests on the Grant administration was notorious even in its own day—but Grant was far from the only president who was hopelessly beholden to such groups. The spoils system, through which politically active men of wealth were rewarded with government appointments for themselves or their hirelings, was openly acknowledged to be the national way of doing business. The great industrialists whose influence was most felt—men such as J. P. Morgan, John D. Rockefeller, Andrew Carnegie and Henry Clay Frick—were all proud, even boastful, of their role in government. As Jay Gould, the great speculator and railroad magnate, put it, "We have made the country rich, we have developed the country." Political control seemed to such men a just reward for their astute business leadership, and during the 1870s and 1880s, the interests of business and the interests of government became almost indistinguishable.

By the end of the 1880s, however, those interests seemed to require redefinition. Because of the dramatically increased output of American agriculture and industry, home markets were acknowledged to be close to saturation even by Republicans, the greatest champions of high tariffs. As a result, unemployment began to rise, labor unrest grew and a farm crisis distorted the idyllic image of a self-sufficient nation. Many politicians sought to lay the blame for such problems at the doorstep of monetary policy. Some favored the free coinage of silver (a loose monetary policy designed to help farmers and workers), while many fought for the gold standard, a tight monetary policy that was popularly perceived as favoring the wealthy. Still others favored bimetallism, a compromise measure whose proponents succeeded only in demonstrating that monetary policy was not at the heart of America's economic woes.

The true explanation of the crisis was far more fundamental than any question of currency. Put simply, rapidly advancing technologies had caused supply to grow far more quickly than demand, thus reducing the time during which America could survive as an economic haven unto herself from a thousand generations (as Jefferson had hoped) to a mere century. There was only one realistic cure for such a condition, but in the United States that cure had always been the stuff of political suicide—expansion of foreign markets for American goods, and with it, the import of cheap raw materials for American factories, a policy that was viewed by many Americans as nothing short of colonialism.

Jefferson's dream of an independent, agrarian-based democracy had been stripped away to reveal an industrial nation that could no longer stand alone economically. But foreign trade was anathema to many Americans, no matter what the truth of their economic plight. If such a program were to be sold to the public it would require a powerful spokesman. And during the 1880s such a man did step to the forefront of American national affairs— James G. Blaine, the "Plumed Knight" from the state of Maine. A brilliant orator and gifted party boss, the bearlike Blaine at first shocked many of his fellow Republican congressmen with his ideas on foreign trade. But as the domestic economic situation became steadily more stagnant and the number of strikes by dissatisfied workers rose, more and more powerful men were willing to listen to this conservative northerner's plans for recovery.

Blaine did not look to Europe or even China for the focus of his program of foreign trade. It was Latin America, with its abundant and cheap raw materials, that he saw as holding the greatest potential. His great dream was a "Pan-American Union," a hemispheric system of trade and economic interdependence—with the United States always in a position of preeminence. When Benjamin Harrison was elected president in 1888 he named Blaine secretary of state, and the Plumed Knight soon made his opinions known in a powerful and much reprinted speech given at Waterville, Maine, in 1890:

"I wish," said Blaine, "to declare the opinion that the United States has reached a point where one of its highest duties is to enlarge the area of its foreign trade. . . . Our great demand is expansion. I mean expansion of trade with countries where we can find profitable exchanges. We are not seeking annexation of territory. . . . At the same time I think we should be unwisely content if we did not engage in what the younger Pitt so well termed annexation of trade."

Blaine's heavy emphasis on American power and predominance made the pill of economic interaction with foreign countries easier for many Americans to swallow; and although his scheme for a Pan-American Union would never come to pass and he himself would die in January 1893, it was Blaine more than any other man who was responsible for the American acceptance of the need for foreign trade. But before such acceptance would become general, the nation would be forced to endure an unprecedented economic depression.

The year 1890 saw more strikes in the United States than any other in the nineteenth century; the farm crisis was continuing; and many politicians were still reluctant to break down protectionist walls, choosing instead to focus on the far less vital (though politically more profitable) issue of gold versus silver. But by tinkering with the American currency system—moving first toward bimetallism and then back to gold—Presidents Harrison and Cleveland only destroyed what little faith there had been in American monetary policy both at home and abroad. In 1893 a run on the Treasury began, which became a run on many American banks, and the nation soon found itself in the midst of a full-scale panic and depression.

James G. Blaine was dead, but his message seemed more relevant than ever. The notion that America was a nation choking on its own inbred economy eventually became widespread, and Blaine's insistence that American expansion was to be purely economic pointed the way for many who believed that while the United States must find a means of recovery, actual colonial possessions were a distinctly un-American option.

One such man was Richard Olney, who became Grover Cleveland's secretary of state in 1895 and was immediately faced with a crisis of significant proportions. Relations with Great Britain, though peaceful, had not prospered during the years of Blaine, who delighted in twisting the British lion's tail in order to satisfy his Anglophobic Maine constituency. The possibility of British aggression in Latin America—still an American nightmare, despite evidence that Britain's now enormous imperial responsibilities had long since precluded such adventurism—was brought up once more in 1895, when a long-standing dispute between Great Britain and Venezuela over the border between the latter nation and British Guiana threatened to turn violent. Washington, citing the Monroe Doctrine, demanded the British submit their grievances to international arbitration. But England's prime minister, Lord Salisbury, had long rejected the Monroe Doctrine on the grounds that it had never been accepted as international law by a power other than the United States. The American demand was rebuffed.

Olney, who had been attorney general prior to taking over the State Department, drafted a vigorous statement of the American position and dispatched it to the American minister in London on July 20, 1895, with instructions that it be relayed to Lord Salisbury. "To-day," Olney wrote, "the United States is practically sovereign on this continent, and its fiat is law upon the subjects to which it confines its interposition. Why? It is not because of the pure friendship and good will felt for it. It is not simply by reason of its high character as a civilized state, nor because wisdom and justice and equity are the invariable characteristics of the dealings of the United States. It is because, in addition to all other grounds, its infinite resources combined with its isolated position render it master of the situation and practically invulnerable as against any or all other powers."

The Olney note caused a sensation. After decades of limited participation in international affairs, the United States had suddenly decided to reenter the scene in a fashion that recalled both Washington's Farewell Address and the Monroe Doctrine. In 1896, Lord Salisbury did finally agree to arbitration, although he did so primarily because of the dangers posed to Great Britain by the rise of the German empire under its new and eminently volatile leader, Kaiser Wilhelm II, and in particular by the kaiser's expression of sympathy to the Boers in South Africa. But to the American people, it was Olney's tough stance that had caused the British to back down. Coming as it did in a year that saw the American economic depression finally easing, the Olney note seemed to confirm an idea that had been bandied back and forth in political circles since Blaine's day—economic recovery rested on expanding foreign markets. And nowhere were those markets more important than in Latin America, where a vigorous maintenance of the Monroe Doctrine would ensure a hemispheric system of prosperity predicated on American predominance—and power.

The United States, which had so recently had cause to question some of its most fundamental principles—including its notion of security as an absolute goal to be pursued in solitude—suddenly found that it was those very principles that would be its salvation. Convinced that they had bested their oldest and most dogged enemy, Americans in 1896 felt that security to be well within reach.

Or rather, most Americans did. But in various parts of the northeastern United States, a trio of powerful intellects were studying their country's international position, and what they saw disturbed them profoundly. They knew that the future economic security of the United States rested on overseas markets; but they also knew that America had few ships with which to carry her own trade, a navy inadequate to protect those merchant vessels and no strategic bases from which to exert influence over the behavior of rival powers. Without such fundamental strengths, said these men, any American confidence in prosperity through foreign trade was a delusion—and any American faith in absolute security was simply naive.

During the Civil War, the Union navy had built up a fleet of hundreds of vessels that was vitally important to the North's eventual victory. But in the postwar years that proud force had been dismantled and ignored, to the extent that when the War of the

Pacific broke out in 1879 between Chile and the combined forces of Bolivia and Peru, each of the combatants could boast a stronger navy than that of the United States. Studying this decline, an obscure, bookish navy officer, Captain Alfred Thayer Mahan, eventually worked his way into a larger study of the world history of maritime force—and what he found astonished him.

The son of a West Point instructor (and a man more fond of libraries than of steam-powered ships), Mahan in 1884 was asked to become a lecturer at the newly founded Naval War College in Newport, Rhode Island, a graduate institution where exceptional officers could achieve the sort of intellectual growth that was often frowned on at the Naval Academy in Annapolis. During his initial residence at the college, Mahan began to realize that "control of the sea was an historic factor which had never been systematically appreciated and expounded." He decided to take this impressive challenge on himself.

Earlier in his life Mahan had been a confirmed anti-imperialist, repelled by the European practice of exploiting the human and natural resources of distant colonies and attracted to noncolonial but commercially expansive ideas. But as he prepared his study of naval history, Mahan began to recognize two fundamental points: no great trading power had ever lacked a strong navy, and strong navies had always required stations abroad. Colonies, Mahan began to see, had often served the needs of naval power, rather than vice versa. It was a seminal discovery for the captain. If dreams of commercial expansion simply could not be achieved without a strong fleet, as history indicated, and if a strong fleet meant overseas possessions (which was doubly true in the age of steam, when a string of coaling stations could mean the difference between naval superiority and humiliation), then the United States must gain such possessions. Mahan himself disdained the word "colonies," and preferred to speak of "coaling stations" and "bases," "posts whose value was chiefly strategic, though not necessarily wholly so"; but however he chose to rationalize his shift in opinion, Mahan had, through his study of naval history, become an imperialist.

The Influence of Sea Power Upon History, 1660–1783, Mahan's first and most famous book, was published in 1890. Most of its pages were devoted to proving the captain's theory of the importance of a strong navy and overseas bases to a flourishing trade—but many were filled with powerful condemnations of the serious strategic vulnerability of the United States. America's divided coastlines, said Mahan, were "neglected and politically weak," and even if the United States were to connect them with a Central American canal, that waterway would bring "the interests of the other great nations, the European nations, close along our shores, as they have never been before. With this it will not be as easy as heretofore to stand aloof from international complications." But such "complications" could only spell disaster, for "the United States has not that shield of defensive power behind which time can be gained to develop its reserve of strength."

The traditional American belief that "the distance which separates her from other great powers" was "a protection," was also, to Mahan, "a snare," because it caused the American people to ignore the question of a navy. But that question would have to be faced, and with it the tangential issue of "foreign establishments, either colonial or military," without which, "the ships of the United States, in war, will be like land birds, unable to fly far from their own shores." In a magazine article that also appeared in 1890, Mahan concisely summed up his anxieties about America's strategic position: "Though distant, our shores can be reached; being defenceless, they can detain but a short time a force sent against them."

This was not a warning that many Americans were particularly interested in heeding. True, the secretary of the navy, drawing on Mahan's still-unpublished theories, had sounded similarly ominous notes in his 1889 annual report. And the Naval Policy Board of 1890 had lectured Congress that, "at present our commerce is carried in foreign vessels," that an interoceanic canal "may be a fruitful source of danger," and that "we are now totally unprepared—even against second-rate powers—to protect our commerce, to prevent blockade of our ports, or to maintain our rights and honor away from home." But the fortunes of the overwhelming majority of the American people would have to dip toward the disastrous before economic need would lead them to embrace en masse such apparently un-American notions as a large peacetime navy, overseas dominions and aggressive competition with other trading powers. Only a relative few were willing to listen carefully to Mahan's lectures or to study closely his written words in 1890.

One of those few, however, happened to be the second most powerful member of the House Naval Committee, and thus in a position to be of some help. Henry Cabot Lodge of Massachusetts had long argued for greater American naval strength, not simply to protect trade but also to assert national prestige, a mission that Lodge approached in a vague, almost mystical fashion. To those who knew him, the approach was not altogether surprising. The overly indulged child of two wealthy Boston merchant clans, Lodge had grown up loving the sea by heritage as well as by inclination. After a youth marked by the usual experiences for boys of his class —tutoring, travel and mayhem—he had cast about for something on which to focus his already impressive intellectual powers. Literature was Lodge's first passion, but when he began to study medieval history under Henry Adams at Harvard, his fascination with politics, world affairs and especially America's future international role became preeminent, and took on an evangelical quality that the fatalistic Adams was often hard put to understand. A gifted orator despite a sharp (many said grating) speaking voice, Lodge rose quickly in Massachusetts state politics, early on stifling qualms over Republican corruption and a tendency toward breaking party ranks. Some, among them Henry Adams, believed that Lodge sold out when he abandoned liberal Republicanism—but the "scholar of politics" maintained that he merely made the practical decisions necessary to give form to his ambitious vision of the nation's future.

One of Lodge's sisters-in-law had married the son of the Naval War College's president, and through this chain the short, wiry, ever-vociferous congressman met the naval prophet, Captain Mahan. For Lodge it was a crucial encounter. "Scholar" or no, he did not possess the kind of hard naval knowledge he needed to argue adequately on behalf of an expanded American presence abroad. Mahan's theories provided him with ammunition for the House Naval Committee's debates, and Lodge's efforts were crucial in ensuring the passage, in the same year that Mahan's book was published, of a Naval Act that included authorization for America's first truly modern battleships.

Lodge shared Mahan's preoccupation with threats to American security in the early 1890s, and perceived those threats as coming not only from America's traditional antagonist, Great Britain, but also from other rising powers who—like the United States—had exhausted their home markets, faced a problem of rapidly rising population and unemployment and were looking outward for solutions. Foremost among such potential enemies were Japan and Germany. After moving up to the Senate, Lodge began to plead various security causes with genuine desperation, among them the immediate annexation of Hawaii. On March 2, 1895, speaking in response to another senator's emphatic statement that "fear of England is the most absurd and ridiculous proposition ever presented on this floor," Lodge rose to lecture his colleagues in a most pedantic—and typical—fashion.

Ordering a large map of the Pacific to be brought into the chamber, Lodge took up a pointer and began to speak, his crisp words snapping through a neatly trimmed beard. To suggestions that the Hawaiian people of the Sandwich Islands were not worthy of American citizenship, Lodge declared, "I do not think that these are the vital questions involved. . . . Those islands, even if they were populated by a low race of savages, even if they were desert rocks, would still be important to this country from their position. On that ground and that ground alone we ought to possess them. That they have a great commerce and fertile soil merely adds to the desirability of our taking them."

Lodge next indicated a series of large red Maltese crosses on his map. "These red crosses . . . are the British naval stations on the Atlantic coast of the United States [Britain's Caribbean colonies]— six powerful, strong places and naval stations. . . . Here, these crosses represent British naval stations in the East and about Australia. Now, everyone can see here at the Falkland Islands is a British naval station. Here is another at Vancouver. Here is another at the Fiji Islands. In the great triangle marked by these three points"—Lodge whipped his pointer at the map for emphasis— "Great Britain does not hold a naval station. There in the center of that triangle, in the heart of the Pacific, where I am now pointing, lie the Sandwich Islands. They are the key of the Pacific."

Pausing only to acknowledge applause from the galleries, Lodge went on to elaborate his point: "Mr. President, it is on account of the military and strategic importance of the Sandwich Islands that I so greatly desire their control by the United States." That importance was hardly confined to quarrels with Britain: "It is well not to forget that there has arisen in the East a new sea power. . . . The Japanese have displayed the qualities of a great fighting race at sea. They understand their future; they realize the prospects which are opening up before them. . . . Remember that they are a new people; they have just whipped somebody [in the Sino-Japanese War of 1894–95], and they are in a state of mind when they think they can whip anybody."

The speech was a remarkable success. It was clear that the growing ranks of Mahanian disciples had found an eloquent and powerful champion in Congress. Lodge, however, had long since made it clear that he had no higher ambition than the Senate; if the problem of American weakness were to be effectively addressed, it would almost certainly have to be done from the White House. As yet, no leader of national stature had shown any inclination to view foreign relations in the light of a powerful navy supported by overseas bases—but with the rise of Theodore Roosevelt, all that would change.

In 1882 Roosevelt, twenty-four at the time, had published a study of the naval campaigns of the War of 1812. The book had been well-received, particularly given the author's age, and had some years later led to an invitation to speak at the Naval War College. It was during this trip that the aspiring author and would-be statesman first heard and met Mahan. The significance of the meeting in the formation of the still-young Roosevelt's political philosophy was critical. Rightfully considering himself a man who had overcome the childhood disadvantages of a slight physique and chronic illnesses in order to enjoy the fruits of the "strenuous life," Roosevelt was quick to spot weakness in men and in nations, and his assessment of America's position in the world in the late 1880s accorded perfectly with Mahan's—and with Lodge's.

Lodge had occasionally found jobs for Roosevelt as a paid author before the start of their respective political careers, and the friendship that had grown up between them was boyish, devoted and marked more than anything else by an awareness of the lack of nationalistic spirit to be found in American society at the time. Roosevelt did not wholeheartedly share the opinion of Henry Adams's younger brother Brooks—who preached that America required an infusion of "barbarian" warrior blood to revitalize herself—and he did recognize that the aggressive militarism of Japan and Germany could probably never take root in the United States. But his sense of American weakness was keen, and his determination to safeguard the nation through a buildup of the navy became all-consuming during the 1890s.

"Preparedness deters the foe," Mahan told Roosevelt in 1897, and the statement became the young politician's credo. As the years passed, the correspondence between Roosevelt, Mahan and Lodge centered less and less on the English threat and ever more on the rising might of Germany and Japan. Roosevelt wrote confidentially to Mahan: "I do not fear England; Canada is a hostage for her good behavior; but I do fear some of the other powers."

He cautioned the captain that "to no one else excepting Lodge do I talk like this." Lodge, too, was more edgy about the Germans than the English, believing that "the German Emperor has moments when he is wild enough to do anything," including "some attempt [at a colony] in South America."

But in 1897 the principal concern of all three was Hawaii. For unlike James Blaine, they saw American expansion in the Far East as equally important to that in Latin America. Mahan's advice on the problem of Hawaii—especially considering the growing Japanese population in the islands—was to "take the islands first and solve afterwards." Roosevelt replied that he took Mahan's "views absolutely, as indeed I do on foreign policy generally," adding that "I am alive to the danger from Japan, and know that it is idle to rely on any sentimental good will towards us."

By the time Roosevelt became ensconced in the Navy Department, he, Lodge and Mahan had decided that the best way to deter aggression, in the face of Congress's continued preoccupation with economic concerns and consistent refusal to support a program of massive naval buildup, was to involve the United States in a war it could be somewhat sure of winning. Much to the delight of all three men, a violent outbreak of the always-simmering independence movement in Cuba in 1895 prompted widespread public support in the United States. American businessmen, on the other hand, were aghast at the prospect of American intervention in what came to be a brutal war between Cuban guerrillas and their Spanish rulers.

The Spanish system of rule had always served American business interests well, and a war was generally perceived as disruptive to the U.S. economy. Yet far from dying down, American popular indignation at the Spanish treatment of the Cubans—who were herded into concentration camps and massacred by the thousands —only grew. Assistant Secretary of the Navy Roosevelt looked to war with Spain in the Caribbean as a chance to "serve notice that no strong European power, and especially not Germany, should be allowed to gain a foothold by supplanting some weak European power."

Mahan, Lodge and Roosevelt, then, were the vanguard of America's aggressive response to expanding European imperialism in the late nineteenth and early twentieth centuries. But even their considerable efforts would have been in vain without the assistance of lesser-known men, primarily in the staff and intelligence corps of the navy, who transformed the broad ideas of their superiors into workable form. Employing the little means at their disposal, these officers constructed specific strategic and tactical plans of operation for their nation's armed forces during the mid- and late 1890s. It was above all their talents—rather than the battle skills of American officers in the field or at sea—that allowed the United States to frustrate the designs of other powers and take advantage of Spanish weakness in 1898.

In the spring of 1896 Lieutenant William Wirt Kimball of the Office of Naval Intelligence was serving temporary duty as staff intelligence officer at the Naval War College. Despite his low rank, Kimball was forty-eight years old (not an uncommon situation in the nineteenth-century navy), a veteran of several intelligence-gathering missions to Latin America and a confirmed advocate of an expanded American naval presence throughout the world. The purpose that Kimball saw underlying that expansion was simple: later in life he would declare that it was "absolutely impossible to wear a sword and sail salt water in Uncle Sam's service for half a century or so without becoming imbued with the feeling that the United States of America is the finest and most glorious thing that ever happened and that it must lead in everything."

Such broad sentiments belied the complexity of Kimball's mind. His ideas on naval policy coincided strategically with those of Captain Mahan; but in the increasingly important areas of intelligence and tactics, he far outstripped his superior. Mahan had focused his studies on the seventeenth and eighteenth centuries, and so became convinced of the primacy of battle- (or capital) ships, the chief instrument of naval power during those periods. Following Mahan's lead, Lodge, Roosevelt and others had centered their calls for naval development on large, heavily armed battleships. But in the mid-1880s Kimball could already see that the development of the torpedo and the submarine might very well change the essential nature of naval warfare. By advocating the building of vessels that could effectively exploit these two new trends, Kimball separated himself from the cult of the battleship.

But it was intelligence and the drafting of war plans that Kimball was most noted for. He had been seconded to the War College in order to assist in drawing up situational problems for a series of war games, and to develop these ideas into contingency plans for actual conflicts. On June 1, 1896, Kimball submitted a paper to the college entitled "War with Spain." Starting from the assumption that hostilities with that country were inevitable because of "the Cuban question," Kimball proceeded to outline "a purely naval war," a "war of blockades, bombardments, harrassments, naval descents on exposed colonies, naval actions whenever they can be brought under fair conditions." Such a war, said Kimball, would be cheap, quick and would allow the Cubans themselves to win independence on the land, "instead of a conquest and occupation of Spanish territory by an organized army of invasion from this country."

Kimball outlined three theaters of operation for such a war: Cuban waters, Spanish home waters, and Philippine waters. The first two were predictable—the third had never been proposed by any planning or policy officer. But Kimball believed that the United States should attack the Philippine Islands "for the purpose of reducing and holding Manila, of harassing trade, of cutting off revenue," and "of occupying . . . the Philippine principal ports," which would be "held until a war indemnity were satisfactorily arranged for." Should the Spanish prove reluctant to do so, "Our government could assure Spain that Manila would have to pay for every merchantman captured."

It was a dramatic leap in American naval strategy. The use of coercion through the seizure of colonies—a feature of British imperial strategy since the days of Sir Francis Drake—was being suggested by an officer of the United States Navy, not for the purpose of spreading democracy, nor even to expand America's economic interests, but simply to cripple the strength and frustrate the designs of an enemy power. Manila Bay was not envisioned as a missionary conquest, but as a simple—and most effective—bargaining chip.

Mahan, in contrast, had concentrated his writings on the need for overseas possessions as a method of supporting American sea power and defending an aggressive trade campaign. Kimball had revealed the other side of the coin, a side that Americans had always rejected as being too purely exploitative—too European—in nature. But the idea that the United States might be able to bring Spain to her knees without ever actually attacking the Iberian Peninsula, or even Cuba, proved attractive enough to override such qualms. As Kimball's plan slowly made its way up the chain of command, being altered slightly at each level to satisfy the vanity of less imaginative officers, the revolutionary feature of Philippine operations was always retained. When the plan finally became official naval policy, though it had been expanded to include land operations in Cuba, a naval attack on Manila was one of its most conspicuous features.

Precisely when Theodore Roosevelt first saw the Kimball plan is impossible to say. But by the time he became settled in at the Navy Department, the assistant secretary was in regular and "intimate" contact with the lieutenant, and in letters to him Roosevelt often referred to "our hopes as to the Spanish business," and worried that those hopes were "a dream." In September of 1897 Roosevelt was preaching the desirability of action against Spain along the lines of the Kimball plan to everyone from Lodge to President William McKinley, who was given personal briefings by the assistant secretary during dinners and horseback rides. In November, Roosevelt wrote to Kimball that a Spanish war would be "one more step toward the complete freeing of America from European dominion." The Philippine action could only hasten this result, and Roosevelt was not the only man who knew it. When he sent his remarkable cable ordering Commodore Dewey to Hong Kong on February 25, 1898, Senator Henry Cabot Lodge was in the office with him, eagerly urging him on.

So great was the desire of Roosevelt and Lodge to humble Spain through the surest and quickest means possible—the Kimball plan —that they did not stop to consider what the United States might do with the captured Spanish provinces once it had them. Following the destruction of the *Maine,* war did at last come, and quickly. The Philippines and Cuba, as well as Puerto Rico and Guam, were seized, and Theodore Roosevelt returned from his adventures in Cuba with the Rough Riders to become governor of New York. But in the meantime the United States had acquired extensive overseas possessions. The Cuban situation was fairly easy to resolve —the war had been fought in the name of Cuban independence, and after a sufficient period of American occupation (enough to ensure future American hegemony over the island) that independence was to be declared. But what of the other areas, especially the Philippines? What was to be done with a bargaining chip when the enemy had already come to terms?

Roosevelt and Lodge were inclined to keep the islands as a way of further expanding America's Pacific influence. But much of the nation was not yet ready to accept such out-and-out colonialism. During the weeks that Spanish and American negotiators met to hammer out a peace treaty in the fall of 1898, the notion that the United States might actually retain the Philippines began to cause protest, especially in intellectual circles. As the controversy spread, the question of what to do with the islands became a nagging nightmare for William McKinley.

The twenty-fifth president of the United States had done his best to avoid the Spanish War, and had only given in when public demand for it became overriding. Author of the famous McKinley Tariff of 1890—a piece of protective legislation designed to keep America's international economic ties at a minimum—McKinley did not share a wholesale imperialist view, and actually had some sympathy for the desire of the Filipinos to rule themselves. But when reports began to come in from Commodore Dewey and others saying that the Filipinos were completely incapable of such self-rule, McKinley was caught in a dilemma. Spain needed money badly, and if the islands were returned to her she would almost certainly sell them off to another power, in all likelihood Germany or Japan. But if the United States went ahead and granted Philippine independence, and the archipelago then fell into confusion and anarchy, any imperial state could and probably would use that instability as an excuse for annexation.

McKinley's confusion in the face of this problem was profound, for these were questions of international strategy and great power politics—unfamiliar terrain to the Ohioan in the White House. After many sleepless nights, the president finally decided that "there was nothing left for us to do but to take them all, and to educate the Filipinos and uplift and civilize and Christianize them." McKinley's belief in America's great mission to spread democracy (though in this case it followed in the wake of global strategic considerations) had allowed him a moral way out, one that was also calculated to gain him additional political support. Following his decision he "went to bed, and went to sleep, and slept soundly, and the next morning I sent for the chief engineer of the War Department (our map maker) and I told him to put the Philippines on the map of the United States."

The saga of the American annexation of the Philippines was to be a bloody one. Filipino resistance to U.S. rule went on until 1902, and during that time hundreds of thousands of natives as well as a considerable number of American soldiers were killed in a war that saw extreme savagery practiced by both sides. William James condemned the American effort, saying that, "There are worse things than financial troubles in a Nation's career. To puke up its ancient soul and the only things that give it eminence among nations, in five minutes without a wink of squeamishness, is worse." Mark Twain thought that, in view of the American suppression of the Filipinos, the American flag ought to have "the white stripes painted black and the stars replaced by the skull and crossbones." But such moral arguments failed to acknowledge the critical shift that was taking place in American political thought—the growth of strategic considerations as a dominant strain in foreign policy.

The Philippines were not annexed for economic gain, but in the cause of American strategic and territorial security. Indeed, administration of the islands would prove to be a costly venture for the U.S. government. Lodge himself said that he saw "very plainly the enormous difficulties of dealing with the Philippines," but expansion of the U.S. presence in the Pacific was viewed as worth the price. The question of precisely what interests the United States hoped to protect through building up military establishments in the Philippines was answered by pro-annexationists with a set of assumptions—the ever more profitable China trade, a naval balance in the Pacific and American prestige were all said to be at stake. But in the years immediately following the Spanish War, more and more Americans began to doubt the validity of such assumptions. The formal annexation of Hawaii—achieved through a joint resolution of Congress that Lodge craftily tacked onto a war appropriations bill in July 1898—only increased such doubts, for the United States now owned what the senator from Massachusetts himself had called "the key of the Pacific." As the struggle to subjugate the Filipinos wound endlessly on, it began to appear that annexation had occurred not so much to protect America's Pacific interests as to forestall the designs of other powers in the region.

In nearly every case, those designs had as their twin goals the achievement of preeminence in the China trade and the establishment of superiority in the balance of naval power in the Pacific. Whether the Philippines could play an important role in denying such a position to any other nation, or whether, as critics charged, the occupation was irrelevant to any real American security interests, would only become apparent over the next decade.

The Western Pacific in 1899 was a checkerboard of delicately balanced American and European holdings aimed primarily at the economic exploitation of the massive market known as the Chinese empire. The Naval War Board, formed to coordinate policy during the Spanish War, knew the importance of the China trade to American manufacturers and merchants, as did McKinley's secretary of state, John Hay. Hay, a thin, brilliant Anglophile given to poetry and nervous illnesses, had been a private secretary in Abraham Lincoln's administration and subsequently American ambassador to Great Britain. His conception of American influence in China as the cornerstone of U.S. Pacific policy seemed to jibe with that of the navy—but from 1899 to 1901 a series of disagreements between the two departments demonstrated on the one hand that America's strategic and economic policies were not always in harmony, and on the other that the Philippine Islands might in fact lack the strategic importance that Lodge and Roosevelt had assigned to them.

In 1899 the European powers were in possession of protectorates and leases in China that heavily compromised the Imperial government. The French wished to spread their influence north from their base of operations in Indochina. The Germans had established themselves at Kiaochow and were angling for a more extensive sphere. The Japanese, already occupying Formosa and the Pescadores, viewed mainland China as a legitimate region for expansion. And the Russians, trading out of Port Arthur, had obvious designs on Manchuria. Only Great Britain seemed to have a genuine interest in maintaining the status quo in China. It was in response to this desire that an Englishman working for the Chinese Customs Service, Alfred Hippisley, approached an old American friend named William W. Rockhill—who also happened to be John Hay's adviser on Far Eastern affairs—in 1899 and inquired as to the American position on China.

Rockhill assured Hippisley that the McKinley administration was first and foremost interested in protecting the integrity of China and maintaining the Far Eastern balance of power; now that the United States had constructed its string of coaling stations (completed with the annexation of Guam in 1898 and the seizure of Wake Island in January 1899), trade was the sole American goal. Hippisley was anxious that the United States make some official statement of its support for the "Open Door," a phrase long used by the British to describe an ideal situation in which all powers had equal access to Chinese ports as well as to each other's spheres of influence there. Rockhill decided, and was able to convince Secretary Hay, that such a statement would be a good idea, given the attitude of the continental European powers. While Hay was on summer vacation, Rockhill drew up a series of notes to be delivered to each of the European governments through America's ministers abroad. In September, Secretary Hay signed the notes and they were dispatched.

A pointed restatement of American unilateralism, the Open Door notes of 1899 said that "the Government of the United States would be pleased" if each European power would pledge that it would not interfere with any other power's Chinese sphere of influence, that it would permit China to collect her rightful tariffs, and that it would, in its leased ports, apply uniform harbor duties on all ships, including its own. Hay, however, waited for no official acceptance from any foreign governments before declaring that he had received "assurances" from all of them that they would maintain "China's rights of sovereignty." The secretary's pronounced emphasis on a unilateral approach to Chinese affairs was underlined in June 1900, when, during the xenophobic Boxer Rebellion, he cabled the American minister in Peking that, "We have no policy in China except to protect with energy American interests, and especially American citizens. . . . There must be no alliances."

The Open Door notes are interesting mainly in the light of subsequent American naval policy, for their effect on other powers was negligible. Hay and Rockhill could only urge respect for the integrity of China if the United States was itself willing to display such an attitude. But the Navy Department had, since the end of the Spanish War, repeatedly said that it desired an American protectorate in China. As early as August 1898, the Naval War Board had been "impressed with the advisability of acquiring a coaling station nearer to central China than is Manila," and in October of 1900 Navy Secretary Long wrote to Hay, commenting on "the desirability of obtaining some station upon the coast of China, or at some other point north of our possessions in the Philippines." Long and those officers below him—including Commodore (now Admiral) Dewey—repeatedly argued that the Philippine position was not sufficient to protect the China trade, especially since the army and navy could not even agree among themselves as to where the development of an American military base in the islands should take place. (The army favored Manila, largely for reasons of creature comforts, while the navy argued for Subic Bay.)

During the debate over whether a Philippine base could be decisive in maintaining America's share of the China trade or if a base in China was also required, the Navy Department made a number of self-contradictory statements that revealed the shady qualifications of the Philippines for that role—and angered many in Washington, including President Roosevelt. In arguing that Subic Bay and not Manila should be the principal American military base in the Philippines, Dewey consistently offered the opinion that "no trade route can be protected by holding the depot to which supplies are bound [in this case Manila]"; yet his position on a China base was precisely the opposite, as was that of Secretary Long. Hay himself was uncertain about the question of a Chinese base, which indicated his own feeling that the Philippines were inadequate to protect trade on the mainland. But W. W. Rockhill, whose influence on Hay was decisive in these matters, lost no time in ruling out a Chinese protectorate. "Everything considered," he said, "I think that it will be a pretty difficult question to settle without giving a rather serious blow to the policy which we have been very consistently following in China." On the basis of this opinion, Hay reluctantly turned down the Navy Department's requests for a China base.

Debate over the American presence in the Philippines was hardly confined to intellectuals in the United States—the strategists themselves could not agree as to the importance or the future role of the islands. All of this left Roosevelt somewhat in a quandary in 1901. "While I have never varied in my feeling that we had to hold the Philippines," he said, "I have varied very much in my feelings whether we were to be considered fortunate or unfortunate in having to hold them." These doubts were destined to grow, not only in Roosevelt's mind, but in the views of other naval strategists who saw that, with the United States holding Pearl Harbor, Midway, Guam and the cable station at Wake—all of which lacked either hostile populations or the need for expensive administrative bureaucracies—the Philippines might indeed be superfluous.

So long as other powers in the Pacific were known to desire them, however, the Philippines would remain a possession that no American president would feel comfortable parting with. During the years following the Spanish War, American lives and dollars were poured into the archipelago (and a native independence movement crushed) largely to prevent a group of islands—whose true importance had been confined to a specific military campaign that had long since been completed—from falling into the hands of any other nation. As to the question of what role the Philippines might play in maintaining a desirable naval balance in the Pacific, that issue came to the fore in the first decade of the twentieth century.

When William McKinley chose Theodore Roosevelt as his running mate in 1900, New York State's political bosses applauded the decision, glad for any chance to get rid of their reform-minded governor. But when McKinley was shot by an anarchist on September 6, 1901, and died eight days later, conservatives throughout the United States shuddered. As Republican boss Mark Hanna said, "I told William McKinley it was a mistake to nominate that wild man at [the] Philadelphia [convention]. I asked him if he realized what would happen if he should die. Now, look, that damned cowboy is President of the United States." Roosevelt's strategic understanding of international affairs had not essentially changed since his days at the Navy Department. With his assumption of national power, that understanding came to dominate American foreign policy.

The results of the Spanish War seemed an unarguable vindication of the theories that Roosevelt had learned from Mahan and Lieutenant Kimball. Spain had been humbled without ever suffering a direct assault at home; Dewey's victory at Manila Bay had prevented Spain's Asiatic fleet from joining her ships in the Atlantic, and so had helped make possible the American victory off Santiago de Cuba in June 1898; and the battleship *Oregon*'s remarkable journey from the Pacific Coast to the Caribbean around Cape Horn in order to play an important role in that victory seemed proof that fast, heavy battleships would play a crucial role in future naval wars.

But to Roosevelt, the American victories raised as many doubts as they eased. In November 1901 the newly installed president received a letter from Lieutenant William Sowden Sims, another of the navy's low-ranking but gifted intelligence officers. Sims had been naval attaché in Paris during the Spanish War and had sent home, in a two-year period, some eleven thousand pages of reports concerning the naval might of the various European powers. Following the war, Sims had discovered that the ratio of shells fired to hits made among the American ships at Santiago was actually worse than that of Dewey's crews at Manila, a fact that he considered so crucial that he risked his career by writing directly to

Roosevelt. The president eventually invited Sims to the White House, and while describing the woeful inferiority of American gun crews, Sims also found time to criticize bluntly the various designs that had been adopted for America's battleships. He considered them "glaringly inferior in principle as well as in details, to those of our possible enemies, including Japan."

Other aspects of America's performance during the war also vexed Roosevelt. The glory of the *Oregon*'s journey around the Horn was soon shown to be less significant than the fact that such a perilous trip had been necessary at all—the importance of a Central American canal to U.S. naval policy was pointed up clearly. Then, too, the navy seemed to require a more efficient command organization; Mahan's emphasis on a mobile, concentrated fleet—based in the Atlantic but prepared for Pacific actions as well—would not allow for the loose system of command that had been the rule after 1865 and during the Spanish War. "It is not likely," said Mahan, "that the United States will ever again be confronted with an enemy as inapt [*sic*] as Spain proved to be"; and against a more accomplished foe, a far better performance would be required. The only area in which the navy's capability had been proved beyond question during the Spanish crisis was the planning of the war itself, and in spite of this (or perhaps because of it) Roosevelt decided that the navy's war planning activities were not sufficiently extensive.

Each of these problems was dealt with during the Roosevelt administration, and with concrete results. Lieutenant Sims was rewarded for his audacity (which he believed a duty, saying that the officer who did not criticize his superiors was "not worth the powder to blow himself to hell") with the post of inspector of target practice, and eventually performed miracles with American gun crews. Battleship design was updated and kept competitive with that of the European powers, even though this meant, as it did for the Europeans, the continual problem of obsolescence, ships that were revolutionary on the drawing board but out-of-date before they were completed. As for a canal, in 1903 Roosevelt took advantage of an American-inspired Panamanian revolution to gain the rights to construct a waterway across that country, typically describing his actions with the remark, "I took Panama." And although the Navy Department could not be fully reorganized to allow the kind of general staff that many officers wanted (such staffs were considered sinisterly "Prussian" by most Americans), the creation of a General Board under Admiral Dewey in 1900 did give much wider sway to war planning activities.

All of these policies reflected Roosevelt's belief that Germany was the preeminent threat to American interests in the Western Hemisphere. For Roosevelt, it was a simple question of dynamics: the Germans, like the Americans, needed to expand and needed overseas possessions. "We are all treading the same path," was his concise assessment, and though the volatile personality of the kaiser might aggravate that condition, the condition itself was perceived as fundamental and entirely natural—none of which lessened the determination of either Roosevelt or the Navy Department to frustrate the designs of the German empire.

That goal was largely achieved during Roosevelt's presidency through a strategy that concentrated the American fleet in the Atlantic, where it could quickly respond to direct German interference in the Western Hemisphere. But the need for such concentration created, in turn, deep anxieties about the balance of power in the Pacific.

Here the range of potential American enemies multiplied to include not only the Germans, but the Russians, the French and the supposedly friendly Japanese, as well. Throughout Roosevelt's two terms, Admiral Dewey's General Board formulated its Pacific contingency planning on the basis of "an ultimate alliance of the United States and two other powers against a coalition of three powers." Germany, of course, represented one enemy; the Russians, because of their known opposition to the Open Door and equilibrium in the Pacific, became a second; and the French, by way of their various pacts with the Russians, filled out the bill. This left the United States, Great Britain and Japan to preserve the Pacific balance, despite the sometime belief of President Roosevelt and other American leaders, notably Senator Lodge, that the Japanese would eventually pursue a policy of aggressive expansion.

Actual events in the Far East and in the United States also made the General Board's coalition plans seem of questionable use. Although the British and the Japanese did sign the first of two general agreements in 1902, this did not prevent Britain, three years later, from recalling her Pacific battleships to meet the growing German challenge in European waters. And the Russo-Japanese War of 1904–5 demonstrated that Japan did not intend to frustrate Russia's annexationist policies in Manchuria so much as take them over. In addition, a series of anti-Japanese riots in California in 1906–7, sparked by successive waves of cheap labor arriving from the Orient, put a severe strain on U.S.–Japanese relations. Many Europeans believed that the United States and Japan would go to war over the issue. And finally, in 1907, Japan signed agreements with the French and the Russians that winked cynically at the Open Door and signaled cooperation in the further exploitation of China.

A wartime alliance with Japan, then, seemed unlikely. But the General Board's continued emphasis on the primacy of the German threat to the Atlantic and the Western Hemisphere made any large-scale solitary or even bilateral (with Great Britain) effort in the Pacific appear unwinnable. The board was therefore reluctant to plan for it. Dewey, speaking for the board, said that if war with Japan came, the United States could not prevent the fall of the Philippines, and perhaps even Guam and Hawaii as well. But he deemed this danger acceptable, and rationalized his position by saying that the United States could always retake those possessions with its Atlantic fleet.

Such a scenario, however, was deeply flawed. It assumed—despite heavy evidence to the contrary—that an American president would become involved in a Pacific war at the cost of exposing the Atlantic Ocean and the Western Hemisphere to the German threat. Yet despite this very questionable assumption, Dewey's was the only plan that was even remotely feasible, barring a drastic naval buildup beyond anything that even Roosevelt and Lodge could have endorsed. In short, the balance of power in the Western Pacific could not realistically be maintained so long as Germany remained the gravest threat to American security.

The inescapability of this conclusion, as well as the continued annoyance caused by the army and navy's squabbling over whether to develop Manila or Subic Bay as the principal American base in the Philippines, led Roosevelt to write in August 1907 that, "in the excitement of the Spanish War people wanted to take the islands. They had an idea they would be a valuable possession. Now they think that they are of no value, and I am bound to say that in the physical sense I don't see where they are likely to be of any value." Indeed, the Philippines were a confirmed danger, in that they tempted Japanese aggression: "They are all that makes the present situation with Japan dangerous. . . . I do not believe that our people will permanently accept the Philippines simply as an unremunerative and indeed expensive duty."

The dissatisfaction of "the people" was most often expressed by the Congress, which consistently refused to appropriate large amounts of money for Philippine fortifications and continually harassed Roosevelt's attempts to build a "big navy." "Little navy" congressmen, mainly Democrats, could not see the purpose of spending increasing amounts of money on ships whose designs were constantly being outdated and whose role, beyond concentration in the Atlantic to meet the German threat, was ill-defined. It was in reaction to this unending congressional opposition, as well as to impress both Japan and Germany of the reality of American naval might, that Roosevelt decided in 1907 on one of the most magnificently symbolic—and arguably useless—acts of his presidency—the World Cruise of the Great Fleet.

In later years, Roosevelt would write that he directed the fleet to circumnavigate the globe so that it would be "clearly understood, by our own people especially, but also by other peoples, that the Pacific was as much our home waters as the Atlantic, and that our fleet could and would at will pass from one to the other of the two great oceans." But the dramatic spectacle of the World Cruise did not hide the fact that America in 1907 was a nation that had not precisely defined its world interests. Roosevelt and the big navy men could not convince Congress and the American people of the value of an unrestrained buildup; Dewey's General Board could not reconcile its requests for funds to fortify Subic Bay with its admission that the fall of the Philippines in a war with Japan would be inevitable; and Roosevelt's desire to prove that the Western Pacific was "home waters" to the Americans did not correspond to his own deeply held conviction that the fleet should remain concentrated in the Atlantic and see to the defense of the Western Hemisphere.

Of far more significance than the World Cruise—though far less publicized—was Roosevelt's exasperated decision in May 1908 to concentrate American forces in the Pacific at Pearl Harbor and to abandon any large-scale fortification and development of either Manila or Subic Bay. It was a move that served to bring American goals far more in line with American capabilities. The infighting and contradictory statements of Roosevelt's own military advisers, as well as the continued opposition of Congress, did not permit the president to fulfill his dream of an America whose interests were worldwide. For the moment, the Atlantic Ocean and the Western Hemisphere were the real vital interests of the United States. Pacific concerns, however else Roosevelt, Lodge and Dewey tried to portray them, remained essentially commercial—and when the General Board finally did formulate its "Plan Orange" for possible operations against Japan, it stated that "the advantages of position are all with Orange [Japan]," and centered the theater of naval operations around Guam, while emphasizing the importance of Midway and the Hawaiian Islands.

Bitter debate over the American presence in the Philippines continued because, as in the case of Texas in 1845, no genuine security argument could be brought forth to silence it. But while able to admit grudgingly that such was the case, Roosevelt and his designated successor, William Howard Taft, would neither withdraw from the islands nor surrender the dream of a radically upgraded navy, one that could truly become what Mahan had called a "shield of defensive power" for America. If offensive operations such as those designed by Lieutenant Kimball were no longer viewed as necessary by the American people, the great fleet was needed, said Roosevelt and Taft, at least to ensure the security of the United States within the hemisphere that it had viewed as vital since the days of James Monroe and John Quincy Adams. From 1909 to 1916 that fleet did indeed remain the focus of passionate controversy—but the spectacle of the First World War would at last provide the big navy men with the security rationale needed to silence debate, and to rally the country behind a policy of dramatic naval expansion.

On August 15, 1916, Democrat Claude Kitchin of North Carolina, majority leader in the House of Representatives, rose to speak on the question of a proposed naval appropriations bill. Kitchin had been among the most determined opponents of a big navy, having done unremitting battle with Roosevelt, Taft and even Woodrow Wilson when Wilson had been brought round to the cause of naval "preparedness" by the German policy of submarine warfare and the sinking of the Cunard liner *Lusitania* on May 7, 1915. In the press, Kitchin had been attacked without mercy for his stand, but until this day he and his allies had prevailed. The August 15 speech, however, was to be the swan song of the small navy.

Kitchin declared that it was "criminal for this House to vote on a proposition that would take hundreds of millions of dollars needlessly out of the Treasury." He recalled his opposition to Republican navy bills, and bemoaned the desertion of many Democrats: "the chairman of the Committee on Naval Affairs, the Secretary of the Navy, and the President and most of my fellow Democrats want me to get up now on this floor and eat my words." Kitchin would not oblige; the bill under scrutiny was "criminal recklessness."

And in truth, the proposed naval bill, already passed by the Senate, represented an armament program such as Theodore Roosevelt or Henry Cabot Lodge would not have dared to propose ten or even five years earlier. It gave Dewey's General Board (as always agitating for drastic increases in shipbuilding) everything it desired, and went one step further: the board had asked for a five-year building program—the proposed bill cut that time to three years. Battleships, destroyers, cruisers and submarines were all to be constructed at a fantastic rate, as Kitchin pointed out:

"The three-year provision of the program requires an increase of appropriations over 7 times more than the total increase by Great Britain in the 10 years prior to the European war, 10 times more than the total increase by Germany or any other nation, except Great Britain, in the 10 years preceding the war, 60 times more than the total increase by Germany in the 5 years preceding the war, and 100 times more than the total increase by Germany in the 3 years preceding the war." To Kitchin, it was an "outrageous, insane program. . . . And Congress votes it! And the Secretary of the Navy approves! And the President will sign!" Kitchin's protests were in vain; on August 29, the great Naval Act of 1916 was passed.

More than anything else, the nightmare of merchant vessels falling prey to unseen German attackers had swung the mood in the United States regarding a naval buildup from one of skepticism to one of avid support. The slaughter of the innocent seemed to have only one remedy—a navy second to none. The German threat, so long propounded by the big navy men, had finally materialized, and those same men were given virtual free rein to indulge their shipbuilding passions.

Their triumph had taken the better part of three decades to realize. Mahan himself was already dead. And Roosevelt, ironically, was no longer intimate with most of those who celebrated the victory of the big navy, chiefly because his fervor for Progressive domestic policies had separated him from the Republican party—even politically from his old friend Lodge. Lodge himself, however, had stayed consistently loyal to the primacy of naval buildup, and so had the officers of the General Board—the grim carnage wrought by Germany's submarines seemed to have vindicated their ceaseless calls to arms. True, a few Americans might still have agreed with Henry L. Stimson, who, as Taft's secretary of war, had mused on "the peculiar psychology of the Navy Department, which frequently seemed to retire from the realm of logic into a dim religious world in which Neptune was god, Mahan his prophet, and the U.S. Navy the only true church"; but far more had joined the ranks of the true believers.

In the First World War itself, as it happened, the mighty new American fleet played a comparatively small role. Only the destroyers that worked the antisubmarine convoy routes of Admiral William Sowden Sims—the man who had taught the navy how to shoot—proved vital in the end. The great battleships that Mahan, Roosevelt and Lodge had dreamed of remained for the most part close to home, guarding the shores of America without ever becoming involved in a significant engagement. Nonetheless, America's decisive role in the war seemed to the American public to confirm the importance of the big navy itself, and the ambitious program of shipbuilding continued even after peace came. Ringed at last by a shield of steel that strategically, tactically and technologically could compete with the greatest navies in the world, most Americans in 1918 felt secure in turning their energies back to the business of business.

But at least one American took scant comfort from the mighty fleet that protected his nation. By the end of the war President Woodrow Wilson, whose shift in advocacy from little to big navy had been so crucial to the latter's victory, had already looked beyond the terror on the seas and seen an extensive new range of threats to American security. These threats did not originate with navies or with expanding boundaries, but in the minds of men. New and radical ideologies were rising in the world, ideologies that offended and endangered Wilson's cherished concept of liberal democracy, and that, if successful, would even come to threaten the political integrity of the nation itself. To do battle with these ideologies, Wilson had already begun to develop a unique mode of American international behavior, one that had led—and would continue to lead—American soldiers and statesmen into unlikely regions on improbable missions.

V

MR. WILSON INTERVENES

1912—1921

ALONG a lonely stretch of the Trans-Siberian Railroad, deep within war-ravaged Russia in the early spring of 1919, two battalions of the U.S. 27th Infantry under the command of Colonel Charles H. Morrow faced an enemy unlike any they had ever seen. A troop of renegade cossacks, headed by a notoriously rugged fighter called Gregori Semenov, had brought up their greatest weapon—a steel-plated, concrete-reinforced nightmare of a train called the *Destroyer*. Colonel Morrow's troops were part of an international force that had entered Russia some six months earlier, with the stated purpose of helping the Siberians end the widespread hunger and administrative disorder that had accompanied the civil war between the new Bolshevik government and its enemies, collectively known as the Whites. This purpose did not, however, conform to the plundering desires of the various cossack bands in Siberia (including Semenov's), who committed every manner of outrage against peasants and local officials and offered as a rationale nothing more elaborate than their opposition to Bolshevism. Colonel Morrow, responsible for maintaining order in the

Lake Baikal region east of Irkutsk, had instructed the blustering
Semenov (a man who claimed lineage from Genghis Khan) to stop
molesting agents of the Trans-Siberian Railroad, the region's sole
means of distributing badly needed food and supplies to the weary
populace. When Semenov had defied this warning, Morrow had
"told him that if he passed a certain point with his armored train
he would blow him to perdition or some similar place." The colonel
had then moved to confront Semenov along the railroad line,
where he was met with the *Destroyer*.

Morrow ordered Semenov to back his train out of the American
sector, and when the cossack leader refused, Morrow brought two
37-millimeter cannon into position. Semenov continued to hold his
ground. Soon Japanese troops, supposed partners of the Americans in this remarkable Siberian expedition, arrived to support
Semenov. Paying only lip service to the broad humanitarian purposes of the intervention, the Japanese had taken the opportunity
to pump almost 80,000 men into Siberia (the Americans, with some
8,500 combat troops, were the only other sizable Allied contingent). The Japanese purpose was obvious. Rather than curbing
social and political instability, the Japanese hoped to spread it, and
so gain greater freedom to secure their hold over neighboring
Manchuria and Eastern Mongolia, as well as to establish a firm
foothold in Siberia itself. The cossacks were their logical partners
in such a scheme. With their help the Japanese brutally fostered a
state of chaos and havoc—as one American officer said of the two
groups, "perhaps the term, team, is a misnomer because the relationship was more nearly that of master crook and paid gun-man."
But on this occasion, the Japanese and the cossacks had chosen the
wrong victim.

Charles H. Morrow was not a man to be intimidated by numbers
or by superior firepower. Twin brother of the governor of Kentucky, and politely referred to by one American diplomat as "an
extremely profane man, [who] grew warm upon the subject of the
Cossack leaders," Morrow was a hard-drinking career officer with
a strong sense of frontier justice, one that he often found use for
in the confusion of Siberia. The overall commander of the American expedition, General William S. Graves, wrote of Morrow that
"he could be genial, he could be politic, he could be stern; and, if
occasion demanded, he could be bluff." The *Destroyer* incident gave
him just such an occasion.

Morrow knew that his two 37s could do little damage to the

heavily armored *Destroyer,* but he was determined that the Japanese and their henchmen should not take advantage of that fact. For hours the standoff continued, the Japanese commanders bemusedly weighing the prospect of actual conflict with American troops. Meanwhile, not far from the railway and not known to any of the antagonists, yet another armed group was considering joining the fray.

In addition to promoting civil order, one of the stated reasons for American involvement in the Siberian intervention had been to assist a large group of Czechoslovakian troops who were stranded in Eastern Russia. During the recent world war these men had fought alongside the Russians against the Central Powers in hope of gaining independence for their country. The Treaty of Brest-Litovsk between the Central Powers and the Bolsheviks, which ended the war in Russia, also ended the Czechs' hopes of cooperating with the Bolsheviks. They were now trying to battle their way to Vladivostok on the Pacific coast of Russia, there to embark by ship to Europe. At first the Bolsheviks had promised these Czechs—estimated at anywhere from fifty to a hundred thousand—safe passage to Vladivostok in exchange for laying down their arms. But the agreement had fallen apart. By May 1918 the Czechs were fighting the Bolsheviks all over Siberia. The arrival in late August and early September of American units determined to assist the Czechs in getting back to Europe was timely, and the Czechs had taken a liking to the Americans, a liking that contrasted sharply with their distaste for all organized Russian authority, whether Bolshevik or White.

News of Colonel Morrow's stand against the Japanese and the cossacks spread quickly, and one nearby group of Czechs, who knew and respected the 27th Infantry's commander, believed that Morrow would indeed go ahead with his threat to attack. These Czech leaders decided that the moment actual fighting began, they would bring a force of ten thousand men to the colonel's aid. A full-scale battle pitting Americans and Czechs against Japanese troops and cossack warriors could have been the only result.

The battle never took place. The Japanese, impressed by Morrow's determination, took over Semenov's train and backed it down the railway away from the American sector. From that moment on, wrote one American, "the Japanese regarded Colonel Morrow as a sort of bomb with the fuse already lighted." And while actual hostilities had been averted on this occasion, the very likelihood of

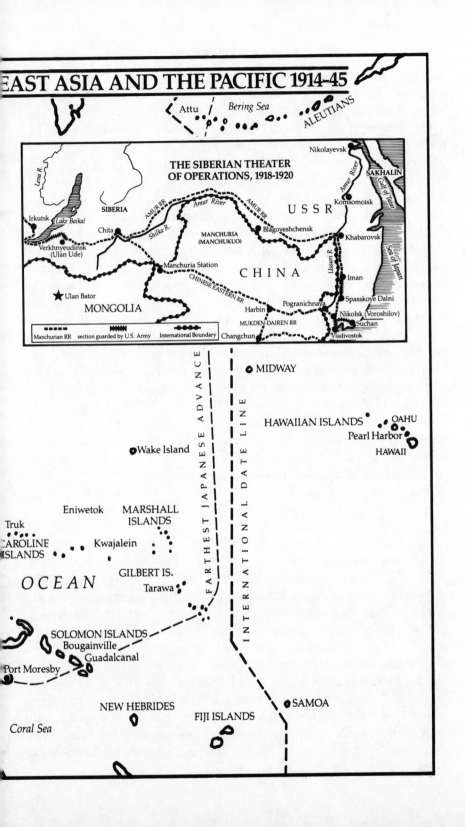

EAST ASIA AND THE PACIFIC 1914-45

Attu   Bering Sea   ALEUTIANS

THE SIBERIAN THEATER OF OPERATIONS, 1918-1920

Nikolayevsk

Lena R.

Amur River

SAKHALIN

Gulf of Tartary

SIBERIA   AMUR RR   Amur River   AMUR RR   USSR   Komsomolsk

Irkutsk   Lake Baikal   Chita   Shilka R.   MANCHURIA (MANCHUKUO)   Blagoveshchensk   Khabarovsk

Verkhnyeudinsk (Ulan Ude)   Manchuria Station   CHINA   Ussuri R.   Iman   Sea of Japan

Ulan Bator   CHINESE EASTERN RR   Spasskoye Dalni

MONGOLIA   Harbin   Pogranichnaya   Nikolsk (Voroshilov)

MUKDEN-DAIREN RR   Suchan

Manchurian RR   section guarded by U.S. Army   International Boundary   Changchun   Vladivostok

MIDWAY

HAWAIIAN ISLANDS   OAHU

Pearl Harbor

HAWAII

Wake Island

Eniwetok   MARSHALL ISLANDS

Truk

CAROLINE   Kwajalein

ISLANDS

GILBERT IS.

OCEAN   Tarawa

SOLOMON ISLANDS

Bougainville

Guadalcanal

Port Moresby

NEW HEBRIDES   SAMOA

FIJI ISLANDS

Coral Sea

FARTHEST JAPANESE ADVANCE

INTERNATIONAL DATE LINE

such action demonstrated both the volatility of the Siberian situation and its immense confusion. It was a confusion that had marked the intervention from the start.

On August 2, 1918, General William Graves, then commanding the 8th Infantry Division at Camp Frémont in California, had received orders "to take the first and fastest train out of San Francisco and proceed to Kansas City, go to the Baltimore Hotel, and ask for the Secretary of War." Graves knew there was a real possibility that this order concerned intervention in Russia. For months the European Allies had been pressing such a project on President Woodrow Wilson as a way of reestablishing the Eastern Front lost by the Treaty of Brest-Litovsk, of preventing any German advances into Siberia and of protecting the massive stores of supplies and matériel that had been stockpiled and were now rotting in the ports of Vladivostok and Archangel while feuding bands cut the Trans-Siberian Railroad to pieces and the population of the interior starved. President Wilson, sensing the dangers inherent in the idea, rejected several formal requests for intervention in the winter and spring of 1918. But when news of the gallant struggle of the Czechs and the emergence of anti-Bolshevik White factions in Siberia reached Washington, the president finally gave in to the Allies—albeit in less than certain terms. This uncertainty was made singularly apparent in the orders that were issued to General Graves when he arrived in Kansas City.

Graves, a circumspect officer accustomed to obeying his superiors without question and to the letter, spent the trip to Kansas City pondering his strange mission. He "feared it meant Siberia," particularly since the army chief of staff had already told him that "if any one has to go to Russia, you're it." This remark had "rather stunned" Graves, but in the face of Russia's deeply uncertain political and military status, a literal-minded officer such as Graves was not an altogether surprising choice. When he arrived in Kansas City he was met by Secretary of War Newton D. Baker at the train station. Their conversation was brief. Baker told the general: "if in the future you want to cuss anybody for sending you to Siberia I am the man." The secretary then handed Graves a sealed envelope and said, "This contains the policy of the United States in Russia which you are to follow. Watch your step; you will be walking on eggs loaded with dynamite. God bless you and good-bye." With that Baker was gone, and Graves left alone to study the remarkable document contained in the envelope.

The Aide-Memoire on Russia of July 17—issued by the Department of State but in fact composed largely by President Wilson himself—implicitly revealed the extent to which ideological threats were fast becoming inseparable from territorial threats. Explicitly, the document was remarkable for nothing so much as its self-contradiction. Stating that it was "the clear and fixed judgment of the United States . . . that military intervention there would add to the present sad confusion in Russia rather than cure it, injure her rather than help her, and . . . be of no advantage in the prosecution of our main design, to win the war against Germany," the Aide-Memoire stated in the same paragraph that "military action is admissible in Russia . . . only to help the Czecho-Slovaks consolidate their forces . . . and to steady any efforts at self-government or self-defense in which the Russians themselves may be willing to accept assistance." Just how the American Expeditionary Force in Siberia (AEFS) was to reconcile those two positions was left to the discretion of General Graves.

In the Aide-Memoire the president also revealed his conflicting feelings about Japan (America's principal partner in the plan) by including a statement that the United States would withdraw its forces if the intervention became "inconsistent" with American goals; but he was equally quick to point out that this statement was not intended to inhibit or influence the actions of Japan or any other ally. In short, Wilson certainly intended the intervention to be a dramatic gesture—but what actual effect he hoped to have on the Russian situation was never made clear.

Despite such ambiguities, General Graves "felt there could be no misunderstanding the policy of the United States." The Aide-Memoire "clearly committed the agents of the United States to a specific line of action," that line of action being, in Graves's view, strict neutrality, a policy of maintaining order by keeping the Trans-Siberian Railroad open and seeing to it that food was distributed. But Graves was to discover that many of his superiors, perhaps even the president himself, did not share such an interpretation. Certainly, the other intervening Allies and the Russian people themselves did not—as became clear soon after the American Expeditionary Force landed in Vladivostok in the late summer of 1918.

The British and the French, deeply disturbed by the rise of radical socialism and communism throughout the world, wanted strong support for the anti-Bolshevik factions in Siberia; the Japanese, in turn, wanted to increase their sphere of influence; the cossacks wanted plunder; the Bolshevik partisans wanted control; the peasants wanted food; and the average American soldier wanted to know what he was doing in Siberia in the first place. Upon arriving in that extreme climate without even adequate winter clothing, the Americans soon became convinced that they were merely a sideshow in the increasingly ideological Great War, and began to refer to themselves as "the forgotten men." It was a vastly bewildering set of circumstances, one that was destined to show its effects in more than physical terms.

As for General Graves, he soon became unpopular with everyone because of his strict interpretation of the Aide-Memoire; unpopularity, however, did not shake his resolve. American troops were ordered to keep the rail lines open in their assigned districts and to discourage anarchy and disorder. No other group, however, was particularly interested in quelling such disorder. Even the peasants whom Graves and his men were supposedly helping sometimes showed their appreciation in bewildering ways—American tobacco tins, given as gifts to the Siberians, often returned in the form of crude homemade grenades. Graves and his men might be neutral; nobody else in Siberia was.

Ministering to their unhappiness with large amounts of vodka and seeking solace in Russian women, the American troops fell victim to widespread alcohol abuse and venereal disease. The general mood turned bitter and despairing. Yet the orders to go home did not arrive until the spring of 1920. In the meantime, officers like Colonel Bull of the Woods Morrow and his men were antagonized by the arrogant Japanese, insulted and taunted by the cossacks and the Whites (who spread rumors that the American troops were "Jews from the East Side of New York City" and therefore pro-Bolshevik), berated by British and French representatives and killed by Russian partisans. Always, the question was why. One American official, having toured the Siberian war zone, summed it up best when he asked, "But,—who in Hell are 'they'? 'They' need help,—financial, economic, military, and need it imperatively. . . . But in the silence of the night I wonder who 'They' are!"

From his earliest days, Thomas Woodrow Wilson had been trained in the art of performance. His father, his "incomparable father," was a Presbyterian minister in Virginia and in Georgia, a man with a stunning gift for oratory and an ego that had been dramatically inflated through years of success in his calling. Young Tommy Wilson, the eldest son, doted on his father obsessively, an intense preoccupation that the father returned; as a boy, Wilson spent many hours either in his father's pulpit or standing in front of a mirror, perfecting the oratorical delivery that his father had mastered, and learning not so much what to say (he was a less-than-average student in school) as how to say it. His gift was style.

Such an upbringing marked Wilson as an ideal candidate for manipulation. For the first three decades of his life, his utter dependence on his father apparently satisfied this craving for direction, and when absent from his father's manse in Georgia for too long, Wilson became racked by nervous, blinding headaches and crippling digestive disorders. In adulthood, these symptoms became chronic, and could only be eased by a return to his father's home for a long rest. Shy, thin, betraying vigor only in his dazzling gray eyes, the young Wilson might have had a happy or at least peaceful life had he followed his father into the clergy; instead, while still a teenager he made the momentous decision to try to enter politics.

As a young man he idolized the British prime minister William E. Gladstone, a figure who combined the righteousness of a cleric with the celebrity of a national leader. Studying Gladstone, Wilson adopted the Briton's crusading zeal—again, paying greater attention to the style of that zeal than to its content. Since Wilson had little money (the quickest means of entering American politics in the decades following the Civil War), a legal path to what he liked to call "statesmanship" seemed indicated. But the law bored Wilson, with its attention to detail and its heavy amounts of study, and when he opened his first practice he was seized by the overpowering depression that had periodically marked his life and would continue to do so for the rest of his days. Leaving the law and entering the academic world—which he often referred to as "minor statesmanship"—Wilson hoped he might enter politics through the back door. But long and boring years at the universities of Wesleyan and Princeton made him nearly despair of his goal. He married Ellen Axson, a compassionate woman who tirelessly ministered to her husband's continuing physical maladies.

Despite these frustrations, Wilson kept abreast of national politics, and by the decade of the 1890s had formulated a system of beliefs that would determine his behavior throughout his career. His ancestors had come to America from various parts of the British Isles, primarily Scotland; growing up in the sheltered seclusion of his father's house, Wilson had become at first familiar with and then dependent on the Anglo-Scottish traditions that had formed his family. Sickly as he was, he shied away from violence and radical actions in life and in politics; the strikes and riots of 1893 disturbed him deeply. He viewed the slow development of orderly, constitutional programs as the only antidote to such dangers. A thorough and enthusiastic reading of the English social scientist Walter Bagehot's application of Darwinian principles to economics and politics solidified his convictions: "In politics," Wilson wrote, "nothing radically novel may safely be attempted. No result of value can ever be reached . . . except through slow and gradual development, the careful adaptations and nice modifications of growth."

Thus the terms "liberal" and "conservative" have a peculiar connotation when applied to Woodrow Wilson. He advocated one goal above all others, social order, and one means of attaining it, representative government. Anyone who threatened that goal and that system—whether from the left or from the right—was anathema to this introverted yet strangely driven man. True, Wilson spoke often of "liberalism"; but his was the liberalism of the nineteenth and even eighteenth century, the liberalism of Edmund Burke, the English political philosopher who chronicled revolutionary France's radical excesses. Wilson's hostility to organized labor during the decade of the 1890s, for example, is well-documented. "We speak too exclusively of the capitalistic class," he said some years after the troubles of the 1890s. "There is another as formidable an enemy to equality and freedom of opportunity as it, and that is the class formed by the labor organizations and leaders of the country."

Wilson's chance to address a national audience—albeit not on the subject of national affairs—finally came when he was elected president of Princeton in 1902. He became involved in a bitter controversy over the social and educational stratification of student life with the dean of the Princeton Graduate School, a quarrel less important in its details than for Wilson's ability to portray himself as a champion of egalitarianism. Having watched with close interest the advances made by the Progressive movement during the domestic upheaval of the 1890s, Wilson started to clothe his opinions in language that betrayed less his distrust of the labor movement than his antipathy toward big business and capitalism. Though he did not win the Princeton battle, he did attract the attention of New Jersey's Democratic political bosses, who made him their candidate for governor and then helped secure his election in 1910. Once in office, Wilson immediately turned on his sponsors in the state machine, a betrayal that netted him praise from liberal Democrats and Progressives throughout the country. By 1911, he was a candidate for the presidency.

The rise had been quick, and understandably so. In oratorical skill Wilson had surpassed his first teacher, his own father, and rivaled his idol Gladstone. His command of rhetoric disguised the second key ingredient of his success: his willingness and ability to shift positions, jettison supporters and use men he disdained if it would advance him. Only one thing was missing from Wilson's remarkable sweep to national prominence in the first decade of the twentieth century. His father had died three months after he had taken over leadership at Princeton, and Wilson felt the loss keenly. The sudden absence of guidance confused him, and though his wife tried to fill the gap, she was far too straightforward and gentle a person to manipulate her husband in the way that Wilson himself craved. His powerful oratory did not suffer, however, and Wilson did find stopgap men to fill the role of advocate and manager during different moments; but he seemed always to feel the need for a stronger, more inspired hand. On November 24, 1911, in a room at the Hotel Gotham in New York, he found one.

It would be difficult to imagine a personality that more perfectly complemented Woodrow Wilson's than Edward Mandell House. A born manipulator, House spent his childhood in Texas stirring up trouble that he might resolve it. "I was a quarrelsome boy," he later recalled. "I used to set boys at each other to see what they would do, and then try to bring them around again." Like Wilson, House spent long childhood hours in front of a mirror, practicing not oratory but the Texan fast draw of a six-gun. For the Texas of House's youth was still rough country, and up to age twelve House showed every sign of pursuing an appropriately strenuous life. But in that year he suffered a head injury, complicated by a case of malaria, that left him subject to periodic bouts of great weakness for the rest of his life. Forbidden by this accident ever to pursue a rigorous or demanding schedule, House sought subtler outlets for his great mental energy.

His first and greatest love was politics—not the near-religious statesmanship of Woodrow Wilson, but the everyday workings of the Texas Democratic machine. But this did not mean that House was not an idealist; far from it. Son of an English immigrant, he had a bent toward constitutional systems that matched Wilson's. It was in their methods that the two men differed. House was irritated by forms and processes; he did not believe that the world's conversion to liberal democracy need be slow, or that existing institutions—even the American Constitution—should stand in the way of a more perfect realization of true representative government. This sense of impatience only increased as House's political experience grew, and it would find its instrument in Woodrow Wilson.

Having inherited enough wealth to satisfy his personal needs, House was left free to devote himself to realizing his highest goal: the election of an American president who shared his views. He trained himself for this task by being the man behind the scenes in the election of no fewer than four governors of Texas, an accomplishment that made this slight, soft-spoken man with the piercing gaze and deceptively easy manner one of the most powerful Democratic party officials in the country. Yet House always remained anonymous, always refused to accept any office in return for his services. One governor did confer on him the honorary rank of colonel, and the nickname—which House himself disliked—stuck. By 1911 he was finished with governors and ready to take on his greatest challenge.

As a younger man, House had written a novel called *Philip Dru, Administrator,* in which an idealistic but tough young politician revamped the American Constitution, pursued a radical policy of political and economic cooperation with Britain, Germany and Japan, and ushered in a period of peace and commercial prosperity that reached its apex with the creation of a world political organization. The novel itself was bad, but Woodrow Wilson found the ideas behind it quite good; and when he met the mysterious "Mr. House of Texas" at the Hotel Gotham in November 1911, the feelings ignited between them released in Wilson the passionate desire for both a confidant and a mentor that had been so painfully missing since the death of his father. "Mr. House," Wilson would later say, "is my second personality. He is my independent self. His thoughts and mine are one." It may be apocryphal that House told a friend after the Hotel Gotham meeting that Wilson would one day turn against him; certainly, House was a shrewd enough judge of human nature to have made such a statement.

After helping to design Wilson's victory against the incumbent President William H. Taft and Theodore Roosevelt, who headed the Bull Moose ticket in 1912, House typically refused any office. Nonetheless, he became the second most powerful man in the country, informally assisting Wilson in his far-reaching program of domestic reform. In April 1913 Wilson demonstrated his flair for dramatic performance by reviving the custom of personally addressing Congress, a practice abandoned by Jefferson as smacking of the Old World. Wilson fought off the bitter attacks of special interest groups and made progress toward dismantling Republican protectionism. He introduced the income tax, created the Federal Reserve System and fought for passage of the Federal Trade Commission and Clayton Anti-Trust acts, all in the first two years of his administration—his devotion to slow evolutionary processes seemed to have been abandoned.

But in reality, Wilson's "New Freedom," though it frightened many in the business community, was not a radical program. The president himself took great pains to say so. "I do not believe in a program of socialism," he had said during the campaign, "but there is no use saying what will not work unless you can say what will work." Pressured by the rising tides of radicalism on the left and on the right, Wilson was desperate to instill a new urgency into his conception of liberal democracy. At home, this meant reform aimed at controlling the abuses of the rich as well as curbing the excesses of organized labor; abroad, it meant a break with imperialism and a new approach to international affairs.

That approach, like Wilson's domestic program and, indeed, like imperialism itself, was derived from a sense of profound anxiety, in this case over the growing power of extremist political groups and movements around the world. In the key foreign policy address of his new administration, given before the Southern Commercial Congress in Mobile, Alabama, on October 27, 1913, Wilson outlined his vision of American behavior in the world, and, most especially, in Latin America. His aim was "the development of constitutional liberty in the world. Human rights, national integrity, and opportunity as against material interests—that, ladies and gentlemen, is the issue which we now have to face." His break with the imperialists seemed complete: "I want to take this occasion to say that the United States will never again seek one additional foot of territory by conquest. She will devote herself to showing that she knows how to make honorable and fruitful use of the territory she has." Trade was to provide the means of exporting American democracy: "I wonder if you realize, I wonder if your imaginations have been filled with the significance of the tides of commerce." In summing up his thoughts, Wilson demonstrated his singular ability to elevate the business of politics to a higher, even a spiritual, plane: "Do not think, therefore, gentlemen, that the questions of the day are mere questions of policy and diplomacy. They are shot through with the principles of life."

It is not difficult to see the influence of Mr. House on these thoughts (although Wilson's own devotion to such democratic ideals can hardly be questioned). House's belief that breaking down trade restrictions between nations would initiate an era of unprecedented peace and prosperity echoed throughout Wilson's greatest speeches, and revealed the fundamental conviction that drove both men—a belief that any people in the world, given economic and political freedom, would choose liberal democracy as their form of government. That economic prosperity might create rather than cure injustice in many countries—that commerce could be as corrupting as it could be civilizing—this was an argument that both House and Wilson rejected as cynical. The simple historical reality that many societies had no constitutional tradition and could not therefore "evolve" toward fully representative government in anything close to the short term was ignored by both men. But mere ignorance of such factors could not lessen their reality, and that reality—as it was so often to do—soon thrust itself into House and Wilson's dream of liberal democracy.

The first signs of trouble came in Mexico. For three decades, that nation had enjoyed unusual (if repressive) stability under Porfirio Díaz. But in 1911 Díaz, realizing that the forces opposed to his rule were growing stronger, left the country. Francisco Madero —a constitutional idealist who was eccentric to the point of mental instability—took over the government and tried to institute reforms. Madero proved far too radical for Mexico's powerful landed class and too moderate for such radicals as Emiliano Zapata and Pancho Villa; in February 1913, Madero's murder was engineered by Victoriano Huerta, an agent of the landowners who was then named president. By organizing bandit groups, Zapata and Villa resisted Huerta's control, and before long the country was reduced to an all-too-familiar state of anarchy, one that as always spelled violence and financial loss for Americans in Mexico. But

more important, President Wilson saw Mexican anarchy as an irresistible temptation to foreign powers (particularly the British,
who had heavy oil interests in Mexico) to increase their influence
there and in Latin America generally.

In March 1913, Wilson—who had refused to recognize Huerta's
government because it was unconstitutional, having seized power
through violence—declared that "consent of the governed" was to
be the "basis of mutual intercourse, respect, and helpfulness between our sister republics and ourselves"; in other words, any Latin
American nation that did not pursue representative government
would receive neither recognition nor money from the Wilson administration. "I am going to teach the South American republics to
elect good men!" Wilson declared in typically didactic fashion.

But such a policy could have no effect if men like Huerta were
able to receive aid from other nations. When reports began to
come into Washington of arms shipments headed for Huerta from
Europe and even Japan, Wilson became certain that chaos in Mexico was being encouraged by thôse powers as a way of gaining
preferential trade status and undermining the Monroe Doctrine.
"The government of Huerta, based upon usurpation and force,"
wrote the president, "would long ago have broken down but for
the encouragement and financial aid derived from its recognition
by other nations, without regard to the wishes or purposes of the
United States." This animosity was reciprocated by the other powers, and aggravated by the fact that the United States had secured
from Panama preferential toll rates for use of the new canal, despite explicit treaty pledges not to do so. As March became April,
the tension centered around Mexico mounted.

When Huertista officers arrested several American sailors in
Tampico on April 9, 1914, and another two days later, Wilson was
given his opportunity for action. He asked Congress to authorize a
forceful response based on an insult to American national honor.
Many senators did not believe that national honor was sufficient
grounds for such a response, and agreed with Senator Henry
Cabot Lodge when he urged the president to base his actions on
the "protection of the lives and property of American citizens."
Wilson answered that "that would widen too much and lead to
war," to which Lodge replied, "I thought it war in any event." The
House passed a resolution supporting the president, but the Senate
debated long and hard. In the meantime, Wilson received a report
on April 21 that a German freighter laden with armaments was

going to land in the Mexican port of Veracruz the next day. Without senatorial authority, Wilson sent American marines into Veracruz and occupied the city.

Wilson's explanation of this action—his implied distinction to
Lodge between military action and actual war, or even formal
intervention—was as important as the occupation itself, for it became the rationale of American international behavior over the
next seven years. Wilson wished to give the Mexicans an opportunity to resolve their internal feuding and arrive at a democratic con-
sensus on their own, but he also perceived that other nations were
by no means willing to stand by and wait for such an orderly process to be carried out. The Mexicans themselves could not, or did
not, wish to resist outside interference. This left the United States
in the position of *enforcing* the kind of noninterference Wilson
believed was the condition best suited to fostering democratic
systems. Here, then, was the great paradox of Wilsonian
foreign policy—only by actively interfering in the affairs of other
nations could the United States lend strength to its advocacy of self-
determination for all peoples.

Through the influence of Argentina, Brazil and Chile, the immediate crisis in Mexico was defused, and the long-term problems
were largely resolved when Mr. House made one of his famous
trips to London to meet with the British foreign secretary, Lord
Grey, and work out a solution in private. The two men, whose
respect for and trust in each other often permitted dramatic results, worked out a deal by which the Wilson administration would
persuade Congress to allow higher toll rates on American ships
passing through the Panama Canal, in return for British cooperation on Mexican policy. Faced by concerted British and American
action, Huerta was effectively isolated, and on August 21, 1914,
August Venustiano Carranza—another conservative strongman,
but one who draped his actions in a "Constitutionalist" shroud and
was therefore more acceptable to Wilson—took power in Mexico
City.

Carranza immediately began to make noises about expelling foreign influences and nationalizing foreign holdings, noises that
frightened American businessmen who had hefty investments in
Mexican mineral industries, especially oil. But Wilson was convinced that the Huerta experience had shown him the way to deal
with such behavior. By isolating corrupt and oppressive rulers
from outside influences, the president believed, the United States

would force them to either reform and adopt democracy or face the certainty of losing power. That such a policy made American interference and, if necessary, intervention a prerequisite to the development of constitutional systems did not disturb the president. Woodrow Wilson was only too ready to "teach" the entire world the virtues of "good government."

The outbreak of the First World War in Europe in August 1914 heightened Wilson's sense of urgency about the American world mission. Not only was the power of the radical right (in this case, the Prussian militarists) on the rise, but Latin America was viewed, as it had been throughout American history, as the most likely site for the expansion of European imperial power. Thus when Nicaragua (a troubled country that had known peace since 1912 only because American marines had been sent in by President Taft) asked Wilson and his first secretary of state, William Jennings Bryan, to grant her protectorate status in 1914, Wilson agreed. The U.S. Senate did not, and would approve no American-Nicaraguan accord until all mention of protectorate status had been removed. But the Bryan-Chamorro Treaty of 1916 did effectively extend a U.S. protectorate over Nicaragua to ensure stability. Similarly, when the ever-unstable nation of Haiti fell into rioting in 1915, Wilson, worried anew about the possibility of German intervention, dispatched marines and imposed a constitution that made Haitian international actions dependent on U.S. approval. In the spring of 1916, Wilson once again imposed his law, this time in the Dominican Republic, which was destined to be run by the U.S. Department of the Navy for the next eight years.

It was in Latin America, then, that Wilson first worked out an active method of responding to those twin fears of internal disorder and external interference that had so plagued his hopes for an international liberal democratic order based on prosperity from free trade. And his seeming successes in that region only strengthened his belief in the rectitude of his crusade. But when he tried to apply these same methods to other parts of the world, he found that not all nations could be so easily steered as the economically dependent states of Latin America. Especially in the ancient and immensely complex world of the Far East, Wilson's missionary doctrines were to founder on the shoals of opposing political traditions, an experience that would cause first consternation and then deep disillusionment in both the president and in his "second personality," Mr. House.

But there was one member of the Wilson administration who, having identified some of the key flaws in the Wilson-House doctrine, was able to foresee such a result; one man who, though consistently loyal to the president, spent much of his considerable energy after 1915 trying to bring American goals more in line with world political realities.

"Mr. Lansing is gray—gray hair, gray eyes, gray suit. Sometimes, like any other man, he wears black clothes; sometimes white. But he is pitched in the key of gray. And grayly he comes and goes." Such was one contemporary magazine's assessment of Robert Lansing, who took over the State Department after William Jennings Bryan resigned in protest over the increasingly forceful tone of President Wilson's notes to Germany concerning the sinking of the *Lusitania* in the spring of 1915. The nation was initially taken by the appointment of Lansing, who had previously been the department's counselor and a virtual unknown; but as the press swarmed around the friends and relations of the new secretary in order to get a better picture of his life and habits, they found precious little material to work with.

Though not particularly secretive, Lansing was far from a public man. The scion of an old Dutch family from upstate New York, Lansing had led a largely uneventful life—and there was every indication that he liked it that way. As a young man he had read for the bar in his own father's law office, where, according to one friend and associate, "he would fool around all day, . . . reading, drawing pictures, and cracking jokes." Reclusive by nature, Lansing disliked arguing cases before an open court, a trait that finally brought him into international law. This inclination was reinforced by his marriage to one of the daughters of John W. Foster, an expert on arbitration who had been one of Benjamin Harrison's secretaries of state. From 1892 to 1910 Lansing served as counsel for various American arbitration committees, honing a knowledge of the intricacies of international law that was both extensive and indicative of his reticent yet powerful intellect.

Lansing was a chronic puzzler, a man whose mind found release in the sports and games of his childhood days (throughout his life his closest friends remained the men he had grown up with in his hometown) and in solving every form of riddle, be it a question concerning the Bering Sea fur-seal arbitration or a daily crossword puzzle. Deeply appreciative of the political and economic system that had allowed his family to attain a position of comfort and social prominence, Lansing was a "Cleveland Democrat," a man of essentially conservative views. One of Wilson's advisers went so far as to accuse him of carrying "conservatism to the point of medievalism," and while this may be an exaggeration, Navy Secretary Josephus Daniels's statement that "he had the point of view of the old-time career diplomat" cannot be argued. "If left to him," Daniels went on, "we would have had war with Mexico and continued the Big Stick Policy, but he would have countenanced no act contrary to old-fashioned diplomatic ethics." Edward House, who admired and respected Lansing despite their occasional differences of opinion, once remarked that the secretary was "something of a Prussian when it comes to serving his country"; but this fervor was always contained, always balanced by a dry and penetrating sense of humor and always regulated by the strictures of law.

It was not a personality that was likely to mesh with that of his chief, and many people were surprised by Wilson's choice of Lansing to succeed Bryan. Not least among these was Wilson's second wife, Edith Bolling Galt. Ellen Axson had died in 1914, and the new Mrs. Wilson was manipulative where the first had been sympathetic, devious where the first had been sincere. Upon announcing to her that he was considering Lansing to replace Bryan, Wilson was met by the former Mrs. Galt's astonished statement that "he is only a clerk in the State Department, isn't he?" Fond of repeating a piece of Washington humor which ran to the effect that the "new way of spelling Lansing" was "H o u s e," Mrs. Wilson tried from the first to influence her husband not to rely on either Lansing or House; she quickly perceived that both men were her rivals in influencing the president.

Lansing understood the central facet of Woodrow Wilson's personality—his desire to be directed, to be presented with creative ideas that he could then unveil to the world. Lansing was fascinated by psychology, and the accomplished caricatures he was fond of drawing during meetings often revealed penetrating insights into the mental and emotional workings of those around him. Disdainful of the spotlight, Lansing quickly learned how to plant ideas in Wilson's mind that the president came to believe were his own. Wilson's initial assessment of Lansing—that he was "not a big enough man, did not have enough imagination . . . and was lacking in initiative"—would in the end prove painfully inaccurate.

The greatest challenge facing the new secretary of state in 1915 was the issue of American neutrality in the world war. Like Wilson and House, Lansing was personally sympathetic to the Allied cause; but recognizing this sympathy for what it was, he made every effort to compensate for it, to be as stern with Britain and France as he was with Germany. This was especially true during the summer of 1916, when Britain's abuse of neutral rights at sea (a policy Britain continued to view as vital to her national security) caused widespread protest within the United States. Looking back on this period, House wrote: "The country has never quite appreciated Lansing. No other Secretary of State had so difficult a task. The years of neutrality before we entered the war presented many delicate and intricate situations, and a false step might have proved disastrous. He made none."

Lansing's chance to pursue a somewhat more creative policy came with the question of the shifting balance of power in the Far East and the rising power of Japan. Wilson's retention of American control of the Philippines (despite his stated disagreements with American imperialists, he believed in the American mission to civilize the islands) had already strained relations with Tokyo. Moreover, when the First World War broke out in 1914, the neutral Chinese somewhat naturally looked to the great neutral, the United States, to protect them from Japanese expansionism. By 1915, then, U.S.–Japanese friction—always compounded by the question of immigration laws and anti-Japanese feeling in the American West—was on the rise.

On January 18, 1915, Japan presented the Chinese government with her Twenty-one Demands. This extraordinary document called for the further extension of Japan's sphere of influence in Manchuria and Eastern Mongolia, for the right to negotiate with Berlin for the disposition of German holdings in Shantung Province (or to seize those possessions, should Japan and the Allies defeat the Central Powers), for control over various industrial works in China and for a pledge that China would not allow any power but Japan to establish military installations within her borders. Wilson considered the Twenty-one Demands deeply offensive, and some Americans called for a forceful support of the Open Door policy. But no one could be sure that if Japanese aims in China were opposed, Japan would not simply join the Central Powers and take what she had demanded. Wilson, caught between his idealistic notion of the integrity of China and his real desire not to harm the Allied cause, was stymied.

Into this situation Lansing brought a fresh approach in the summer of 1915. Defining American interests in the Far East as commercial rather than political, the secretary shied away from Wilson's heavy emphasis on moral issues. Seeking out House, Lansing held a series of discussions with the president's alter ego that revealed a strong similarity of opinions on Far Eastern questions. Both sympathized "with the Japanese aspirations for colonization in Manchuria." To demand that a rising empire such as Japan's forgo attaining its own sphere of influence (especially in view of the utter inability of the Chinese government to maintain order within China proper, much less Manchuria and Mongolia) would, they concluded, only weaken the American position with regard to Wilson's vigorous interpretation of the Monroe Doctrine as establishing a legitimate American sphere of influence in the Western Hemisphere. Neither Lansing nor House wished to see Japan expand into China proper, but both were convinced that such developments could be avoided only if the United States were willing to accommodate Japanese ambitions in other places.

To this end, Lansing began to talk of turning the Philippines over to the Japanese, and again he found House sympathetic. Certainly, the American government would want guarantees from the Japanese as to Philippine governmental autonomy; but the islands had no clearer strategic value in 1915 than they had had in 1902, and Lansing shared Theodore Roosevelt's belief that the American occupation only endangered Japanese-American relations. Disposal of the Philippines, however, did not meet with Wilson's approval. In the face of this refusal Lansing sought other ways of both appeasing and controlling Japan.

After unsuccessfully trying to channel Japanese ambitions into international economic arrangements that would force Chinese trade concessions, Lansing next turned to direct bilateral negotiations with a special envoy from Tokyo, Viscount Ishii. The Lansing-Ishii Agreement of November 1917, by which the United States recognized "that Japan has special interests in China, especially the part to which her possessions are contiguous," has often been portrayed as an attempt by the secretary of state to pay lip service to the idea of the Open Door while actually acquiescing to Japanese designs in Manchuria, Mongolia and China itself. But the Open Door had never had any great effect on actual conditions in China; the powers to whom John Hay had addressed his circular had largely gone ahead with their exploitative programs. Moreover, while Lansing did intend to give tacit U.S. approval to Japanese moves in Manchuria and Mongolia, he always considered this the limit to what the American government could tolerate—any Japanese expansion into China proper, especially into the German holdings in Shantung, was viewed by Lansing as unacceptable. The Lansing-Ishii Agreement was, in fact, an attempt to both recognize political realities in the Far East and salvage a real measure of safety for the Chinese, neither of which the Open Door had been able to do. In addition, Lansing hoped that the successful completion of his negotiations would strengthen the power of Japanese moderates in Tokyo, men who were firmly committed to controlling the ambitions of the military-expansionist faction.

Despite Lansing's signal achievement, the question of the Far East continued to disturb President Wilson, who viewed the secretary's efforts to work out a complex solution to an equally complex problem with impatience. Wilson craved a gesture that might convince both the Chinese and the Japanese that a successful future lay in respecting national integrity and constitutional systems—but in both China and Japan, as Lansing perceived, there was no historical foundation for such gestures. Lansing had tried to work out a realistic solution and received only the president's scorn in return; it was not the last time that the secretary would feel the sting of presidential ingratitude.

Despite Lansing's reluctant but measured attempts to delineate American neutrality, despite House's many trips to the capitals of Europe and despite Wilson's 1916 campaign slogan, "He kept us out of war," the president went before Congress on April 2, 1917, to ask for a formal declaration of hostilities against Germany. Certainly, the resumption of unrestricted submarine warfare (which had been suspended since early 1916) by the German government in February 1917 contributed heavily to this momentous decision. But there were other grave issues involved, issues that clearly revealed Wilson's growing anxiety over instability and extremism in the world and the possible effect of such elements on the United States.

The first of these involved Mexico. In 1915, Wilson had attempted to offer Mexican President Carranza something other than a negative inducement to reform by giving de facto recognition to the dictator's regime and, in November of that year, allowing his troops to cross American borders to attack the bandit

Pancho Villa, who continued to resist the power of the landowning class. Villa, in retaliation, crossed into the United States and, on March 9, 1916, attacked the town of Columbus, New Mexico, murdering seventeen people. Wilson quickly responded by dispatching ten thousand men under General John "Black Jack" Pershing into Mexico to search for Villa. Pershing never caught his quarry (though he did manage to become involved in minor clashes with Carranza's men), and the main effect of the American expedition was to unite more Mexicans in the struggle against outside intervention.

By the late fall of 1916, Carranza had almost completed his long-promised constitution. This document favored a program of strident nationalism (and nationalization), and gave lesser attention to genuine reform, further angering Wilson and alarming American business interests. But it was in February 1917 that the Americans were given their greatest cause for concern. A telegram from the German foreign minister, Arthur Zimmermann, to Germany's representative in Mexico City was intercepted in Washington. The telegram proposed Mexican cooperation in the German war effort, in return for which Germany would assist Mexico in recovering the lands she had lost during the Mexican War—California, New Mexico and Arizona. The Zimmermann telegram confirmed Wilson's greatest fear—that radical elements would use instability in Latin America to thwart American objectives and threaten American security.

And there was more to come. In March 1917 the Romanov dynasty in Russia was overthrown and replaced by a Provisional Government that created a constituent assembly, called for land reform and abolition of the social and political structures of the country and rededicated itself to a vigorous prosecution of the war against Germany. Wilson, though generally relieved and encouraged by these developments in Russia, also believed that such fateful events would require more enlightened and articulated guidance than could be found in either Paris or London. While the president had long believed that the creation of constitutional systems of government throughout the world would be a slow affair, events refused to follow his evolutionary schedule. A certain anxiety over this dilemma was reflected in his April 2 War Message.

First acknowledging that "German submarine warfare against commerce is a warfare against mankind," he went on to pledge that "our motive will not be revenge or the victorious assertion of

the physical might of the nation, but only the vindication of right."
The policymakers in Berlin "have played their part in serving to
convince us at last that that Government entertains no real friendship for us and means to act against our peace and security at its
convenience. That it means to stir up enemies against us at our
very doors the intercepted note to the German Minister at Mexico
City is eloquent evidence."

But it was in reference to "the wonderful and heartening things
that have been happening within the last few weeks in Russia" that
Wilson displayed both his anxious hope for a new era and the
peculiar misunderstanding—even ignorance—of the facts that so
often marked his idealism: "Russia was known by those who knew
it best to have been always in fact democratic at heart, in all the
vital habits of her thought. . . . The autocracy that crowned the
summit of her political structure, long as it has stood and terrible
as was the reality of its power, was not in fact Russian in origin,
character, or purpose; and now it has been shaken off and the
great, generous Russian people have been added in all their naïve
majesty and might to the forces that are fighting for freedom in
the world, for justice, and for peace. Here is a fit partner for a
league of honor."

Just over one year after making this remarkably inaccurate statement, Woodrow Wilson would order thousands of American
troops into Russia, where they would work in effective support of
those same reactionary elements whose overthrow had initially
given him such satisfaction. His resonant call that "the world must
be made safe for democracy" was irrelevant to a situation in which
democracy had little precedent or foundation, a situation that released political and social forces devastating enough to convince
Wilson that radicalism might do more than compete with liberal
democracy around the world—it might ultimately defeat it, even
in that greatest bastion of constitutional government, his own
United States.

The eventual seizure of power by the Bolsheviks under Lenin
and Trotsky in St. Petersburg on November 7, 1917, caused confusion and eventually alarm in Washington and in the governments of Western Europe. The Russian Provisional Government
had fallen largely because the Allies had steadfastly demanded
Russian participation in the war as a condition for financial and
material assistance, despite the exhaustion of the Russian people.

Every Allied nation had its own indigenous socialist or communist movement, and most of the Allies believed with Wilson that in fighting the Central Powers they were not only combating the radicalism of the right, but were also demonstrating the ability of representative government to withstand assaults from any extreme. Lenin's Bolshevik victory deeply imperiled this viewpoint, and many in the West believed that the best approach to what was happening in Russia was simply to ignore the group that had caused it.

On December 7, 1917, Secretary of State Lansing wrote that "the best thing to do [about the Bolsheviks] is to let things alone as far as it is possible to do so. . . . The Russian situation is to me an unanswered and unanswerable riddle. . . . The especial characteristics of the idealists who are masters in Petrograd are lack of any sentiment of nationality and a determination, frankly avowed, to overthrow all existing governments and establish on the ruins a despotism of the proletariat in every country. . . . It seems to me that Russia is about to be the stage on which will be acted one of the most terrible tragedies of all history. Civil war seems certain. . . . I believe that the Russian 'Terror' will far surpass in brutality and destruction of life and property the Terror of the French Revolution." Both Wilson and House initially agreed with this diagnosis and this prescription. The Bolshevik Revolution, in their minds, was a phase in Russia's internal upheaval, one that, if left to itself, would eventually lead to a more enlightened form of revolutionary government.

This attitude was underlined by Wilson in his Fourteen Points speech on January 8, 1918. In an eloquent attempt to establish the United States as the foremost advocate of a publicly formulated, just settlement of the war—"open covenants of peace, openly arrived at"—Wilson declared that though the power of the Russian people might be "shattered, . . . their soul is not subservient. They will not yield in either principle or in action. Their conception of what is right, and what is humane and honorable for them to accept, has been stated with a frankness, a largeness of view, a generosity of spirit, and a universal human sympathy which must challenge the admiration of every friend of mankind; and they have refused to compound their ideals or desert others that they themselves may be safe."

But on March 3, 1918, the Bolsheviks did indeed "desert," signing the Treaty of Brest-Litovsk with Germany and removing Russia from the war effort. Fear that what had happened in Petrograd and Moscow could happen in any European capital (or even in the United States) spread among the Western Allies. So far as conservatives in the British and French governments were concerned, there were now two enemies to be dealt with—the Central Powers and Soviet Russia. Immediately after the signing of Brest-Litovsk, the Allies began to step up their calls for intervention in Russia to aid those groups who were carrying on the fight against Bolshevism in the south and in Siberia.

Neither Wilson nor Lansing based their repeated refusals to participate in such projects on any belief that the Bolsheviks might become acceptable Russian rulers. Rather, they felt that intervention might drive those elements of the Russian people who were not yet supporters of Bolshevism into the Soviet camp. This would be especially true if intervention involved the Japanese, for whom the Russians had nothing but distrust. The British and the French argued that there was the larger question of reestablishing the Eastern Front, but Lansing dismissed such ideas in March—"as to the military benefit to be gained, there is no evidence that it would be of any magnitude or potency." When the Allies spread rumors that the Bolsheviks were arming Austro-German prisoners of war in Siberia to combat their internal enemies, Lansing coolly dismissed the reports, correctly believing them to be unfounded.

None of which meant that Wilson and Lansing did not want to find a way of acting to defeat Bolshevism in Russia. What they required, however, was solid evidence that there were Russians who would welcome such intervention, and that such groups might have a reasonable chance of success. When reports of large-scale resistance to Soviet authority in Siberia—including the valiant campaign of the stranded Czechs—reached Washington in April, Wilson wrote to Lansing: "I would very much value a memorandum containing *all* that we know about these several *nuclei* of self-governing authority that seem to be springing up in Siberia. It would afford me a great deal of satisfaction to get behind the most nearly representative of them if it can indeed draw leadership and control to itself."

The jump in thinking, the distortion of facts involved in this statement, was characteristic of the president. Wilson desired that the anti-Bolshevik groups in Siberia be democratic; accordingly, he began to perceive them as such even before he had any sound information on which to base this opinion. In fact, the "nuclei" of which he spoke were grouped primarily around czarist military officers—most notably Admiral Aleksandr V. Kolchak—and represented aristocratic elements who hoped to play on the traditional loyalties and fears of the Russian peasants in order to return Russia to the world of the Romanovs. Yet Wilson sensed that a response to Bolshevism was needed, and might well be made by the other Allies even if the United States refused to participate. The president could not abdicate American influence in such an important undertaking; yet he needed to justify his conduct morally. In seeing the Siberian groups as he wished to see them, Wilson therefore rendered the Allied intervention meaningless from the start.

How fully Wilson and Lansing agreed to the Siberian intervention as a way not only of combating Bolshevism but also of containing Japanese expansionism is difficult to know. Lansing himself did not fear possible Japanese annexation of Siberia; during the height of the intervention he wrote in exasperation, "[T]he Japanese are not fools. They know that a white race would never submit to the domination of a yellow race. To take the sovereignty or economic control of Eastern Siberia would mean endless trouble for Japan, as the Siberians would never rest until they had driven the Japanese out of the country." Lansing's great concern was not Japanese expansionism, then, but the strong probability that a Japanese military presence in Siberia would drive the population of the region into the arms of the Bolsheviks. When the secretary finally did agree to the idea of intervention, it was as much to police the activities of the Japanese army as anything else. In addition, Lansing had been able to convince Wilson of the need for heavy amounts of economic aid to the Siberians, as well as for an American Railway Commission whose engineers would assist local Russian officials in ensuring that food and supplies reached the Siberian peasants. This, Lansing always felt, was the only effective way to combat Bolshevism.

For Wilson far more than for Lansing, the Siberian intervention was an idealistic and characteristically dramatic gesture, one whose inherent confusion was clearly embodied in the Aide-Memoire of July 17, 1918, that was finally delivered to General Graves. Even after American troops had arrived in Siberia, Lansing continued to remind the president that Bolshevism was "preeminently an economic and moral phenomenon," and therefore "not to be conquered by force." But such complexities were largely lost on Wilson, who desired more sweeping solutions.

When American troops arrived in Siberia in the late summer of 1918, they found that the Japanese, already present in great force, were pursuing the policy of disruption that would mark their entire stay; in addition, the Russian peasants had no great affection for the White authorities who were trying to impose their rule over Siberia. Graves, the ever-blunt American commander, began calling almost immediately for American withdrawal, saying that the confusion in Siberia was "growing worse daily. . . . We are by our mere presence helping establish a form of autocratic government which the people of Siberia will not stand for and our stay is creating some feeling against the allied governments because of the effect it has." Wilson, however, had committed himself to intervention. "My policy regarding Russia is very similar to my Mexican policy," the president said. "I believe in letting them work out their own salvation, even though they wallow in anarchy a while." But the essential fallacy that underlay Wilson's Mexican policy also weakened the Russian intervention—only active American intervention could allow the Russians even the appearance of self-determination. And all the while, in Russia as in Mexico, anarchy spread.

The Allied sense of urgency, which might have been expected to diminish after the conclusion of the armistice with Germany on November 11, 1918, was in fact prolonged by the Bolsheviks of the new Russia. When negotiations opened in Paris, wrote American economic representative Herbert Hoover, "Communist Russia was a specter which wandered into the Peace Conference almost daily." Conflicting plans on how to deal with the possible spread of Bolshevism took up almost as much Allied time and energy as did creating the terms of peace; indeed, such plans would ultimately influence those terms to a remarkable degree.

To Woodrow Wilson the Great War itself had never been as important as the kind of peace that would be made after it. In this respect, Bolshevism appeared as a grave ideological threat to his long-held vision of spreading liberal democracy throughout the world. For this reason alone, the undermining of Soviet power continued to be one of the main features the president hoped to embody in the coming settlement.

In September, without consulting either Lansing or House, Wilson had authorized the publication of a series of documents that purported to show that Lenin and Trotsky were in the service of

Imperial Germany. The documents were almost certainly forgeries. Lansing believed them so, as did House, and when the latter went to discuss the matter with Wilson, he told the president that "their publication meant a virtual declaration of war upon the Bolsheviki Government." Wilson "admitted this." True, the president did advocate the convening of a peace conference to settle the Russian civil war; but when the Soviets included unrequested concessions in their acceptance of the idea (concessions that might have been useful to the Allies had their desire to negotiate been genuine), Wilson joined the other Western leaders in using this slight breach of protocol to reject Bolshevik participation. And when a young American diplomat, William Bullitt, returned from a secret trip to Russia to say that he believed the Soviets were willing to moderate their activities and propaganda, Wilson refused to receive him.

Meanwhile, reports concerning the brutally reactionary nature of the Kolchak government in Siberia continued to come in from General Graves; but the president was in no mood to listen. By February 1919, Wilson was involved in the battle with the Allies, and later the U.S. Senate, over the League of Nations—a struggle that would cost him both his health and his mental stability. The story of Wilson's pursuit of an international organization of free states, and how he sacrificed to Allied demands many of the terms he himself had once called necessary for a just peace, was the ultimate expression of the president's desire to resolve international complexities through sweeping measures. Faced with the often vindictive designs of the French on Germany, as well as with the increasingly vengeful demands of his own people, Wilson steadily came to believe that the actual terms of the Versailles peace treaty were less important than the need to include a "covenant" for an international organization that would, in the future, clear up any imperfections of the peace. How such a League of Nations would magically resolve what could not be agreed on at Paris was never explained. Wilson, faced with circumstances that made him agree to terms that deviated ever more widely from his liberal democratic prescriptions, began to retreat into a world largely of his own making.

That retreat was to cost him the most important friendship of his life, that of Edward House. House had been disposed toward an international organization of nations ever since writing *Philip Dru;* his ideas on the subject had largely guided Wilson's actions.

But House knew—as did Wilson—that many compromises would have to be made at Paris to get the Allies to agree to such a project. Along with the president he submitted to the scrapping of the terms for a less vindictive peace. German territory was occupied by France, unbearable indemnities were imposed on the German people, and the Allies fairly fell over one another in the rush to gain "mandatory" control of the colonial possessions of the Central Powers. Wilson, the man to whom the defeated and small nations of Europe had looked for justice or at least restraint, made scant attempts to check any of these moves, and ultimately blamed House for allowing them to happen. The president simply could not tolerate the evidence of his own self-betrayal. As John Maynard Keynes, serving on the British delegation, wrote:

"The disillusion was so complete that some of those who had trusted most hardly dared speak of it. . . . The President was no hero or a prophet; he was not even a philosopher; but a generously intentioned man, with many of the weaknesses of other human beings, and lacking that dominating intellectual equipment which would have been necessary to cope with the subtle and dangerous spell-binders . . . face to face in Council—a game of which he had no experience at all. . . . [I]n fact the President had thought out nothing; when it came to practice, his ideas were nebulous and incomplete. He had no plan, no scheme, no constructive ideas whatever for clothing with the flesh of life the commandments which he had thundered from the White House."

Amid these unhappy proceedings, the protesting voice of Lansing went unheeded. Upon learning that the Japanese had threatened to refuse participation in the League of Nations unless they were given control of the German holdings in Shantung (a move long viewed by the secretary of state as unacceptable), and further that Wilson had agreed to accept a Shantung settlement in order to placate Tokyo, Lansing was outraged. Referring to the league as "a plaything of the President's mind which he takes to bed with him," Lansing went on to say, "my policy would have been to say to the Japanese: 'If you do not give back to China what Germany stole from her, we don't want you in the League of Nations.' " At Paris, Wilson would not even listen to Lansing's objections; and when the secretary cornered House and told him "that to give [Shantung] to Japan was to barter away a great principle," House "replied, 'We have had to do it before.' " Lansing answered, "with some heat, 'Yes, it has been done and it is the curse of this Conference that that method has been adopted.' " Lansing's sense of public service prevented him from taking his case to the newspapers, but when he returned home to face Congress he made his objections plain, and sealed his fate within the Wilson administration.

Throughout the peace conference, American soldiers remained in Siberia, the embodiment of their president's increasing fear that though the power of the radical right had been defeated, the radical left was still to be dealt with. Returning home to defend the League of Nations and the Treaty of Versailles—a treaty that would be difficult for Americans to support, not least because it obligated the United States to continuing international cooperation and collective security—Wilson took every opportunity to harp on the subject of the menace of the left. "Bolshevism is steadily creeping westward," House had noted early in 1919, and though he had fallen from grace by the time Wilson embarked on his speaking tour of the western United States in September, Wilson echoed this sentiment everywhere he went. "My fellow citizens," he told an audience at Kansas City, "it does not make any difference what kind of minority governs you, if it is a minority. . . . The men who now are measurably in control of the affairs of Russia represent nobody but themselves."

In Des Moines, the president related his version of the Russian Revolution, saying that following the Bolshevik takeover, "in other parts of Europe the poison spread. The poison of disorder, the poison of revolt, the poison of chaos. And do you honestly think, my fellow citizens, that none of that poison has got in the veins of this free people? . . . [M]oney coming from nobody knows where is deposited in capitals like Stockholm to be used for the propaganda of disorder and discontent and dissolution throughout the world, and men look you calmly in the face in America and say they are for that sort of revolution. . . . It is the negation of everything that is American, but it is spreading and so long as disorder continues, so long as the world is kept waiting for an answer of the kind of peace we are going to have . . . that poison will steadily spread, more and more rapidly until it may be that even this beloved land of ours will be distracted and distorted by it."

On September 25, 1919, Wilson—exhausted by his losing campaign to rally public support for the Treaty of Versailles—collapsed in Pueblo, Colorado. Suffering a stroke on his return to Washington, the president survived, half-paralyzed and emotionally unbalanced. For much of the remainder of his term, a small clique centered around the First Lady was in effective control of the executive branch of government. Then, on November 19, American unilateralists led by Henry Cabot Lodge defeated the Treaty of Versailles in the Senate. But, despite Wilson's warning, revolution and social disintegration did not follow.

To the American troops in Siberia, however, such questions were immaterial. All they wanted to know was when they were going home.

Secretary of State Lansing was just as strongly anti-Bolshevik as his president—but as always, he tempered that avidity with reason. "Communism," he wrote at the time of Wilson's western tour, ". . . brings man down to a dull, drab level. It says, 'Work because you ought to work for others.' It sounds wonderfully fine. It smacks of Christian altruism. But it won't do, because man is not naturally an altruist, and no law or system can make him so." This same realism dictated Lansing's policy toward the Siberian intervention in the fall of 1919. Informed repeatedly by American representatives that "the Kolchak government has failed to command the confidence of anybody in Siberia except a small discredited group of reactionaries, Monarchists, and former military officers," and faced with the growing outrage of Congress over the unauthorized military action, Lansing overrode his own disposition toward further support for the Whites and advised withdrawal of American troops on December 23. When Admiral Kolchak was defeated and executed early in 1920, the secretary of state wrote tersely: "We simply did the best we could in an impossible situation."

The men of the American Expeditionary Force in Siberia had long known of that impossibility. All had felt its effects in some way, but Colonel Charles H. Morrow and his "Wolfhounds" (a nickname given to the 27th Infantry by Russian peasants, who marveled at the Americans' speed in recapturing escaped prisoners) had been at the forward edge of the American presence in Russia, and for over a year had lived a life that was particularly bizarre—and dangerous. Colonel Morrow had constructed an elaborate camp for his men in the Siberian interior, and spared no effort to protect them and alleviate the hardship and confusion that constantly attended their duties. "I think we've got to hand it to Colonel Morrow," wrote one private years after his return. "Old 'Bull of the Woods' seemed more intent on bringing all us rookies home safe and sound than anything else."

As the men of the AEFS began to return home, they brought with them reports of unusually high incidences of mental instability and even insanity among their comrades. In October 1919, the *San Francisco Examiner* had written angrily of these reports, and commented: "None of us knows why they were sent away to Siberia. None of the men themselves knows why he went, why he fought, why he saw mates fall or stricken of melancholia." The *Examiner* went on to quote one returning American official as saying, "For God's sake tell the American people to get the railroad corps out of Siberia as soon as possible or they will all go crazy. . . . They are going to pieces mentally."

More than the severe climate of Siberia was responsible for this condition. Far from home on an unknown mission, the men of the AEFS endured circumstances that vividly brought to life the confusion that underlay their dispatch. General Graves himself was to write that, "I was in command of the United States troops sent to Siberia and, I must admit, I do not know what the United States was trying to accomplish by military intervention." It was probably of little consolation to the veterans of the campaign to learn that their president had himself been emotionally impaired by the conflicting ideas and motives that had prompted his approval of intervention. And when Wilson did regain enough strength to write of this period, he still could not bring himself to confess to any weakness in his reasoning:

"The world has been made safe for democracy," he declared in 1923. "But democracy has not been made safe against irrational revolution. The supreme task, which is nothing less than the salvation of civilization, now faces democracy, insistent, imperative. . . . The United States, as the greatest of democracies, must undertake it. . . . The sum of the whole matter is this, that our civilization cannot survive materially unless it be redeemed spiritually. It can be saved only by becoming permeated with the spirit of Christ and being made free and happy by the practices which spring out of that spirit." In the end, the preacher reemerged to eclipse the politician.

The Siberian intervention was the purest expression of Wilson's preoccupation with the threat of hostile ideologies to liberal democracy both at home and abroad. The "Red Scare" of 1919, during which bombings and race riots broke out in Chicago and New York, culminated in the arrest by the attorney general of hundreds of anarchists and socialists, many of whom were deported to Russia. The scare had been aggravated by Wilson's rhetorical denunciations of Bolshevism and by his calls for an active American effort to halt its spread—yet in Siberia itself, violence and chaos persisted not only during the intervention but long after the departure of American troops. The failure of the Siberian expedition was soon forgotten, however, as Washington withdrew from active political engagement in the affairs of Europe and turned to what it perceived as the more pressing issues of hemispheric security and worldwide disarmament.

A half century after they were written, the final thoughts of General Graves on what he called "America's Siberian Adventure" still have a distinct pertinency:

"The absence of information from the United States and the Allied Governments, about military intervention in Russia, indicates that the various Governments taking part in the intervention take very little pride in this venture.

"Who can blame them?"

V I
A RECKONING IN THE EAST

1921–1941

THE skies were clear above the eastern section of China's vast, muddy Yangtze River on the morning of December 12, 1937. As Lieutenant Masatake Okumiya of the Japanese navy's Second Combined Air Group led his six dive-bombers into the Changchow air base after an early morning run on targets outside the Nationalist Chinese capital of Nanking, he hoped that his group would be able to take further advantage of the day's ideal weather conditions. Since July, the undeclared war between Japan and China—which had broken out largely because the Chinese at last seemed determined to stem the tide of foreign expansion into their nation that had been going on for decades—had offered many Japanese naval pilots their first chance for real action. During the Yangtze campaign they had demonstrated an enthusiasm that overshadowed their inexperience—as well as some occasional errors in judgment. But their commander, Rear Admiral Teizo Mitsunami, was a proud officer, a rising star in the imperial service, and he was delighted with the overall performance of his men during the drives against what almost all Japanese viewed as the impossibly arrogant chauvinism of Chiang Kai-shek's Nationalist forces. Mitsunami was especially pleased that his navy pilots had outshone their army counterparts; even during as important an operation as the Yangtze campaign, the rivalry between the Japanese army and navy could not be concealed.

Once on the ground in Changchow, a small town midway between Nanking and Shanghai, Lieutenant Okumiya was told to report for an operational briefing. Along with twenty-three other pilots, Okumiya was informed by an intelligence officer, Captain Morihiko Miki, "that an advance Army unit had reported seven large merchant ships and three smaller ones fleeing the capital [Nanking], loaded to capacity with Chinese troops. . . . Ground forces were unable to reach them, so it was requested that the naval air arm make an attack." There was, Miki went on, a danger that some of these ships might belong to foreign neutrals, such as Great Britain or the United States—but the Chinese had long ago adopted a tactic of putting out American and British flags to lure Japanese troops close, only to then spray them with machine-gun fire. "You should not," Miki warned, "attack the ships if you know definitely that they are American or British. But if you are suspicious that they are Chinese hiding under neutral flags, attack." Okumiya and his fellow pilots, "thrilled" with this latest opportunity, returned to their planes and flew west, heading for the point on the Yangtze where the supposedly Chinese ships had been sighted—unaware that they had been duped into provoking an international incident by their own comrades in the Japanese army.

The "advance Army unit" of which Okumiya spoke was part of a larger formation that had bravely and determinedly fought its way around Nanking and captured the town of Wuhu upriver, beginning the process of encirclement that would eventually doom the Nationalist Chinese capital. These troops were under the command of Colonel Kingoro Hashimoto, one of the most notorious of Japan's ultranationalist army officers. Hashimoto had but one passion—the forceful expansion of the Japanese empire in Asia and the Pacific—and he had pursued that goal for the better part of a decade with every form of military and political violence that his fertile mind had been able to concoct. In 1930 he had founded the "Cherry Society," a group of restive young army officers whose stated purpose was "national reorganization, by armed force if necessary," and who saw the sacrifice of their own lives in that cause as analogous to the falling of cherry blossoms—glorious death giving way to life, in this case the life of a reinvigorated, drastically expanded Japanese empire.

Hashimoto had been involved in two violent schemes to place expansionists in control of Japan's government in the first half of the 1930s, attempts that never got past the planning stages. But in February of 1936 he had been involved in still another plot, one that had caused a national crisis in Japan. The conspirators had attempted to assassinate the prime minister and had succeeded in killing other high officials who, they believed, were betraying Japan through their obedience to big business interests (whose greed for profits precluded, in Hashimoto's mind, proper devotion to national honor) as well as through their efforts to come to terms peacefully with Japan's two great rivals in the Far East—Great Britain and the United States. None of the officers involved in the plot was ever severely punished (which indicated the rising power of such groups in Japan), and Hashimoto was no exception. For plotting to kill his nation's leaders, the colonel had simply been reassigned to duty in China.

Following the outbreak of the undeclared Sino-Japanese War of 1937, Hashimoto had looked beyond the immediate goal of China's defeat to other opportunities for his homeland. Adopting an aggressive attitude toward those citizens of nonbelligerent nations that he came into contact with during his military exploits in China, Hashimoto secretly hoped to spark an incident that might force his government to confront the fact that England and America—through their support of the Open Door policy and the "integrity" of China—stood in the way of Japan's great destiny and could only be removed by force. On December 12, Hashimoto was presented with an ideal opportunity to realize his ambition.

As the situation in Nanking had become increasingly dangerous in the first week of December, the American ambassador and most of his staff had left the city, leaving behind a small group to conduct business, attend to the needs of those Americans who had not yet departed and, if the situation deteriorated rapidly, supervise a full evacuation. To assist in this effort, the gunboat U.S.S. *Panay*, one of eight vessels that made up the American Yangtze Patrol, was ordered to stand by outside the city. The *Panay* was a small, flat-bottomed, lightly armed vessel (boasting only two 3-inch guns and eight .30-caliber machine guns), but with her whitewashed hull, mahogany paneling and brass railings she was a comfortable and impressive ship, one that had always been adequate for the job

of protecting American interests and citizens on the Yangtze—
adequate, that is, until the invasion of Japanese forces. When the
fighting around Nanking finally did grow too dangerous for
American nationals on December 11, the Americans boarded the
Panay (along with two Italian journalists) and the ship headed
upriver, moving steadily farther from Nanking because of Japanese artillery fire. At this point, the officers of the *Panay* believed
that the Japanese shells that frequently dropped dangerously close
to their ship and to three Standard Oil tankers that were traveling
under her protection were simply the result of poor Japanese
marksmanship. They did not know that the advance army units
around them were commanded by Colonel Hashimoto.

About twenty-five miles above Nanking, the *Panay* finally an-
chored on the morning of December 12, her captain feeling that
the situation at that distance from the capital was safe. The Standard Oil tankers followed suit. All four vessels were carefully observed by Japanese troops onshore. One junior-grade Japanese
officer even came aboard the *Panay* to ask rather arrogantly if he
could search the ships for Chinese troops. His request was refused
by the *Panay*'s skipper in only slightly more polite language. The
Japanese officer left, and the troops ashore seemed to lose interest.
Within minutes of this departure, however, Captain Miki in
Changchow received the fateful intelligence report from an "advance Army unit" that there were Chinese troops fleeing up the
Yangtze on a series of ships, and that the navy air arm should
attack if possible.

It may never be known whether Colonel Hashimoto actually
dictated that report—but it would certainly have been passed to
him before transmission to the naval air units. Whether it was a
deliberate lie on the colonel's part or the fortuitous mistake of a
lower officer, Hashimoto let the erroneous report be sent. Very
soon after, Lieutenant Okumiya and his fellow pilots were joyously
on their way to attack what they thought were retreating enemy
troops. Not only would Hashimoto at last get his incident, but he
would also use the navy—the navy, which had always lagged behind the army in its ultranationalism—to do the job.

The Japanese planes sighted the four ships at just past 1:30 P.M.
on that Sunday afternoon. They attacked immediately, the
bombers staying at a high altitude and the fighter-bombers coming
in lower to drop their payloads and strafe the ships with machine
guns. If any of the pilots did see the huge American flags that the

crews of the *Panay* and the Standard Oil ships had painted and draped over their decks and awnings, they almost certainly thought back to the words of Captain Miki: "if you are suspicious that they [the crews] are Chinese hiding under neutral flags, attack." Young pilots in their first real war, many of these Japanese officers would later explain that in the heat of the moment they never even saw the American flags. This would seem a near impossibility, yet it was a story they stood by through intense questioning by their own superiors. Within minutes of their first run, the *Panay* was sinking, and her crew, many of them (including all the officers) badly wounded, was being ferried to shore on motor launches. Two of the Standard Oil tankers were aflame, and the third was crippled. One tanker captain was already dead. The Japanese success seemed complete, but the enthusiasm of the young pilots only mounted.

As the Americans made for shore, more were wounded when the Japanese planes returned to strafe their quarry. Hiding among the muddy marshes and reeds of the riverbank, the stunned American sailors watched as the planes continued to search and fire. Soon a Japanese army patrol boat appeared, moving in on the sinking *Panay* and spraying it with machine-gun fire. The Japanese crew then boarded the American vessel, even though the *Panay*'s colors were still clearly visible. Finally, the planes and the patrol boat departed. But for the crew of the *Panay* it was only the beginning of a two-day nightmare of roaming through the Chinese countryside, carrying the wounded and seeking safety. When they finally did find it aboard a British vessel, two American sailors and one of the Italian journalists had died of their wounds.

Colonel Hashimoto, meanwhile, had not been idle. Never to be outdone by the navy, and perhaps to make doubly sure that he would get his incident, he had ordered his artillery units upriver to fire on the British gunboats *Ladybird* and *Bee,* killing one British sailor. Having committed this further outrage, Hashimoto suddenly disappeared into the Chinese countryside. Whether he knew that a quick and sharp response to his actions was possible, either from the British and Americans or from his own government, or whether his immediate superiors had simply told him to lay low until the crisis that would inevitably result was resolved, nothing was seen or heard of this audacious, brutal officer in the weeks that followed the attacks on the Yangtze. He may have participated in the subsequent "rape of Nanking," during which Japanese army forces committed every manner of outrage against Chinese civilians on a huge scale; certainly, it was an episode suited to Hashimoto's talents. But there was no official effort to either locate or reprimand him.

This did not please the Japanese navy, which expressed its deepest regrets for the *Panay* attack to the emperor (there was speculation that someone involved would have to take the path of hara-kiri) and transferred Admiral Mitsunami in disgrace to staff duty at home. Navy Vice Minister Admiral Isoroku Yamamoto explained that, "We have done this to suggest that the Army do likewise and remove Hashimoto from his command." The army had no such intention, and the civil government of Japan—trapped between the two battling services and a public enthusiastic over its victories in China—was paralyzed.

When word reached Washington of the surprise sinking of the *Panay* and the shelling of the British vessels, there was widespread shock—though relatively little disbelief. Americans generally and their government officials in particular had long sympathized with the plight of the Chinese, and previous Japanese outrages—most notably Japan's acquisition of Shantung on the Chinese mainland at the Paris Peace Conference in 1919 and the contrived invasion of Manchuria in 1931—had convinced many Americans that the seemingly democratic system the Japanese had created in the late nineteenth and early twentieth centuries, with its parliamentary Diet, its prime minister and its cabinet system, was deeply imperiled by the fanaticism of the military expansionists. From the outset, then, the *Panay* incident was seen in Washington as further evidence of a profound shift in the nature of the Japanese government.

President Franklin Roosevelt certainly shared this view. He immediately ordered Secretary of State Cordell Hull—a dignified, slightly lisping Tennessean whose devotion to economic internationalism and legalistic systems of world peace sometimes masked a signal capacity for toughness—to deliver a stiff message to the Japanese ambassador, who appeared in Hull's office on December 17. The ambassador tried to tell Hull that the incident had not been as extreme as had been reported; and he reiterated the sentiments of his own foreign minister, Koki Hirota, who had told American ambassador Joseph C. Grew in Tokyo that it was his "wish to do everything in my power to maintain good relations with the United States." But Hull was not buying either the effort to downplay the *Panay* attack or the attempt at conciliation. "I said," the secretary later recalled, "that if Army and Navy officials in this country were to act as the Japanese had over there, our Government would quickly court martial and shoot them." Elaborating on the astonishment of the Roosevelt administration, Hull asked the Japanese envoy if "these wild, runaway, half-insane Army and Navy officials were going to be properly dealt with."

Clearly, failure to carry out such punishment would indicate to the American government that the Japanese officers in question had acted with official sanction from Tokyo. Hull told the ambassador that President Roosevelt wished his shock at the incident to be relayed to the emperor personally, that the United States was preparing a full account of the incident according to the evidence then being collected and that the Japanese government should issue a full statement of regret, an offer of compensation and an outline of methods to ensure that no such behavior would occur in the future.

Meanwhile, at a meeting of Roosevelt's cabinet on the same day, possible responses to the Japanese attack were discussed. Roosevelt's aging secretary of the navy, Claude A. Swanson, wanted war immediately, and, wrote Interior Secretary Harold L. Ickes, "undoubtedly he is talking for the admirals." Ickes himself, a Theodore Roosevelt Progressive who had a curmudgeon's temperament and an exceptionally keen mind, saw Swanson's point. "Certainly war with Japan is inevitable sooner or later," he wrote in his diary, "and if we have to fight her, isn't this the best possible time?" But Roosevelt and Hull were not convinced. "As Swanson continued to shout for war in his feeble old voice," Ickes recalled, "the President remarked that he wanted the same result that Swanson did [Japanese moderation] but that he didn't want to have to go to war to get it."

Roosevelt was convinced that the *Panay* incident was evidence of a grand design on the part of the Japanese to "force all the Westerners out of China" and thus clear the field for their own economic and political expansion; but despite this belief, the president ultimately heeded the warnings of those, like Hull and Ambassador Grew, who felt that a stiff response to the bombing—such as economic sanctions or military moves—would push the United States into a war it was not prepared for and did not want. Already the American public, though as outraged as their president by the sinking, had made its position clear—an editorial in the *Christian*

Science Monitor summed up the general reaction best when it wrote, "The gunboat *Panay* is not the battleship *Maine*." As always, Roosevelt's first concern was to prevent his policy from running too far ahead of public opinion—sanctions and military moves were ruled out.

Yet there was the persistent feeling in the administration that *some* response had to be made, and when Treasury Secretary Henry Morgenthau, Jr.—a longtime FDR aide who had served under Roosevelt during the latter's term as governor of New York —suggested the idea of seizing Japanese assets in the United States, the president was delighted with the idea. Morgenthau was ordered to investigate the details—but when he returned to the Treasury Department, he found that many members of his own staff, including and especially Assistant Secretary Wayne Taylor, were reluctant to assist him. Like the American public, Taylor and other Treasury officials wanted to avoid war at any cost, an attitude that Morgenthau—who was ready for an immediate declaration of hostilities—found infuriating. "[T]hey've sunk a United States battleship and killed three people," he railed at his assistant. "You going to sit here and wait until you wake up here in the morning and find them in the Philippines, then Hawaii, and then in Panama? Where would you call a halt? . . . How long are you going to sit there and let these fellows kill American soldiers and sailors and sink our battleships?" Taylor's answer was simple and to the point: "A helluva while."

Morgenthau did develop a plan for seizing Japanese holdings in the United States, but by the time he was ready to present it Roosevelt had lost much of his enthusiasm for retaliatory action. The public determination to keep the *Panay* from becoming a *casus belli* had been expressed with ever greater determination as details of the attack were published—many believed that the sinking was cause not for war, but for a complete withdrawal of the two to three thousand U.S. troops stationed in China. Then, too, Roosevelt had Europe to contend with. The brutality of Mussolini's forces in Italy's war against Ethiopia in 1935 and Hitler's repudiation of the Versailles treaty and subsequent reoccupation of the Rhineland in 1936 all pointed toward the possibility of a new European war, as did the conflict of Fascist and Loyalist forces in Spain. In Roosevelt's view, it was no time to mount a major American effort toward resolving the complexities of the Far East. On Christmas Eve, 1937, the official Japanese apology for the *Panay*

incident arrived in Washington, offering a reparation settlement
of $2,214,007.36. President Roosevelt accepted both the apology
and the settlement. He was eager to return to some sort of a status
quo with regard to Japan so that he could concentrate his energies
both on the economic depression that continued to plague the
United States and on systems for peace that could counter worldwide aggression without resorting to force.

While Roosevelt accepted the Japanese apology and reparations
payment so as not to provoke Tokyo, he refused to acknowledge
any legitimacy to Japanese grievances against the Chinese government or to Japan's growing need for natural resources. In addition, FDR wanted to maintain the American security perimeter in
the Pacific established by William McKinley and Theodore Roosevelt and upheld by Woodrow Wilson. Finally, FDR's response reflected the influence of American civic and political leaders who
sought legalistic and moralistic solutions to international disputes,
an influence that had become dominant during the past two decades.

The American rejection of the League of Nations in 1920 had
demonstrated a refusal on the part of the United States to associate
itself further with an international political system that, it was
widely felt, had produced the First World War. Following the return of the Republican party to national leadership in 1921, more
and more Americans came to regard that war as having been not a
crusade for democracy, but the final embodiment of the evils of
the European balance of power and the inevitable result of an
international financial system that was geared to reap profits from
vast war machines. Increasingly, peace groups sprang up in the
United States during the early years of the 1920s, movements that
were dedicated to finding systems of international behavior that
could deter and even prevent nations from turning to war as a
method of redressing grievances.

None of this implies that a majority of Americans rejected participation in affairs outside their own nation. From the time of
James G. Blaine's "annexation of trade," the United States had,
whether by design or circumstance, created a perimeter of worldwide interests that could not be ignored or abandoned. True, many
Americans by 1921 did not feel entirely comfortable with such a
perimeter. The brutal annexation of the Philippines, the interventions in the Caribbean and Latin America that had often (as in the

cases of Nicaragua in 1912, Haiti in 1915 and the Dominican Republic in 1916) led to de facto American administration of so-called "sister republics," as well as the increasing activities of American commercial and business concerns throughout the world, had created a moral and political position for the United States that many of her citizens found singularly unsuitable. Yet at the same time, retreat from this new perimeter was viewed by almost all national leaders as impossible. The efforts of Robert Lansing and Colonel House, for instance, to transfer control of the Philippines to Japan (and thus stabilize relations with that nation and conditions in the Far East generally) had never been taken seriously by President Wilson or by anyone else. Having created an American perimeter of interests, it seemed, even those liberal democrats who might have questioned its extent could not countenance its dismantling. American prestige, the mission to spread democracy, the need for overseas markets—all of these ensured that America would hold on to her new world position.

The resultant dilemma—the revulsion at such international political practices as had produced the First World War combined with the need to hold onto a perimeter that had been gained through disturbingly similar methods—deeply affected the American conception of national security in the 1920s. Not least of these effects was a desire to develop systematic solutions to complex international issues. The balance of power, imperialism and all their attendant evils were viewed by the American peace groups and their representatives in Congress as essentially a system, an ancient, reprehensible order based on exploitation and war. The efforts of such diverse men as Theodore Roosevelt and Woodrow Wilson to improve that system by participating in or modifying it had not only tainted the American character but had proved a threat to American security by drawing the nation irresistibly into World War I. If the United States was truly to lead the way out of the warlike labyrinth that had so dominated world affairs for centuries, it seemed logical now to stop trying to improve the old system and introduce a new one—which is precisely what Senator William Borah of Idaho set out to do.

A "prairie Progressive," a skilled speaker and an unmistakably American individualist, Borah prided himself on his iconoclasm. He could rarely be identified with any one faction in Congress; his opinions were always his own, and generally outspoken. When, in December 1920, he introduced a resolution calling for a general disarmament conference among the powers of the world, many inside Congress and out were surprised. This was, after all, a man who had violently opposed any participation in the League of Nations, which aimed, among other things, at just such a program of disarmament. But as his resolution was passed and Borah agitated further for a conference, the difference between the two concepts of disarmament—his own and the League's—became clearer. The league, in addition to disarmament, required obligation, membership, participation; Borah was clearly angling for a more unilateral (if no less pacifist) solution. Instead of an international congress, the Senator from Idaho wanted an international system of law; instead of practical commitments, he wanted moral standards, standards that each nation would be expected, but not *required,* to uphold.

It was an idea that immediately seized the imagination of the American people, for it seemed to offer an ideal resolution to their dilemma—a simultaneous abandonment of traditional international relations without any obligation to adjust America's world position. With dramatic passion, peace groups, women's groups, what sometimes looked like representatives of the entire nation laid siege to Warren Harding's White House and demanded a disarmament conference. In November 1921 they got one.

The Washington Naval Conference produced three treaties that seemed of momentous significance. The first, or Four-Power, Treaty, was concluded between the United States, Great Britain, France and Japan, and by its terms each nation pledged to respect the rights of the others in the Pacific and to resort to consultation rather than to force as a method of resolving differences. The second of the treaties, the Five-Power, added Italy to the list of participants and established a ten-year ban on the building of capital ships (battleships and aircraft carriers), setting a ratio for the amount of tonnage each power could have in that category: for every five tons of capital tonnage the United States and Britain possessed, the Japanese could have three, the French and the Italians 1.67. In agreeing to their inferior position, the Japanese secured pledges from the United States and Britain not to construct any military bases west of Hawaii or north of Singapore. Finally, the third or Nine-Power Treaty was yet another reaffirmation of the Open Door policy and the integrity of the Republic of China.

Hailed throughout the United States and the world as a monumental new step toward peace, the Washington Treaties were in reality full of loopholes that finally rendered them meaningless. First, they limited only the number of capital ships the powers were allowed, when recent experience had shown that cruisers and destroyers would be key in future naval wars (almost immediately after the conference, Britain and Japan launched a race in the construction of cruisers). Then, too, further restatements of the Open Door policy could do no more for the "integrity" of strife-ridden China than had John Hay's original enunciation of it in 1899. And the tacit admission of Great Britain and the United States that the defense of such ports as Hong Kong and Manila Bay was impossible could hardly be expected to calm Japanese expansionists. True, the Japanese did attempt to show further good faith at Washington by agreeing to end their occupation of Shantung—but only after extracting economic concessions from the Chinese that made actual occupation superfluous.

But the greatest fallacy of the Washington Treaties lay in their nonbinding status. None of the signatories was obliged to force the others to obey any of the treaties' terms, for this would have been viewed as warlike. Instead, the power of moral censure—world-wide public condemnation—was relied on to shepherd wayward nations back into the ranks of the peaceful. But even this fatal flaw was viewed among the peace groups as an affirmation of the world's rejection of coercion and war as methods of international behavior. With the Washington Naval Conference, then, the legalistic-moralistic school of American policy-making signaled a shift in the general American attitude toward national security that would grow over the next ten years—the replacement of unilateral interventionism with legalistic-moralistic approaches.

The extent to which this shift was permitted by the destruction of what had been the paramount threat to American and Western Hemispheric security prior to 1918—the Imperial German Navy—cannot be overestimated. Great Britain and the United States were now fast allies in the cause of peace, despite frequent disputes over exactly how to achieve and maintain that goal; and there was no other power in the world, including Japan, that could mount a serious attack on the Western Hemisphere. Americans, therefore, could afford the luxury of hiding behind the moralism embodied in the Washington Treaties.

Encouraged by the euphoria and immense popularity of the Washington Conference, increasing numbers of American leaders joined the ranks of the legalistic moralists. Elder statesmen such as Secretary of State Charles Evans Hughes and former Secretary of War and State Elihu Root—both noted legal experts—hailed the beginning of a new age and joined ranks with younger statesmen and lawyers in trying to ensure that an international system based on neither a balance of power nor an obligatory system such as the League of Nations might be given a chance to eliminate warfare as a method of settling disagreements. The general notion was that much as other social ills had been "outlawed," so, too, could war be.

But the traditional American reliance on unilateralism was never too far beneath the surface of this new legalistic approach. Masked by the absence of any overpowering threat to American security, that reliance nonetheless made itself felt during the 1920s, as in the case of Calvin Coolidge's dispatch of marines to Honduras in March 1925 to put down civil disorder and protect American interests. Still another revealing case of traditional American behavior came with the question of entry into the World Court. In January 1926, with pressure from peace groups mounting for American participation in the Court, the Senate approved the idea but attached a rider that made its approval valueless—the United States would only join if the Court would agree not to offer any opinions on matters relating to U.S. security. American participation on these terms was, quite predictably, refused.

But the legal moralists were not defeated. In 1927, the brilliant French foreign minister Aristide Briand, deeply concerned about the weak defensive posture of his nation, decided that if he could definitely eliminate the United States as a future source of military troubles, France would have that much more strength available to devote to traditional threats. Sensing the American national mood, Briand offered Coolidge's secretary of state, Frank B. Kellogg, a pact in which France and the United States would mutually pledge never to go to war with each other. Kellogg, a notoriously profane and cynical man, was put in a position that angered him. At home, the by-now powerful peace groups applauded Briand's idea. But critics (and Kellogg tended to agree with them) argued that such a pact defied George Washington's great admonition to avoid not only entangling alliances but "habitual hatred" and "habitual fondness" for other nations. Kellogg agonized long and hard over whether or not to accept Briand's proposal, angrily cursing the Frenchman as well as the peace groups that surrounded his State

Department offices. Then, in December, the secretary devised a way out of the trap.

Capitalizing on the popularity of Briand's idea, Kellogg suggested that other powers be included in the pact—that, in fact, it be made universal. The peace groups were delighted with Kellogg's counterproposal. Briand was anything but: a universal pact was as useless for his real purposes as no pact at all. Yet now it was Briand who had been put in the uncomfortable position of either accepting Kellogg's offer or appearing to act against the cause of peace. He chose the former course, and in August 1928 the Kellogg-Briand Pact, or Pact of Paris, was signed. Born out of a Frenchman's desire to apportion his military strength more effectively and an American's desire to preserve effective freedom of action, and signed by all but four nations, the pact banned war as a method of settling international disagreements—with two very key provisions. First, like the Washington Treaties, it was nonbinding, involving no obligation on the part of any signatory to enforce its terms. Second, it excluded from its moral pronouncements those wars that could be represented as defensive, which, for the United States, meant any security threat to the Western Hemisphere.

Such shortcomings, however, could not flag the worldwide enthusiasm with which the pact was met. It was the high tide of the legalistic-moralistic movement, and the absence of any major flare-ups encouraged those in the United States who thought they might at last have found a method of attending to their nation's security without using the tools that had embittered native populations in Latin America and Asia, caused extensive bloodshed throughout the world and given the lie to the idealistic visions of such men as Woodrow Wilson.

But the dream was very soon destined to be shattered. As threats to the new legalistic-moralistic system of international relations began to surface, many men and women responded by seeking ways to give teeth to a series of agreements that, by their very nature, could have no teeth. And in this struggle no one person's efforts were more considerable, sincere and ultimately ill-fated than those of Henry L. Stimson, a courageous New York lawyer whose personal nature was anything but pacifistic.

In August 1917, as the United States was busy marshaling and expanding its armed services for war in Europe, Secretary of War

Newton Baker had received an unusual visitor in his Washington office. That the man was an army major who had been working overtime at the Army War College preparing himself for field duty and was now requesting assignment to the front lines in France was no surprise; but the fact that the man was almost fifty years old, one of the nation's top courtroom lawyers and had been Taft's secretary of war, did give Secretary Baker pause. At his age and with his experience, Henry Stimson could easily have avoided active service in the First World War, or certainly have been assigned to the safety of staff duty; but as he himself would later put it, "my ancestors, when in service, have been in the fighting branch; moreover I felt that my former attitude toward this war and our part in it, made it necessary that I should now evidence my faith by works, and show that I was willing to do what I said others should do, and stake my life for the cause." Secretary Baker was initially suspicious that Stimson's motives were political. But as the honesty of the former secretary's intentions became more apparent, Baker decided to give Stimson what he wanted: a promotion to lieutenant colonelcy and assignment to France in an artillery unit. Stimson would later boast that his regiment fired the first American artillery round of the war. If so, it was a most appropriate coincidence.

Since 1905, Stimson's life had been a record of service, of tireless devotion to his nation carried out in a righteous manner that some found insufferable but all conceded was genuine. Like Robert Lansing, he had been born into an old New York family that could trace its American roots back to the seventeenth century, and like Lansing, he, too, eventually chose the law and public service as his careers—but there the similarities between the two men ended. Stimson's mother had died when he was only eight, and his father —a remarkable man who gave up a life in business when his wife became ill and took up the study of medicine in Paris under Louis Pasteur—had been so shattered by the loss that on returning to New York he sent young Henry and his sister to live with their grandparents and devoted himself to emergency room work in the city's "houses of relief." The elder Stimson eventually became a renowned surgeon, displaying a tremendous capacity for midlife career change that he would pass on to his son.

After happy preparatory years at Phillips Academy, Andover, Massachusetts, Stimson attended Yale and then went on to the Harvard Law School, where he found "an atmosphere both inside the halls of the university and outside in its yard which was re-

markably different from that in New Haven. In the classrooms of
the Law School there was a spirit of independent thinking unlike
anything I had met before." This was a remarkable era at Harvard,
which numbered among its professors the likes of William James
and Josiah Royce, and Stimson took full advantage of every opportunity. He also began a series of trips to the western United States
that would result in a lifelong passion for the outdoors and a
"strenuous life" that was much like Theodore Roosevelt's; it was
not the only similarity between the two men. In 1891, Stimson was
admitted to the bar and became a clerk in the office of Elihu Root,
the great American legalist and statesman, who was destined to
have a profound effect on his new associate.

A young girl from Connecticut, Mabel White, proved the object
of Stimson's determined affections, and he pursued their long
courtship with a singleness of purpose that was typical. They were
married in 1893, but before the marriage Stimson suffered an
attack of mumps that left him sterile. Children being an impossibility, the Stimsons (much like the James K. Polks of a half century
earlier) withdrew into a world of secret and deep devotion, Mabel
accompanying her husband on his amazingly strenuous wilderness
excursions and keeping up with his passion for all manner of
sports. Stimson became a noted courtroom lawyer, an advocate of
rare speaking and debating ability, and his practice prospered accordingly.

Stimson had developed an interest in politics early on, but until
the age of thirty-seven confined his participation to New York City
district affairs. But when Theodore Roosevelt, for whom Stimson
had unbounded admiration both as a man and as a Republican
Progressive, became president and appointed Elihu Root secretary
of state, the likelihood of a call to higher government service
greatly increased. In 1905, that call came. Stimson was summoned
to Washington and offered the post of United States attorney for
the Southern District of New York. Stimson took the job and immediately joined in Roosevelt's campaign of trust-busting and
rooting out corruption in the business community. Noted for
his reluctance to seek publicity—a reluctance that often bordered,
as it would in the future, on hostility toward the press—Stimson pursued his work in the manner of a vigorous crusader. Critics were quick to tag him as self-righteous, but in measuring his
goals and achievements during the heyday of Theodore Roosevelt's trust-busting, it is difficult not to argue that Stimson's zeal

produced concrete public benefits that transcended simple self-aggrandizement.

In addition, there were elements to Stimson's personality that always undercut the obvious charge of arrogant pomposity. A certain delicacy of features and expression betrayed a character that was privately far more complex and philosophical than the public man was willing to display; the lifelong, deeply touching devotion to his wife tempered the martial air that governed his professional dealings; and despite the fact that his intensity of purpose resulted in chronic gastroenteritis and insomnia (or perhaps because it did), he maintained a desperate longing for the releases of humor and recreation. Later in life, as a member of Herbert Hoover's cabinet, he would often complain that he "never knew such unenlivened occasions as our Cabinet meetings. When I sat down and tried to think it over, I don't remember that there has been a single joke cracked in a single meeting . . . , nothing but steady, serious grind, and a group of men sitting around the table who apparently had no humanity for anything but business. I am afraid I am too much of a loafer and enjoy my recreation too much to be able to stand this thing perpetually."

Stimson's term as secretary of war under William H. Taft was largely uneventful, but he nonetheless found the subsequent return to private life disappointing. Having missed out on actual combat in the Spanish-American War because his National Guard unit never made it to the fighting, Stimson was determined to get into the thick of the 1917 fray and satisfy a lifelong craving for his "baptism of fire." Then, after gaining this experience, he returned to New York and his law practice, which continued to bring him a handsome living. But in 1927, his nation called him yet again, and President Coolidge found Henry Stimson, as ever, ready to serve.

In 1925 Coolidge had decided to withdraw those American marines still stationed in Nicaragua, holdovers from the interventions of William Taft and Woodrow Wilson. But a seeming conspiracy of circumstances quickly formed to force the return of the troops to Nicaragua. The Mexican government instituted a broad program of nationalization, prompting American businessmen and conservatives to charge that Mexico had gone Bolshevik; moreover, its leaders were trying to spread Bolshevism throughout Central America—most notably in Nicaragua, where, the Americans said, Mexican socialism was the inspiration behind a new group of rebels who had plunged their nation into renewed civil strife. Coolidge ordered the American marines back to Managua in an effort to silence the criticism of these conservatives—and in doing so provoked the outrage of still other Americans, who saw this latest action as disturbingly reminiscent of Woodrow Wilson's attempts to impose democracy and protect American business interests through intervention. Coolidge found himself in the midst of a domestic debate centering on Nicaragua.

In January 1927, Under Secretary of State Robert Olds aggravated this situation by declaring that "the Central American area down to and including the isthmus of Panama constitutes a legitimate sphere of influence for the United States, if we are to have due regard for our safety and protection. . . . We do control the destinies of Central America and we do so for the simple reason that the national interest absolutely dictates such a course. There is no room for outside influence other than ours in the region. . . . The action of Mexico in the Nicaragua crisis is a direct challenge to the United States."

While remarkably candid, opinions such as Olds's offended peace groups and noninterventionists, and Coolidge needed some way to calm the growing criticism. He eventually decided that along with the marines, he would dispatch to Nicaragua a special envoy, one who would be given a free hand to make whatever deals were necessary to end the crisis. That envoy was Henry Stimson.

On arriving in Managua in April 1927, Stimson quickly held a personal meeting with the military leader of the Nicaraguan rebels at a small village called Tipitapa. Responding to Stimson's pledge of American-supervised free elections, the majority of rebel generals agreed to lay down their arms. Only the ambitious, charismatic Augusto Sandino, who kept up the fight against government troops and American marines in the mountains of the north, resisted Stimson's adroit diplomatic settlement.

But Sandino's resistance meant little in the short term. With the truce signed and peace returning to most of Nicaragua, Stimson returned home to be congratulated by his president for ending the cruel Nicaraguan civil war—and thus furthering the cause of American security by stabilizing a key portion of the Central American subcontinent without resorting to military intervention. The 1928 elections in Nicaragua were among the fairest in that country's history. There was a new feeling both within the United States and in Nicaragua that American influence might mean a great deal more than simple economic exploitation, and much of that feeling was identified with Stimson.

Throughout the Nicaraguan affair, Coolidge's special envoy had made use of diplomatic techniques that would become his trademarks—an ability to meet given situations head-on and to view them without the clouding of ideology; a capacity for tough, personal negotiation; and a lawyer's gift for reconciling American self-interest with the ambitions of second parties.

Coolidge next made use of Stimson by dispatching him to the Philippines as governor-general, giving him the same broad powers that he had used so effectively in Nicaragua. Stimson's administration of the Philippines—whose government had deteriorated badly over the past two decades—was not unlike his handling of the Nicaraguan crisis. He met personally with Philippine nationalist leaders and opened the doors of his governor's palace for the first time to prominent native figures. He rooted out corruption in the civil administration and supported relaxed trade regulations with the United States. But despite all these conciliatory moves, he consistently and firmly ruled out any question of Philippine independence. Neither were the Filipinos capable of it—he often referred to "the Malay tendency to backslide" when left on their own —nor, more important, was it in the interest of the United States to relinquish control of the islands and thereby lose influence in the Western Pacific. Stimson's faith in the importance of America's defensive perimeter was unshakable.

In recognition of his already considerable career of public service, Stimson was appointed secretary of state by Herbert Hoover in 1929. One of the new secretary's first acts was to complete the job he had begun at Tipitapa and initiate a phased withdrawal of American marines from Nicaragua. The rebellious Sandino continued to wage a savage fight against his former commander, José María Moncada, but the job of fighting the remaining insurgents was increasingly turned over to the new Nicaraguan National Guard and its commander, Anastasio Somoza. When General Moncada tried to run for a second term in 1932 (which was forbidden by the Nicaraguan constitution), Stimson played a key role in ensuring that he did not. The 1932 elections were even fairer than the 1928 had been, and when the old anti-American Juan Sacasa was elected, President Hoover and Secretary Stimson placed no obstacle in his path.

The return of the marines from Nicaragua seemed further

proof to many in the United States that the eras of big-stick diplomacy and worldwide interventionism were over, and had been replaced by the rule of law. Stimson, through his association with
men like Elihu Root, his great fame as a lawyer and his forceful
but peaceful forays into diplomacy, had by the time of his appointment as secretary of state in 1929 become closely identified with the legalistic-moralistic school of American foreign policy.
He had been a supporter of both the Washington Treaties and
the Kellogg-Briand Pact, and his experiences had only confirmed
in his own mind the possibility that world peace and American
security could be attended to through international law rather than
through violence and bloodshed.

But in 1929, Stimson and the rest of the nation, like Woodrow
Wilson, Robert Lansing and Edward House before them, were to
learn that what seemed workable in the West could often prove
sadly irrelevant when dealing with the endless violence of the Far
East.

In 1929 the province of Manchuria—covering an area larger
than the American Pacific Coast states—was the nexus of expansionist and nationalist designs on the part of China, Japan and the
Soviet Union. Nominally Chinese, Manchuria had in fact been
ruled for many years by a warlord, except in those areas where the
Russians and the Japanese "administered" the Chinese Eastern
Railway and used that administration as an excuse to set up established zones of control. Rich, fertile and sparsely populated, Manchuria represented a valuable prize for all three nations. But while
Nationalist China and Soviet Russia, each caught in the grip of
dramatic domestic transformations, could afford to turn away
from that prize and satisfy their own needs within the vast expan-
ses of their homelands, Japan, an island nation whose industrial
establishment and concurrent thirst for raw materials were expanding constantly in the first decades of the twentieth century,
could not afford to let the Manchurian opportunity pass.

The worldwide economic collapse of 1929 underscored this
point. No nation was hit harder by that collapse than Japan. As the
walls of economic protection went up around the other powers,
Japan, deeply dependent on imports and exports, found itself
against a wall. Lacking an imperial system on a scale such as Britain's, the Japanese were forced to guard their few external holdings and spheres of influence with particular determination. When

Chiang Kai-shek decided to assert himself over the issue of Manchuria in 1929 and attacked the Russian sector of the Chinese Eastern Railway, the Japanese feared that they might be the next target of Chinese nationalism; and without her Manchurian holdings, Japan could not have hoped to maintain even a low level of economic equilibrium.

Much of this was lost on Secretary of State Stimson and his advisers. Within the State Department, experts on the Far East tended to be "China hands" such as Dr. Stanley K. Hornbeck, chief of the Far Eastern Affairs division. Hornbeck had taught at various colleges, in both the United States and China, and his pro-Chinese sympathies, while scholarly, were never very effectively veiled. Departmental knowledge of the still-unrecognized Soviet Union lagged behind that of China, but it was growing through the efforts of men like William Bullitt. Knowledge of the social and governmental traditions of Imperial Japan, however, was abysmally low. Lacking statesmen with Chiang Kai-shek's talent for selling his cause to the American public, the Japanese could not help but contribute to this unhappy state of affairs.

In November 1929, Stimson sent a note to the Chinese and the Russians, citing the Kellogg-Briand Pact (which both nations had signed) and preaching the virtues of negotiation and peace. The replies he received were the first indication that the legalistic-moralistic approach to international relations might be in trouble. Chiang Kai-shek spouted the rhetoric of offended Chinese nationalism and asserted his nation's historic rights in Manchuria—rights that the Chinese had been unable to exercise for decades. And the Russians, in a very curt reply, reminded Stimson that the United States had not even recognized the Soviet Union yet and ought to attend to its own affairs. The Soviets then launched a counterattack in Manchuria and the fighting escalated.

If the legalistic moralists felt any momentary doubts, however, they were largely calmed by the January 1930 meeting of the London Naval Conference. Called to expand the 1921 Washington terms to cover cruisers and other noncapital ships, the conference did little more than offend the French by continuing to assign them a low naval ratio and allow the Japanese to achieve parity in submarines, destroyers and heavy cruisers. The world naval race was still on, but the new words of peace coming out of London had a soothing effect in America, where peace groups and statesmen alike continued to believe that the world was turning away from war. President Hoover and Secretary Stimson heightened this effect in June, when, in the face of the economic crisis, they began to talk of helping the struggling European nations by putting in place a one-year moratorium on all payments of reparations and war debts left over from World War I. Hope for peaceful international cooperation was still alive.

But on the night of September 18, 1931, it received a near-fatal blow in Manchuria. The Japanese troops sent to the mainland had always represented the most extreme faction of the Imperial Army, and it was the belief of such men that the retreat from Shantung and the unequal terms of the Washington and London naval treaties had been national disgraces; on his return from London in November 1930, Prime Minister Yuko Hamaguchi had been shot and mortally wounded by one of these outraged extremists. As Japan's economic plight became more severe, one conclusion became increasingly clear even to the most moderate Japanese leaders: the key to recovery lay overseas. Such moderates might argue timing and methods with the army extremists, but they could not—and did not—question this underlying assumption.

On September 18, units of the Japanese army in Manchuria placed a small bomb on a strip of railway track near the town of Mukden, in the Japanese sector. The bomb went off, doing little damage, but the Japanese troops blamed the Chinese army for the incident and immediately moved against them. Within days, the Japanese were running rampant throughout Manchuria, shocking many of their own leaders at home. The United States quickly aligned itself with China (whose strident nationalism Stimson had criticized only two years earlier), and demanded that the government in Tokyo stop the attacks.

The demand was further demonstration of the general American ignorance of Japanese affairs. Japan's cabinet system was structured so that the army and navy ministers (each selected from their respective services by the army and the navy) were the only cabinet officers besides the prime minister to have direct access to the emperor; by resigning their posts, these two officials could destroy any ruling cabinet, and if the government refused to condone policies supported by the military, the admirals and generals could refuse to supply new ministers. Such a structure left the power of the elected Diet and even of the prime minister himself gravely constricted. But American officials acted on the assumption that a constitutional government implied civilian control. The realization that this might not be so came slowly in Washington, and brought with it a paralyzing uncertainty.

For no one was this more true than for Stimson. At a cabinet meeting on October 9, he found President Hoover reluctant to issue any condemnatory statements involving Japan, even if they were in accord with the Nine-Power Treaty and the Kellogg-Briand Pact. Hoover wished, said Stimson, to avoid getting "ourselves into a humiliating position, in case Japan refused to do anything to what he called our scraps of paper or paper treaties." Stimson was taken aback. "The question of 'scraps of paper' is a pretty crucial one. We have nothing but 'scraps of paper.' This fight has come on in the worst part of the world for peace treaties. The peace treaties of Modern Europe, made out by the Western nations of the world[,] no more fit the great races of Russia, Japan, and China, who are meeting in Manchuria, than, as I put it to the Cabinet, a stovepipe hat would fit an African savage." Despite these feelings, Stimson intended to apply those same treaties to the crisis: "they [the Chinese and the Japanese] are parties to those treaties and the whole world looks on to see whether the treaties are good for anything or not."

On January 7, 1932, Stimson sent a note to the governments of China and Japan, saying that the United States would not recognize any treaty between the two countries that endangered "the international policy relative to China, commonly known as the open door policy." More significant, the United States "does not intend to recognize any situation, treaty or agreement which may be brought about by means contrary to the covenants and obligations of the Pact of Paris of August 27, 1928." Authorship of this doctrine of nonrecognition was eventually claimed by Hoover, though it came to bear Stimson's name. In fact it was little more than a new twist on Woodrow Wilson's Latin American policy, with one great difference—Wilson had been dealing with countries that were economically dependent on the United States; Stimson had no such leverage with Japan or even China. The war in Manchuria went on, and as his unilateral message continued to be ignored, Stimson sought help in the form of British support. London, however, would offer nothing. On January 11 *The London Times* approved this course, saying that it did not "seem to be the immediate business of the Foreign Office to defend the 'administrative integrity' of China until that integrity is something more than an ideal."

For the Hoover administration, there were two obvious choices:

continue to state the legalistic-moralistic line without backing those statements up through economic or military action, or take disciplinary steps and accept that they might lead to hostilities. At a crucial cabinet meeting on January 26, Secretary of War Patrick Hurley argued for a tough stance, regardless of the possibility of war. Hoover replied that "he would fight for [the] Continental United States as far as anybody, but he would not fight for Asia." Stimson agreed, with perhaps a twinge of reluctance. Hurley countered that the "principle" of Stimson's January 7 note, if taken literally, " 'would prevent our annexing any territory in this hemisphere,' and asked if the President was prepared for that." Hoover said he was; and Stimson "pointed out that the United States had ceased to be an annexing power." The secretary of war was unconvinced, and "said to the President, 'I don't see how you can support the holding of the Philippines if you hold those principles.' " Stimson, betraying his own confusion, "then pointed out that the Philippine question was different. We did not hold them by assimilation or force." For one of the country's best courtroom lawyers, as well as an ex-governor-general of the Philippines who had always fought against home rule for the islands, it was a deeply flawed line of argument. But the weakness of his position in the Manchurian crisis offered Stimson no other. The secretary of state saw Hoover again later that day, and once again told him that he "was against putting any threat into words."

The Japanese answer to this policy came in the form of bombing raids on the international city of Shanghai. On February 23, Stimson restated his doctrine of nonrecognition in an open letter to Senator Borah that reviewed the history of the Open Door, and tried desperately to make up in moral force what it lacked in practicality. Meanwhile, the League of Nations was meeting to consider action against Japan; it assigned the Lytton Commission to study the problem. In May, Japan created the puppet state of Manchukuo in Manchuria, and placed the last of the Manchus on the throne of what was obviously an effective Japanese colony.

Stimson could talk all he wanted to about the "mad dogs" who had taken control in Tokyo, but the facts were far more complicated. Many Japanese moderates knew that the United States and the League of Nations were not prepared to condone Japan's forceful control of Manchuria; yet since 1929 it had become apparent, given the attitudes of Russia and China, that control could only be exercised through such force. Given the vitality of such control to the empire's survival, Japanese leaders had limited options. Thus, when the Lytton Commission declared that Manchukuo was an illegal creation and the Japanese angrily stormed out of the league, it was less a demonstration that the moderates in Japan had lost power (an impression created by the fall of a largely moderate government in 1931) than that many key moderates had, in the face of Western intransigence, changed their views and their tactics.

There were very few in the United States who had foreseen this possibility, but of those few at least one was close to Stimson. Elihu Root, the secretary of state's former mentor, had been in touch with his ex-clerk as far back as November 14, 1931, soon after the Mukden incident. "Rather to my surprise," Stimson recorded, "Mr. Root is more sympathetic with Japan than with China; and he is very fearful lest we do not recognize her real claims to Manchuria." The aging Root had seen what the secretary could not—that "the status quo" (Stimson's own, often-repeated term) in the Far East was not retrievable—indeed, insofar as Manchuria went, it had not existed for decades. To try to imagine otherwise was merely to postpone a reckoning with the increasingly dynamic Japanese empire that was surely unavoidable. That reckoning need not be war; but it certainly could not be a return to the status quo, for the status quo spelled national ruin for the overpopulated, depleted archipelago of Japan. Somehow the Japanese would have to be accommodated. Yet the overwhelming force of the legalistic-moralistic school was against any such accommodation as long as Japan's militants were allowed to indulge in openly aggressive behavior. Neither Hoover nor Stimson felt they could contradict this popular sentiment; and rather than threaten a military response, they imposed vastly increased tariffs on Japanese imports. This action dealt a heavy blow to the Japanese economy. In the face of this American behavior, the Japanese people and their leaders became increasingly truculent, nationalistic and violent. A crisis could hardly be avoided.

But rather than accept this view and adjust to it, Stimson chose to believe in the power of public censure—and he fully intended to pass his commitment to legalistic moralism on to the next generation of American leaders.

The morning of January 9, 1933, was rainy and cold at Highhold, the Stimsons' estate on Long Island. The secretary of state

rose early in order to catch a nine o'clock train that would take him
north, up the Hudson Valley. By the time he reached the small
town of Hyde Park, the rain had turned to snow that was sticking
on the ground. Getting into a waiting car, Stimson was driven some
three miles to the home of the governor of New York and new
president-elect of the United States, Franklin Delano Roosevelt.

Stimson found the big Roosevelt house that overlooked the
Hudson River "in a good deal of confusion from the accumulation
of packages both during Christmas and after the campaign." The
"general furnishings," Stimson felt sure, would not have met with
his own wife's approval: "They gave the impression of confusion,
and this was even so of a large room which they had built on and
which they were evidently very proud of. It was a beautiful room
in shape and size and had his [Roosevelt's] library of books in it,
but it did not give the impression of calm and simplicity."

Stimson had never before met Roosevelt, who received him
"with great cordiality." The purpose of the meeting, one that had
been agreed to only reluctantly by President Hoover, was to give
the two men a chance to discuss continuity in foreign policy, a
subject that greatly concerned Stimson. They talked "from eleven
o'clock when I got there through luncheon which we had entirely
alone and down on our drive back to New York, on which we were
alone." Their conversation touched on every important aspect of
current American policy—Latin America, the economic crisis, disarmament—but no subject occupied more of their time than did
the Far East.

As a boy at Groton, Franklin Roosevelt had first been introduced
to the subject of America's world position through the works and
theories of Alfred Thayer Mahan. His doting mother, the indomi-
table Sara Delano, once commented that her son knew Mahan's
The Influence of Sea Power Upon History almost by heart. From these
studies the young Franklin developed his first suspicions of Japan
as a threat to American interests in the Far East. Then, as an
undergraduate at Harvard, Roosevelt had learned of the famous
writings of Japan's Baron Tanaka, calling for a hundred-year campaign of Japanese imperial expansion. The story stayed with him.
When he became assistant secretary of the navy in the Wilson administration, he very nearly got himself into deep trouble by revealing classified information concerning the naval strength of
various powers, including Japan, to Wilson's big navy foes.

But during the League of Nations struggle and the subsequent swing toward legalistic moralism, Roosevelt—ever the political pragmatist—had moderated his naval nationalism with calls for international peace and cooperation. His battle with polio resulted in national celebrity when, at the Democratic convention of 1924, he bravely made his way to the podium on a pair of crutches to place New York governor Al Smith's name in nomination. His own election as governor of New York had been the result in 1928, and by 1932, with his defeat of Herbert Hoover, Franklin Delano Roosevelt had become closely identified with those who wished to meet the Great Depression with a willingness to experiment with radically new programs. In the realm of foreign policy, moreover, his ideas and intentions were far from established. He had, at the insistence of such influential American nationalists as publisher William Randolph Hearst, distanced himself during the campaign from Wilsonian internationalism; but whether this was a genuine transformation no one could say. It was this uncertainty, to a large degree, that had prompted Stimson's desire to meet with the president-elect.

Somewhat to his surprise, Stimson found that he and Roosevelt agreed on all major issues, and that on the question of the Far East their opinions ran especially close. Roosevelt "fully approved of our policy," Stimson recorded, and his "only possible criticism was that we did not begin it earlier." Stimson described the entire history of his dealings with Japan, China, Russia and the League of Nations at some length, and Roosevelt "said that it was his belief that Japan would ultimately fail" in her designs on Manchuria. Roosevelt expressed faith in the economic sanctions against Japan being considered by the League of Nations. Neither man seems to have suggested that without American participation (the United States sold Japan a large portion of the oil and scrap iron needed for her war machine) those sanctions could have no meaning; nor did they note, though they must have known, that no American leader, given the anti-League attitude prevalent in the United States, could possibly have participated in such a program.

After agreeing that the maintenance of the American fleet at Hawaii and the American military presence in the Philippines were crucial, Stimson once again demonstrated his fundamental misunderstanding of the Japanese government by calling it "a temporary reversion by Japan to the old position of a feudal, military autocracy." Roosevelt apparently shared this misconception; like Stimson, he failed to see that it was the seeming liberalism of Japanese moderates in the economically happier days of the 1920s that had been "temporary."

Thus all the key elements of Stimson's Far Eastern policy—the doctrine of nonrecognition, the related belief that Japan's behavior could be affected by international public opinion, the maintenance of a military and political status quo in the region and a mistaken faith in Japanese liberalism—were accepted by Roosevelt.

The two men met again in Washington on January 19, and as their harmony of beliefs spread from Far Eastern affairs to include Stimson's Latin American policy of relying increasingly on local leaders to preserve hemispheric stability (even if those leaders proved to be somewhat less than democratic), Roosevelt remarked to the secretary that, "We are getting so that we do pretty good teamwork, don't we?" Stimson "laughed and said 'Yes.' "

Within months, however, Stimson would be gone and Cordell Hull would be ensconced at the State Department. With his deep faith in lower tariffs and international trade agreements as the best method of treating the world's ills, Hull seemed to bring a new approach to American diplomacy; but in fact, Roosevelt would always stay far more in line with Stimson's ideas than with his own secretary of state's. Blending Stimson's strain of legalistic moralism with the more blatant economic nationalism of such close advisers as Rexford Tugwell and Raymond Moley, Roosevelt devised an approach to foreign policy that he hoped would allow him effective freedom of action while wrapping that freedom in a shroud of moral pronouncements—it was an approach as elusive as the man himself.

This first became apparent at the meeting of the World Economic Conference in London in the summer of 1933. The goal of the conference was to ease the international economic crisis through lowering trade restrictions and stabilizing currency rates. Secretary Hull, a disciple of such solutions, left the United States with a plan for international reciprocal trade agreements that he thought had his president's backing; but before the secretary even reached London, Roosevelt had repudiated it. Concerned above all with solving domestic problems, Roosevelt had become deeply worried that lowering trade restrictions would hurt the American economy. He went on to reject any stabilization of currency rates, and on July 2 delivered a stinging message to the American delegation and the conference generally, stressing the importance of national programs to international economic recovery.

Some economists, such as John Maynard Keynes, saw Roosevelt's point in refusing to cooperate internationally when currency and trade conditions were unfavorable. Nonetheless, the president's note doomed the London Conference and created great bitterness, both abroad and in Cordell Hull. Hull's ego was somewhat assuaged by his prominent role at the Montevideo Conference of the Pan-American states in December, at which the nations of the Western Hemisphere formally renounced intervention in one another's internal affairs and applauded America's new "Good Neighbor" policy. But the Montevideo declaration signaled more Roosevelt's willingness to leave Latin American stability in the hands of local strongmen than it did any momentous shift toward internationalism. And when Hull finally did convince Roosevelt to push for the power to negotiate reciprocal trade agreements early in 1934 that resulted in the Trade Agreements Act, the president worked hard to ensure that the legislation would continue to afford him wide freedom of action to work out arrangements that would primarily benefit the United States. All in all, it was difficult to argue Raymond Moley's statement that "the strategy of the situation" was "to let Cordell Hull talk one thing re tariffs while the army is marching in another direction."

Roosevelt's long struggle over the issue of neutrality legislation between 1935 and 1937 was yet another expression of the president's desire to ensure American freedom of action through methods similar to those advocated by the legalistic moralists. By 1935 many Americans wanted a blanket statement of the American position in regard to future foreign wars, a formal detailing of the terms of neutrality that would prevent future presidents from being drawn into such conflicts as World War I. The first Neutrality Act of August 1935 put a mandatory embargo on shipments of "arms, ammunition and implements of war" to all foreign belligerents, but left it up to the president to determine what the "implements of war" were, to decide when and if to withhold American protection from citizens traveling on belligerent vessels, and to declare precisely when the act should be invoked. A compromise between the Roosevelt camp, who wanted the executive to have the power to define neutrality (and thus discriminate against those nations it viewed as potential enemies), and those who demanded a posture of complete American neutrality in all foreign conflicts, the act satisfied no one. It would be revised in 1936 and again in 1937, outlawing loans to belligerents and installing a "cash-and-carry" system for belligerent nations doing business in the United States. But the essential conflict between the two schools of neutrality, the Rooseveltian and the absolutist, remained largely unchanged throughout this period.

On October 2, 1935, Roosevelt revealed the complexity of his attitudes toward neutrality and nationalism in a speech at San Diego. Stating that it was "not surprising" that many Americans feared being dragged into another war similar to "the folly of twenty years ago," the president went on to say that in "the face of this apprehension the American people can have but one concern —the American people can have but one sentiment: despite what happens in continents overseas, the United States of America shall and must remain, as long ago the Father of our country prayed that it might remain—unentangled and free." But typically, Roosevelt immediately stood this argument on its head by declaring, "Yet in our inner individual lives we can never be indifferent, and we assert for ourselves complete freedom to embrace, to profess and to observe the principles for which our flag has so long been the lofty symbol."

The apparent contradiction in these statements was given form during that same October by the American response to the Italian war against Ethiopia. According to one story recounted by his close aide and friend, Harry Hopkins, "The President said that world sympathy was with Ethiopia. His certainly are. He scanned the news dispatches and everything favorable to Ethiopia brought a loud 'Good.' " Roosevelt activated the same neutrality law he had formerly criticized, knowing that by withholding arms and preventing Americans from traveling on Italian cruise ships he would be effectively damaging Italy's war effort. But by the terms of that same act, American oil could and did continue to flow to Italy. In this instance, though the legislation proved useful to FDR's personal goals of inflicting some degree of punishment on Italy, the oil shipments prevented any significant hindrance of Italian aggression.

When civil war broke out in Spain in July 1936, Roosevelt was quick to ask Congress to extend rather than restrict the terms of the Neutrality Act in order to make it cover civil disorders and thereby bar any American influence in that conflict, either direct or indirect. In this case, his interest was not the cause of the underdog but the prevention of another European war. As Secretary Hull later recalled, "Our policy had nothing to do with our views on the right or wrong side in the Spanish Civil War. We were not judging between the two sides." To Roosevelt and Hull, the preeminent consideration was "our own security," and that security seemed deeply threatened by the possibility that the United States might be dragged into another European conflict. The presence of German and Italian troops in Spain only heightened this concern. Roosevelt's determination to remain aloof from the struggle by following the British and French lead in a policy of nonintervention, though it angered many Americans who viewed such alignment as being leaguelike, proved unmovable.

The Italian and Spanish experiences showed not only Roosevelt's acceptance of the legalistic-moralistic line on neutrality and internationalism, but also the remarkable extent to which the president viewed European affairs as the principal source of future threats to American security. Certainly, this outlook was influenced by his uncanny ability to sense the public mood—his actions during both the Ethiopian and the Spanish civil wars (neither of which were publicly viewed as cause for extreme American interference) stayed well within the bounds demanded by public opinion. Yet Roosevelt's reactions to these European crises were far more than mere deference to the public will, and his recognition of the Soviet Union in 1933, his unsuccessful attempt to get the United States into the World Court in 1935 and his many direct messages to Hitler and Mussolini gave further proof of a deep personal tendency to view Europe as the most potentially dangerous area of the world for U.S. interests.

All of which made Roosevelt, like Stimson before him, inclined to pursue a policy based on the preservation of American interests and the status quo in the Far East. But the Far East, since 1933, had become far more volatile than the region Stimson had once tried to manage.

In April 1934, Japanese Foreign Minister Eiji Amau had announced the "Amau Doctrine," which stated that Japan had special rights in Eastern Asia and was opposed to any other nation giving aid to China. The doctrine had obvious parallels to the 1823 pronouncement of James Monroe and John Quincy Adams, and Japanese statesmen made the most of those parallels. Henry Stimson, out of the State Department at the time but still greatly interested in the Far Eastern question, tried to draw a distinct difference between the Amau and Monroe doctrines by once again declaring that American policy with respect to the Caribbean and Latin America "has been to maintain the status quo," while, "on the contrary, judged by the action of the Japanese government and the statements of many of their leaders, their policy has been to overthrow the status quo in Manchuria to Japan's own advantage." Privately, President Roosevelt agreed with this assessment; publicly, the American government made no forceful response to Amau's statement, thereby hoping both to calm Tokyo's apprehensions about Western designs in Asia and to dampen the ambitions of Japanese expansionists.

Instead, the American silence only encouraged those in Japan who preferred to assert the empire's special rights in the Far East with even more force than Amau had. In December 1934, Tokyo denounced the terms of the Washington and London Naval treaties. Yet another naval conference had been scheduled for late 1935, with the proviso that if the participants could not reach agreement on revised terms, the existing treaties would expire. The Japanese seemed ready to abrogate the treaties unless they were granted full naval parity with the United States and Great Britain. Some considered the Japanese threat a bluff; but in January of 1936, Japan did walk out of the London meeting when the British and Americans attempted to stick to unequal naval ratios.

The February 1936 mutiny of extremist army officers in Tokyo (among them Colonel Kingoro Hashimoto) against high-level moderates in the imperial cabinet revived Western fears that the Japanese government was falling increasingly under the sway of the new breed of army officers, with their semimystical blend of socialism, militarism and fanatical devotion to their emperor. That many of the conspirators escaped severe punishment meant more to foreign observers than the fact that key Japanese officials and high-ranking officers—including General Hideki Tojo, then serving in Manchuria—denounced the attempted coup d'état as inexcusable.

And when hostilities broke out between Chinese and Japanese troops in July of the following year, those same Western observers —including Henry Stimson and Franklin Roosevelt—saw them as further links in the chain of Japanese aggression. Roosevelt chose to ignore any Chinese responsibility for the fighting, and once again to make clever use of the Neutrality Act: finding that no formal state of war existed between the two nations, he allowed arms shipments from America to reach Chiang Kai-shek. This only made it more difficult for Japan's moderates to check the army's extreme behavior in the Chinese war, behavior that included summer bombings of Chinese cities and a subsequent heavy loss of civilian life; for with world opinion growing ever more hostile, more and more Japanese started to doubt that their program of economic and political expansion could be carried out peacefully.

In response to expanding aggression in both the Far East and Europe, President Roosevelt delivered one of the most powerful, eloquent and ultimately confusing speeches of his career on October 5, 1937, in Chicago. Citing the decline of the "political situation in the world," Roosevelt went on to say that the "high aspirations expressed in the Briand-Kellogg Peace Pact and the hopes for peace thus raised have of late given way to a haunting fear of calamity. . . . Innocent peoples, innocent nations, are being cruelly sacrificed to a greed for power and supremacy which is devoid of all sense of justice and humane considerations." The problem was easy enough for Roosevelt to define—but when it came to solutions, the president was far more uncertain, and in his uncertainty he echoed the legalistic moralists: "There must be a return to a belief in the pledged word, in the value of a signed treaty. There must be recognition of the fact that national morality is as vital as private morality." Then came the crux of the speech:

"It seems to be unfortunately true that the epidemic of world lawlessness is spreading. When an epidemic of physical disease starts to spread, the community approves and joins in a quarantine of the patients in order to protect the health of the community against the spread of the disease. . . . [T]he will for peace must express itself to the end that nations that may be tempted to violate their agreements and the rights of others will desist from such a course."

Because of these last statements, there was immediate speculation throughout the country that in his "Quarantine Speech," Roosevelt—despite his emphasis on "the pledged word"—might be departing from the legalistic-moralistic reliance on the power of public opinion and opening the way for the kind of economic sanctions and perhaps even military moves that Herbert Hoover and Henry Stimson had always ruled out.

Yet at a press conference on the very next day, Roosevelt was quick to say, "Look, 'sanctions' is a terrible word to use. They are out of the window." When asked if that meant the president would rely on future world conferences, Roosevelt answered, "No; con-

ferences are out of the window. You never get anywhere with a
conference." There followed questioning on the subject of neutrality: "How can you be neutral if you are going to align yourself with
one group of nations?" Roosevelt replied, "There are methods in
the world that have never been tried yet." "But at any rate,"
pressed one exasperated reporter, "that is not an indication of
neutral attitude—'quarantine the aggressors' and 'other nations of
the world.' " Roosevelt's answer to this was perhaps the most characteristic statement he had yet made: "I can't give you any clue to
it. You will have to invent one."

We know now that Roosevelt in fact had no specific plan for
countering the actions of what he called the "bandit nations"—
Germany, Italy and Japan—at the time of the Quarantine Speech.
Instead, he was trying to urge the nations of the world to find new
ways of controlling aggression and at the same time to get a reading of American public opinion on the subject. It was that reading,
when it came, that caused him to back away from forceful action.
Though many American citizens shared Roosevelt's shock at the
behavior of Japan, Germany and Italy and liked the overall tone
of his speech, few were ready to support programs that might lead
to war. Roosevelt would later remark of this period that "It's a
terrible thing to look over your shoulder when you are trying to
lead—and to find no one there." As a result, any stiff response to
Japanese moves in China was ruled out, despite the objections of
Secretaries Ickes and Morgenthau.

This discrepancy in American behavior—the deeply offensive
labels applied to Japanese leaders combined with an apparent unwillingness to act either diplomatically or militarily on those sentiments—only caused confusion in Tokyo. When the League of
Nations called the Brussels Conference in November 1937, to discuss Japan's behavior (the United States attended as a guest
power), it was not surprising that the Japanese refused to participate. The feeling of being increasingly ostracized from the world
community i¹ duced Tokyo not to rejoin the ranks of international
cooperation but instead to sink further into a mood of defiance.
That Roosevelt apparently considered the Chinese Nationalists
(who had exhibited brutality and chauvinism of their own) "inno-
cents" aggravated this trend, and alienated an increasing number
of responsible Japanese moderates.

The American response to the sinking of the *Panay* added to
Tokyo's confusion. Roosevelt condemned the attack in strong lan-

guage, and believed its perpetrators had official sanction. Yet in the end he accepted the Japanese apology—which showed every sign of being deeply sincere—and the reparations payment. Once again, there seemed to be little consistency in American policy. What the Japanese could not know was that this shifting of the U.S. position was a further sign of Roosevelt's desire for a return to the status quo in the Pacific so that he could concentrate on Europe.

After the *Panay* attack, the president did dispatch Captain Royal E. Ingersoll of the navy's War Plans Division to London to discuss joint strategy with Britain in the event of a Pacific war—but Ingersoll left Washington *after* Roosevelt had accepted Japan's apology and payment, and his talks never amounted to any concrete contingency plans. Indeed, when the Joint Army and Navy Board produced its revised "Plan Orange" in 1938, it envisioned a defensive Pacific effort by the United States, and drew a triangular "position in readiness" between Alaska, Hawaii and Panama. Strategically, then, the Philippines and the American military presence in China meant as little as they ever had; but Roosevelt's strong language continued to alienate Japanese leaders.

Prominent among those in Tokyo so affected was Prince Fumimaro Konoye, who by late 1938 had become prime minister. The scion of an established aristocratic family, Konoye was disdainful of Japan's big businessmen and was favorable to socialist domestic policies. A complex man, slight and exceptionally insightful, Konoye was until the mid-1930s a confirmed moderate—but this had not prevented him from delivering regular warnings to the world about the inevitably tragic consequences of Western intransigence in the Far East. Konoye always hoped to solve these problems through negotiation and compromise, but by 1938 he realized this might no longer be possible.

On November 3 of that year, with the Japanese army apparently successful in China, Konoye announced a "New Order" in the Far East, one that would put Japan in a position of regional leadership and have as its object the steady removal of prejudicial Western influences and concessions. In the same statement, Konoye said that Japan would consider herself released from the obligations of any and all previous treaties, and would no longer support the policy of the Open Door.

Konoye seemed to have timed his message well. Both the United States and Great Britain were preoccupied with the deteriorating

European situation—the German annexation of Austria and the Munich Pact on Czechoslovakia had both taken place earlier that year. It was true that by early 1939 a rising number of American leaders, including Stimson, were criticizing Roosevelt and demanding a firmer stand in regard to Japan. The former secretary of state, having admitted the failure of legalistic moralism to affect Japanese behavior in 1931, had begun to swing around toward a policy of economic coercion, which, however, bypassed any program that might effectively have accommodated the Japanese by granting them predominance in such vital regions as Manchuria and thereby discouraged further aggression. In urging this policy, Stimson was joined by many thoughtful Americans. But despite such growing sentiment, Konoye correctly guessed that even these domestic critics of American policy saw European instability as the central threat to American security.

When the U.S. Joint Army and Navy Board began to formulate its "Rainbow Plans" for the defense of the Western Hemisphere in May 1939, it based all of its assumptions on the primacy of the Nazi threat, further demonstrating the rising American concern with Europe. The only real action taken by Roosevelt in Far Eastern affairs during this period was the July announcement that in six months the United States would terminate its 1911 trade agreement with Japan—a step hardly likely to moderate, or even affect, Japanese behavior. Finally, when European hostilities broke out in September 1939, Roosevelt's attention was even further diverted from Japanese expansionism in Asia.

The unclear signals emanating from Washington—all based on a desire to preserve a Far Eastern equilibrium that had long since been shattered—placed even moderates such as Prince Konoye in the position of being encouraged to pursue a policy of expansion through military actions rather than diplomatic initiatives. On the one hand, the Roosevelt administration talked repeatedly of the evils of Japanese aggression. On the other, although the president and his advisers wanted to avoid a Pacific war that the American people would not support and that could only drain resources away from the job of aiding the European Allies in their struggle against the Axis and preparing U.S. forces for a German attack at sea or in the Western Hemisphere, they made no significant effort to bargain with Tokyo. Absence of any serious diplomatic initiative added to Japan's sense of defiant isolation and augmented the rising power of her military extremists, who continued to declare that Tokyo could seek a reckoning with the United States only through force.

The deterioration of Allied fortunes in Europe in the spring of 1940 gave renewed impetus to Japanese expansion in Asia. The defeat of France eased Japan's thrust into Indochina, where she could threaten the oil fields of defeated Holland's holdings in the East Indies. Several presidential advisers continued to tell Roosevelt that only by embargoing shipments of oil and scrap metal to Japan could the United States hope to affect Japanese behavior. But Secretary Hull, still acting in the belief that Japanese moderates somehow could and would restrain the militarists, rejected such schemes. Ambassador Joseph Grew in Tokyo echoed this view, and when Roosevelt finally did agree to a preliminary embargo on oil and scrap in July, it was so limited as to be virtually meaningless. Throughout this period, diplomatic contacts between the two nations continued to be fruitless. The United States refused to accommodate the Japanese in East Asia or the Pacific; Japan could not survive without either such an accommodation or forceful expansion; the fighting in China went on.

In late July, Prince Konoye amplified his New Order declaration by proclaiming the "Greater East Asia Co-Prosperity Sphere," in which Japan was to replace the Western nations as the driving force behind Far Eastern commerce and politics. At the same time, Konoye appointed General Hideki Tojo—a confirmed expansionist although never a radical in the Hashimoto mold—as war minister. Soon thereafter Ambassador Grew, in his famous "Green Light" message, reversed his longtime stand and warned that "continued patience and restraint on the part of the United States may and probably will lead to developments which will render Japanese-American relations progressively precarious." Interior Secretary Ickes, still arguing for a complete embargo on oil shipments to Japan, pointed out that, "We didn't keep Japan out of Indo-China by continuing to ship scrap-iron, nor will we keep her out of the Dutch East Indies by selling her our oil."

Japan's signing of the Tripartite Pact with Germany and Italy on September 27, 1940, was also ominous—yet even this development led to no serious diplomatic initiatives on the part of the United States. The prevailing sentiment in the Roosevelt administration was that any threat to the security of either the United States or Latin America would come from Germany—Hull himself believed that the "danger" of German penetration in "the Western Hemisphere was real and imminent." Chief of Naval Operations Harold Stark and Army Chief of Staff George Marshall stressed this point to Congress in November 1940, when they advocated a "Germany first" strategy.

As American support of Great Britain was stepped up early in 1941, Secretary Hull finally did engage in two sets of negotiations with Japanese diplomatic representatives, one in the spring and one in the fall. Each set of talks revealed Hull's fundamental misunderstanding of Japan's position and yet at the same time Japanese willingness to consider solutions that, while they would have forever precluded any return to a Far Eastern status quo, might have avoided a serious rupture between the two governments. Certainly, during these talks with Hull, the Japanese always asked for terms that would have placed them in an advantageous, even predominant, position in the Far East. But the opportunity to negotiate a lesser accommodation of the island empire had long since passed, as was evident by Prince Konoye's resignation in October and his replacement as prime minister by General Tojo.

Unwilling or perhaps unable to accept all this, Hull discounted the Japanese proposals, and on December 7, 1941, Americans felt the full effects of their unwillingness to come to a reckoning in the East. The bombing of Pearl Harbor had been years in the making. It was doubtless impossible that during a few short weeks in November, Cordell Hull and the special emissaries of the Japanese government could have countered the effects of such longstanding conditions. President Roosevelt—who never wanted war in the Pacific, but who had, largely through his fixation on Europe and his static diplomatic approach to Japan, all but eliminated any other solution—was presented with the greatest threat to American security since the burning of Washington in 1814.

It was singularly appropriate that as he turned to meet that threat, Roosevelt did so with the aid of a man who had had a profound influence on his own policies toward the Far East and toward the American perimeter of interests generally. On June 19, 1940, Henry Stimson had been in his law office in New York when the telephone rang. "I was called up by the President who offered me the position of Secretary of War," Stimson recorded. Roosevelt "said he was very anxious to have me accept because everybody was running around at loose ends in Washington and he thought

I would be a stabilizing factor in whom both the Army and the public would have confidence."

Stimson proved far more comfortable with, and effective in, the post of secretary of war during the coming great crisis than he had been as a spokesman for the legalistic-moralistic movement. Roosevelt, too, found in war a situation that reconciled many of the apparent contradictions in his foreign policy. And both men drew one overriding lesson from the experiences of the 1920s and 1930s and the subsequent Japanese attack on Pearl Harbor: events that threatened American security, even on the perimeter of U.S. interests, must always evoke an immediate and forceful American response. Dynamic opponents would have to be met with dynamic policies, not moral invective. This was the great legacy of the Stimson-Roosevelt era—and it would dominate American foreign policy in the decades following World War II.

V I I

DEFINING THE PERIMETER

1945–1968

"SOMEWHERE across the broad globe the armed forces of some Communist power were expecting soon to go into action." In late May and early June of 1950, intelligence reports to this effect reached the desk of George F. Kennan, the U.S. State Department's leading Soviet expert. The reports left Kennan frankly "puzzled." He had recently stepped down as the head of State's Policy Planning Staff after a series of disagreements with his superiors over U.S.–European relations and the role of his staff in policy formulation, and he was due to leave the department altogether at the end of June. But Kennan had spent his life studying the Soviet Union in particular and communist behavior generally —any report that indicated a significant move on the part of the USSR or one of its client-states was entirely too tantalizing to ignore. Kennan and his fellow Russian experts had immediately undertaken an "intensive scrutiny" of the disposition of the Soviet Union itself, and this study had "satisfied us that it was not Soviet forces to which these indications related. This left us with the forces of the various satellite regimes, but which?"

Despite a soft-spoken manner and a fragile physical constitution, Kennan was an intellectually vigorous foreign service officer, renowned for his detailed research and eloquent reporting. With characteristic intensity he set about determining which communist nation was preparing for aggression. "Summoning the various experts to the table," he later recalled, "we toured the horizons of the Soviet bloc." Possibilities were discussed and discarded, and eventually the subject of Korea came up. In 1945 that peninsula—the focus of Russian, Chinese and Japanese ambitions during the nineteenth and early twentieth centuries—had been divided at the 38th parallel between the forces of the United States and the Soviet Union following the surrender of Japan. The division had supposedly been for military purposes alone, each of the victorious allies assigned the task of disarming Japanese troops within its zone. But in the years since the surrender the arrangement had taken on a political dimension, with both the United States and the Soviets setting up client regimes under repressive strongmen.

Considering the possibility of an attack by North Korea against the southern republic, Kennan and his colleagues were informed by the Pentagon and by General Douglas MacArthur's headquarters in Tokyo that the idea was out of the question. Despite the withdrawal of most American occupational forces in 1948, the Republic of Korea could stand up to communist aggression. Indeed, the military told Kennan, "our greatest task . . . was to restrain the South Koreans from resorting to arms to settle their differences with the north." The possibility of aggression from the North was therefore discarded; but this offered Kennan no comfort, for "nowhere else . . . could we see any possibility of an attack, and we came away from the exercise quite frustrated." In such a state of mind, Kennan left for his farm in Pennsylvania on the morning of Saturday, June 24.

On that same Saturday, Kennan's chief, Secretary of State Dean G. Acheson, was winding up a week of speeches, press conferences and cabinet meetings with a welcome day of rest at his own farm, Harewood, in Sandy Springs, Maryland. Acheson was prevented from ever leaving the world of official Washington completely behind by a special white telephone that had been installed at Harewood and hooked up to the White House switchboard. It rang several times that Saturday, breaking the summer stillness and calling the secretary away from the gladiola garden that consumed much of his free time. But none of the news was momentous, and

Acheson did manage to get "some hours of gardening and a good dinner" in before retiring to read himself to sleep. The only further source of annoyance were the "movements of security officers changing guard during the night," a sound that "echoed through that small house." Acheson was not used to such heavy security, but it had become a necessary precaution—the secretary's frequent clashes with the communist-hunting Senator Joseph McCarthy and his followers had produced hate mail, some of it threatening. It was "a regimen not conducive to relaxation," but Acheson, a man with a deeply ingrained sense of humor, made the best of a bad situation as night descended on Harewood.

Meanwhile, one of Acheson's lesser lieutenants, W. Bradley Connors, in charge of public affairs for State's Division of Far Eastern Affairs, was at home in his Washington apartment. At just past eight in the evening Connors received a call from Donald Gonzales, Washington bureau chief of United Press International. Gonzales said he had received word from UPI's correspondent in South Korea that an attack had been launched across the 38th parallel by the North Korean communists; UPI was looking for confirmation. Connors broke off the discussion and immediately tried to call the American embassy in the South Korean capital of Seoul. But because of the time difference, the switchboards in Seoul were closed down. Connors left his apartment and made straight for the State Department.

At 9:26 Connors was at his post to receive a cable from John J. Muccio, the American ambassador in Seoul: ACCORDING KOREAN ARMY REPORTS WHICH PARTLY CONFIRMED BY [American] K[orean] M[ilitary] A[ssistance] G[roup] FIELD ADVISOR REPORTS NORTH KOREAN FORCES INVADED R[epublic] O[f] K[orea] TERRITORY AT SEVERAL POINTS THIS MORNING. . . . IT WOULD APPEAR FROM NATURE OF ATTACK AND MANNER IN WHICH IT WAS LAUNCHED THAT IT CONSTITUTES ALL OUT OFFENSIVE AGAINST ROK. Muccio cited artillery, infantry, armor and amphibious attacks at several points along and below the 38th parallel; the South Koreans were apparently already in retreat. Connors immediately got on the phone and contacted his chief, Assistant Secretary of State for Far Eastern Affairs Dean Rusk, who that night was a guest of Washington columnist Joseph Alsop.

Some months earlier Rusk had won Secretary of State Acheson's "high respect and gratitude" by offering to take over the Far Eastern desk, a position that had turned into a controversial post after

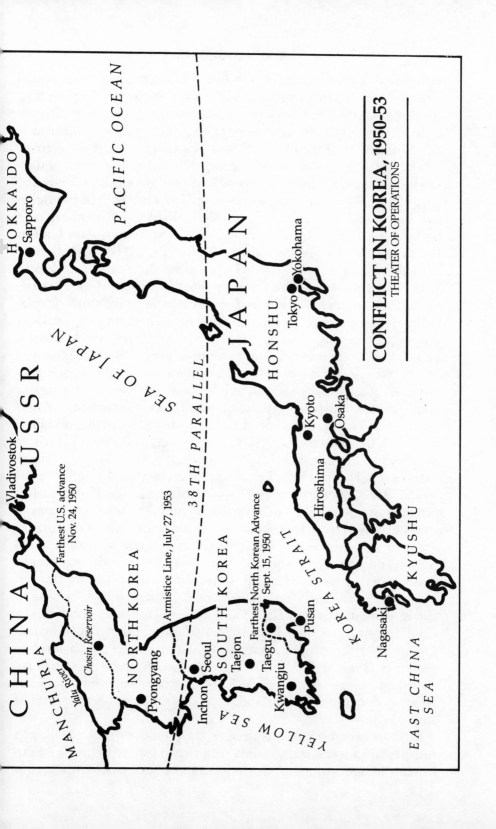

CONFLICT IN KOREA, 1950-53
THEATER OF OPERATIONS

PACIFIC OCEAN

HOKKAIDO
Sapporo

U S S R
CHINA
Vladivostok

SEA OF JAPAN

JAPAN

HONSHU

Tokyo
Yokohama

Kyoto
Osaka

Hiroshima

38TH PARALLEL

Farthest U.S. advance
Nov. 24, 1950

MANCHURIA

Yalu River

Chosin Reservoir

NORTH KOREA

Pyongyang

Armistice Line, July 27, 1953

Inchon Seoul

SOUTH KOREA

Taejon

Farthest North Korean Advance
Sept. 15, 1950

Taegu

Kwangju

Pusan

KOREA STRAIT

YELLOW SEA

KYUSHU

Nagasaki

EAST CHINA
SEA

China had been "lost" to communism through the victory of Mao Tse-tung in 1949. Pro-Nationalist (or simply anticommunist) Americans, especially in Congress, had blamed the loss on ineptitude or possibly even treachery at the State Department. Rusk, often inscrutable behind a tight smile, had served as an intelligence officer in China under General Joseph "Vinegar Joe" Stilwell during the Second World War, and he had cited his experiences in the region in making the offer to take over Far Eastern Affairs. Acheson had been happy to accept, calling Rusk's offer "above and beyond the call of duty"—praise that the secretary, who himself had taken much of the heat for the China loss, did not offer lightly.

Rusk's own view of world affairs during the years since World War I led him to read the reported North Korean attack as of the utmost importance. "There never was a balance [of power], if by balance we mean equilibrium," he had recently said of the interwar years. "If by balance we mean contending forces which express themselves at times in war and at times in peace, then we have had several basic rearrangements of the balance of power in one generation." Rusk's stark view of the balance of power as unreliable and ever-changing meant that any communist advance in any part of the world could and indeed must be viewed as potentially dangerous. The assistant secretary immediately left Alsop's for the State Department.

He arrived to find that the assistant secretary for United Nations affairs, John Hickerson, and Ambassador-at-Large Philip C. Jessup had also been called in. The three immediately telephoned the secretary of state at Harewood. Acheson shared the alarm of his subordinates, and ordered that the secretary-general of the United Nations be notified of the attack and asked to schedule an emergency meeting of the Security Council for the following day. In addition, the chiefs of staff of the armed services were to be located and informed. As the various top military men were tracked down, a sense of dramatic urgency spread throughout the government—and when Hickerson, pursuant to Acheson's order, got through to Secretary-General Trygve Lie at the United Nations, the latter received the news of the North Korean action with the somewhat astonished statement: "My God, Jack, this is war against the United Nations."

Rusk, Hickerson and Jessup next got in touch with the Pentagon and began to work out possible American responses to the North Korean attack. Acheson, in the meantime, put through a call to

Independence, Missouri. President Harry S Truman had gone home for the weekend to attend to family business, and when Acheson's call came through he had just finished dinner and was in his library. "Mr. President," Truman heard Acheson say, "I have very serious news. The North Koreans have invaded South Korea." Truman's first reaction was "I must get back to the capital," but Acheson urged him to wait until more was known. The secretary informed Truman that he had requested an emergency session of the UN Security Council, at which he hoped to secure condemnation of the North Korean attack; but for the moment, American actions hinged on the effectiveness of South Korea's resistance. Truman, as was generally the case, approved both Acheson's actions and his advice, and each of the two men went uneasily to bed. But in Washington, at the State and Defense departments, it was only the beginning of a long night of waiting, planning and endless telephoning.

By eleven-thirty the next morning, it was clear that the South Koreans were in deep trouble, and Acheson called Truman to tell him so. A North Korean tank column was moving relentlessly toward Seoul; it was already time to start thinking about evacuating the city. As Truman ordered his presidential plane readied for the trip back to Washington, Acheson got into his convertible and drove top down to the State Department, where waiting reporters noticed that the usually punctilious secretary was carrying, not wearing, his jacket; the trouble must be real, indeed.

In his office, Acheson was quickly briefed on further developments. The military situation had only gotten worse, but diplomatically, the United States had already scored a victory: the UN Security Council had approved an American resolution condemning the North Korean attack as "a breach of the peace." Passage of the resolution had been allowed by the absence of the Soviet delegate, who, Acheson assumed, was continuing the Russian boycott of council sessions that had been prompted in February by the UN's refusal to admit the People's Republic of China. Because of the Russian absence and for the first time since its creation, the UN seemed ready to vote for concrete action to counter aggression; as the reality of this became clear, Acheson had all staff and messages kept out of his office for two hours while he considered its deep implications.

At the same time, President Truman was thinking hard about the Korean situation as he returned to Washington. "In my generation," he later wrote, "this was not the first occasion when the strong had attacked the weak. I recalled some earlier instances: Manchuria, Ethiopia, Austria. . . . Communism was acting in Korea just as Hitler, Mussolini and the Japanese had acted ten, fifteen, and twenty years earlier. I felt certain that if South Korea was allowed to fall Communist leaders would be emboldened to override nations closer to our own shores." At that point, Truman radioed Acheson to be at Blair House (the White House was being renovated at the time) that night for dinner along with his advisers and all top defense personnel. Truman had already made his decision: "If this was allowed to go unchallenged it would mean a third world war, just as similar incidents had brought on the second world war."

At dinner that night, Truman found his cabinet and advisers in unanimous agreement with his assessment. Acheson led the way, spelling out his belief that "we could not accept the conquest of this important area by a Soviet puppet under the very guns of our defensive perimeter with no more than words and gestures in the Security Council." Force was the only answer to such a threat; collective force, if the UN could be made to act quickly enough, unilateral force if it could not. Specifically, Acheson recommended that General MacArthur be authorized to give the South Korean army all the matériel it required, that the air force be directed to cover the evacuation from Seoul, and that the U.S. Seventh Fleet be sent into the Formosa Strait to ensure that neither Mao Tsetung nor Chiang Kai-shek use the Korean hostilities as a cover for operations against his opponent.

The following day, Acheson added to his suggestions by including direct American air support of South Korean ground actions and additional troops for American garrisons in the Philippines. But the secretary did not stop there. He proposed increased American aid to the French in Indochina, on the chance that Korea might be only the first of several communist attacks in Asia. He also recommended that the United States sponsor a Security Council resolution calling on any and all UN members to aid South Korea. Acheson, on the advice of George Kennan, was betting that the Soviets would continue to boycott the council sessions. And the bet paid off. On June 27 Acheson got his resolution and with it international sanction for American action, sanction that he greatly prized but had not waited for—American warplanes were already at work in the skies above Korea, swift and grim testament to

Truman's and Acheson's determination that the errors of the 1930s should not be repeated during their term of leadership.

Throughout the rest of the week, the lessons of the thirties haunted not only policymakers in Washington but military officers in the Far East as the fighting continued to go badly for South Korea. By Thursday, June 29, General MacArthur's personal representative in South Korea was reporting that despite American air support the status quo antebellum could not be restored without the deployment of American ground forces. In typically reckless fashion, General MacArthur himself visited the front and returned to Tokyo to confirm that without the intervention of American troops, there would be disaster in Korea. Truman wondered whether such American intervention would not lead to a similar response on the part of one of the communist powers; Acheson informed him that "it was State's view that while the Chinese might intervene, the Russians would not." MacArthur was asking for one brigade immediately, to be built up to two divisions. Acheson strongly urged the president to assent. On Friday morning, June 30, the decision was made—American ground forces would go to the front. As Acheson later recalled, "We were then fully committed in Korea."

The decision met with remarkably wide-ranging support both within and outside the administration. The American public and America's allies alike applauded the speedy resolve of Truman and Acheson—but the secretary of state had experienced enough professional and public scorn in his long career to know that such feelings might change. If the day should ever come when the decision to go to war in Korea without consulting the Congress were viewed as a mistake, Acheson (an accomplished lawyer) would want precedents with which to refute any allegations of wrongdoing. To this end, the secretary prepared a relatively short but key memorandum on the "Authority of the President to Repel the Attack in Korea," which was delivered to Truman and the Congress on July 3.

Listing eighty-five specific instances in which presidents of the United States had ordered American troops into action without congressional authority, the Acheson Memorandum was a powerful exposition of the expanding nature of American national security during the first 170 years of the nation's history. Citing constitutional authorities such as William Howard Taft and Charles Evans Hughes as well as a number of other Supreme Court justices, Acheson argued that "The basic interest of the United States is international peace and security. The United States has, throughout its history, upon orders of the Commander in Chief of the Armed Forces and without congressional authorization, acted to prevent violent and unlawful acts in other states from depriving the United States and its nationals of the benefits of such peace and security." The memo read like a solid legal brief, cogent, well-researched and leading to the central point: "The continued defiance of the United Nations by North Korean authorities" represented "a threat to international peace and security, a threat to the peace and security of the United States and to the security of United States forces in the Pacific."

But it was in its use of precedents that the Acheson Memorandum was especially revealing. Beginning with the expulsion of pirates from Amelia Island and "the protection of American citizens and American territory" in "the Spanish Floridas in 1817," Acheson compiled an impressive case history of American unilateralism. It included action in Hawaii in 1893, when the United States sought to frustrate the designs of the British and the Japanese; President Taft's occupation of Nicaragua in 1912; and Woodrow Wilson's long history of intervention in Mexico, the Caribbean and Central America. It was an overwhelming list, in the face of which it would have been difficult to argue that Truman's action in Korea was in any way illegal or even outside the realm of established American behavior.

Yet the decision to intervene in Korea was not merely in keeping with the American tradition; it dramatically broadened and amplified the same. By directly tying American security to the southern portion of a peninsula that had historically been of little or no importance to the United States, Truman and Acheson knowingly extended the perimeter of American vital interests and signaled to the world that they would be constantly on the alert for any threat to that perimeter. The president, the secretary of state and their subordinates all believed they had learned the lessons of Munich and the lessons of Pearl Harbor. On June 30 they acted on that conviction, and brought to a forceful crescendo the expansion of American security interests that had begun in 1941.

Personally and professionally, Joseph Stalin was as obsessed as any American leader of this or any other period with the idea of making his nation safe from foreign threats. As a ruler, Stalin was the spiritual inheritor not only of Lenin but of the czars, who had seen their own empire crisscrossed by would-be conquerors since its creation. When Germany once again assaulted Russia in 1941— opening a campaign that would destroy seventeen thousand Russian cities and towns and cost twenty million Russian lives—the Soviet leader became determined that, following the expulsion of the Germans, he would forever seal off the avenues of invasion that had plagued his nation for centuries.

In the West, to Stalin this meant firm control over Poland, once a fierce invader in its own right, and, in modern times, a tempting pathway to Russia because of its weakness. It meant, too, a dominant voice in the affairs of the Balkan nations, whose squabbles had dragged Russia into the tragedy of the First World War. And above all, it meant the final breaking up of Germany and its transformation into a neutral, unarmed state that would never again be allowed to ravage the Soviet Union. As for the East, the American Ambassador, Averell Harriman, summed up Stalin's approach in a note from Moscow: "Japan has for two generations been a constant menace to Russian security in the Far East and the Soviets wish now to be secure from this threat." Such a goal rested on control not only of Mongolia and Manchuria, but of at least the northern portion of Korea and several key islands in the northwestern Pacific. Added to these larger security concerns were others, equally long-standing—Afghanistan, northern Iran, and control of the Dardanelles, to respond to Russia's need for a warm-water port.

But if Stalin inherited the traditional goals of Russian security, he did not inherit czarist methods of achieving them. Under the czars, Russia had been an active participant in the European balance of power. Her security had depended on the negotiating skills of her diplomats and on a willingness to commit to alliances with other powers, as well as on the strength of her armies. But because of Russia's isolation brought on by the 1917 Bolshevik Revolution, Soviet leaders had been forced to adopt a more unilateral style in international affairs. Lenin and Trotsky had tried to interact with outside powers, but had been answered with the Siberian intervention and an economic blockade. All of these experiences convinced Stalin that Russia's security was her own affair, and, more specifically, *his* own affair, to be pursued in the only way left to him by the noncommunist world—unilaterally.

This as much as any other single factor made Stalin's Russia an effective rival of the United States. By 1941, both nations had arrived, by radically different paths, at similar goals—security that would not depend on the actions of other powers. It is consequently a misperception to regard Soviet-American relations during and after the Second World War as strictly a "mirroring" process. Rather, each nation was on a course that paralleled the other's, a condition most dramatically demonstrated by the fact that in that fateful year of 1941 both suffered devastating surprise attacks.

Perhaps no American better understood Stalin's concept of security—its legitimate as well as its illegitimate dimension—than Franklin Delano Roosevelt. Both men hoped that postwar arrangements would be determined by great power policies. FDR had already embodied this advocacy in a call for a system of "Four Policemen"—the United States, the Soviet Union, Great Britain and China—that he hoped would safeguard international peace. But by late 1943 the president realized that the Chinese government of Chiang Kai-shek was too weak to serve as a member of any such system. At the Teheran Conference in November–December, he abandoned it in favor of the United Nations, a body, however, that would effectively be controlled by a Security Council, where the "Four Policemen" would hold permanent seats. Stalin correctly interpreted this as American acceptance of the notion that postwar affairs would be managed primarily by the Big Three, and that the United Nations itself would be little more than a forum for debate. This belief was solidified by the Russian leader's meeting with Roosevelt and Churchill at the Crimean city of Yalta in February 1945.

The Yalta Conference at which the Big Three reached preliminary agreement on postwar arrangements in Europe and the Far East saw each of the participants seeking a position that would afford his nation maximum security from future threats. In the Far East, Stalin traded recognition of Chiang's Nationalist government and a pledge to declare war against Japan for territorial concessions in a series of negotiations that were both characteristic and revealing. Unconvinced that the Chinese communists under Mao could win and above all obsessed with closing off traditional lines of attack into Russia, Stalin bartered away international communist solidarity for Soviet national security.

But it was in settling the postwar disposition of Europe, and especially Eastern Europe, that the Big Three did their most controversial work. Just before the conference, Averell Harriman had written to Washington, saying that "The overriding consideration in Soviet foreign policy is the preoccupation with 'security,' as Moscow sees it. This objective explains most of the recent Soviet actions which have roused criticism abroad," including "the sponsorship of puppet regimes in all contiguous countries." Churchill had already agreed to such puppet regimes in Romania and Bulgaria; but when Stalin set up a government that was an obvious Soviet client in Poland—the nation for which, as Churchill said at Yalta, Britain "drew the sword"—the British prime minister's deepest suspicions concerning Soviet intentions were fully aroused.

For his part, Stalin sensed that Churchill wished to construct a *cordon sanitaire* around Russia, and quickly countered that for the Soviet Union, Poland was "not only a question of honor but one of security[,] . . . of the life and death of the Soviet State." The Russian premier repeatedly emphasized that twice in a generation Germany had been able to invade Russia because of Polish weakness; Churchill, in turn, complained that the present Soviet-backed Polish government did not represent "even one third of the Polish people." The two European leaders thus reached an impasse—one that seemed especially designed for the talents of Franklin Roosevelt.

Roosevelt fully understood Stalin's fear that a nonaligned Polish state might be a temptation to future conquerors. "We want a Poland that will be thoroughly friendly to the Soviets for years to come," he told Stalin and Churchill. "This is essential." Such a statement seemed to indicate tacit agreement to Stalin's plans for Poland and for Eastern Europe generally, and indeed, there is much to suggest that Roosevelt was prepared to cooperate with the Russian leader *provided* Stalin would make certain concessions to the American president's position as leader of the free world. Foremost among these concessions was the question of free elections in Eastern Europe.

Along with the Far Eastern settlements, plans for the United Nations and agreement on the amount and type of reparations to be demanded of Germany, the final Yalta Accords included a "Declaration on Liberated Europe," which provided that elections would be held in those nations of the continent that had been occupied by the Axis powers. Reporting to the Congress on the results of the conference on March 1, 1945, Roosevelt stressed this provision—but also took pains to prepare the American people for what might well be de facto Soviet control of Poland and Eastern Europe. "Throughout history," he said, "Poland has been the corridor through which attacks on Russia have been made. . . . And you must remember, also, that there had not been any Polish government before 1919 for a great many generations." Referring to Eastern European nationalists such as the leaders of Yugoslavia as "prima donnas," Roosevelt seemed ready to accept effective Russian control of Eastern Europe if Stalin would allow at least the semblance of free elections and thereby protect the American president from charges that he had abandoned the cause of freedom in a large portion of the world.

But following Yalta, elections in Eastern Europe were delayed, Soviet control over the region was forceably tightened and Churchill's criticism of Russian behavior in Poland grew more pointed. Roosevelt, too, became deeply concerned about Russian ambitions. Privately, FDR was heard to express the extreme view that Stalin "has broken every one of the promises he made at Yalta." At the same time, the American president feared that Churchill's stand on Poland might expose England and the United States "to the charge that we are attempting to go back on the Crimean decision." Clearly, what had seemed a masterly set of compromises at Yalta had within weeks been deeply endangered by the ambiguous language in which it was framed.

With the issues thus unsettled, Roosevelt suddenly suffered a cerebral hemorrhage in Warm Springs, Georgia, and died on April 12, 1945. What this meant for the United States and for the world was simply and eloquently summed up by Harry Hopkins: "Well —he isn't there now, and we've got to find a way to do things by ourselves." Roosevelt had shared his characteristically pragmatic understanding of the Yalta accords and of how best to deal with Joseph Stalin with precious few people—and this group did not include his little-known vice-president.

Harry S Truman had no history of sympathy for the Soviet Union. Following the Nazi invasion of that country, the Missouri-born machine politician had remarked, "If we see that Germany is winning we ought to help Russia and if Russia is winning we ought to help Germany and that way let them kill as many as possible . . ." Although he did think to add, "I don't want to see Hitler victorious under any circumstances," the remark was revealing, reflecting the attitude of a man whose only experience at dealing with other nations had been service in an artillery regiment in France during World War I. Truman's mastery of the mechanics of foreign policy was destined to grow during his years at the White House, but his fundamental prejudices never truly changed.

This attitude brought the new president into direct confrontation with several members of the cabinet that he inherited from Franklin Roosevelt, most notably Secretary of War Henry Stimson. The failure of legalistic moralism and the part he himself had played in it had caused a dramatic shift in Stimson's point of view toward international relations during the Second World War. While paying lip service to the idea of the United Nations, he, like FDR, preferred all major questions to be settled by the great powers before other nations were included in any discussions. Fundamental to this attitude were recognition of the legitimacy of Russian security goals and an acceptance of Soviet hegemony in Eastern Europe based on the nonconflicting interests of Russia and the United States. "Our respective orbits do not clash geographically," Stimson wrote of the two nations in April 1945, "and I think that on the whole we can probably keep out of clashes in the future."

But at a decisive cabinet meeting on April 23, 1945, Stimson was somewhat shocked to find that Truman's natural inclination was to follow the tough-minded advice of men such as Navy Secretary James Forrestal and former ambassador to Moscow W. Averell Harriman. In Forrestal's forceful mind America's two great historic fears—of European expansionism and hostile ideologies—merged in the form of a Soviet Union whose power was now global, and he consequently believed "that we ought to be more firm with the Russians and hold them up." Harriman, who had been shocked by years of firsthand exposure to Stalin's domestic brutality, also called for "strong words by the President on a strong position." Stimson quickly countered that, while a tough policy might work on smaller questions, Poland and Eastern Europe were "too big to take chances on." Rather, the secretary of war supported Admiral William D. Leahy—FDR's chief of staff and a man who was far from sympathetic to Soviet concerns—when the latter declared that "the Yalta agreement was susceptible to two interpretations."

Truman, however, rejected such opinions, and following the meeting acted on those personal inclinations that Forrestal and Harriman had done so much to reinforce. The United Nations Conference was meeting in San Francisco, and on his way to address it, Soviet Foreign Minister Vyacheslav M. Molotov stopped in to visit with the American president. The meeting quickly turned sour. Truman demanded to know why the Russians had failed to live up to their word on Poland; Molotov replied diplomatically that he was certain all differences between the United States and the Soviet Union on that subject could be worked out. Truman then "replied sharply that an agreement had been reached on Poland and that there was only one thing to do, and that was for Marshal Stalin to carry out that agreement in accordance with his word."

Molotov was indignant, and made no attempt to hide it. "I have never been talked to like that in my life," he said.

"Carry out your agreements," Truman answered tersely, "and you won't get talked to like that."

Whether or not Soviet behavior in Poland and Eastern Europe was in fact a breach of the Yalta accords, or whether, as Admiral Leahy suggested at the April 23 cabinet meeting and as Roosevelt's own behavior before his death seemed to indicate, those accords were open to two interpretations, has been debated since the time the agreements were first made public. But the April 23 meetings with the cabinet and with Molotov indicate that not two weeks after Roosevelt's death and before the actual surrender of Germany, Truman was prepared to identify the Soviet Union as a future source of threats to American security. Victory in the war had, by military necessity, extended the perimeter of American defensive interests; and Truman was determined to see that that perimeter did not contract after the peace, leaving behind it a vacuum of power in a devastated world, a vacuum into which only one power could move—the Soviet Union, inspired by an ideology inherently hostile to American democracy.

Secretary Stimson continued to protest against Truman's position after the April 23 meeting, but in vain. "Some Americans," Stimson wrote on April 26, "are anxious to hang on to exaggerated views of the Monroe Doctrine and at the same time butt into every question that comes up in Central Europe. . . . Our position in the western hemisphere and Russia's in the eastern hemisphere could be adjusted without too much friction." But such an adjustment implied a basic acceptance of the diplomatic principle of spheres of influence, and spheres of influence sounded, to many Americans, suspiciously like another European system of international relations—the balance of power. As far as Truman was concerned, the United States had not fought a great war to set up a new system based on the balance of power; and the president confronted the Russians with these sentiments in his meetings with Stalin at Potsdam in July–August 1945.

But if Truman was not prepared to deal with issues of international security through the creation of spheres of influence, an approach that might have satisfied Stalin, there were also indications that the United States would place only limited faith in any system of collective security. The alliance with Britain was tested early on, when the United States loaned London a desperately needed $3.75 billion on harsh terms that greatly compromised British economic integrity, and hence British power.

In negotiations over the United Nations themselves, American representatives also revealed that America's freedom of action was not to be compromised. The UN Charter's Article 51, composed by Assistant Secretary for Latin American Affairs Nelson Rockefeller and Republican Senator Arthur Vandenberg, stipulated that signatory nations would be allowed to form and join regional defense pacts so long as those pacts did not violate other articles of the charter. At a stroke, the United States both assumed the role of champion of collective security and made certain that should that collective voice ever dissent too greatly from its own, U.S. national security would not be threatened.

In these instances, the Truman administration committed America to a broad range of economic and diplomatic programs that, while rejecting any participation in a system of spheres of influence, reinforced the traditional American reliance on a unilateral approach to national security. In doing so, it also echoed the rhetoric of both Woodrow Wilson and the legalistic moralists. Like the statesmen of the twenties and thirties, and like Wilson himself, Truman was a man of genuine personal commitment to the ideals of collective security—but like all those predecessors, he was never finally prepared to see American security rely solely or even fundamentally on such a system. In short, if Truman did not share Roosevelt's finesse, his penchant for power politics or his intricate understanding of the need for international cooperation, he certainly shared his former chief's ability to reconcile two apparently contradictory positions on the issue of national security.

Further evidence of Truman's determination to place American security above all other considerations was offered throughout 1946. Stalin's famous speech on February 9 of that year, which celebrated the victory of Soviet arms and the vigor of the Soviet state, contained passages that deeply shocked listeners in the West, including the American president. After blaming the recent war on "the development of world economic and political forces on the basis of monopoly capitalism," Stalin went on to insist that "the Soviet social system has proved to be more capable of life[,] . . . more stable" and "a better form of organization of society than any non-Soviet social system." To many in Washington, it sounded like a blatant challenge, "The Declaration," as Justice William O. Douglas called it, "of World War III."

A more tempered though hardly more cheerful outlook was offered by George Kennan (then serving in the Moscow embassy), who was ordered by the State Department to give an assessment of Stalin's February 9 speech. Pleased with the chance to express himself fully, Kennan sent to Washington on February 22 the most wordy cable in State Department history, dubbed and forever known as "the Long Telegram." Despite its verbosity, the cable's central theme was relatively succinct: "At the bottom of the Kremlin's neurotic view of world affairs is [a] traditional and instinctive Russian sense of insecurity." Soviet leaders were bent on undermining the West, said Kennan, in order to ensure their own security; they were therefore primarily most "sensitive to [the] logic of force," and at the same time "impervious to [the] logic of reason." As a response, Kennan stressed a program based not on military adventurism but on rehabilitating the "health and vigor of our own society," so that the Russians would be met at all contested points by the only thing they understood—strength.

The Long Telegram heightened the anti-Soviet suspicions of men like James Forrestal (who adopted it as his credo) and these suspicions now spilled over into the question of postwar Germany. It had originally been the hope of all three victorious allies to establish in that largely shattered nation a unified, neutral state whose powerful industries would be partially dismantled and the rest of them internationally supervised. But many officials in Washington now felt that Stalin's real purpose in calling for a unified, neutral Germany was to create a state that could easily be absorbed into the Soviet orbit. Acting on this fear, the Western Allies began to rethink their strategy on Germany, and to view the Western zones of occupation as a potential bulwark against the spread of communism.

The Truman administration's steady process of identifying the Soviet Union as the primary source of future threats to American security culminated with the submission of a report by the president's special counsel, Clark Clifford, in the fall of 1946. Starting from the position that the Soviets believed conflict with "the capitalist states" to be "inevitable" and that "the aim of current Soviet policy is to prepare for the ultimate conflict by increasing Soviet power," the Clifford Report went on to state that "the U.S.S.R. is seeking wherever possible to weaken the military position and influence of the United States abroad" and was pursuing this goal "with speed, consistency and boldness." American policies, said the report, should match the Soviets by being "global in scope" and heavily reliant on increased military spending, for "a direct threat to American security is implicit in Soviet foreign policy . . ."

On receiving the report, Truman ordered all ten copies of it locked up; while he accepted its findings, he believed they might cause a national furor. For, unlike most of the administration, the American public was still largely confused about the nature of the Soviet threat, and had by no means accepted its primacy. But within five short months, Truman was able to change the national mood, with the help of a brilliant lieutenant capable of sounding an alarm that few Americans were able to ignore.

As a boy in Middletown, Connecticut, during what he later described as "the golden age of childhood," Dean Gooderham Acheson had a pony that did not share its master's passion for imaginative games. "Mean, as well as lazy, and uncooperative," Acheson wrote of the animal, "he knew who was afraid and who would fight back. The timid did well to feed him sugar on a tennis racquet; but he was as gentle as a lamb if one had one's fist cocked for a fast punch in the nose." The lesson stayed with Acheson throughout his life; and when he became the most gifted American statesman of the postwar era, he would often approach his adversaries with that same fist cocked, ready to bargain, but equally ready to deliver a fast punch.

The "golden age of childhood" of which Acheson spoke could, he felt, be definitely fixed at "the last decade of the nineteenth century and the first few years of the twentieth, before the plunge into a motor age and city life swept away the freedom of children and dogs, put them both on leashes and made them prisoners of an adult world." Acheson's early days were full of pastoral amusements, hiking, fishing—and above all, mischief-making. His father, the town's Episcopal pastor and a British citizen, was firm but not punitive with the prankish boy, allowing ample freedom of behavior; and when Dean was forced to leave this idyllic world for the confines of the Groton School, the effect was heartbreaking. "To adapt oneself to so sudden and considerable a change," he later wrote, "required what is now called a 'well-adjusted' personality. Mine apparently was not. At first through surprise, ignorance and awkwardness, later on and increasingly through wilfulness, I bucked the Establishment and the system. One who does this fights the odds. The results were predictable, painful, and clear."

None of Groton's various punishments, however, could take the spirit out of Dean, and following his graduation he decided to season himself with a term on a Canadian railroad gang, an experience he remembered as "one of the most important few months of my life." Learning self-reliance among the tough rail workers, Acheson returned east to attend Yale, where his spirited idiosyncrasies were allowed wide room for growth. He displayed no particular intellectual prowess, but developed his general rowdiness into a somewhat more refined panache. But refinement or no, one quality remained consistently strong in Acheson from his youth through his college days and, indeed, to the end of his life: humor, a humor that was always displayed in a sprightly pair of eyes and an irrepressible grin.

Dedication finally overtook Acheson at Harvard Law School, where, under the tutelage of Felix Frankfurter, his considerable intellectual talents at last began to show themselves. Frankfurter recommended Acheson to Supreme Court Justice Louis D. Brandeis as a suitable clerk. Marriage to a tall, artistic and shrewd young woman from Michigan, Alice Stanley, produced children and an apparently happy family life, and as he became more established Acheson decided to grow a mustache. Rarely has such a seemingly superficial decision had such an effect. The mustache, which Acheson liked to flare up at its ends, not only betrayed its wearer's British heritage, but heightened the impression of superiority that often estranged Acheson from those who did not share his quickness of mind. It has been said that the mustache gave him the appearance of an English brigadier, and indeed, though his own Anglophilia was far from rampant, the term was appropriate—for despite his intellectual condescension, Acheson was middle class and proud of it, an able subordinate willing to faithfully serve a qualified superior.

During his first years in Washington, that superior was Justice

Brandeis, of whom Acheson later said, "to him truth was less than truth unless it were expounded so that people could understand and believe." Acheson himself did not have the common touch that would have permitted him to become the public expounder of truth; nor, during his initial period of governmental service at the Treasury Department, did he approve of Franklin Roosevelt's attitude toward such dispensation. To Acheson, FDR "condescended," generally displaying an attitude that was "patronizing and humiliating. To accord the President the greatest deference and respect should be gratification to any citizen. It is not gratifying to receive the easy greeting which milord might give a promising stable boy and pull one's forelock in return." Acheson left Roosevelt's administration in a dispute over monetary policy, but FDR was impressed with the gentlemanly as well as the intellectual qualities that the younger man displayed during the disagreement, and before the end of World War II Acheson was back in government, serving as assistant secretary of state for economic affairs.

Acheson's private opinions concerning international relations were already well-formed. He had been deeply touched by Woodrow Wilson's struggle and failure during the League of Nations debate in 1919, but such sympathy did not blind his insight; Wilson had failed because the League of Nations had been too much of an ideal, admirable but useless unless backed by the kind of practical strength Americans traditionally relied on to ensure their own security. At the same time, Acheson was aware of the decline of the European balance of power. In a speech at Yale in 1939, he cited that decline as responsible for the rise of fascism. The deterioration of the British empire and the Pax Britannica were especially to blame for the collapse of world order. And in the face of that collapse, "one conclusion stands clear and inevitable at the outset. We must make ourselves so strong that we shall not be caught defenseless or dangerously exposed in any even possible eventuality. . . . I think it clear that with a nation, as with a boxer, one of the greatest assurances of safety is to add reach to power. To this end we need a navy and air force adequate to secure us in both oceans simultaneously." Acheson went on to outline an international economic order stabilized by expanded trade, heightened liberalism and finally American might—already, the idea of a Pax Americana was germinating in his mind.

When talk of a United Nations became widespread, Acheson approached it, typically, with skepticism as well as approval. He still had little patience with idealistic systems of peace that were based on the power of morality. Only strength and determination could make the UN an effective instrument, and by the close of World War II Acheson had become convinced that if that determination did not stem from the leadership of the United States, the new world organization was as doomed to failure as the last: "In the Arab proverb," he said of the United Nations some years later, "the ass that went to Mecca remained an ass, and a policy has little added to it by its place of utterance."

This sense of tempered realism also determined Acheson's attitude toward the Soviet Union. By 1945 Acheson (now under secretary of state) was disposed to support Henry Stimson's view that accommodation with the Russians was possible provided certain hard facts were recognized. When Stimson, after the successful testing of the atomic bomb, went so far as to suggest that the United States actually share the secret of atomic power with the Soviets, many were shocked; but Acheson supported him. "At the present time," Acheson wrote to Truman in September 1945, "the joint development of this discovery with the U.K. and Canada must appear to the Soviet Union to be unanswerable evidence of an Anglo-American combination against them. To their minds, there is much other evidence of this."

The Soviet Union, Acheson went on, "must and will exert every energy to restore the loss of power which this discovery has produced. It will do this, if we attempt to maintain the policy of exclusion, in an atmosphere of suspicion and hostility, thereby exacerbating every present difficulty between us." Acheson considered such developments unfortunate, since he could not "see why the basic interests of the two nations should conflict." But "any long range understanding based on firmness and frankness and mutual recognition of each other's basic interests seems to me impossible under a policy of Anglo-American exclusion of Russia from atomic development. If it is impossible, there will be no organized peace but only an armed truce."

It is ironic that Acheson himself was destined to become one of the chief architects of that "armed truce." But within a year of his communication to Truman on atomic energy, Acheson abandoned Stimson's program of accommodation with the Russians (much as Stimson, in an earlier era, had shunned Elihu Root's call for accommodation of Japan) and joined with those who saw in Soviet behavior far more than simply the determined prosecution of a program of national security. And as Acheson's opinions changed, he drew closer, both personally and professionally, to Truman. The man from Independence fit Acheson's idea of a proper president far more than Roosevelt had. Truman, like Acheson, was a confirmed member of the middle class, a man who had made his own way to the top and did not display the haughty affability of the patrician; to Acheson he was always "the captain with the mighty heart," and the bond between them became unbreakable. Indeed, it was Acheson who was primarily the author of the doctrine that would bear Truman's name, filling much the same role that John Quincy Adams had played for James Monroe in 1823—and producing the most important American foreign policy declaration since that same Monroe Doctrine.

The doctrine itself was prompted by turmoil in the Eastern Mediterranean. In October 1944 Winston Churchill had concluded a secret agreement with Stalin that guaranteed British hegemony in Greece—a nation long viewed by Britain as vital to the security of her empire—in return for Russian control of Romania and Bulgaria. Throughout the Second World War, Greece had been riven by civil conflict—between resistance partisans and Nazi occupation forces, on the one hand, and native factions of the left and right, on the other. In the winter of 1944–45 the British had made a concerted effort to keep Greece's extreme leftists (including the Greek Communist party) out of the government in Athens, and had aided those factions within the center and the right that supported a return to the prewar constitutional monarchy—and British control. In the spring of 1946 the right won an overwhelming victory in the first postwar parliamentary elections, which the left for the most part boycotted, and in September the monarchy was restored. This act brought the Greek communists to the verge of full-fledged revolution and to the leadership of the forces of the wartime Popular Front.

These developments occurred against an ominous backdrop. During the Second World War, Britain and the Soviet Union had occupied Iran in order to prevent her vast oil resources from falling into German hands. This arrangement had been scheduled to end in March 1946—but when that date arrived, the Soviets were slow to withdraw their forces. Truman had considered this action a possible prelude to an open breach with the Soviets. Dean Acheson, among others, agreed that the United States should insist upon Soviet withdrawal, without, however, threatening military action. Largely because of American firmness, the Soviet Union withdrew its troops.

In August, however, Stalin had sent a note to Turkey demanding that Ankara fulfill a 1936 treaty obligation to allow the Soviet Union a strong voice in the future administration of the Dardanelles. Largely because Turkey had cooperated economically with the Axis during World War II (although Ankara did declare war on Germany in 1945 in order to gain admittance to the United Nations), FDR and Churchill had agreed to allow Russia such a role in Turkish affairs. But by 1946 both Britain and the United States had decided that giving the Russians a voice in such a key strategic locale would be a serious mistake. Truman had dispatched American warships to the Eastern Mediterranean and Stalin had backed down—but the crisis had further polarized Soviet-American relations.

When the United States therefore received word on February 21, 1947, that Britain, because of her domestic economic plight, would be forced to suspend all aid to the governments of Greece and Turkey in six weeks, the message was interpreted by the Truman administration as the first great test of American resolve. The sudden withdrawal of British power would leave behind it the vacuum that Truman had always feared, one well-suited to Soviet penetration. Throughout the administration, the immediate assumption was that Greece would succumb to Bolshevism, that the Greek communists were controlled by Stalin (and Yugoslavia's Tito) and that general disorder in the region would be used by the Russian leader as a pretext to impose favorable treaty terms on Turkey.

It has since been learned that Stalin had only contempt for the Greek communist insurgency, which began in earnest in early 1947. He told a group of Yugoslavs at the time, "What do you think, that Great Britain and the United States—the United States, the most powerful state in the world—will permit you to break their line of communication in the Mediterranean Sea! Nonsense. And we have no navy. The uprising in Greece must be stopped, and as quickly as possible." But none of this was known in Washington, where the Greek crisis was seen as a crucial test of Soviet opportunism versus American determination not to let poverty, devastation and anarchy compromise freedom.

For six days the Truman administration generally and Undersecretary of State Acheson in particular worked to formulate a plan of aid for Greece and Turkey, and on February 27 members of the cabinet assembled at the White House to explain the package to congressional leaders. Secretary of State George C. Marshall spoke first but, as Acheson recalled, "flubbed his opening statement." The members of Congress were unconvinced that Greece and Turkey were vital to American security, and Acheson saw his program begin to slip away. "In desperation" he asked Marshall to let him speak. "This was my crisis. For a week I had nurtured it. These congressmen had no conception of what challenged them; it was my task to bring it home." Acheson proceeded to paint a colorful but stark picture of the situation in the Eastern Mediterranean, saying that American failure to act "might open three continents to Soviet penetration. Like apples in a barrel infected by one rotten one, the corruption in Greece would infect Iran and all to the east. It would also carry infection to Africa through Asia Minor and Egypt, and to Europe through Italy and France, already threatened by the strongest domestic Communist parties in Western Europe. The Soviet Union was playing one of the greatest gambles in history at minimal cost. It did not need to win all the possibilities. Even one or two offered immense gains. We and we alone were in a position to break up the play."

Acheson's oration was a stunning success. The formerly reluctant congressmen sat in silence for long minutes, and then Senator Arthur Vandenberg said solemnly: "Mr. President, if you will say that to the Congress and the Country, I will support you and I believe that most of its members will do the same." All that was left, then, was to turn Acheson's words into a presidential address of equal power and eloquence. The under secretary of state went straight to the job, and by March 12 the speech was ready for a joint session of Congress.

Truman, pointing out that the "integrity" of Greece and Turkey were "essential to the preservation of order in the Middle East," went on to describe a worldwide struggle in terms that were vintage Acheson and in some cases direct lifts from the under secretary's suggested draft. "At the present moment in world history nearly every nation must choose between alternative ways of life," and America could not afford to stand aloof from that process: "I believe that it must be the policy of the United States to support free peoples who are resisting attempted subjugation by armed minorities or by outside pressures. I believe that we must assist free peoples to work out their own destinies in their own ways." Echoing Acheson's "rotten apple" scenario, Truman performed brilliantly and, more important, with effect.

Appearing before Congress to testify in defense of the proposed aid bill in the days following Truman's speech, Acheson revealed the more temperate and pragmatic side of his own worldview. When several congressmen expressed concern about the United States taking up the massive obligation of the fight for freedom throughout the world, the under secretary replied, "It is true that there are parts of the world to which we have no access. It would be silly to believe that we can do anything effective in Rumania, Bulgaria or Poland. You cannot do that. That is within the Russian area of physical force. We are excluded from that."

Such tacit acceptance of sphere-of-influence politics disturbed some senators, and in answering them Acheson displayed his own attitude toward the Soviets at this time: "Senator, I think it is a mistake to believe that you can, at any time, sit down with the Russians and solve questions." Problems in Soviet-American relations would have to be "worked out over a long period of time and by always indicating to the Russians that we are quite aware of what our own interests are and that we are quite firm about them and quite prepared to take necessary action."

Clearly, then, there were in Acheson's mind practical limitations to the policy of countering communism. But these were not the reasons for the success of the Truman Doctrine. It was in their use of what the historian John Lewis Gaddis has described as "shock therapy" that Truman and Acheson were able to bring not only congressional but public opinion in line with administration goals. On May 22 the Greek and Turkish aid bill—destined to include an American military mission to Greece—was signed into law, and in future crises, Truman and Acheson turned again and again to the tactic of universalizing threats to American security in order to attain limited goals.

Throughout the spring and summer of 1947, Soviet-American relations continued to deteriorate, and the Truman administration reacted characteristically. On June 5, 1947, Secretary of State George Marshall announced an American formula for the economic relief of Europe—the Marshall Plan—that hinged on U.S. predominance and was thus viewed by the Soviet Union as a direct threat to its own security. On July 2, Soviet Foreign Minister Molotov walked out of the Paris conference convened to work out the terms of American relief, saying that the proposed American plan would eventually restore the power of Germany, split Europe in two and place the western sector of the continent under American control.

In that same month, George Kennan, at the urging of James Forrestal—now the nation's first secretary of defense—published an expanded version of his Long Telegram in *Foreign Affairs* magazine. Using the pseudonym "X," Kennan once more analyzed "The Sources of Soviet Conduct," saying publicly that "Soviet pressure against the free institutions of the Western world is something that can be contained by the adroit and vigilant application of counter-force at a series of constantly shifting geographical and political points. . . ." Kennan's words could be read in a distinctly military light (although he would later claim that he did not intend them as such), and for Forrestal as well as others, they pointed the way toward further consolidation of American security through an expanded defense establishment.

In July the National Security Council and Central Intelligence Agency were created with the passage of the National Security Act, and September saw the signing of the Rio Pact, by which the United States and the nations of Latin America agreed, under Article 51 of the UN Charter, that an "armed attack by any State against any American State shall be considered as an attack against all the American states. . . ." This broadening of the Monroe Doctrine met with almost universal approval in the United States, reflecting the strong belief that, the United Nations notwithstanding, Western Hemispheric security remained the business of the nations of that hemisphere, and of the United States in particular.

By appealing to tradition, then, the Rio Pact met with approval, but because of that same tradition, the Marshall Plan ran into strong opposition. A significant number of Americans could not be made to see that American security rested on the revival of Western Europe—especially the western portion of Germany, so recently a confirmed enemy. The Russian menace had not yet been acutely felt in that part of the continent, and the Truman administration's statements that European poverty was an inducement to communism did not prove strong enough to persuade the American Congress to part with over $7 billion in aid.

Because of this, Truman once more went before a joint session of Congress on March 17, 1948. Dean Acheson had temporarily left the administration for financial reasons and returned to private practice, but the president's special message was framed in language that his foreign policy mentor would doubtless have approved. "Rapid changes are taking place in Europe which affect our foreign policy and our national security," Truman announced in somber tones. "Since the close [of the Second World War], the Soviet Union and its agents have destroyed the independence and democratic character of a whole series of nations in Eastern and Central Europe." To counter this Soviet campaign, Truman recommended immediate approval of the Marshall Plan, universal military training and the reenactment of selective service.

Truman's ability to shock the nation was once again successful. Within two weeks the Marshall Plan had been approved and American negotiators were working with British and Canadian representatives on the idea of a North Atlantic Treaty Organization (NATO). And in June the London Conference on West Germany —composed of the United States, Great Britain, France and the Benelux countries—agreed to permit a West German assembly whose task it was to draw up a constitution, make sure that control of the vast industrial establishments of the Ruhr Valley was kept in the hands of the Western allies and arrange for the continued and indefinite presence of American occupational forces in West Germany. The first step in this remarkably bold program was the release of a new, West German deutsche mark.

That the Kremlin would be stunned by such an obvious move to divide Germany and revitalize the western sectors was predictable. The neutralization of a unified Germany had been one of the foundations of Stalin's own security program. But few suspected that the Russians would react to the project with the speed and determination with which they did. On June 23, 1948, the Western powers announced that the new German currency would circulate in West Berlin as well as in the Western zones of occupation; the next day, the Red Army cut all overland entry into West Berlin and shut do. n that part of the city's electrical power. The Berlin blockade had begun.

The second great test of American international resolve, the blockade elicited statements from U.S. officials that foreshadowed the reaction to North Korea's invasion of South Korea two years later. In response to the Russian move, the American armed forces in Germany devised one of the most ingenious campaigns in the nation's history—the Berlin airlift. Avoiding military confrontation with the Russians altogether, the U.S. Air Force ferried thousands of tons of food and other supplies into West Berlin every day, turning Stalin's attempt to force a more satisfactory German arrangement on the Western Allies into one of the Russian leader's worst diplomatic defeats.

American control of the volatile European situation continued to deepen in the fall of 1948. In September the new West German Assembly convened under Konrad Adenauer and the United States continued its steady movement toward NATO participation. On September 21, Secretary of State Marshall announced, "In every field . . . the Russians are retreating. . . . We have put Western Germany on its feet and we are engaged in bringing about its recovery in such a way that we can really say that we are on the road to victory." West Berlin, like Greece, Turkey and Western Europe generally, had been successfully incorporated into the American perimeter of vital interests, and American confidence rose accordingly—as did Stalin's suspicions that the West intended to frustrate his plans for Soviet security.

But if the Truman administration could claim "victory" abroad, it very nearly suffered ignominious defeat at home. The November 1948 election, pitting the president against Republican internationalist Thomas Dewey, was a close affair—and no one watched the election returns with greater interest than Dean Acheson. Staying up all night and growing ever more ebullient as Dewey's apparent victory crumbled, Acheson celebrated Truman's victory with a highball breakfast. The former under secretary of state had good reason to be cheerful: although he did not yet know it, the election signaled his own return to and control of the State Department.

"You had better be sitting down when you hear what I have to say," Truman told Acheson when the two met in Washington at the end of November 1948. "I want you to come back and be Secretary of State. Will you?"

Acheson was "utterly speechless." In a daze, he asked about Secretary Marshall, who, Truman then explained, was leaving office after having a kidney removed. Acheson protested that he was not qualified for the office; Truman answered that he "could say the same of himself. But the fact was that he was President and he did want me to be Secretary of State." Truman's reelection had given him the opportunity to ignore political appointments and put the man he most trusted at the helm of American foreign policy. Acheson could hardly decline.

The spring of 1949 saw Acheson in complete control. In March, Truman unexpectedly asked for the resignation of Defense Secretary James Forrestal, Acheson's principal rival in the realm of national security. The president had been losing confidence in Forrestal ever since the latter's earlier opposition to American recognition of Israel, one of Truman's proudest and boldest moves. (Forrestal subsequently underwent a severe mental collapse, and committed suicide in May.) In April, the North Atlantic Treaty—which Acheson, both in and out of office, had fought vigorously for—was signed in Washington, and the Soviets, in part because of internal economic instability as well as strains in the Eastern bloc such as the "rebellion" of Tito's Yugoslavia, were forced to lift the Berlin blockade in return for minor concessions. And in May, at a Council of Foreign Ministers meeting in Paris, Acheson's belief that negotiation with the Russians was at this point all but useless was borne out by a complete absence of useful discussion.

But the new secretary of state and his chief were given precious little time to enjoy their successes. The victory of Mao Tse-tung in China prompted Acheson to prepare for Truman during the summer of 1949 a massive State Department review of Chinese-American relations, one that blamed the loss of China to communism largely on Chiang Kai-shek's corruption and stated that the United States could not at present have any effect on domestic Chinese affairs. To many Americans in and out of Congress—especially to those with ties to the immensely powerful China Lobby, which wanted to see Chiang restored to power on the mainland—such a pragmatic policy seemed outright abandonment of a longtime ally and appeasement of the communists, and the belief that the secretary of state considered Asia of secondary importance became widespread.

In an attempt to alter this perception, Acheson gave a speech before the National Press Club on January 12, 1950. Speaking from notes, the secretary of state tried to stress the point that China was not yet wholly in the grip of the Soviet Union. Declaring once again that China's swing to communism was largely that nation's own affair and that, so long as the Soviet Union did not try to take advantage of it, the United States would have to remain somewhat disinterested, Acheson went on to outline what he believed to be the cornerstones of U.S. policy in Asia. Describing an American "defensive perimeter" that ran "along the Aleutians to Japan and then goes to the Ryukyus," and from there stretched to the Philippine Islands—restating a position adopted by the Joint Chiefs of Staff—Acheson stressed that there were limits on American Far Eastern policy options, especially in the South Pacific and Southeast Asia, where domestic turmoil was rampant. Farther north, however, in the Philippines and Japan, American policies could achieve more substantial results because American influence was far more established. To perpetuate this state of affairs, Acheson urged that American aid, especially to Korea, be continued. But once again, Acheson and Truman met with a Congress anxious to take a hard rhetorical line on world communism but reluctant to assume the economic burdens of such a global commitment. Soon after Acheson's speech, Korean aid for the year 1951 was rejected in the House.

At the same time, Truman and especially Acheson faced even greater domestic challenges. In January, the largely unknown Senator Joseph McCarthy of Wisconsin selected anticommunism as the foundation on which he would build his national reputation. On February 9, 1950, McCarthy delivered a speech in Wheeling, West Virginia, in which he declared that "the State Department, which is one of the most important government departments, is thoroughly infested with Communists." The idea struck a chord, providing many Americans with an adequate explanation for the disaster of Mao Tse-tung's victory. The junior senator from Wisconsin referred to Acheson as a "pompous diplomat in striped pants," and McCarthy's wild rampage eventually led to a series of hearings in the Senate.

Acheson answered McCarthy with a series of caustic asides—in his memoirs he would refer to this period as "The Attack of the Primitives"—that only further enraged the senator and his followers. Acheson soon became the primary target of the witch hunters. Throughout the struggle, Truman stood by his secretary of state, saying that "If Communism were to prevail in the world today—as it shall not prevail—Dean Acheson would be one of the first, if not the first, to be shot by the enemies of liberty and Christianity." But McCarthy had captured the public's attention, and by late spring Truman's public opinion rating was at its lowest point since April 1948.

In the midst of this storm, the president and the secretary of state were presented with a policy document of signal importance in American history. On April 7, 1950, Paul Nitze, head of the National Security Council, submitted to the president a comprehensive study of America's world position and overall policy options—NSC-68. The document focused on the primacy of the Soviet threat, and delineated the nature of that threat in terms that made the Truman Doctrine and the work of George Kennan pale by comparison. "[T]he Soviet Union," it announced early on, "unlike previous aspirants to hegemony, is animated by a new fanatic faith, antithetical to our own, and seeks to impose its absolute authority over the rest of the world. . . . The Kremlin regards the United States as the only major threat to the achievement of its fundamental design," and the "implacable purpose of the slave state to eliminate the challenge of freedom has placed the two great powers at opposite poles. . . . The assault on free institutions is world-wide now, and in the context of the present polarization of power a defeat of free institutions anywhere is a defeat everywhere."

The universalization of threats to American security, which had animated Truman and Acheson since the days of the Greek crisis, was accorded the highest importance; and it was no longer "an adequate objective merely to seek to check the Kremlin design, for the absence of order among nations is becoming less and less tolerable. This fact imposes on us, in our own interests, the responsibility of world leadership. . . . [T]he cold war is in fact a real war in which the survival of the free world is at stake."

Even George Kennan was stunned, both by the report's conclusions and by the increases in military spending it recommended. Kennan had already tangled with Acheson on the subject of NATO—the former head of the Policy Planning Staff had opposed American participation on traditional grounds (he saw NATO as an "entangling alliance") as well as for practical reasons of cost. Now, Kennan's policy of containment was being transformed into a massive military program of a type that he had consistently disparaged. Kennan argued that Stalin's freedom of movement externally was being severely constricted by internal Russian factors, especially the task of postwar reconstruction. But Acheson supported the findings of NSC-68 and actively campaigned for their acceptance.

Such acceptance would, of course, mean huge tax increases to cover greatly increased military expenditures, and it was here that

Acheson and Truman once again found the going hard. The American public might enjoy the theatrics of Senator McCarthy, but when it came to paying higher taxes to fight the communist menace abroad, there was widespread reluctance to do so. Acheson toured the country, drumming up support in typical fashion—as one governor put it, "He scared hell out of us." On May 1 President Truman was able to approve $10 million in military assistance for the French and their noncommunist native allies in Southeast Asia, who were fighting a tough battle against the nationalist forces of the Viet Minh (including communists under Ho Chi Minh). Little more than that, however, seemed immediately possible.

For a variety of reasons, then, the North Korean invasion of South Korea on June 24 was fortunate for the administration. The onslaught itself provided ample rationale for a national security program like that outlined in NSC-68; it gave added impetus to the West Europeans to rearm West Germany within a new defensive organization; and by responding to the communist move quickly and aggressively, Truman and Acheson silenced cries that they had abandoned Asia while at the same time providing themselves with ammunition for the battle against Senator McCarthy. The defense of the newly expanded perimeter of American vital interests seemed assured; from 1951 to 1953 the projected defense budget increased from $22.3 billion to $50.4 billion. Four years later, when someone commented to Dean Acheson that, as far as helping the administration to achieve its goals, "Korea came along and saved us," the former secretary answered simply, "I think you can say that."

Dean Acheson's life was often touched by irony, and this was certainly so when he cited the American expedition into the Spanish Floridas in 1818 as a precedent for the response to the Korean invasion. For in sending General Douglas MacArthur to Korea, Acheson and Truman repeated the error of Adams and Monroe —they turned an American military commander with his own notions about security loose in a situation over which they themselves had little control.

On September 15, 1950, MacArthur reversed the drift of events in Korea by carrying out a brilliant amphibious assault at Inchon, behind the North Korean lines. The landing and subsequent rout of communist forces back across the 38th parallel brought many more American citizens and congressmen into the already sizable

MacArthur cult, and in the face of this, Truman and Acheson were reluctant to slow the general's drive into North Korea. They did warn him not to continue should he encounter Russian or Chinese troops, but these orders were subsequently modified. MacArthur was told to continue only if he believed he had a reasonable chance of success. The general, of course, always believed he had a reasonable chance of success, and pressed on.

On October 2, *The New York Times* reported that the foreign minister of the People's Republic of China, Chou En-lai, had warned that China would "not stand aside" if North Korea were invaded. But Truman and Acheson could not—and would not—stop the overwhelming juggernaut that was MacArthur's northward advance. Swept up by their own rhetoric and enticed by the idea of actually "rolling back" communism and unifying Korea under a "democratic" government, the president and his secretary of state ignored Chou's warning. On November 21, American troops reached the Yalu River, the border between North Korea and China. Five days later, the Chinese counterattacked in force, killing large numbers of American and United Nations troops. Within three weeks, the forces of the West were once again below the 38th parallel, and this time it was Chou En-lai who was speaking of the unification of Korea—as all communist.

The decision to allow MacArthur to cross the 38th parallel and advance to the Yalu was the greatest blunder of the Truman-Acheson years, and in later years, Acheson admitted as much in a private letter. "If you ask, as you do," the former secretary said in 1960, "why we all sat around like paralyzed rabbits while MacArthur carried out this nightmare, you will find [the answer] . . . in the development of the power and position of an American theater commander" in the century since the Civil War. "Our weakness was MacArthur," Acheson concluded, "and we deserve all you say for not knowing and in not acting sooner." The idea that MacArthur could successfully break through the static lines of the Cold War caused momentary exhilaration in Washington, and neither Truman nor Acheson was immune to it; but when that euphoria had passed, the administration found itself in a perhaps even more dangerous situation than it had encountered on June 24.

The debacle at the Yalu did not prompt any doubt of the need for a universal response to communist aggression on the part of either Truman or Acheson, but following the disaster both men knew better than to support a policy of worldwide liberation. That portion of NSC-68's recommendations remained out of reach. Thus when MacArthur, in an effort to compensate for his own overconfidence and subsequent failure, began to talk publicly about full-scale war against communist China as the only way to win the Korean War, Truman and Acheson began to think about bringing the venerable general home. Finally, when MacArthur publicly disagreed with Truman's policy of not allowing the Nationalist Chinese to participate in the Korean fighting, the president did relieve MacArthur of command.

Public furor erupted—and again, Truman and Acheson were accused of taking a soft line on Asian communism. When MacArthur went before a Senate hearing to declare that Truman's Korean policy amounted to "appeasement" and that the fight against communism was a "global proposition" in which "you can't let one-half of the world slide into slavery and just confine yourself to defending the other," his public support rose dramatically. "What I advocate," the general said, "is that we defend every place, and I say that we have the capacity to do it. If you say we haven't, you admit defeat."

MacArthur's testimony was followed first by that of the Joint Chiefs of Staff and then by Secretary Acheson's, and the statements of these men made it clear that the general was talking less about defense in his call for a war against China than about offense (or outright aggression). It soon became apparent that the Truman administration was, in fact, committed to a policy of holding the line against communism worldwide. JCS Chairman Omar Bradley surprised listeners by not only disagreeing with MacArthur, but by terming a war against China as "the wrong war, at the wrong place, at the wrong time, and with the wrong enemy." General Bradley advocated the limited Korean action as the best possible course.

But it was Acheson who finally turned the Senate and the nation against MacArthur. His testimony was by far the longest of any witness, well over six hundred pages in length. With remarkable patience he endured questions on Korea as well as on subjects that were not even related to the war, but mere reflections of the personal hostility many senators felt toward him. America had responded to the North Korean attack, Acheson explained, not because South Korea was of any "strategic" importance to the United States in a purely military sense; rather, American security had now been defined in terms that transcended strategic concerns to encompass considerations of ideology. It was therefore important for America to demonstrate the strength of the free world by actively repelling communist aggression throughout the globe, even in places deemed militarily unimportant. Acheson's commitment to this goal was obvious. By the time the Senate hearings were over, MacArthur had lost his case.

It was for MacArthur's successor, General Matthew Ridgway, to finally push the Chinese Communists back to the 38th parallel and there establish a line of defense that would eventually become permanent. This freed Acheson to spend the remainder of his term as secretary of state consolidating the American position in both Europe and Asia. Learning the lesson of MacArthur's advance to the Yalu, Acheson concentrated on strengthening the position of the free world rather than trying to break up the communist bloc. At home, the "Attack of the Primitives" went on, but following his success in the MacArthur hearings, Acheson's position was immensely strengthened.

In 1950 the secretary of state had made a statement concerning the activities of Senator McCarthy, which illuminated his attitude toward the business of communist hunting at home: "I don't ask for your sympathy," he told a group of newspaper editors. "I don't ask for your help. You are in a worse situation than I am. I and my associates are only the intended victims of this mad and vicious operation. But you, unhappily, you by reason of your calling, are participants." Yet it was the final irony of Acheson's years at the State Department that he and his chief were in some degree responsible for the growth of anticommunist hysteria that swept the country and the West during their term in office.

Both Truman and Acheson designed pragmatic, realistic programs that they felt were necessary to combat what they perceived as a significant challenge to American and Western security; and that both men understood the limits as well as the obligations of their anticommunist programs became clear during the congressional hearings on the Truman Doctrine, during the Berlin crisis and finally during the MacArthur hearings. But it was the tactic of employing inflated rhetoric to justify ever more expansive means of protecting American security, rather than any refined sense of limitation, that so profoundly affected Acheson's and Truman's successors.

With the victory of the Republican party under Dwight D. Eisenhower in the 1952 election, American foreign policy was placed in the hands of a man who employed anticommunist rhetoric to an extent that even Dean Acheson considered extreme. John Foster Dulles, like Woodrow Wilson, under whom Dulles had studied at Princeton, was a minister's son who possessed a true flair for dramatic public speaking but was somewhat uncomfortable with intimate personal relationships. An intellectually facile and immensely successful international lawyer, Dulles had served on the American delegation to the Paris Peace Conference in 1919, where he had seen Wilson's ideals come into sharp conflict with the more pragmatic policies of Robert Lansing, a breach that had especially personal ramifications for Dulles—Lansing was his uncle. From the time of the Versailles Conference until his death in 1959, Dulles's life was dedicated to reconciling the apparently contradictory points of view of these two men.

To this end, Dulles worked hard during the 1920s and 1930s to integrate his own natural inclination toward liberal idealism into a generally more pragmatic outlook than Wilson had betrayed. In a speech delivered in 1922, for instance, Dulles told his listeners that "Moral distinctions [in international affairs], though pleasing to those who draw them, are hard to sustain in fact, and I know of no historic reason to justify our approaching these problems of international relations with the complacent assumption that we are party to a clashing of the forces of good and evil, and that solution is to be found in the moral regeneration of those who hold views contrary to our own. All nations are inherently selfish and we are no different than any others."

Dulles's lifelong effort to combine Wilsonian idealism and the pragmatism necessitated by the complex realities of international politics resulted in broad inconsistencies in both his personal statements and in his policy initiatives. When nominated for the post of secretary of state, Dulles announced at his Senate confirmation hearings that "The threat of Soviet communism is not only the gravest threat that has ever faced the United States, but the gravest threat that has ever faced what we call western civilization." Because of this, "a policy which aims only at containing Russia is, in itself, an unsound policy; . . . It is only by keeping alive the hope of liberation, by taking advantage of whatever opportunity arises, that we will end this terrible peril which dominates the world." To Dulles, the struggle between the United States and the Soviet Union was "an irreconcilable conflict."

That Dulles meant to act on such opinions seemed evident in his determination not to respond to the tentative diplomatic overtures initiated by Joseph Stalin's successor, Georgi Malenkov, early in 1953. The new American secretary of state instead pushed hard for a further strengthening of West Germany and the NATO alliance. And in January 1954 Dulles once again appeared to give new force to a program of countering communism worldwide when he publicly detailed a policy of "massive retaliation," hinting that communist powers guilty of aggression—either directly or through client states—could not rule out the possibility of an American nuclear response.

But neither Dulles nor President Eisenhower was in fact willing to risk even limited nuclear conflict, and their talk of massive retaliation was to a large degree designed to compensate for the general perception that the American public, after Korea, would not support large-scale conventional responses to communist aggression.

The president and his secretary of state found themselves in a severe dilemma: if conventional land conflicts were opposed by large numbers of Americans, and if "massive retaliation" offered the unacceptable possibility of nuclear holocaust, how could the United States attend to its security in those regions of the world viewed as vital? This problem was compounded by the increasing frequency of internal communist uprisings throughout the world —such as Ho Chi Minh's struggle against the French in Vietnam —that were far more difficult to portray to the American public or to the United Nations as "aggression" than the North Korean attack against South Korea had been.

Dulles spelled these problems out at a May 1954 cabinet meeting. "The nibbling," he said, referring to worldwide communist activity, "has already reached the point where we can't see much more territory go to the Communists without real danger to ourselves. The problem, of course, is where to draw the line. . . . It's not difficult to marshal world opinion against aggression, but it is quite another matter to fight against internal changes in one country. If we take a position against a Communist faction within a foreign country, we have to act alone. We are confronted by an unfortunate fact—most of the countries of the world do not share our view that Communist control of any government anywhere is in itself a danger and a threat."

Dulles soon formulated a resolution to this policy dilemma, one that belied his public talk of worldwide "liberation" and "massive retaliation." It came in the form of covert subversion, first tested in Iran in 1953. Fearful that Iran's nationalist premier, who had taken over the British-controlled oil industry despite the objections of the shah, was leading his nation into the communist camp, Washington supplied arms and matériel to the shah and his supporters, who successfully reestablished control over the Teheran government.

The most extensive use of covert subversion came a year later, in the Central American nation of Guatemala. For over a year the president of that impoverished country had been moving steadily toward a program of socialization and nationalization, and when, in May 1954, Guatemala received an arms shipment from the Soviet bloc, Dulles decided to move forcefully against what he perceived as communist penetration of the Western Hemisphere. In June, President Eisenhower gave the green light for a CIA-backed coup that put an obscure but pro-American Guatemalan military officer in power. The operation was little more than a CIA field exercise. But the success of the Guatemalan coup was of key importance to both Dulles and Eisenhower; with both large-scale land operations and "massive retaliation" eliminated as American options, covert subversion seemed a solution that might garner the fruits of the first policy without incurring the risks of the second.

Eisenhower and Dulles next turned to the problem of Southeast Asia. The Geneva Conference on Indochina in July 1954 established a truce between Ho Chi Minh and the French, who had been decisively defeated at the Vietnamese town of Dien Bien Phu only weeks earlier. The Geneva Accords also temporarily partitioned Vietnam at the 17th parallel (with the French withdrawing south of that line); recognized Cambodia and Laos as independent nations; restricted both North and South Vietnam from joining any military alliances or permitting any additional military bases in their territories; and called for Vietnamese national elections within the next two years to determine the country's ultimate status.

Dulles immediately declared that the United States could not accept the Geneva Accords, explaining to British Foreign Minister Anthony Eden that, even if the settlement were carried out faithfully, America could not tolerate "the guaranteeing of the subjection of millions of Vietnamese to Communist rule." The secretary of state did say that the United States, despite its disapproval, would not try actively to subvert the accords—but given the recent success in Guatemala, such a statement seemed little more than disingenuous.

As indeed it was. On September 8, 1954, the Southeast Asia Treaty Organization—SEATO—was forged under American leadership. Even before the signing of this regional defense pact, the United States had dispatched a military mission to South Vietnam that had assisted in bolstering the new, independent regime of Ngo Dinh Diem and initiated efforts to discredit Ho Chi Minh among the Vietnamese populace. Such efforts could be defended by the United States on the grounds that it had not been signatory to the Geneva Accords—but SEATO's adoption of a protocol that extended defensive protection to South Vietnam represented an undeniable subversion of those agreements. Over the next two years, that process of subversion would continue—and would eventually plunge Vietnam into a savage civil war.

In undertaking these policies of subversion, Dulles demonstrated the pragmatism that always balanced his dramatic talk of universal "liberation." Action taken to counter any possible communist takeovers—as in Guatemala and South Vietnam—was embarked on only in areas of marginal strategic interest to the Soviet Union. Further evidence of this aspect of Dullesian policy was offered in the fall of 1956, when rioting broke out in Poland. Soviet Communist party leader Nikita Khrushchev's denunciations of some of the more repressive aspects of Stalinist rule had caused many Eastern Europeans to think that the time was ripe to demand greater freedoms from their leaders, and in Poland they took to the streets to do so. Given the American secretary of state's public statements, it was only natural that many citizens in both the East and the West looked to Dulles to champion this cause.

But in October, Dulles explained on national television that "our contribution to it [Polish freedom] isn't one of actually intervening and meddling, because that kind of thing, that interference from abroad in the affairs of another country, often is counter-productive. Our job is only as exponents of freedom to keep alive the concept of freedom." For a man who had come to office talking of liberation, this sounded suspiciously like tacit acceptance of sphere-of-influence politics. This view was dramatically underlined later in that month, when widespread rioting also broke out in Hungary, and the Soviet Union sent in troops and armor to put down the rebellion. No significant American response was made to the Hungarian Revolt, and many claimed that Dulles had abandoned the cause of freedom behind the Iron Curtain.

But Dulles's apparent reluctance to act within what Acheson had called "the Russian area of physical force" only increased his desire to defend—and even expand—American interests in the Third World. On October 26, 1956, Ngo Dinh Diem announced a new constitution for the Republic of South Vietnam just at the moment when free elections were to have taken place in both the northern and southern sections of that country. Dulles once again backed Diem up, thereby fully subverting the Geneva Accords. Diem's South Vietnam, from which the French had by now completely withdrawn, had no chance for survival without heavy American aid, and Dulles saw to it that that aid was delivered. The United States was now, as Acheson said of Korea, "fully committed" in South Vietnam.

This commitment brought with it criticism, both at home and abroad. But during the Suez crisis in that same fall of 1956 Dulles once again revealed that the interests of America's allies would be ignored when they came into conflict with American security goals. Dulles believed that the Anglo-French demand that Egyptian President Gamal Abdel Nasser return ownership of the British-controlled Suez Canal Company (which Nasser had nationalized in July) might force Egypt into the communist camp. The secretary of state condemned first the demand and then the Anglo-French-Israeli invasion of Egypt that followed it. By employing economic coercion against the allies, Dulles eventually forced an end to the military action, and supported a UN resolution granting control of the Suez Canal to Egypt.

The fall of 1956 was a dividing line in the American quest for absolute national security. In Indochina, the U.S. commitment to unilateral intervention was finally undertaken; in Eastern Europe, the hope that the Western democracies would roll back the Soviet empire was dispelled by American inaction and Soviet tanks; in Suez, the United States not only abandoned its allies but actively opposed them. Above all, the mid-1950s saw a hardening of the trend by American policymakers to view nationalistic struggles in the Third World as an extension of the conflict between the United States and the Soviet Union. Without question, John Foster Dulles expanded the perimeter of American vital interests, especially in the Pacific and Southeast Asia; but that expansion did not conform to his own talk of liberation and rollback. Dulles's principal legacy

was less an extension of actual conflict than an expansion of rhetoric, accompanied by a global system of pacts and minialliances
that were meant to demonstrate America's commitment to the
global struggle against communism. The Eisenhower administration simply would not assume the awesome burdens of open conflict against either indigenous or Soviet-backed communist
movements in remote corners of the world. That task was to be
undertaken by the men who succeeded Eisenhower and Dulles.

By the time John F. Kennedy entered the White House early in
1961, Dean Acheson had become one of the most respected elder
statesmen of the Democratic party. In choosing a secretary of state,
Kennedy sought and followed Acheson's advice, nominating the
same Dean Rusk who had served Acheson so well at the Far Eastern desk. Time had not, however, moderated Acheson's worldview. He had greatly disliked John Foster Dulles personally
(stunning a group of friends after Dulles's death with the remark,
"Thank God Foster is underground") and held him in contempt
professionally, complaining that Dulles was not forthright enough
in standing up to communism and had elected instead to hide
behind a rhetorical smokescreen. During the three years of Kennedy's presidency, Acheson urged the strongest possible responses
to Soviet adventurism and communist uprisings along the perimeter of America's interests. He always rejected a policy of rollback
but insisted that encroachments on the free world must be met and
checked as they had been in Korea.

But, perhaps because he had been so long out of power, Acheson
seemed not to comprehend that the nature of the communist
threat had changed significantly in the years since Korea. By 1963,
large-scale, conventional aggressions had increasingly given way to
nationalist guerrilla uprisings that were woven, often inextricably,
into the civilian fabric of Third World nations. Such movements
could rarely be defeated by even large numbers of conventional
troops. To Acheson, however, the best way to fight communism
was still to dispatch American armed forces to contested points in
numbers sufficient to maintain the lines of containment. For this
reason, he supported Kennedy's expansion of the American presence in South Vietnam. Just as he felt he had correctly applied the
lessons of Pearl Harbor to Korea, so did Acheson feel that an
accurate reading of the lessons of Korea indicated American maintenance of the territorial and governmental integrity of the Saigon

regime. Securing the perimeter of American interests was no less vital to Acheson in 1963 than it had ever been—and if defense of that perimeter required American support of South Vietnam, then it was an expense that the nation could ill afford to spare.

Kennedy's assassination brought to power a man even more impressed by Acheson's concept of universalism than Kennedy had been. Lyndon Baines Johnson had been born on a failed dirt farm in rural Texas and battled his way out of bitter poverty by becoming first a teacher, then a noted political operator, and finally a congressman, senator and vice-president. Always gregarious, often vulgar, though sometimes remarkably gracious, Johnson retained vivid memories of his youth during the Great Depression, memories that contributed to a sincere conviction that the evils of poverty, ignorance and repression could most effectively be fought by a vigorous democracy ready to devote its blood and its wealth to the cause. Both were poured readily into Vietnam during the opening months of Johnson's presidency, and in August 1964 the American Congress gave its seal of approval to this policy when it overwhelmingly passed the Tonkin Gulf Resolution, authorizing Johnson to take all necessary steps to repel aggression in South Vietnam. This included extensive strategic bombing north of the 17th parallel.

But by 1967, with the number of American servicemen stationed in Southeast Asia climbing into the hundreds of thousands, it had become apparent to critics both in and out of government that the war in Vietnam was neither the clear-cut containment of communist aggression that President Johnson claimed nor the winnable conflict that the Joint Chiefs of Staff believed was possible. Johnson had surrounded himself with advisers whose foreign policy views had been largely formed during their years of service under Harry Truman—men such as Dean Rusk and Clark Clifford—and these men, like Acheson, endorsed the validity of the Vietnam undertaking. But other veterans of the Truman years, including George Kennan, were already warning that an American obsession with proving the strength of the free world in Southeast Asia would dangerously weaken the United States both morally and economically. In addition, critics argued that the American military effort ignored many fundamental features of the Vietnamese situation. Unlike the Korean conflict, they said, the lines of the Vietnamese war were fluid. The 17th parallel was a largely artificial boundary, one that could neither interdict the movements of the native South

Vietnamese communist rebels, the Vietcong, nor prevent infiltration by large numbers of North Vietnamese forces. Victory in such a war could almost certainly not be won through conventional battlefield engagements.

Popular criticism of the war was heightened by President Johnson's continued bombing north of the 17th parallel in an effort to demonstrate to the North Vietnamese the full cost of continued aggression. The bombing eventually became the focus of widespread domestic protest in the United States, and as the American B-52s failed to achieve their goal of making the North Vietnamese drop their efforts to unite Vietnam militarily, the ranks of the doubters within the administration grew. But Johnson would not break faith with Dean Acheson's principle of the need for a universal response to communist aggression. Despite the growing domestic discontent and the appalling loss of both American and Vietnamese lives, the war and the bombing went on.

Even by the summer of 1967, Acheson himself was still making comparisons between Vietnam and Korea. "I am writing about Korea now," he told a friend, referring to his memoirs, and "The more I watch this war [Vietnam] the more parallels I see to Korea and the more I admire my Chief [Truman]." To Acheson, the few differences that did exist between the Korean and Vietnamese experiences arose in large part from the personal contrasts between Johnson and Truman. "LBJ has not HST's courage," Acheson wrote to Anthony Eden, and was therefore "the one to blame" for America's domestic and international problems. Nor did Acheson agree with Johnson's policy of massive strategic bombing: "We have run out of useful targets aside from [the] population," he wrote. "It is just not worth the casualties and the pilots know this. LBJ's problem is how to stop. I have argued the point with him and while he won't admit it, this is the problem." Despite these opinions, Acheson continued to favor America's overall military commitment in Vietnam, and when he, along with a group of other distinguished foreign policy experts, was called to the White House to be briefed by civilian and military officials on the Vietnamese situation in November 1967 he reiterated his support.

Acheson's convictions, like those of many other supporters of the war, were deeply shaken by the Tet Offensive that exploded in January 1968. Just as American generals and administration spokesmen were claiming that victory was close at hand, the Vietcong and North Vietnamese army struck at American positions not only on the front lines but deep inside South Vietnam. The attacks were repelled, but at heavy cost, and the psychological effect on American troops and American citizens was devastating. To Acheson, it was an indication that not only he but President Johnson as well had been given false information by the JCS, and that the Vietnamese situation might be far bleaker than its supporters had supposed. The former secretary of state intended to make his new doubts clear to President Johnson as quickly as possible.

Called to the White House in February 1968, Acheson found Johnson obsessed with the ongoing siege of American marines at the Vietnamese town of Khe Sanh, a battle that was disturbingly reminiscent of the doomed French stand at Dien Bien Phu fourteen years earlier. Acheson attempted to voice his worries, but Johnson was not interested in doubts, and the president's unwillingness to listen eventually caused Acheson to walk out of the meeting and return to his law office. When Johnson's assistants called him there and said that the president wanted to know why he had walked out, Acheson answered acidly, "You tell the President—and you tell him in precisely these words—that he can take Vietnam and stick it up his ass."

Few remarks could have been better calculated to gain Johnson's ear. The president asked Acheson to return to the White House, and Acheson complied, telling Johnson on his return that "the Joint Chiefs of Staff don't know what they're talking about." Acheson said that if Johnson wanted any further advice from him, he would have to agree to allow the former secretary of state full access to all available reports on the Vietnam situation, and not merely to selected information designed to create support for the war. Johnson agreed. During the coming weeks, Acheson grilled numerous American officials who had been in Vietnam and pored over mountains of data concerning the war—and as he did, his thoughts not only on Vietnam but on the containment of communism generally began to evolve.

In March, Acheson wrote that he had "completed the second stage (High School) of my Vietnam education—a most remarkable one, from a rare and probably unequaled faculty—which has confused some of my earlier simple conclusions and shown the difficulties to be even greater than I thought." Seldom had Acheson's pragmatism been more admirably demonstrated; out of power and in his late sixties, the man who had been the force behind the Truman Doctrine and the Korean War was now willing not only to relearn Asian politics but to reconsider his views on the Cold War. Acheson did not favor immediate withdrawal from Vietnam, but he did believe that definite limits on the American effort must now be set. Beyond a certain point, the goal of ensuring an independent South Vietnam could not justify the current vast expenditure of American lives and dollars. Ends and means were becoming increasingly unbalanced; and when Acheson again met with Johnson at the White House in mid-March, he told the president point-blank that the Joint Chiefs of Staff were leading him "down the garden path."

By the end of March, Acheson had moved even further in this direction. Believing that there was no real political power base on which to build in South Vietnam—that the Saigon regime was corrupt, inefficient and detested by many of the South Vietnamese themselves—Acheson determined that a definite timetable for American disengagement must be set. Again called in to the State Department and the White House for a series of briefings, along with other elder foreign policy advisers—collectively known as the "Wise Men"—Acheson stated his view succinctly: "We can no longer do the job we set out to do in the time we have left, and we must take steps to disengage." A majority of those present at the meeting agreed with Acheson's assessment.

The effect on President Johnson was considerable. Johnson considered Acheson and those who shared his views "intelligent, experienced men. I had always regarded the majority of them as very steady and balanced. If they had been so deeply influenced by the reports of the Tet offensive, what must the average citizen in the country be thinking?" Johnson soon announced a partial halt to the bombing of North Vietnam—and his own determination not to seek another term in office.

In January 1969 the prosecution of the Vietnam War was handed over to the Republican party and to Richard Nixon, who also sought Dean Acheson's advice. Although Acheson found to his surprise that he could actually tolerate conversation with Nixon —who as one of the nation's great communist-hunters had been an object of Acheson's deepest scorn—he disagreed with Nixon's expansion of the conflict to all of Indochina. Not that this increased Acheson's sympathy for those who were only too willing to give the communists the benefit of the doubt. "The fact of the matter is," he wrote in March 1971, "that the credibility gap, both ways—that is my disbelief in the government and my disbelief in the media—

is complete. I don't believe that a half dozen people anywhere know what the real facts are. . . . My conclusion for over a year is that we should stop talking, testifying, denouncing and invading— and move steadily out."

In October of that same year, Acheson died quietly in his study after a day of gardening. American withdrawal from Vietnam was still long years away, but Acheson's final calls for disengagement were, nonetheless, singularly important. The men who most dramatically expanded the American military presence in Southeast Asia all believed that they were keeping faith with the tenets of anticommunism set forth by Acheson and his chief, Harry Truman, during the opening years of the Cold War. The Vietnam War —the most tragically divisive American experience since the Civil War—was, to a very real extent, the logical conclusion of the Truman Doctrine, which relied so heavily for its domestic support on the power of rhetoric. To the very end, Acheson himself remained a realist, a man personally unhampered by the constraints of dogma; but the legacy of universalism led his successors to define the American perimeter in terms that the nation itself could not ultimately endorse.

In Vietnam, the means employed finally exceeded any reasonable ends that could be attained in a region of the world that was always of marginal strategic significance to the United States. Yet disengagement from Southeast Asia was an idea that deeply disturbed many American leaders, even some who favored it. In defining the perimeter of U.S. interests in the years after World War II, American statesmen had not so much created a new world as projected American ideas about security onto an already existent (if largely devastated) international community. The forceful response of the United States to the possibility of communist penetration in Greece and Turkey, in Western Europe and in Asia was at one with an American tradition that had seen in its evolution the establishment of secure continental boundaries in North America, numerous military interventions in Latin America and the Caribbean, the annexation of the Philippine Islands and a subsequent expansion of American interests in the Pacific.

In questioning the U.S. presence in Vietnam, therefore, critics called for a fundamental reexamination not only of America's involvements overseas in the post–World War II era but of the nation's traditionally expansive definition and pursuit of national security itself. In 1950, Dean Acheson had chronicled the course of that pursuit in his memorandum on the authority of President Truman to repel communist aggression in South Korea. Yet by the late 1960s Acheson himself had been forced by the experience of Vietnam to question some of the underlying principles of that memo, especially the notion that American leaders could and indeed should react decisively—and if need be militarily—in foreign countries whose security they had identified with that of the United States. That Acheson, in the years before his death, felt immensely out of place in the changing world around him is understandable. The perimeter that he had done so much to define—and that had once seemed the clear frontier of American security concerns— had by the time of his death become a zone of uncertainty fraught with danger not only to the territorial integrity but to the moral authority of the United States.

But it was not on the perimeter alone that American leaders faced perplexing challenges in the 1960s. With the rise of Third World rebellions that were nationalistic, often socialist and in some cases openly aimed at the installation of communist regimes, American policymakers perceived new threats to the security of the United States in the Western Hemisphere—a region that no American leader, Democrat or Republican, realist or ideologue, had ever been able to view as less than vital.

V I I I

SECURING THE HEMISPHERE
1965–1986

LATE on the night of April 24, 1965, the United States Caribbean Amphibious Task Force—six ships in all—cruised quietly into the waters off Santo Domingo, capital city of the Dominican Republic. Aboard the task force's flagship, the helicopter carrier *Boxer*, 1,800 American marines waited in the sultry Caribbean darkness to learn whether they were involved in a mere exercise or if in fact they would be going ashore. Fighting could be heard in the distant city, civil warfare of a type that was all too familiar to Santo Domingo— political factions were battling each other within a populace whose long exposure to tyranny, repression and poverty had made it more than willing to take to the streets in outbursts of frustrated violence. Few of the Caribbean Task Force's officers and men had any idea of what had caused the fighting in Santo Domingo that night, and as they stood by waiting for further instructions, their superiors in Washington tried to sort out the situation—with notably poor results.

The American ambassador to the Dominican Republic, W. Tapley Bennett, was a socially adept career diplomat with a limited understanding of Dominican affairs—so limited, it would seem, that when the Santo Domingo revolt broke out he was visiting his sick mother in Georgia. There had been rumors that trouble might break out in the Dominican capital, but since the assassination of longtime dictator Rafael Trujillo in May 1961, it seemed to Bennett that such rumors were constantly circulating. A few of them had even come true: Trujillo's family had been violently expelled following his death; the man who had subsequently been elected president, the firmly democratic but economically inept Juan Bosch, had been overthrown by a military coup in October 1963; and a military junta had then placed Donald Reid Cabral in office. Reid Cabral's efforts to reorganize the country's economy (still recovering from the remarkable larceny of the Trujillo family) had alienated both the Right and the Left and killed off what little popularity he still enjoyed in the country. But Ambassador Bennett believed that all this would be dealt with in the upcoming June 1965 elections, and so left for home feeling little if any apprehension. Apparently, he did not yet realize that in Santo Domingo, elections were not the established way of doing national business.

Because of the ambassador's misreading of events, the United States was caught off-guard on April 24 when a group of young Dominican officers took control of two key military bases in the Santo Domingo area, captured the army chief of staff and called for the return of Juan Bosch. Senior Dominican military officers, seeing a chance to rid themselves of Reid Cabral (who had been battling their exorbitant military pension schemes) *and* to purge the armed forces of idealistic young troublemakers, had then chosen to betray their president by seizing control of the San Isidro air base on the eastern outskirts of Santo Domingo and establishing yet another military junta.

Despite its surprise at such developments, Washington might have been willing to write all this off as just another Caribbean outburst, save for one key factor—Cuba. In 1959, Havana had been "lost" to communism, and by 1965 only the narrow waterway known as the Windward Passage and the tiny, weak nation of Haiti separated the Dominican Republic from the forces of Fidel Castro. To Latin American experts in Washington, the night of April 24 was truly momentous—was communism, having gained a foothold in the Western Hemisphere, now making a new bid for expansion?

President Lyndon Johnson was most especially fearful that this might happen. The fact that the rebellious Dominican officers were calling for the return of a constitutionally elected president meant little to Johnson, who immediately interpreted the Dominican crisis as an opening for Castroism and communism. He attributed this danger—which prompted the immediate dispatch of the Caribbean Task Force to Dominican waters—as much to the chaos brought on by the revolt as to any deliberate scheming on the part of the rebellion's leaders. In this view he was most strongly supported by Under Secretary of State for Economic Affairs (and former head of State's Latin American desk) Thomas C. Mann. Mann, who had been a minor participant in the American-backed Guatemalan coup of 1954, had clearly revealed his own view of the correct American role in Latin American affairs in a June 1964 speech. Dispensing with the remnants of Wilsonian idealism, Mann declared that it was not the duty of the United States to reinstate or even, in some cases, to defend constitutionally elected presidents; had such a course been followed in Guatemala, for instance, "we would have been obliged to do everything in our power . . . to restore a Marxist-Leninist. . . ." Rather, it was the job of the United States to halt the infection that had taken root in Havana half a decade earlier. Mann believed that anarchy in the Dominican Republic would soon place communists in control of the revolt, if they were not there already; and on the third day of the rebellion, that possibility became even more likely.

Monday, April 26, saw violence spreading in Santo Domingo as the Dominican air force began to bomb rebel-controlled areas, killing civilians, and the rebels opened up their armories to the people in the city, arming anyone who could carry a gun. To President Johnson, Secretary of State Dean Rusk, Undersecretary Mann and Ambassador Bennett this was proof positive that the communist influence on the rebellion was rising—only communists, they believed, would indiscriminately arm civilians. The Caribbean Amphibious Task Force was ordered to continue standing by to evacuate Americans and other foreign nationals, while in Fort Bragg, North Carolina, the 82nd Airborne Division was put on full alert.

By Tuesday, Santo Domingo was in utter chaos. Foreigners massing for evacuation at the Hotel Embajador in the western sector of the city were terrified when armed Dominicans began shooting up the hotel lobby. Perhaps the most disturbing aspect of the incident was that no one could tell if it was the rebels or the soldiers of the San Isidro senior military junta who had started the trouble. But despite such incidents, Ambassador Bennett, now back at his post, did not request a landing of U.S. marines to protect Americans and other foreign nationals. The ambassador was far more interested in thwarting the aims of the rebels than he was in playing the role of neutral peacekeeper. To this end, he allowed American military attachés to advise the junta at San Isidro while he refused a rebel request for a U.S.–sponsored cease-fire on Tuesday afternoon. By Tuesday night rebel fortunes were fading in the face of the planes and tanks of the military junta. Ambassador Bennett still did not feel that American troops needed to land (despite the violent disorder that may have endangered American lives) and President Johnson accepted his judgment, nonetheless keeping U.S. troops at the ready.

Ambassador Bennett expected that during the night of Tuesday-Wednesday the military forces at San Isidro would press their advantage and crush the rebels. He was disappointed. The leaders of the junta had no desire to squander their cherished tanks in dangerous street fighting, and the rebels were thus given time to regroup. At this point, Ambassador Bennett suddenly decided that American lives were in fact in danger. On Wednesday afternoon Bennett urged the leader of the junta to request a landing of American troops. The request, as later described by Senate Foreign Relations Committee Chairman J. William Fulbright, who conducted a lengthy investigation into the Dominican affair, was made "on the ground that this was the only way to prevent a Communist takeover; no mention was made of the junta's inability to protect American lives. This request," Fulbright said, "was denied in Washington, and [the junta] was thereupon told that the United States would not intervene unless [the Dominican military] could not protect American citizens present in the Dominican Republic." Thus the junta "was told in effect that if [it] said American lives were in danger the United States would intervene. And that is precisely what happened."

Washington's sudden willingness to move on the matter had been prompted by President Johnson's increasing conviction that the Dominican Republic was being lost to communism. The importance of this lay not only in its regional implications but in its international and domestic American ramifications as well. With the American military commitment in Vietnam rising steadily, Johnson could not afford to deviate from the path of a universal response to communist aggression and thus open himself up to charges of weakness and inconsistency. The cost would be great—as one Johnson administration official remarked at the time, "One more outbreak and we would be out of business." This attitude produced something of a siege mentality in President Johnson—the Dominican crisis, he said, was "just like the Alamo." In typical fashion he went on: "Hell, it's just like you were down at that gate, and you were surrounded, and you damn well needed somebody. Well, by God, I'm going to go—and I thank the Lord that I've got men who want to go with me, from [Secretary of Defense Robert] McNamara right on down to the littlest private who's carrying a gun."

At just past 6:00 P.M. Wednesday, the decision was made and the marines aboard the *Boxer* were ordered to prepare to go ashore—all this, despite the fact that by Wednesday evening the CIA had not been able to identify any more than three communists among the leadership of the Dominican rebels. The only remaining question was whether or not to secure the approval of the Organization of American States (OAS) before going in. It was an idea that was never taken too seriously. Johnson himself had said that "The OAS couldn't pour piss out of a boot if the instructions were written on the heel." And one White House aide, asked why the administration did not even try to obtain the sanction of the hemisphere's collective security agency, answered, "It was getting close to cocktail time, which is not the best moment to be rounding up OAS ambassadors." In truth, Johnson could not afford to ask for OAS sanction—he had already decided that the intervention was necessary, and OAS condemnation of the landing would only have been an awkward embarrassment.

At about 7:00 P.M. some four hundred American marines took up positions around the Hotel Embajador in Santo Domingo, and at 8:40 their commander in chief went on national television to inform the American people that U.S. troops had landed in the Dominican Republic to protect American lives. No mention was made of any communist threat. Thursday morning found American marines establishing a safe evacuation zone around the Hotel Embajador and trying to fight off snipers while the Dominican military leaders at the San Isidro air base still showed marked reluctance to press their struggle.

Given the involvement of U.S. troops, their reluctance was understandable. Clearly, the United States meant to thwart the aims of the rebels and do the junta's job for them. As for Juan Bosch, the man in whose name all the trouble had been started, he had been politely told by American officials to stay in his place of exile, Puerto Rico—the fact that the rebels were calling for his restoration was enough to make Bosch seem highly unreliable to many of Johnson's advisers. As Thursday night fell and the San Isidro junta remained militarily ineffectual, President Johnson decided to take the full plunge: the 82nd Airborne began to land at San Isidro, in order to prepare the way for a full-scale American occupation. During the next twelve hours over two battalions of America's premier combat troops landed at the junta air base.

Within the United States, criticism of the invasion became steadily more pointed as the military buildup at San Isidro continued. In the face of this criticism, Ambassador Bennett began to compile a list of "known" communists in the Dominican rebel movement. At the White House, meanwhile, President Johnson, Secretary of State Rusk, Defense Secretary Robert McNamara and National Security Adviser McGeorge Bundy met with a noted former ambassador to the Dominican Republic, John Bartlow Martin. Johnson, and especially Bundy, felt it was urgent that an independent adviser such as Martin (who was by no means convinced that the Dominican revolt was a cover for communist subversion) travel to Santo Domingo and report on the situation. Bundy—who earlier in life had been the coauthor of Henry Stimson's memoirs and edited a collection of Dean Acheson's speeches and writings—was concerned that American military units were very soon going to be forced into large-scale action, and he wanted to be sure that they would have a clear goal.

Rusk, too, stated his opinion, as Martin later recalled it, "that it was a very serious matter to start shooting up a capital city with American troops." Martin quickly interjected, "That's the last thing we want to have happen, Mr. President," to which Johnson answered sharply, "No, it isn't. The last thing we want to have happen is a communist takeover in that country." As Martin left the Cabinet Room, he turned to Bundy and asked, "How much time do you think we've got before they [the American troops] start shooting, taking the place, you know?" Bundy answered simply, "You might have forty-eight hours, but I doubt it."

Ultimately, time was of little consequence. Martin reached San Isidro, where "U.S. planes were landing and taking off every two or three minutes. U.S. soldiers were setting up tents and unloading supplies. U.S. Jeeps and trucks roared across the base and around the hangars. This was a troop buildup. Within a couple of days we had something like twenty-one thousand troops in Santo Domingo —nearly as many as we then had in Vietnam." Meeting with the leaders of both Dominican factions, Martin quickly became convinced that Ambassador Bennett was essentially correct: the rebellion was being exploited by Castroite and communist forces. Perhaps the rebellion had been democratic in the beginning, Martin later wrote, but "in a flash it had changed. . . . Blind fury and anarchy overwhelmed the city. Dominican troops killed Dominican troops. Dominican civilians killed each other. . . . In those senseless hours, all ideals vanished. . . . Men and women like these have no where to go except to the Communists. All other doors are shut."

Why "all other doors" should be so "shut" Martin did not say, but his evaluation was enough for Johnson. On May 2, 1965, the president once again went on national television to explain the dramatic troop buildup in the Dominican Republic. This time he fully elaborated on the communist threat. The speech was laced with inaccuracies and bizarre exaggerations that Johnson apparently believed (as one longtime aide said of the president, "The first victim of the Johnson whopper is always Lyndon Baines Johnson"). According to the President's May 2 version of events, Ambassador Bennett had been ordered home not to visit his ailing mother but to discuss the volatile Dominican situation; the Dominican embassy staff had early on called for American military help, saying that if it did not come, American citizens "will die in the streets" (no such communication had ever been made); but most important of all, the revolution had taken a "tragic turn" because "Communist leaders, many of them trained in Cuba, seeing a chance to increase disorder . . . took increasing control." The United States intended to thwart this plan forcefully, for "the American nations cannot, must not and will not permit the establishment of another Communist government in the Western Hemisphere." The following day, addressing an AFL–CIO group, Johnson said, " . . . we don't propose to sit here in our rocking chair with our hands folded and let the Communists set up any government in the Western Hemisphere."

When the American embassy in Santo Domingo published its list of supposedly known communists in the Dominican rebel movement, American reporters on the scene went to work, quickly identifying many of the persons on the list as either out of the country, already in jail, known *anti*communists, or even, in one or two cases, dead. American credibility in the Dominican crisis began to crumble, and administration officials rushed to salvage it. Secretary of State Dean Rusk played down the numbers issue, saying at a news conference, "I am not impressed by the remark that there were several dozen known Communist leaders and that therefore this was not a very serious matter. There was a time when Hitler sat in a beer hall in Munich with seven people."

In addition, there were diplomatic efforts to offset the anti-communist tone of the invasion. McGeorge Bundy traveled to the Dominican Republic and tried to work out a middle-ground solution to the crisis, an effort that was sabotaged by Undersecretary Mann, who saw no room for a middle in Latin America and the Caribbean. As various OAS members stepped up criticism of the unilateral American intervention, President Johnson agreed to the creation of a multilateral OAS force, to be commanded by a Brazilian general and incorporating U.S. troops—but by this time, the job had been done. The rebels had been defeated, and the presumed communist threat deterred.

In September 1965, the U.S. House of Representatives, delighted with the success of the Dominican operation, passed a resolution declaring that the danger of "subversive domination" by "international communism and its agencies in the Western Hemisphere" was a flagrant violation of the Monroe Doctrine and overrode any inter-American pledges not to intervene in each other's affairs. In other words, large-scale, open American intervention in Latin America, officially repudiated by Washington since the days of Henry Stimson and Franklin Roosevelt, was once again an option.

When a new president for the Dominican Republic was finally selected in the spring of 1966, he turned out to be one of Rafael Trujillo's old associates, Dr. Joaquín Balaguer. Juan Bosch condemned the solution and became bitterly anti-American; civil disorder in the Dominican Republic diminished but did not disappear; and neither the standard of living nor the economic stability of the tiny nation underwent any dramatic increase. But the principal goal for which American troops had fought had nonetheless been secured—whatever else he may have been, Balaguer was no communist.

The importance of the Dominican intervention extended beyond the realm of U.S.–Latin American relations and into the overall American quest for national security. Not since Woodrow

Wilson had an American president been so willing to use U.S. troops to determine directly the outcome of internal dissension in another nation of the hemisphere—and even Wilson had justified his interventionism on moral grounds. Lyndon Johnson, despite his rhetoric, had a far weaker commitment to liberal democracy in Latin America. His was an even more traditional approach to the problems of the region, one that viewed U.S. security as the central motivating factor in hemispheric affairs, that saw the Latin republics often as little more than likely targets for foreign subversion and that did not shrink from the use of massive force in order to achieve its goals. Johnson's dramatic action in the Dominican Republic was nothing more or less than the culmination of a century-and-a-half-long search for a successful way to subordinate the goals of Latin American nationalists to the preeminent concern of the United States for hemispheric security.

The threat of British imperial designs in the Western Hemisphere that had so disturbed America's Founding Fathers in the late eighteenth and early nineteenth centuries created an air of mutual distrust in U.S.–Latin American relations that was to endure for generations. The great Latin American leaders—Francisco de Miranda, José de San Martín, Simón Bolívar—all hoped that the United States would champion their struggles against the Spanish Crown; but American leaders from Alexander Hamilton and Thomas Jefferson to John Quincy Adams believed that the former Spanish colonies were unlikely to create, in Adams's words, "free or liberal institutions of government." Faced with such an attitude, it was only natural that the Latin Americans would seek assistance elsewhere—but when they obtained it, even in highly limited ways, from Great Britain, American suspicions ran high.

For if the republics of Latin America were truly doomed to bad government, as North American leaders believed, then that bad government would in turn create an instability that would eventually lead not to British aid but to British annexation. From the beginning, then, Washington's goal was not so much to play a beneficially influential part in Latin American affairs as to exclude the influence of other powers from the region. This policy is perhaps best exemplified by an incident in 1826, just three years after John Quincy Adams and James Monroe had warned the empires of Europe to stay out of the Western Hemisphere, when the U.S. delegates to Simón Bolívar's pan-American Congress of Panama arrived too late to participate in the proceedings. Such events deeply embittered men like Bolívar—but his objections, like those of his successors, were ignored in Washington.

In the late 1840s, when the issue of digging an isthmian canal in Nicaragua was being talked up by shipping lines and businessmen in both the United States and Great Britain, President James Polk tried to persuade the five republics of Central America (Guatemala, El Salvador, Nicaragua, Honduras and Costa Rica) to resist British influence by working in concert. But, then as now, the five Central American states were bitterly suspicious of one another, and Polk's plan was answered in 1849 not by cooperation but with a request from Nicaragua, El Salvador and Honduras to join the American Union. One of Polk's successors, Franklin Pierce, entered office saying that he would "not be controlled by any timid forebodings of the evils of expansion"; coming on the heels of the Mexican War and the Central Americans' request to join the Union, this statement aroused deep concern in Great Britain, which had imperial possessions in Belize, the Miskito Coast of Nicaragua and the Bay Islands nearby. England's prime minister, Lord Palmerston, was himself ready to take a firm stand against U.S. expansionism in Latin America and the Caribbean, and in America there was equal determination to stand up to "John Bull" in the south just as Polk had done in the northwest over the issue of Oregon.

The 1850 Clayton-Bulwer Treaty, by which the United States and Great Britain agreed to be partners in any Nicaraguan canal scheme, did little to ease these deep-rooted tensions. Of far greater significance over the next decade were the actions of American "filibusterers," independent adventurers who traveled to Latin and especially Central America to seek their fortunes through trade, plunder and politics. The greatest of all these filibusterers was William Walker, "the grey-eyed man of destiny," who was backed by the financial resources of Cornelius Vanderbilt and actually managed to have himself named president of Nicaragua for two years. The incident would have been merely bizarre had the United States not recognized Walker. But British indignation at such actions was real and dangerous. Only the reluctance of the British public to enter yet again into hostilities against the United States prevented a serious breach.

In 1860 Great Britain began the process of begrudgingly assenting to American hegemony in the Western Hemisphere by officially relinquishing control of Nicaragua's Miskito Coast and the Bay Islands (although Britain retained Belize). But this did little to ease the now-fixed American fear that, with the northwest boundary of the United States secure, it was from the south that future threats would come. This fear prompted Secretary of State William Seward's tough bargaining stance in talks with France over Napoleon III's ill-fated Mexican adventure during the American Civil War, and those talks once again revealed the essential American attitude toward Latin America. Seward had little interest in internal Mexican strife caused by generations of class and racial conflict between Indian peasants and Spanish oligarchs. His only concern was to exclude other powers from the region, and once that was assured, Mexico's importance to him disappeared.

The American fear of European, and especially British, intrusion into Latin America sprang up several more times in the nineteenth century, particularly during the British-Venezuelan boundary dispute of 1895. That disagreement led to Secretary of State Richard Olney's remarkable statement during the Cleveland administration that the United States was "practically sovereign on this continent, and its fiat is law upon the subjects to which it confines its interposition." Although Olney's counterpart in the administration of Benjamin Harrison, James G. Blaine, had attempted to play down such arrogance by stressing a reborn Pan-Americanism as the key to mutual prosperity in the hemisphere, even he could not help but reveal his American chauvinism from time to time. This was most true in the case of his famous "annexation of trade" speech in 1890, which demonstrated Blaine's desire to closely tie the economic fortunes of Latin America to the leadership of the United States.

The drastic expansion of American economic interests in Latin America and the Caribbean that had started with the "decade of the filibusterers" was given a strong boost by Blaine's Pan-Americanism and heightened Washington's desire for stability in Latin America. And certainly, U.S. intervention in Latin America during the late nineteenth and early twentieth centuries often coincided with the interests of American business. Interventionism also conflicted with those same interests on many other occasions, disturbing established governmental systems that were favorable to U.S. business. The examples of Cuba in 1898 and many of Woodrow Wilson's crusading policies represent only a portion of these cases. The pattern of American behavior in Latin American affairs can only be fully understood if we bear in mind that while American business often profited by Washington's efforts to ensure hemispheric security, it rarely prompted them—such practices had long been in use and represented a tradition of active response to the threats of European interference generally and of British imperialism specifically.

Although the British threat had largely disappeared by the end of the nineteenth century, the American tendency to view Latin America as a region susceptible to foreign penetration by its own internal weaknesses remained firmly in place. When the rise of the Imperial German Navy became the principal concern of men such as Henry Cabot Lodge and Theodore Roosevelt, it was therefore only logical they should view Latin America and the Caribbean as the most likely locales for German aggression. Germany's defeat did allow momentary relief from Latin American anxieties in Washington, but the new threat of Bolshevism, imported into Central America by Mexico's revolutionaries, revived those fears and sparked American intervention in Nicaragua, to which it was feared Mexico's radicalism would spread.

But by the late 1920s, statesmen such as Henry Stimson could see that the supposed "socialism" of Mexico was nothing more than a facade, and that America in fact had no great rival for control of the hemisphere. For the first time, Washington felt comfortable with the idea of letting Latin Americans tend to their own affairs. The resulting Good Neighbor policy was prompted more by the absence of perceived threats than by any particular concern with improving the lot of Latin Americans in general. This is best attested to by Franklin Roosevelt's tolerance of such dictators as Rafael Trujillo in the Dominican Republic and Anastasio Somoza in Nicaragua, both of whom FDR was said to have dismissed at different times with the same revealing remark: "He's a son of a bitch, but he's ours."

The first century of American anxieties over Latin America and the Caribbea i had always been general. Cuba, however, had consistently been cause for particular concern. The island that Jefferson believed could "fill up the measure of our political well being" and that John Quincy Adams called "indispensable to the continuance of the integrity of the Union itself" continued to disturb the thoughts of American leaders even after Presidents Polk and Pierce were frustrated in their efforts to buy it. Although the United States pledged itself to Cuban independence following the

Spanish-American War, Senator Orville Platt of Connecticut proposed an amendment to the 1901 U.S. Army appropriations bill
that strongly compromised that pledge. The Platt Amendment,
soon signed into law, stated that Cuba could not enter into any
treaties that the United States considered compromising to the
island's independence; that Cuba could not go into governmental
debt; that the United States would be allowed to maintain a large
naval and military base at Guantánamo Bay on the southern coast
of the island; and, most important of all, that should Cuban internal stability break down, the United States would be justified in
intervening to restore it.

Deeply offensive to Cuban nationalists, the Platt Amendment
remained in effect until 1934—the same year, it so happened, that
an aggressive strongman came to power in Havana through a revolt of Cuban noncommissioned officers. Fulgencio Batista at first
ruled through puppet presidents, but when a Cuban constitutional
convention set elections for 1940, Batista entered the lists and was
promptly elected. For four years Batista ruled legally, and when
he was defeated in the 1944 elections he allowed his opponent to
take office. Cuba, it seemed, might actually be on the road to democracy.

In March 1950, just before the outbreak of the Korean War, the
State Department's George Kennan went on a fact-finding tour of
Latin America. His conclusions had important implications both
for U.S. policy in the Western Hemisphere and for any hopes for
Cuban democracy. The danger in Latin America, as everywhere
else, was communism, said Kennan; and if Stalin should overrun
Europe, then "Latin America would be all we would have to fall
back on." The huge task of rebuilding Europe and Japan was
draining American resources away from the nations of the Western Hemisphere; but since the era of James G. Blaine it had been
those resources that had encouraged stability in Latin America—
without the money, there was little hope for regional security. Yet
the reconstruction of Europe and Asia was of primary importance.
The United States in this respect faced a severe dilemma, one to
which Kennan offered a solution that eventually became the principal guideline for U.S. policy in Latin America during the next
generation. In fighting communism in the Western Hemisphere,
Kennan said:

"The final answer might be an unpleasant one, but . . . we should
not hesitate before police repression by the local government. This

is not shameful since the Communists are essentially traitors. . . . It is better to have a strong regime in power than a liberal government if it is indulgent and relaxed and penetrated by Communists."

The Good Neighbor policy had been dropped. A new threat, perhaps more powerful than any of its predecessors, had revived American fears that Latin American instability would lead to subversive foreign penetration and thereby threaten the security of the United States itself. Washington believed it did not have the money to promote democracy or the troops to intervene directly in hemispheric affairs. The job of ensuring stability would have to be left to Latin American leaders alone, and more often than not, this meant military dictators acting with the support of Latin America's still-powerful landed oligarchies.

Certainly, this was the case in Cuba. In 1952 Batista once again entered the presidential race but, sensing early on that he would not be elected, seized presidential power by force. Ruling with the support of Cuban landowners and American businessmen, Batista ignored his country's constitution for two years and, whenever criticism arose, cited his strong opposition to communism. In 1954 he staged an election in which he ran unopposed, thus restoring at least the appearance of legitimacy to his rule.

But domestic Cuban discontent rose. In November 1956 the eloquent Cuban nationalist Fidel Castro returned to his country from exile in Mexico and began to organize guerrilla bands in the Cuban mountains. Batista immediately embarked on a brutal campaign to crush this opposition, killing some twenty thousand Cubans over the next two years and torturing many more. As Castro's following grew, some American businessmen in Cuba began to sense a change in the political climate of the country. This development was crucial, for at the time of Castro's revolt American interests owned a large percentage of the Cuban sugar industry as well as a controlling share of the country's mining firms and public utilities. Castro had not yet been confirmed as a Marxist-Leninist and his popularity in Cuba was unarguable; Washington, hoping it could capitalize on the nationalist drive behind the revolution, made no significant move to maintain Batista when Castro seized power in January 1959.

It was a decision that would be long and harshly debated during the years that followed. At first it seemed a creative and successful choice—Castro was welcomed into power by the Cuban people and made no immediate, serious moves against U.S. business interests. But when Castro ordered summary executions of many Cuban military officers and other Batista supporters, he lost much of his appeal, especially to Americans. Castro explained that he was simply consolidating his position; but his followers began to heighten their anti-American propaganda, and Castro finally did make preliminary moves to seize U.S. holdings in his country.

Cuba's principal export, sugar, had long enjoyed duty-free status in the United States, and Washington now began to talk of changing that unless Castro moderated his policies. The effect was predictable. In the face of even hinted American coercion, Castro rallied his supporters to ever more ardent nationalism—and to socialism. Programs of land redistribution and industrial nationalization were put in place, and American suspicions about the new Cuban leader reached a peak.

In February 1960 Castro and Soviet Chairman Nikita Khrushchev signed the Russo-Cuban Trade Agreement. The Soviets agreed to supply oil and technical experts in exchange for Cuban sugar. Russian trade, which before the revolution had accounted for only some 2 percent of overall Cuban dealings, was soon running at 80 percent. In July 1960, Cuban sugar was cut from the American market altogether, leaving Castro fully dependent on Soviet assistance. More and more Cuban refugees came into the United States, with stories of an idealistic Cuban revolution betrayed by the communist Castro. By the end of 1960 President Dwight D. Eisenhower had agreed to allow the CIA to secretly train anti-Castro Cuban guerrillas in Guatemala.

Whether the United States could have changed the outcome of the Cuban revolution through a more moderate policy, or if in fact Castro had committed himself to a thoroughly socialist revolution far earlier than he wished Americans in Cuba and Washington to suspect, has remained a debate with no foreseeable conclusion. Eisenhower's decision to train the anti-Castro guerrillas, however, was a gambit whose denouement came relatively soon—and was nothing if not decisive. When John F. Kennedy was inaugurated in January 1961, he announced a massive new program of economic and technical assistance for Latin America known as the Alliance for Progress; but even more quickly, he decided to sever all relations with Castro's Cuba and to maintain Eisenhower's covert CIA operation in Guatemala. Less than a month after the announcement of the Alliance for Progress, the CIA reported that their Cuban guerrillas were ready to mount a countercoup against Castro if the United States was ready to supply transportation and air support. Kennedy assented.

On April 17, 1961, the 1,500 Cuban exiles landed at the Bay of Pigs on Cuba's southern coast. The promised U.S. support failed to materialize, and Castro, grasping the importance of timing, fell on the guerrillas and destroyed them almost immediately. The incident was more than an indication of Castro's power and popularity—it was one of the worst humiliations suffered in recent years by an American president. The U.S. role had been obvious, and Khrushchev lost no time in reminding Kennedy on April 18 that the American president had given the Soviet Union public as well as private assurances that no such anti-Castro project was to be undertaken: "How are we to understand what is really being done by the United States now that the attack on Cuba has become a fact?" The denunciation was coupled with a warning: "As for the U.S.S.R., there must be no mistake about our position. We will extend to the Cuban people and its Government all the necessary aid for the repulse of the armed attack on Cuba. We are sincerely interested in the relaxation of international tension, but if others go in for its aggravation, we will answer in full measure."

President Kennedy was well aware of how drastically the Bay of Pigs disaster had both damaged American effectiveness in international relations and bolstered Castro's now firmly Marxist government. Privately, Kennedy voiced his deep regret at having allowed the project to proceed: "How could I have been so far off base?" he asked. "All my life I've known better than to depend on the experts. How could I have been so stupid, to let them go ahead?" But Kennedy was reluctant to display such sentiments to Khrushchev. On the same day that he received the Soviet leader's message, Kennedy sent back a reply, telling Khrushchev that the Russians were "under a serious misapprehension in regard to events in Cuba. . . . Where people are denied the right of choice, recourse to such struggle [as the Bay of Pigs] is the only means of achieving their liberties." Kennedy also matched the international tone of Khrushchev's warning: "I have taken careful note of your statement that the events in Cuba might affect peace in all parts of the world. I trust that this does not mean that the Soviet government, using the situation in Cuba as a pretext, is planning to inflame other areas of the world." Kennedy reminded his counterpart that "free peoples in all parts of the world do not accept the claim of historical inevitability for Communist revolution. What your government believes is its own business; what it does in the world is the world's business."

Both Eisenhower and Kennedy, then, believed that the loss of Cuba to the Soviet bloc represented a tremendous threat to American security. Largely because of the success of the 1954 Guatemalan exercise, each of them also believed that CIA-backed subversion would work; neither adequately appreciated Castro's genius for leadership or the very real extent of his popularity. The Bay of Pigs only strengthened that popularity, and by the spring of 1961, America was faced with one of its worst national nightmares come to life—the island of Cuba tied to a mortal enemy. At this point, hemispheric security evolved from a goal into an obsession.

True, Kennedy did try to restore some liberal democratic elements to the security-dominated hemispheric policy of the United States by creating the Alliance for Progress; but he very soon came to realize that Latin American social and economic problems were even more staggering than they had been in Woodrow Wilson's day ("almost insuperable," in Kennedy's own words) and he had doubts that they could be solved by any American aid program. But the more fundamental problem—how to keep communism, now that it was firmly entrenched in Cuba, confined to that island—could not be viewed as insoluble. To do so would be to acknowledge that the United States must learn to live with a constant threat just ninety miles from its own shores, and Kennedy was not the man to break so fundamentally with a century and a half of American tradition. After 1961, Cuba's role as the focus of U.S. security concerns in Latin America was solidified; future American efforts in the region would generally have as their basis the prevention of "another Cuba."

This policy was privately spelled out by President Kennedy when Dominican dictator Rafael Trujillo was assassinated in May 1961. There were "three possibilities" for a future Dominican government, said JFK, "in descending order of preference: a decent democratic regime, a continuation of the Trujillo regime or a Castro regime. We ought to aim at the first, but we really can't renounce the second until we are sure that we can avoid the third." On December 2, 1961, Fidel Castro further polarized the situation by announcing publicly, "I am a Marxist-Leninist, and I shall be a Marxist-Leninist until the last day of my life." The lines had be-

come ever more sharply drawn—and the mutual antagonism between the two countries soon pushed the entire world to the very
brink of disaster.

In part because of the fall of Cuba, and in part because of other
aggressive Soviet moves throughout the world—such as the construction of the Berlin Wall in August 1961—President Kennedy
and his secretary of defense, Robert McNamara, felt the need to
bolster American public confidence throughout the first eighteen
months of their administration by frequently speaking of America's growing advantage in strategic nuclear weaponry. By the summer of 1962, Khrushchev had become deeply disturbed by such
statements, and decided that a Soviet countermove was necessary.
Just how or where the Russian leader would choose to do so was
not clear—but Kennedy felt sufficiently uneasy about the Cuban
situation to warn the Soviets in mid-September 1962 not to try to
install nuclear weapons of any kind in Cuba. On October 3, the
U.S. Congress echoed their president's concern by passing a joint
resolution declaring that the regime of Fidel Castro was trying to
export communism into other nations of the Caribbean and Latin
America, and that this contravened not only the Monroe Doctrine
but the charter of the OAS and the 1947 Rio Pact as well. The
United States, said the resolution, was therefore justified in stop-
ping that spread "by whatever means may be necessary . . ." The
document did not rule out another invasion attempt.

Despite such ominous moves and countermoves, it nonetheless
came as an enormous shock to the members of Kennedy's cabinet
to learn on October 14, 1962, that American U-2 spy planes had
photographed missile-launching sites under construction in Cuba.
Further photos even showed a partially assembled Russian ballistic
missile on the ground. Kennedy immediately interpreted this development as a Russo-Cuban test of American will; as one of the
president's advisers put it, "Every country in the world, watching
so audacious an action ninety miles from the United States, would
wonder whether it could ever thereafter trust Washington's resolution and protection."

Quickly, an Executive Committee, or "ExCom," was formed to
study the problem and decide on an appropriate response. The
ExCom included Secretaries Rusk and McNamara, National Security Adviser McGeorge Bundy and other key cabinet members, as

well as a group of out-of-government experts whose opinions were viewed as vitally important in formulating an American plan of action. Chief among this group was Dean Acheson. The ExCom's work was made all the more difficult by the need to conduct its business in absolute secrecy; revelation of the events in Cuba might cause a national panic.

Acheson, as he would later do in regard to Vietnam, recalled Korea in strongly advising President Kennedy to order an immediate air strike to destroy the Cuban missile installations; but such a strike ran the risk of killing not only Cuban civilians but Russian technicians as well. At the urging of Attorney General Robert Kennedy—who likened the proposed American air strike to the Japanese attack at Pearl Harbor—JFK eventually settled on the idea of a naval blockade of Cuba (and he was even secretly prepared to take American missiles out of Turkey if the Soviets would remove theirs from Cuba). On October 22, 1962, the president went on national television to inform the American public of what had transpired and what he intended to do about it.

Speaking in level tones that did little to disguise his own understanding of the enormity of the danger facing the world at that moment, Kennedy announced that he had "unmistakable evidence" that a "series of offensive missile sites is now in preparation" on Cuba, which he called "that imprisoned island." The purpose of these bases, he continued, "can be none other than to provide a nuclear strike capability against the Western Hemisphere." This, according to Kennedy, was a violation of all inter-American pacts, as well as of the Monroe Doctrine and Congress's recent joint resolution.

Next, Kennedy harkened back to several of his Democratic predecessors. Like Truman and Acheson, he recalled the totalitarian threat of the 1930s, which, said the president, "taught us a clear lesson: Aggressive conduct, if allowed to grow unchecked and unchallenged, ultimately leads to war." The United States, while it did not wish war, especially nuclear war, would not "shrink from that risk at any time it must be faced." Then, explaining his response to the Soviet-Cuban move, he echoed Franklin Roosevelt by forgoing the term "blockade" and inserting the word quarantine: "a strict quarantine on all offensive military equipment under shipment to Cuba is being initiated." Ships found to be carrying such goods would be turned back; others could proceed. In addition,

Kennedy pledged to maintain U.S. surveillance of Cuba and to seek collective condemnation of the new missile sites by both the OAS and the United Nations.

One section of Kennedy's address especially revealed the catastrophic dimensions of the Cuban missile crisis: "It shall be the policy of this nation to regard any nuclear missile launched from Cuba against any nation in the Western Hemisphere as an attack by the Soviet Union on the United States, requiring a full retaliatory response upon the Soviet Union." Worldwide nuclear war now depended on the actions of Cuba's ruler. In an attempt to undercut Castro, Kennedy appealed to the Cuban people—just as Franklin Roosevelt had appealed to the peoples of Italy and Germany—to reject this latest gamble: "These new weapons are not in your interest. They contribute nothing to your peace and well-being. They can only undermine it."

If anyone had ever doubted the key place Cuba held on the security perimeter of the United States, that doubt was dispelled by Kennedy's dramatic address. During the following week, American and Soviet ships faced each other in the Caribbean Sea, while Kennedy and Khrushchev exchanged notes, desperately seeking a way out of war. The missiles, Khrushchev repeatedly maintained, were purely for defensive purposes. Kennedy dismissed this argument as preposterous. Finally, on October 27, the Russian leader blinked, and admitted that "mistakes . . . have been made in the history of our state," and that Russian leaders, including himself, "have not only acknowledged them but sharply condemned them." The implication was that placing missiles in Cuba might have been one such mistake. If Kennedy would agree to end the blockade and issue a pledge that the United States would not again sponsor or participate in an invasion of Cuba, said Khrushchev, the missiles would be withdrawn. Kennedy agreed to the terms, but demanded that the pledge not to invade be conditional on American on-site inspection of the dismantling of the Cuban missiles. Such inspection never occurred, and Kennedy therefore did not consider the pledge binding.

Kennedy had participated in one of history's greatest tests of will and won, but despite the unbinding nature of his pledge not to invade Cuba, it became apparent that the president would now concentrate on containing rather than actively undermining Castro. Cuba nonetheless remained fixed in his mind as a symbol of American vulnerability. On November 18, 1963, just four days before his death, Kennedy spoke in Miami and declared that "We in the Western hemisphere must use every resource at our command to prevent the establishment of another Cuba in this hemisphere, for if there is one principle which has run through the long history of this hemisphere it is our common determination to prevent the rule of foreign systems or nations in the Americas."

For Kennedy, a policy to prevent foreign intervention in the hemisphere had always had an economic as well as a military side, although neither had proved a marked success. This lack of any appreciable result helped to convince his successor that the subordination of economic development to military security in Latin America was an absolute. It was this subordination that determined Johnson's response to the 1965 Dominican crisis; and in November 1966, Johnson spelled out his views publicly, in a speech that had important implications not only for Latin America, but for the entire perimeter of American security interests:

"There are 3 billion people in the world and we have only 200 million of them. We are outnumbered 15 to 1. If might did make right they would sweep over the United States and take what we have. We have what they want. . . . We have had to show it couldn't be done in Korea. We may have to show it can't be done in other parts of the Pacific. We are showing right now it can't be done in Vietnam. Four hundred thousand of our young men, the flower of our manhood, the very tops, are out there.

"It is better to do it there than it is in Honolulu."

The stewardship over American foreign policy of Richard Nixon and his national security adviser (later secretary of state), Henry A. Kissinger, saw yet another swing in the American attitude toward Latin America, this one back toward limited interest and, in cases where action was deemed absolutely necessary, covert operations. Both Nixon and Kissinger were inclined to view world affairs in terms of great power politics. In Kissinger's elaborate system of balancing the powers, there was little room for the nations of Latin America. Like Nelson Rockefeller, who undertook a special mission to Latin America for Nixon in 1969, Kissinger was most comfortable assigning responsibility for hemispheric stability to Latin America's established rulers, and was disturbed by any threat to that policy.

This became fully evident during the 1973 crisis in Chile. In 1970, radical socialist Salvador Allende had been elected president

of a Chile increasingly controlled by oligarchs and American businessmen. Allende's initial efforts to restructure his country's land
ownership system as well as to limit American influence caused
alarm in Washington, where he was perceived as the next Castro.
Various methods of eliminating Allende were discussed, but it was
not until September 1973, when the Chilean military—with American approval if not direct American assistance—staged a coup
against their president, that Nixon and Kissinger's consistent efforts to undermine Allende (who died during the coup) became
known.

But these efforts had never been as significant as anything undertaken by Johnson, Kennedy or even Eisenhower. Kissinger re-
portedly viewed Chile as "a dagger pointing at the heart—of
Antarctica," and when he had received a Chilean emissary three
months before the military coup in Santiago he had lectured his
visitor with studied contempt. "You come here," Kissinger said,
"speaking of Latin America, but this is not important. Nothing
important can come from the South. History has never been produced in the South. The axis of history starts in Moscow, goes to
Bonn, crosses over to Washington, and then goes to Tokyo. What
happens in the South is of no importance." The Chilean emissary,
stunned, told the American secretary of state that he knew "nothing of the South." "No," Kissinger replied, "and I don't care."
Nixon's successor, Gerald Ford, accepted Kissinger's assessments;
and as American attention turned away from Latin America in the
early to mid-1970s, the economic and political stability of the region once again deteriorated. The grisly work of right-wing police
and murder squads as well as of leftist terrorists turned much of
the Western Hemisphere into a tragically familiar bloodbath, centered especially on the Central American nations of El Salvador
and Nicaragua.

Jimmy Carter's inauguration in January 1977 signaled yet another swing of the pendulum of U.S. Latin American policy. The
soft-spoken, reflective former governor of Georgia wanted to put
renewed emphasis on the hemispheric problems of poverty, ignorance and human rights violations, and two of his principal advisers—Cyrus Vance at the State Department and Andrew Young at
the United Nations—supported this goal. The conclusion of the
Canal Zone Treaty in 1978, by which the United States pledged to
gradually shift control of its most valued waterway to the Republic
of Panama over the next twenty-two years, was a momentous turn-

ing point in U.S.–Latin American affairs, and seemed to herald a new era full of fresh possibilities.

But the fact that the treaty was ratified in the Senate by only one vote demonstrated the reluctance of many American leaders to abandon a security-dominated policy in the hemisphere. And Carter himself ultimately proved unable to escape the pressing need to attend to American security by stressing above all else the need for hemispheric stability. Although Carter's human rights rhetoric undoubtedly had beneficial effects in countries such as Brazil and Argentina, and although the Canal Zone Treaty did improve U.S.– Latin American relations generally, the president was nonetheless stymied when faced with leftist revolutions in Central America. In Nicaragua and El Salvador, the forces of stability were clashing with revolutionaries who demanded the kind of reforms that Carter himself seemed to be calling for; yet Carter, whatever his other dissimilarities to John Kennedy, Lyndon Johnson and Richard Nixon, was no more willing than they had been to tolerate the kind of revolutionary chaos that might lead to another Cuba. But while Carter inherited the great Latin American dilemma of his predecessors, in the face of it, he waffled.

This was especially true in the case of Nicaragua, where in 1979 the ruling Somoza family was finally deposed by the radical Sandinistas. The Somozas had based their power on control of the Nicaraguan National Guard, a force created and trained by American marines during the late 1920s and early 30s. The National Guard's principal antagonist at that time had been the same Augusto Sandino who had defied Henry Stimson's negotiated peace of Tipitapa. Sandino was eventually murdered by the National Guard, and, despite his own record of brutality to uncooperative Nicaraguan peasants, became a celebrated martyr. By the late 1970s, Sandinista opposition to the Somozas' exacting and repressive rule was gaining ground, and President Carter himself was not unsympathetic to the rebels' grievances. Nevertheless, the Sandinista leaders were Marxists, and Soviet-Cuban adventurism had recently been on display in many parts of the world, particularly Afghanistan and Angola.

In order to forestall any possible opening for the Soviet Union or Cuba in Central America, Carter and his national security adviser, Zbigniew Brzezinski, began clandestine efforts to maintain Anastasio Somoza Debayle in power in Nicaragua, while simultaneously trying to persuade the dictator to moderate his human rights policies. But brutality was the very essence of Somoza's rule; and as Nicaraguan violence heightened, a frustrated Carter tried to get the Organization of American States to intervene. It was a fruitless effort. Finally, Somoza fell and the Sandinistas assumed power in Managua.

In order not to repeat the Cuban experience of twenty years earlier, Carter immediately tried to extend his hand to the Sandinistas by sending $20 million worth of aid to Nicaragua. In September 1979 he asked Congress for another $70 million—but the American Congress was by that time both mystified by Carter's apparently contradictory Latin American policies and alienated by his conduct on a number of other issues. The aid measure was not passed until the middle of 1980, and by then the Sandinistas, perilously near bankruptcy, had sought aid from Castro and in turn the Soviet Union.

Carter had no more "lost" Nicaragua than Eisenhower and Kennedy had "lost" Cuba, but the fact that Marxism had finally made the leap from a Caribbean island to the American mainland was nonetheless cause for alarm and even near panic among many American leaders. Events in El Salvador did little to ease this heightened fear. Throughout the 1970s that country, with its most respected leaders in political exile, had been ravaged by a brutal civil war. In 1979 a group of junior military officers overthrew the ruling regime and tried to introduce moderate reforms, while at the same time pledging to prosecute the struggle against leftist guerrillas. But these young officers faced the same dilemma that the United States itself often had: economic and land reform in El Salvador would alienate most of the army (who were closely tied to the country's oligarchy) and thereby render any effort to combat the leftist rebels a near hopeless task. Unable to act, the reformers fled the country within a few months, and a military junta took over.

President Carter once again revealed that his main concern was for Latin American stability. He asked Congress for aid for the Salvadoran junta, while he characteristically stressed his intention to see to it that the junta instituted reforms. Predictably, the reforms got nowhere, while the American aid went to reinforce the junta's rule. Carter, who feared both the domestic and international effects of another leftist takeover in Central America, hesitated to reverse his policy yet again—but when a group of four women, including two American Maryknoll nuns, were raped and murdered by Salvadoran government soldiers, he had no choice but to cut off aid. In 1980 the president was bogged down in a quagmire of contradiction and disappointment, the celebrated achievement of the Canal Zone Treaty long since forgotten and the upcoming American national election deeply in doubt.

Carter's Republican opponent in the 1980 election, Ronald Reagan, made much of the Central American issue. Placing public emphasis on the security aspect of that region's affairs, Reagan early on revealed a preoccupation with Nicaragua that matched America's earlier Cuban obsession and betrayed the would-be president's overall view of world affairs. "Let's not delude ourselves," he said in an interview during the campaign. "The Soviet Union underlies all the unrest that is going on. If they weren't engaged in this game of dominoes, there wouldn't be any hot spots in the world." Reagan's universalist attitude toward the threat of international communism was a throwback to the hyperbole of NSC-68 —"When did the cold war ever end?" he asked rhetorically—and signaled a return to American reliance on unilateral intervention, both overt and covert, to attain U.S. security goals in the Western Hemisphere.

Keeping Carter's program of aid to the anti-leftist government of El Salvador in place, the newly inaugurated President Reagan quickly authorized the CIA to train anti-Sandinista Nicaraguans in Honduras. These so-called "contras" included not only ex-Sandinistas disillusioned by the authoritarian turn their revolution had taken, but former supporters of Somoza as well—a highly heterogenous group, remarkably similar in composition to the anti-Castro Cubans who had tried to invade at the Bay of Pigs in 1961. Despite such an ominous precedent, Reagan felt that the policy was of utmost importance—Managua had recently increased its support of guerrillas in El Salvador, and once again the principal problem for an American executive was the containment of communism in the Western Hemisphere.

In pursuing this goal, Reagan saw no need to employ complex policies such as John Kennedy and Jimmy Carter had tried to pursue, which aimed not only at halting the spread of communism but also at addressing the larger problems of repressive political systems and backward economies. Reagan viewed such attempts as self-defeating, and any failure to counter the Sandinistas and shore up the anticommunist government in El Salvador, the president believed, only damaged American credibility elsewhere. Attempting to rally the country behind his policy of political and, if necessary, military involvement in Central American affairs, Reagan washed over the example of the Bay of Pigs and emphasized the direct threat to U.S. security that he perceived as inherent in the Central American crisis: "If we cannot defend ourselves there," he told a joint session of Congress in April 1983, "we cannot expect to prevail elsewhere. Our credibility would collapse, our alliances would crumble. . . ." Three months later Reagan authorized a presidential commission headed by former Secretary of State Henry Kissinger to travel to Central America and formulate appropriate U.S. policies for the region. But while the commission was doing its work, the arming and training of the contras went on.

In July 1983 the Contadora group of Latin American nations—Mexico, Venezuela, Colombia and Panama—called for pan-American talks to find a peaceful solution for the problems of Central America. Cuba's Fidel Castro cautiously accepted the idea of such talks, provided that all parties, including the United States, agreed to abide by their findings. In Nicaragua, President Daniel Ortega made a similar commitment. And in Washington, President Reagan praised the effort as admirable—but made no move to pursue the initiative. Four years later, the presidents of the five Central American countries signed a plan to end hostilities in the region. Once again, Reagan rhetorically endorsed the effort, but later termed the plan fatally flawed and was reluctant to lend his support to its provisions. He had in fact no intention of allowing a multilateral solution in Central America that might compromise the interests of U.S. security, and preferred instead to rely on a policy of arming the Salvadoran government and attempting to subvert the Marxist regime in Managua.

Meanwhile, the tiny nation of El Salvador continued to be racked by violence that was, even by Central American standards, horrifying. Right-wing death squads murdered with impunity anyone even suspected of aiding the leftist guerrillas; and those same guerrillas maintained their control over El Salvador's hinterland as much through terror as through the persuasiveness of their politics. Neither the government nor its opponents were able to gain any significant military advantage; but despite this deadlock, the Reagan administration chose not to initiate or pursue meaningful diplomatic solutions throughout 1983.

January 1984 saw the release of the Kissinger Commission's Report on Central America. Its conclusions were nothing if not predictable, reflecting both Washington's obsession with hemispheric security and Kissinger's own tendency to view Third World conflicts as mere extensions of big-power conflict. The report's chief concern was that America's "credibility worldwide is engaged." In characteristic universalist fashion, failure in Central America was perceived as damaging to overall American security interests: "The ability of the United States to sustain a tolerable balance of power on the global scene depends on the inherent security of its land borders." Internal conditions in countries like El Salvador were dealt with simplistically: ever greater military support was required to sustain the government and give it a chance to hold elections and reforms. To the commission, however, the central issue was not the solution of domestic Central American inequities, but the "erosion of our power to influence events worldwide that would flow from the perception that we were unable to influence vital events close to home."

Hoping to lend greater legitimacy to his increasingly controversial Central American policy, President Reagan agreed to American sponsorship of Salvadoran elections in the spring of 1984. In a May runoff vote, José Napoleon Duarte, a Christian Democrat, was elected president and pledged to end the violence in his country and make governmental participation more broadly based. Yet Duarte's hopeful beginnings were soon deeply endangered by the continuing desire of the Salvadoran army to suppress the leftist rebels. Reagan, meanwhile, could argue as had Woodrow Wilson that he was helping to teach all of Latin America the virtues of "good government"; but, again like Wilson, Reagan had already revealed the essence of his approach to hemispheric affairs—unilateral intervention—in another part of the region.

In October 1983 American military forces, in a highly secret operation, had stormed the tiny Caribbean island of Grenada. The domestic Grenadian circumstances that prompted the invasion were almost as complex as had been those in the Dominican Republic in 1965, but both cases shared one overriding factor: a group of native military officers deposed the government and could not demonstrate to Washington's satisfaction that they were free of communist influence. There were also important differences between the 1965 and the 1983 American operations: in Grenada, the United States acted in cooperation with the Organization of Eastern Caribbean States (although the United Nations and even some of America's allies subsequently condemned the action); and in Grenada, too, the officers heading the new regime were avowed Marxists and there was at least some evidence that Castro intended to take advantage of the revolutionary chaos— Cuban advisers were captured during the militarily flawed but ultimately successful American campaign. But the essential rationale was the same in both cases, and dramatically demonstrated that America's traditional attitude toward hemispheric security had changed very little over two decades—indeed, over one and a half centuries.

Yet if the attitude and its attendant policies had changed comparatively little during that time, their rate of success had diminished. Since the end of World War II the larger South American nations, most notably Chile and Argentina (always a locus of anti-American sentiment) had proved troublesome indeed to the United States' pursuit of its perceived security requirements. In the Caribbean, Castro's takeover of Cuba seemed the final thwarting of the hopes of generations of American presidents, while the export of Marxist revolution to the Latin American mainland underlined the growing irrelevance of traditional American security considerations to Latin American nationalism. The Western Hemisphere, whose stability had so long been seen in Washington as the first requisite of U.S. security, was clearly slipping away from American control.

The loss of Cuba, so long dreaded as a vital blow to U.S. security, in fact proved manageable, once American interests were clearly spelled out during the 1962 missile crisis. The threats to the Panama Canal and Caribbean sea-lanes that had often been predicted as consequences of a hostile takeover in Havana did not materialize. But Latin American suspicions about U.S. motives and methods were greatly heightened by the anticommunist actions undertaken by Washington after Castro's victory. Similarly, the loss of Nicaragua did not drastically affect American security—Managua's swing to Marxism proved less of a regional irritant than did the contra war supported by the Reagan administration and funded to a large extent by various shadowy American private backers.

In truth, the Latin American crisis of the post–World War II era had far more to do with domestic social stratification and economic mismanagement than it did with the spread of Marxism. By the time of the American invasion of Grenada, many key Latin American countries—most notably Brazil, Argentina and Mexico—had sunk so deeply into debt to foreign governments and banks that there seemed little likelihood of their ever making good on the loans. Much of the income of these nations was needed to pay off the interest on their debts. Wealthy Latin Americans, especially in Mexico, took funds out of their unstable native economies and deposited them abroad, creating staggering liquidity problems. At the same time, their poorer countrymen fled in growing numbers from domestic violence and unemployment to the sanctuary of the United States. A hemispheric crisis was no longer imminent—it had arrived with devastating force.

Yet in the face of these dislocations, President Reagan chose to downplay economic issues and to heighten his anticommunist policies toward Latin America generally, and toward Nicaragua especially. Like so many American leaders before him, Reagan had been frustrated by Latin American complexities; in Reagan's case he turned to traditional Cold War universalism as a way of ensuring U.S. security in the hemisphere. But at the same time, Reagan sensed the inadequacy of past approaches to the broader issues of American national security, and began to look beyond the hemisphere for innovative ways to make America safe from foreign threats. In this search he finally turned not to other allies or to other regions of the globe, but to the heavens themselves, and there he perceived a security that might, at long last, prove absolute.

I X

STAR WARS—THE SEARCH FOR ABSOLUTE SECURITY

1967–1986

DR. Edward Teller, America's foremost thermonuclear physicist, first met Ronald Reagan in Sacramento shortly after Reagan's election as governor of California in the fall of 1966. Teller later described this initial meeting as "not at all close," but "successful," in that he was able to convince Reagan to pay a visit to his base of operations, the Lawrence Livermore National Laboratory. Located some forty miles east of San Francisco, Lawrence Livermore was at the core of America's thermonuclear research program, and at the time of the meeting between Dr. Teller and Governor-elect Reagan, the laboratory's activities were focused on a project that proved to have special appeal for California's new chief executive —nuclear defense against Soviet missiles and warheads.

Reagan arrived at Lawrence Livermore's maze of multistoried institutional buildings and low-level sheds on a late winter morning in 1967, soon after his inauguration. He was immediately taken to a general briefing on the laboratory's various programs, particularly an upcoming test in Alaska of a large, ground-launched nuclear weapon that was designed to destroy incoming Soviet missiles.

Reagan, deeply interested, interrupted to ask "maybe a dozen questions," according to Teller, all of which were "sharp, pointed, [and] technical." Teller was impressed by Reagan's apparent grasp of subjects "about which he could not have known a great deal." Subsequently, Reagan attended a lunch with some twelve members of the laboratory's staff—"a politically mixed group"—where Teller was further impressed (as most of America would one day be) by the fact that Reagan "got along with everybody."

Neither Reagan nor Teller could have known that within a decade and a half the seeds planted during the governor's visit to Lawrence Livermore would germinate into one of the most controversial defense debates in American history, one that would bring America's two-century-old quest for security to a spectacular turning point. Elected in 1980 as the nation's fortieth president, Ronald Reagan became the greatest spokesman for American invulnerability since the dawn of the nuclear era; and in assuming that role, he relied for technical support on many of the inventive minds that staffed the Lawrence Livermore Laboratory.

It was not altogether surprising to find Edward Teller at the center of such developments. Fifty-nine years old at the time of Reagan's visit, Teller had during his long career been involved in some of the twentieth century's most astounding scientific and technological breakthroughs—and controversies. A precocious boy born of middle-class Jewish parents in Budapest, Teller had early on demonstrated a marked penchant for iconoclasm. At the age of six, informed by a teacher that "in the beginning God created the heaven and the earth," Teller asked pointedly, "Who created God?" This central desire—to probe into some of life's greatest mysteries—proved to be more than mere boyish curiosity; it subsequently dominated Teller's personal and professional life.

Bored by the simplicity of childhood mathematics and science, fascinated by the futuristic visions of novelist Jules Verne, Teller grew up with firsthand experience of political turmoil and ethnic bigotry. First in Hungary and then during his college years in interwar Germany, Teller watched nominally socialist governments give way to deeply anti-Semitic totalitarian regimes. Amid this uncertain atmosphere, Teller pursued his scientific interests, and within a remarkably short span of years his distinctive face, dominated by a pair of brooding, bushy eyebrows, could be found in group photographs of Europe's foremost physicists.

Teller's great gift was not for the design of apparatus but for the outlining of principles. "Edward is a physicist with a fantastic creative mind," a colleague later said of him. "He understands the beauty of a piece of music. But for God's sake, don't ask him to design a trumpet." By the time of his emigration to the United States in 1935 Teller was putting his talents to work alongside the likes of physicists Enrico Fermi and Leo Szilard, trying to unleash the tremendous energy that was believed to be contained in the heart of the atom. With his great facility not only for physics but for mathematics and chemistry as well, Teller was invaluable to colleagues for his advice, assistance and unique ability to stand back and view problems with greater detachment than almost any of them could achieve.

As a member of the team assigned to create a deliverable atomic bomb at Los Alamos, New Mexico, Teller worked under Robert Oppenheimer during the final years of World War II. But Los Alamos was devoted to a specific question of applied physics, and proved too confining for Teller's expansive genius. The experience did, however, give him a chance to pursue the goal with which his name would later become most closely associated: thermonuclear power.

Following World War II, Teller worked harder than any other man for the development of an American thermonuclear device. Put simply, what Teller envisioned was the use of an atomic fission bomb such as those dropped on Hiroshima and Nagasaki to create, in a confined space, a heat so great that it would cause the fusion of hydrogen isotopes, such as occurs constantly in our own sun. The power of such a device would be many times greater than that of an atomic bomb, perhaps hundreds of times greater; and some scientists (such as Robert Oppenheimer) who agreed with Teller that fusion—or hydrogen—bombs were feasible considered it morally wrong to work for their creation. When the Los Alamos Laboratory dragged its heels on thermonuclear projects, Teller pressed the American government for the establishment of a second national laboratory devoted to nuclear research. In 1952, he got his way. Named for physicist Ernest O. Lawrence, a pioneer in cyclotron research and, like Teller, a nuclear weapons enthusiast, the Lawrence Livermore National Laboratory's guiding spirit was and would remain Edward Teller.

Teller's aggressive attitude toward weapons work was grounded in his own belief that no lasting peace with the Soviet Union could be achieved. The Russian reluctance to put all nuclear research under the open control of an international agency (Teller firmly opposed policies of scientific secrecy), the Soviets' reliance on espionage to obtain scientific information, and his own earlier experiences with fascism masquerading as socialism in interwar Europe, all combined after 1945 to convince Teller that the Soviet Union was an implacable enemy of the United States.

This conviction gave a great sense of urgency to Teller's work at Lawrence Livermore, and by October 1952 the laboratory was ready to test "Mike," Teller's and America's first successful thermonuclear device. A bizarre sixty-five-ton apparatus, "Mike" triggered a blast equivalent to ten million tons of TNT (10 megatons) and vaporized the Pacific island of Elugelab. Teller's staff at Lawrence Livermore next set about the task of turning "Mike" into a deliverable bomb, while Teller himself became involved in a bitter debate with many of his fellow physicists.

Amid the communist scare rampant in 1953, Robert Oppenheimer's security clearance—the effective work permit of those involved in nuclear research—was canceled because of his longstanding personal friendships with known communist sympathizers. Teller, called to testify at Oppenheimer's hearing, gave testimony that Oppenheimer's liberal supporters in the scientific community—of whom there were many—considered damning. Already shunned for his extreme conservative views and his aggressive push for the creation of the hydrogen bomb and the Lawrence Livermore Laboratory, Teller now found himself almost completely isolated professionally. Former friends and colleagues went out of their way to avoid and even disparage the "father of the hydrogen bomb"; but this in no way detracted from Teller's determination to make Lawrence Livermore an integral part of America's defense and security establishments.

During the late 1950s and early 1960s, with Lawrence Livermore turning out ever more sophisticated hydrogen bombs and missile warheads, Teller became increasingly uncomfortable with one salient aspect of international relations: the nuclear balance of terror between the United States and the Soviet Union. The idea that the only safeguard against worldwide holocaust was the presumption that neither the United States nor the Soviet Union would launch a nuclear attack against the other because it faced the certainty of a massive retaliatory strike was intolerable to Teller. He still had enough faith in technology to believe that a way out of such a scenario of mutual suicide—generally known as the policy of "deterrence"—could be discovered. He also had enough fear of the Russians to believe that they were working relentlessly to gain the capacity to launch a "preemptive" nuclear strike against the United States, one that would destroy the American capacity for retaliation. In a 1962 book, *The Legacy of Hiroshima,* Teller spelled out his further anxieties about Russian intentions:

"The Communists have a clearly understood, openly announced, and firmly held revolutionary aim: World domination. They pursue this aim with deep conviction, with impressive zeal, with religious fervor. . . . No matter how often the United States sends strongly worded diplomatic notes, Russia knows that we will not launch the first nuclear attack. This leaves the field of ambiguous aggression open to them. Russia can support Communist revolutionary movements in the Congo or Cuba secure in the knowledge that the United States will not retaliate with nuclear bombs dropped on Russia. . . . Ambiguous aggression may not appear to conquer the world for Russia in a hurry; but step by step, nation by nation, convert by convert, it will conquer the world eventually. And this our policy of mutual deterrence does not deter."

If the United States could not make a nuclear response to Soviet aggression credible because of its own fear of Soviet retaliation against the American heartland, then there was, to Teller's way of thinking, only one option left: defense, especially against Soviet intercontinental ballistic missiles (ICBMs). To this end, Teller became a strong advocate of antiballistic missiles (ABMs), which were designed to intercept and destroy Russian ICBMs. "It would be wonderful," Teller wrote, "if we could shoot down approaching missiles before they could destroy a target in the United States."

Such a defensive shield would free the United States for the task of countering Soviet aggression worldwide without the fear of nuclear attack; but antiballistic missiles were quickly revealed to be prohibitively expensive, unreliable (their explosions and subsequent radioactive fallout might be as destructive to American citizens as to Russian missiles) and ultimately unrealistic—many critics likened the idea of trying to intercept missiles with missiles to trying to defend one's self from a speeding bullet by shooting it down with one's own gun. But Teller would not be swayed from the idea of a defensive shield: "we certainly must continue to look for a satisfactory missile defense system."

In 1967, this search had led Teller and his staff to the development of a large nuclear device designed to intercept Soviet warheads in the "terminal" phase of their flight, that is, when they reentered the earth's atmosphere. When Governor Ronald Reagan came to Lawrence Livermore early that year, he was fascinated to learn of such plans. "We showed him all the complex projects," Teller later said of Reagan's visit, "and there was no skimping on time." Although the two men "did not discuss space"—that is, the idea of actually basing defensive weapons in outer space—during this particular visit, by 1980 space had been incorporated into Teller's vision of a nuclear defense, and had made its way into Reagan's rhetoric as well.

During his first term, President Reagan—after soliciting extensive technical advice from Teller—presented to the American people the idea of a defensive shield against nuclear weapons as not only desirable but possible. Through both land- and space-based defenses, Reagan said, the nuclear dilemma of deterrence could indeed be resolved, and the country could return to a time when its security did not depend on the actions and attitudes of the Kremlin's leaders. For two generations Americans had lived with the risk of destruction—the *relative* security—offered by the nuclear balance of terror; now they were to be returned to a time when their security was their own province, dependent solely on their own will.

Within those two generations, however, the problems of both American and world security had changed dramatically. And although President Reagan, by seeking to nullify those changes, was able to strike a deeply sympathetic chord in the American people, no amount of revisionist or optimistic rhetoric could change the circumstance that the American quest for absolute security had reached a historical crisis point.

An intimate connection between the science and defense communities of the United States has characterized American history since the administration of Thomas Jefferson. In March 1802 the first public funds set aside by the Congress for any comprehensive study of the sciences were incorporated into the creation of the Army Corps of Engineers and the Military Academy at West Point. In subsequent decades, it was often the army—and particularly the Corps of Engineers—that was responsible for breakthroughs not only in public works, but in topographical, natural and other studies as well. Sometimes, as in the case of John Charles Frémont's expeditions to California in the 1840s, these scientific projects were combined with military missions aimed at enhancing the national security of the United States—indeed, any undertaking that could fulfill such a twofold function stood a better chance of gaining government backing than its purely scientific competitors.

The industrial revolution of the mid- to late nineteenth century provoked a rapid evolution of military thought throughout the world, and in the United States that evolution tightened the bonds between science and the armed services. With the victory of the industrially powerful Union in the Civil War, heavy reliance on the most scientifically advanced methods of warfare was confirmed, and the technological strain that had always been present in America's efforts to guarantee her security was significantly strengthened. The first strong evidence of this was the work of Alfred Thayer Mahan, who stressed technical advances in shipbuilding as well as tactical innovations in outlining ways to make the United States Navy a world-class military force.

With the rise of Mahan's disciples, such as Henry Cabot Lodge and Theodore Roosevelt, and the gradual acceptance of their strategic doctrines, it also became clear that the newly accentuated technological side of American military theory had as its central aim *defense*. With the rapid expansion of America's perimeter of vital interests during the imperialist period, and the resultant multiplication of possible threats to American national security, this emphasis on defense as the best remedy to a broadened sense of vulnerability was reinforced. It is not surprising that when Lieutenant William W. Kimball—whose strategic plan for the conquest of the Philippines and Cuba was accepted and used by the Navy General Board during the Spanish-American War—put forward tactical innovations (primarily submarines and torpedo boats) that were *offensively* oriented, they were largely ignored by the navy's high command. The cordon of massive battleships that Mahan, Lodge and Roosevelt strove to create was a weapon with a primarily defensive purpose, and one which relied heavily on psychological impression rather than actual military efficacy for its power.

Nothing better demonstrates this than the terror wrought by German U-boats (a distinctly offensive weapon) during the opening years of the First World War. Largely immune to the big guns of the heavily armored battleships, the U-boats were ultimately defeated not by America's floating fortresses but by the destroyer convoys of Admiral William S. Sims—a tactical rather than a technological innovation, and one whose success did little to alter the deeply rooted American reliance on defensive military systems designed by America's renowned scientists and engineers.

The American preoccupation with defensive military ideas was further highlighted during the interwar period. Though the big battleships had played a limited role in World War I, the United States Navy (like that of all the great powers, except Japan) continued to place its hopes for security in the mammoth steel ships. General William "Billy" Mitchell, commander of the American Expeditionary Air Force in Europe during the war, returned home to plague his less imaginative superiors with unremitting claims that the battleships were obsolete behemoths that could easily fall prey to up-to-date planes launched from aircraft carriers. It was these latter offensive weapons, said Mitchell, that must be developed. The navy's reply was a 1925 court martial. In the U.S. Army, meanwhile, similar lessons from World War I were also disregarded. Officers such as George S. Patton maintained that the future of land war lay in rapid, highly mobile units of tanks supported by infantry; but again, defense proved the dominant consideration in American military thought, and armor was accorded no significant role.

The disaster of Pearl Harbor seemed to demonstrate clearly the folly of America's military fixation with using technology to develop weapons—and hence strategies—that were oriented almost solely toward defense. The great battleships, as Billy Mitchell had predicted, were tragically decimated by Japan's carrier-launched aircraft. It was only the fortunate fact that America's own carriers were not in Pearl Harbor on December 7, 1941, that saved the nation from an even greater blow. And when American ground forces first arrived in North Africa, they were cut to pieces by the Afrika Korps of Germany's Erwin Rommel, a man who had built a worldwide reputation in Poland and France by proving that technologically and numerically superior forces could be defeated by bold offensive tactics. The arrival of George Patton helped to balance and eventually overturn this situation. Besides being a tactical innovator himself, Patton could call on the virtually limitless resources of the United States, an industrial advantage that not even the German panzer commanders could overcome indefinitely.

It was not tactical innovation, however, that was to be remembered as the symbol of America's final victory in World War II, but a breakthrough in science and technology. The mushroom clouds that appeared over Hiroshima and Nagasaki on August 6 and August 9, 1945, symbolized the resurgence of the bond between science and security in the American defense establishment. So great had been the faith of American leaders not only in the military but in the diplomatic power of the atomic bomb that President Harry Truman believed he could use the invention to coerce Joseph Stalin into more temperate behavior following the war. When Secretary of War Henry Stimson brought news of the successful testing of an atomic device to Truman at the Potsdam Conference on July 16, 1945, the president's attitude toward negotiations with the Russians altered dramatically. "He was a changed man," Winston Churchill said of Truman. "He told the Russians just where they got on and off and generally bossed the whole meeting."

Yet Truman quickly discovered that the Russians would not comply with his demands, despite the existence of the bomb. A month and a half after the Potsdam Conference, Truman's secretary of state, James Byrnes, met with Russia's Vyacheslav Molotov at the first Council of Foreign Ministers meeting in London. Byrnes, a South Carolinian, was known to place great faith in the diplomatic persuasiveness of America's new atomic power; and Molotov, aware of this, humorously but pointedly inquired as to whether Byrnes was carrying an atomic bomb in his "hip pocket," a favorite expression of the American secretary of state's. "You don't know Southerners," Byrnes told Molotov. "We carry our artillery in our hip pocket. If you don't cut out all this stalling and let us get down to work, I am going to pull an atomic bomb out of my hip pocket and let you have it." Byrnes was somewhat unprepared for Molotov's reply—the Soviet foreign minister simply laughed.

Both Molotov and Joseph Stalin seemed to recognize from the beginning the key weakness of America's atomic might—its effective postwar disutility. The explosions over Hiroshima and Nagasaki had been horrible in their scope and lasting in their legacy of radiation poisoning; so shrewd a man as Stalin could quickly infer that it would take an event of dramatic magnitude—at least equal to the Japanese attack on Pearl Harbor—to bring an American atomic strike against the Soviet Union. Stalin also knew that his own scientists were far closer than the Americans believed to developing a Russian atomic bomb. All the Russian leader need do was avoid a cataclysmic breach with the United States until that development was completed, and then the world's two great powers would be placed on terms of terrible but undeniable equality.

Henry Stimson was the first American statesman to understand the full complexity of this situation. On September 11, 1945, Stimson submitted a memorandum on the subject of the control of atomic energy to President Truman, one that contained deep implications for America's policy regarding the Soviet Union. "To put the matter concisely," the secretary of war wrote, "I consider the problem of our satisfactory relations with Russia as not merely connected with but as virtually dominated by the problem of the atomic bomb. . . . *Those relations may be perhaps irretrievably embittered by the way in which we approach the solution of the bomb with Russia. For if we fail to approach them now and merely continue to negotiate with them, having this weapon rather ostentatiously on our hip, their suspicions and their distrust of our purposes and motives will increase.*" (The italics were added by Stimson himself.) The secretary of war proposed that the United States, after consultation with Great Britain, directly approach the Soviet Union and offer to share its knowledge and to work jointly toward control of the new energy, moving atomic research away from military and toward peaceful uses. As to the issues of internal Russian policies and Soviet behavior in Eastern Europe, Stimson told Truman:

"I still recognize the difficulty and am still convinced of the ultimate importance of a change in Russian attitude toward individual liberty but I have come to the conclusion that it would not be possible to use our possession of the atomic bomb as a direct lever to produce the change. I have become convinced that any demand by us for an internal change in Russia as a condition of sharing in the atomic weapon would be so resented that it would make the objective we have in view less probable." Such Russian resentment would also be aroused, Stimson said, by asking the Russians to join in an international effort to control and develop atomic energy:

"*I emphasize perhaps beyond all other considerations the importance of taking this action with Russia as a proposal of the United States—backed by Great Britain but peculiarly the proposal of the United States. Action of any international group of nations, including many small nations who have not demonstrated their potential power or responsibility in this war, would not, in my opinion, be taken seriously by the Soviets.*"

Ten days after submitting this memo, Stimson left the War Office permanently, and most of those who had supported the views contained in his last major communication—such as Dean Acheson—significantly shifted their stands during the following two years. The bitterness that Stimson had predicted did indeed settle over

Soviet-American relations. True, that bitterness had additional causes, and once the Soviets had been alienated Stimson did favor taking a tougher line with them. But his perception of a unique diplomatic opportunity in September 1945, based on a frank assessment of postwar realities as well as of the Russian attitude toward great-power relations, nonetheless had tremendous value.

President Truman, however, chose to place his trust in a policy of confrontation. As late as 1947 Stimson was still able to write, "I do not share the gloomy fear of some that we are now engaged in the preliminaries of an inevitable conflict." But Truman and the future secretary of state Dean Acheson remained unmoved, confident of American military superiority, deeply suspicious of Soviet intentions and determined to demonstrate American resolve.

Truman's military experts had told him that it might be twenty years before the Russians would be capable of developing an atomic bomb; the news that they had exploded such a device in August 1949 therefore came as a deep shock. Stalin had his atomic parity, although the United States still possessed a superior delivery system with its massive fleet of bombers. But in May 1951 the Russians took another dramatic step into the nuclear age when they successfully detonated a thermonuclear device designed by physicists Andrei Sakharov and Igor Tamm. Like Edward Teller's "Mike" of the following year, the Russian apparatus was not yet a deliverable bomb—but by August 1953 the Soviets had overcome that obstacle as well.

The United States continued to emphasize its superior delivery capacity, but the rapid Russian advances had already caused President Truman to confront a new dilemma that made all such considerations uncertain—deterrence. Truman's attempt at atomic diplomacy had failed because nothing Stalin did had been deemed grievous enough to warrant the horrors of an atomic attack. And so, even before the Russians had reached the atomic age, deterrence was taking shape in the form of the disutility of the American bomb. Stalin had quickly learned to act within the limits of what Edward Teller later described as "ambiguous aggression," never pushing the United States beyond the point where an atomic attack would be justifiable—America's powerful new weapon continued to have no effect on conventional diplomacy; nor did the new Soviet weapons.

But the development of the Russian bomb nonetheless put America on disturbingly equal terms with the Soviet Union, and when Dwight Eisenhower entered the White House early in 1953, he quickly announced a military "New Look," which put increased emphasis on America's atomic arsenal. Secretary of State John Foster Dulles, meanwhile, seemed to indicate a lowering of the "nuclear threshold"—the point at which an atomic war would be unleashed—in January 1954 when he threatened "massive retaliation" if American world interests were seriously imperiled. In fact, Eisenhower and Dulles's attempts to escape the dilemma of deterrence were no more successful than Truman and Acheson's had been, and by 1956 both the president and his secretary of state were willing to admit as much. In January, Dulles—who twenty-four months earlier had said that "the way to deter aggression is for the free community to be willing and able to respond vigorously at places and with means of its own choosing," including the possibility of "massive retaliatory" strikes—told *Life* magazine that "The ability to get to the verge without getting into the war is the necessary art. If you cannot master it, you inevitably get into war. If you try to run away from it, if you are scared to go to the brink, you are lost."

That "the brink" was clearly delineated was evident during the 1956 Hungarian uprising. And Eisenhower openly abandoned the prospect of nuclear superiority in his "New New Look" military program of that year, which stressed a policy of deterring Soviet attacks against the United States by maintaining an adequate retaliatory arsenal. Russia's development of the hydrogen bomb and the steady improvement of its delivery systems had forced even the Republican administration to accept the essential logic of deterrence: that neither the United States nor the Soviet Union could use nuclear weapons, even against opposing client states, when faced with the certainty of a retaliatory strike against their own territory.

This position was spelled out by Air Force Secretary Donald Quarles in August 1956, when he labeled nuclear war "an unthinkable catastrophe for both sides." "Neither side," Quarles went on, "can hope by a mere margin of superiority in airplanes or other means of delivery of atomic weapons to escape the catastrophe of such a war. Beyond a certain point, this prospect is not the result of the *relative* strength of the two opposed forces. It is the *absolute* power in the hands of each. . . ." In other words, absolute destructive power meant that both the United States and the Soviet Union would have to learn to live with relative security.

Not only was the de facto security of the nation imperiled, but its ultimate goal of invulnerability seemed hopelessly beyond reach. Few American leaders had ever promised that absolute security was *immediately* attainable, but fewer still had been willing to hazard the opinion that it might not *eventually* be achieved. Yet since 1945 neither national political party had been able to formulate a policy that could reconcile the goal of absolute security with the fact of deterrence (although neither Truman nor Eisenhower felt able to acknowledge as much openly)—and very soon, the deep official and public anxiety brought on by this conundrum was dramatically heightened.

In August 1957 the Soviet Union announced the successful testing of its first intercontinental ballistic missile. Unmanned, extremely fast and wholly expendable, the ICBM posed a significantly greater threat to the United States than had bombers. Two months later, in a further demonstration of the full meaning of their new power, the Soviets launched a man-made satellite into orbit around the earth atop an ICBM—*Sputnik.* In the words of Edward Teller:

"Sputnik caused fear. It was painfully apparent that Russia, capable of throwing a satellite around the earth, could also launch a device armed with an atomic or a hydrogen bomb. Watching Sputnik flash overhead in the night, Americans realized as never before that our nation was in the range of Russian rockets—rockets that could carry the terrible destructiveness of nuclear weapons from launching pad to target, from continent to continent, from hemisphere to hemisphere in twenty minutes."

Faced with this unprecedented threat, many Americans tried once again to escape the strategy of deterrence and reset America's sights on the goal of a security that would be unaffected by the actions of the world's other nuclear power. This effort was ignited in no small part by a key 1959 magazine article published by Albert Wohlstetter of the Rand Corporation. "The notion," Wohlstetter wrote, "that a carefully planned surprise attack can be checkmated almost effortlessly, that, in short, we may resume our deep presputnik sleep is wrong and its nearly universal acceptance is terribly dangerous." He went on to declare that America could not afford to rely on bombers or missiles alone for her security. Instead, she would have to construct a vast range of nuclear delivery systems—bombers, ICBMs, intermediate-range missiles, submarine-launched missiles (SLBMs)—in order to ensure that a Soviet preemptive strike would be made impossible.

Wohlstetter's emphasis on the feasibility of a preemptive strike alarmed many sectors of the American government, but it also suggested to those who had never been comfortable with the reality of relative security that the United States could escape the end-game of deterrence by building its own nuclear arsenal to the point where an *American* preemptive strike would be possible. In other words, the desire for absolute security was still powerful; and in the early 1960s, it was placed back in the hands of America's scientists and engineers.

Perhaps the most disturbing aspect of the policy of deterrence to many American leaders was that it depended on the continuous evolution of offensive military thought, and seemed to preclude the long-sought goal of an impenetrable defensive shield with which to protect both the perimeter and the homeland. When John Kennedy was inaugurated in January 1961, he was determined not only to address the issue of American nuclear vulnerability by increasing the nation's offensive power, but if possible to escape the balance of terror by developing technologically advanced systems of defense. Kennedy, himself a World War II naval hero, was haunted by the nightmare of a nuclear Pearl Harbor, and when he learned of preliminary plans for development of an American antiballistic missile system, he was eager for details. But Kennedy did not share Edward Teller's seemingly limitless faith in nuclear technology (indeed, the two men were often at personal odds); and when he received a full description of the radioactive fallout that would probably result from even a successful ABM shield, he turned away from the panacea of defense and back toward deterrence.

Two other developments reinforced this trend. The first was the Cuban missile crisis of 1962, which highlighted the essential irrelevance of nuclear weapons to conventional diplomacy even when those weapons were themselves the cause of a diplomatic crisis. Kennedy's success during the Cuban affair had as much to do with his willingness to meet Khrushchev's adventurism forcefully through the conventional avenues of tough bargaining and a naval blockade as it did with any implicit threat to launch a nuclear strike against Russia. The Soviet leader's withdrawal of Russian missiles from Cuba over the protests of Fidel Castro was prompted largely by a fear of international and domestic humiliation, in addition to the prospect of nuclear annihilation.

The second key development of the early 1960s was the rapid improvement of submarine-launched ballistic missile (SLBM) design. True, submarine-launched missiles remained relatively inaccurate, compared to intercontinental missiles, and therefore could play little if any role in a preemptive strike, which by definition required pinpoint accuracy to destroy the enemy's missile-launching capability. But because the nuclear submarines that carried these upgraded missiles could remain at sea for extended periods of time and were difficult to track and virtually impossible to destroy, their value as a weapon of retaliation was almost limitless. With further development of such weapons, many scientists—including Kennedy's science adviser, Dr. Jerome B. Wiesner—concluded that deterrence represented the limit of any significant technological contribution to nuclear strategy. In 1964, Dr. Wiesner, together with Herbert F. York, who had been the first director of the Lawrence Livermore Laboratory, published an important article in *Scientific American* that stated:

"Both sides in the arms race are thus confronted by the dilemma of steadily increasing military power and steadily decreasing national security. *It is our considered professional judgment that this dilemma has no technical solution.* If the great powers continue to look for solutions in the area of science and technology only, the result will be to worsen the situation." As for the possibility of an antimissile defense, Wiesner and York declared that such a system would have to be "truly airtight," something they considered highly improbable if not impossible.

Also in 1964, Defense Secretary Robert McNamara defined the attitude of Lyndon Johnson's administration toward deterrence by outlining a policy of what he called "mutual assured destruction." The unfortunate acronym of this policy—MAD—soon became a catchphrase in the nuclear debate. Critics charged that the Russians intended to outwit McNamara's MAD by successfully developing an effective antiballistic missile system. McNamara conceded that possibility, while insisting that it was remote, and said that the United States would continue its own research into antiballistic missile defenses.

But the most important American reaction to the unknown—

and thus all the more worrisome—level of Russian ABM advances was the 1966 decision to go ahead with the development of multiple independently targetable reentry vehicles, or MIRVs. The United States could now place numerous warheads atop one intercontinental missile, dramatically increasing its offensive power; it could also put both live and dummy warheads atop the missiles, thereby making it even harder for the Russians to be sure that their ABM system would offer complete or even partial safety. The development of a multiple warhead missile system was supported by both advocates and critics of deterrence. On the one hand, these new weapons seemed to heighten the possibility of assured destruction (at least some live warheads, it was believed, would always penetrate even an extensive ABM system); alternatively, the vast increase in the number of precision warheads gave new life to the idea that one or the other of the nuclear superpowers could launch a successful preemptive strike.

That the Johnson administration considered multiple warhead missiles primarily a weapon of deterrence rather than of first strike was made clear by McNamara in a speech in September 1967. "The cornerstone of our strategic policy continues to be to deter deliberate nuclear attack upon the United States, or its allies," said the secretary of defense, "by maintaining a highly reliable ability to inflict an unacceptable degree of damage upon any single aggressor, or combination of aggressors, at any time during the course of a strategic nuclear exchange—even after absorbing a surprise first strike." Neither the Soviet Union nor the United States, according to McNamara, at present had the capacity to launch a successful preemptive strike; indeed, given the presence of submarine-launched missiles on both sides, such a capacity seemed no longer attainable. Once again citing the disutility of nuclear weapons in world affairs, McNamara stated that "Unlike any other era in military history, today a substantial numerical superiority of weapons does not effectively translate into political control or diplomatic leverage"—technological advances had not changed the central characteristics of the nuclear age that Henry Stimson had perceived less than a month after Hiroshima. "In the end," McNamara concluded, "the root of man's security does not lie in his weaponry. In the end, the root of man's security lies in his mind."

During the following year, the Soviet Union apparently accepted McNamara's logic and virtually abandoned further ABM development, concentrating instead on their own MIRV program. And in 1969, former National Security Adviser McGeorge Bundy summed up the outgoing Democratic administration's final acceptance of deterrence. "There is an enormous gulf," Bundy wrote in *Foreign Affairs,* "between what political leaders really think about nuclear weapons and what is assumed in complex calculations of relative 'advantage' in simulated strategic warfare. Think-tank analysts can set levels of 'acceptable' damage well up in the tens of millions of lives. They can assume that the loss of dozens of great cities is somehow a real choice for sane men. They are in an unreal world. In the real world of real political leaders—whether here or in the Soviet Union—a decision that would bring even one hydrogen bomb on one city of one's own country would be recognized in advance as a catastrophic blunder; ten bombs on ten cities would be a disaster beyond history; and a hundred bombs on a hundred cities are unthinkable. Yet this unthinkable level of human incineration is the least that could be expected by either side in response to any first strike in the next ten years, *no matter what happens to weapons systems in the meantime.* . . . To put the proposition quite simply, each great power must move from a zealous concern for its own advantage to a sober acceptance of parity."

Once again, Americans were faced with the promise of relative security, but this time not only in the short term, but for the foreseeable future. And once again, there were many American leaders who were unwilling to accept such a prospect.

The 1972 Strategic Arms Limitations Treaty (SALT I) was negotiated and signed by the United States and the Soviet Union against a backdrop of increasingly effective weapons of deterrence. For its part, the United States was considering development of a new bomber, the B-1, to replace its fleet of aging B-52s, as well as the new, intercontinental Missile Experimental (MX), which it was hoped could be made safe from a Soviet preemptive strike through either increased hardening of the silos that stored the missiles or by making the missiles themselves mobile and frequently rotating their location. Perhaps more significant than either of these were plans for a new nuclear submarine and submarine-launched missile, the Trident class, as well as advances made in cruise missile technology. The United States had long had the capacity to build these air-breathing, ground-hugging cruise missiles that could frustrate Soviet ABM systems; but in 1970 dramatic leaps in guidance systems, turbofan engines, microelectronics, range and, most important of all, radar reflection made such weapons markedly more effective. Like submarine-launched missiles, the cruise missiles had limited accuracy and were primarily a weapon of deterrence.

It is not surprising, then, that by the beginning of the 1970s Richard Nixon and Henry Kissinger were publicly placing emphasis on nuclear "sufficiency" rather than superiority. The SALT I agreements limited both the United States and the Soviet Union to two bases of a hundred antiballistic missile launchers each, reflecting the growing belief that ABMs were a destabilizing force and ought not to be built, because, despite their flaws, they might still tempt one nation into false confidence and a preemptive strike. In addition, SALT I called for a five-year freeze on the development, testing and deployment of intercontinental and submarine-launched missiles.

But President Nixon made a deliberate effort to exclude multiple warhead vehicles—the MIRVs—from the agreement, principally because he felt that the United States enjoyed an advantage over the Soviets in this area. Neither he nor his advisers were yet willing to accept fully the notion of complete nuclear parity—"sufficiency," in this case, apparently meant a small but significant American edge. With an effective missile shield still out of reach, Nixon and his successor, Gerald Ford, pursued an aggressive policy of MIRVing American missiles, until by the mid-1970s the warhead capability of America's ICBM force had been increased some six times over. Yet not even this dramatic increase in power—by the end of the decade the United States possessed some 9,400 deliverable warheads, compared to about 6,000 for the Soviet Union—could silence the claims of critics that the United States was falling behind in the nuclear arms race.

The 1970s were, in fact, dominated by talk of a nuclear "window of vulnerability," a new fear that the United States was leaving itself open to a Soviet preemptive strike. Yet the technical and strategic arguments against antiballistic missile systems were still too powerful to overcome. The only answer seemed to be heightened deterrence, and in the face of this supposed need—and in response to claims by America's European allies that a deterrent force based solely in American territory and on American delivery systems could not guarantee the safety of Europe, especially given the recent Russian installation of medium-range missiles on Europe's borders—the United States began to install intermediate-range ballistic missiles in Europe.

President Jimmy Carter endured a heated controversy over this deployment, and many conservative Republicans, including Ronald Reagan, claimed that even the new European-based missiles were not a sufficient guarantee of safety for the United States and its perimeter of vital interests. Carter negotiated a new strategic treaty with the Russians, SALT II, which pledged further talks for the reduction of nuclear stockpiles; but the American Senate had been impressed by the "window of vulnerability" rhetoric (and alarmed by the Russian invasion of Afghanistan), and SALT II was never ratified.

The fall of 1980 proved decisive in the development of American nuclear strategy. First, Ronald Reagan, running on a platform that pledged to upgrade America's offensive and defensive capabilities, was elected president. Days later, in the Nevada desert, a team from the Lawrence Livermore Laboratory tested a new device, code-named "Dauphin," that used a hydrogen bomb to transform high-radiation X rays into focused beams of immense destructive power. The X-ray laser, as it was called, had long been viewed as technically unfeasible, but its riddle was finally solved by a brilliant young scientist at Lawrence Livermore, Peter Hagelstein. Working under Dr. Lowell Wood, a protégé of the aging but ever-vehement Edward Teller, Hagelstein gave new hope to the idea of a defensive shield against ICBMs. Each X-ray laser, mounted either on an orbiting satellite or atop an American ICBM, could conceivably eliminate tens, perhaps hundreds, of incoming missiles and/or warheads.

The vague dreams that Ronald Reagan and Edward Teller had discussed at Lawrence Livermore fourteen years earlier seemed to have taken a large step toward realization. Not long after the 1980 election, Reagan met with Senator Harrison Schmitt, chairman of the Senate's Subcommittee on Science, Technology and Space. "The meeting lasted about twenty minutes," Schmitt later said. "We were talking about science and technology in general. Then, about halfway through the session, he made a statement that he was concerned that we could not just keep building nuclear missiles forever—that ultimately their proliferation would get us into trouble. He asked what I thought about the possibility of strategic defense, especially with lasers."

A year after his inauguration, Reagan met again with Dr. Teller, and over the next year they would meet three more times. In addition, Reagan sought the advice of military men interested in the idea of building a defensive shield against strategic nuclear weapons (these meetings did not, however, include some of the Pentagon's top officers). By March 1983, Reagan felt ready to take his case to the public.

In a dramatic restatement of the American quest for absolute national security, President Reagan announced on television on March 23, 1983, not only an ambitious buildup of American conventional and nuclear weapons but also his intention of placing renewed emphasis on strategic defense and once again trying to overcome the relative security of deterrence. "Wouldn't it be better," Reagan asked the American public with simple logic, "to save lives than to avenge them?" As to who would be assigned this awesome task, the president left no doubt: "Let us turn to the very strengths in technology that spawned our great industrial base and that have given us the quality of life we enjoy today. . . . I call upon the scientific community in our country, those who gave us nuclear weapons to turn their great talents now to the cause of mankind and world peace: to give us the means of rendering nuclear weapons impotent and obsolete."

It was a leap in logic and a bending of facts reminiscent of Woodrow Wilson. No one—not even Edward Teller—had ever believed that nuclear weapons themselves could be made "obsolete"; indeed, Lawrence Livermore's only successful instrument of strategic defense, the X-ray laser, was itself powered by a thermonuclear explosion. The idea of strategic defense, before Reagan's speech, had been directed against intercontinental missiles alone, and to be sure, later in his talk, Reagan returned to this theme: "I am directing a comprehensive and intensive effort to define a long-term research and development program to begin to achieve our ultimate goal of eliminating the threat posed by strategic nuclear missiles." But this was not the section of Reagan's speech that would be most remembered. "Rendering nuclear weapons impotent and obsolete"—this became the rallying cry for America's new Strategic Defense Initiative (SDI), or, as it was popularly to be labeled, the Star Wars program.

Reagan's speech touched off an immediate storm of controversy. Critics contended that a program such as the president had outlined, because it could defend only against ICBMs, offered no protection from other nuclear threats. McGeorge Bundy, George Kennan, Robert McNamara and SALT negotiator Gerard Smith joined voices to complain publicly that the SDI program, even if it could be made effective against ballistic missiles, "entirely excludes from its range any effort to limit the effectiveness of other systems —bomber aircraft, cruise missiles, and smuggled warheads." At least one former member of Reagan's cabinet, former Secretary of State Alexander Haig, Jr., admitted that the speech had been a poorly thought out blunder: "The White House guys," Haig told an audience at the Lawrence Livermore Laboratory, "said, 'Hey, boss, come on. You're going to make a big splash. Big P.R. You're going to look like the greatest leader in America. Get out there and give that speech.' And he did. But the preparation had not been made. I know the aftermath the next day in the Pentagon, where they were all rushing around saying, 'What the hell is strategic defense?' "

Answers to that question came relatively quickly from the administration, but were confused in their content. Reagan established an official agency, the Strategic Defense Organization, under Lieutenant General James A. Abrahamson, a persuasive speaker who made it clear from the beginning that the SDI's primary function was to create a new strategic balance that would encourage both the United States and the Soviet Union to "reduce significantly or even eliminate ballistic missile forces." Yet when asked if that meant that he intended to share Star Wars research with the Russians, Reagan was often hesitant and contradictory, sometimes indicating a willingness to cooperate, other times retreating from such a position.

Then, too, there seemed a lack of any clearly defined technological course for the SDI to take. The initial concept had rested on the success of the X-ray laser; but soon after his speech, Reagan— worried about the possibilities of radioactive fallout and nuclear firestorms in the atmosphere—decided to pursue *non*nuclear defenses. This led not only back to ABM technology but toward the development of electromagnetic and particle weapons, scientific wonders that were generations away from development, if in fact they were feasible at all. All of this made it ever more clear that the SDI could not, in anything approaching the foreseeable future, offer protection from anything other than a limited number of strategic ballistic missiles; and as this conclusion became more inescapable, the ranks of technical critics swelled. The Center for

Defense Information summed their arguments up best when it called the SDI "a program that even its strongest proponents concede will provide only a limited defense against one type of nuclear attack. It will build a leaky roof on a house with no walls."

At the core of the problems surrounding the Star Wars program were issues of psychology and politics. In February 1984 Defense Secretary Caspar Weinberger—the cabinet member who most strongly shared President Reagan's dream of strategic defense—revealed the true cause of the administration's sense of urgency about the SDI program: "If we can get a system," Weinberger told the Senate Armed Services Committee, "which is effective and which we know can render their weapons impotent, we would be back in the situation we were in, for example, when we were the only nation with the nuclear weapon and we did not threaten others with it." From the beginning, then, the Star Wars program was an effort to recapture an age of American supremacy, one during which the goal of absolute security had seemed within reach. Reagan and Weinberger identified this period as the four years between Hiroshima and the development of the Russian atomic bomb, despite the fact that the American bomb had lost its utility immediately after the surrender of Japan and had never regained it.

This effort was by no means confined to nuclear strategy. Within the Western Hemisphere, Reagan had already asserted interventionist policies that he thought had traditionally assisted the cause of liberal democracy in Latin America, but that in reality had usually embroiled the United States in difficult foreign entanglements without appreciably affecting any Latin American inclination toward democracy. In other parts of the world, Reagan sought to expand the influence of the United States through policies that had a similar military orientation—and brought similarly frustrating results. More often than not what resulted was a policy of bluster and bluff, the rhetoric of an assertive America but the actions of a cautious politician.

When Israel invaded Lebanon in June 1982, heightening a long and savage conflict, Reagan was unable to significantly moderate the situation through diplomacy and instead dispatched United States Marines to Beirut as part of an international peacekeeping force. The troops remained in the face of what became a Lebanese civil war. Like so many of his predecessors, Reagan was seeking to "police" a nation that seemed incapable of governing itself; but when a suicide truck bomb destroyed the U.S. Marine barracks in October 1983, the American effort was revealed as futile. In the following year Reagan withdrew the marines, after losing a total of 262 servicemen and failing to affect the outcome of the Lebanese fighting.

The Reagan administration's assertive policies were, then, truly global in scope, if not in effect. Indeed, when asked in February 1983 which areas of the world he considered most important in America's new effort to return to a position of unequaled strength, Defense Secretary Weinberger answered, "All of them." Such unshakable universalism had been viewed as impractical by a broad range of American interventionists—from John Foster Dulles to Lyndon Johnson—and even Weinberger himself seemed later to qualify this position by imposing precise conditions on the dispatch of American forces abroad. Nonetheless, there was every sign that Weinberger's original statement had the complete support of President Reagan, who clung tenaciously to the theory that the Soviet Union (which he had once termed an "evil empire") was at the heart of all international disorder.

Given such a worldview, the importance of defense became primary. Edward Teller had written in 1962 that "If the Communists should become certain that their defenses are reliable and at the same time know that ours are insufficient, Soviet conquest of the world would be inevitable." Teller ignored the fact that not only American history but modern military history had long since demonstrated that *no* defense could ever be truly reliable for more than a fleeting time; but Reagan accepted Teller's judgment, and structured his approach to both arms development and arms control negotiations around the central fixture of the SDI.

In the early 1970s, Richard Nixon had been able to secure agreement on SALT I with the Soviets by using ABMs—a system he knew could never truly protect either America's citizens or her nuclear missiles—as a bargaining chip. But Ronald Reagan had no intention of making such use of the Star Wars program. When Soviet negotiators at the 1984 strategic arms talks in Geneva began to predicate all significant Russian concessions on American willingness to state publicly that the SDI weapons under development would not be deployed and that further research would be limited, President Reagan steadfastly stood by his program. Indeed, Reagan moved discussion away from eventual deployment of a comprehensive shield and toward the immediate deployment of a partial, nonnuclear shield, even though such deployment involved air- and land-launched missiles that would be scarcely more effective than earlier missile defenses, that would seriously endanger the 1972 SALT treaty on ABMs and that had little to do with the revolutionary scenario with which he had so aroused the nation in March 1983.

As the technology involved in the SDI changed, so too did its political purpose. Reagan had initially hoped that a comprehensive missile defense would eliminate the possibility of nuclear war by convincing the Russians that they would not be able to significantly damage the United States even if they launched a surprise strike. In other words, the Russians would be discouraged from attack by the *certainty* of failure. But as a comprehensive shield was revealed to be infeasible and a partial shield took its place, Reagan began to put forth the theory that the SDI would prevent a Russian attack by making Moscow *uncertain* of whether or not enough U.S. missiles would survive a Russian preemptive strike to make possible an effective American counterstrike. Thus what Reagan had originally envisioned as an escape from the nuclear balance of terror eventually became simply another manifestation of that balance; without admitting it, Reagan had been led back to the logic of deterrence.

But the president persevered, and in so doing again demonstrated that his commitment to the Strategic Defense Initiative was something very much more than a diplomatic ploy. And in truth, Reagan's vision was a heartfelt embodiment of America's search for invulnerability, the most ambitious in the nation's history. In setting higher goals than his predecessors, the president popularized a program with more technical deficiencies (but greater psychological appeal) than any of its defensive antecedents—and in refusing to acknowledge those flaws, he magnified nearly every unstable aspect of relations between the nuclear powers.

EPILOGUE

FOR more than two centuries, the United States has aspired to a condition of perfect safety from foreign threats. Alarmed by even potential dangers to the nation's security, Americans have forcefully responded to both real and imagined assaults against our own borders as well as against those of foreign nations and provinces whose security we have seen as either strategically or politically linked to our own. In this endeavor, we have steadily expanded the scope of our efforts, extending our protection to other states until the perimeter of our security interests ranges from the Elbe River to the Yellow Sea. Yet the goal of absolute security has constantly eluded us.

Rather than trying to accommodate the national interest to this apparent truth, however, each generation of American policymakers has rejected the measure of relative safety handed down by its predecessors and has attempted to move America closer to a condition of absolute security. The territorial integrity offered the new nation by the Treaty of Paris in 1783 did not provide sufficient security for the war hawks of 1812, who tried to remove the British presence from North America altogether; an expanded but still uncertain western border was unacceptable to James Polk, who established the American presence on the California coast and the Rio Grande; well-defined continental boundaries meant little to men such as Henry Cabot Lodge and Theodore Roosevelt, who viewed an American presence in the Pacific as vital to the nation; and predominance in the Western Hemisphere, in much of Europe and in parts of the Western Pacific and East Asia proved too little to quiet America's fears during the Cold War.

In this sense, the pursuit of national security has steadily grown in scope. Expanded territorial holdings and political influence have brought with them an expanded range of threats. These new and heightened dangers have demanded a commensurately greater expenditure of American resources. Yet when these new expenses have been paid and a greatly increased measure of territorial and strategic security has seemingly been attained, we have, by and large, found ourselves exposed to a new array of foreign threats. To cope with these dangers, America has steadily expended an ever greater share of her national wealth and resources until—by the end of the 1980s—she finds them stretched to the very limit.

At the same time, Americans—today as yesterday—remain uneasy with "permanent alliances" that might inhibit their search for absolute security. The Reagan administration's decision to pursue the Star Wars program over the objections of many European leaders—who fear that the SDI will destroy the psychologically unsettling but nonetheless tangible stability afforded by nuclear deterrence—echoes the determination of past generations of American unilateralists to safeguard the republic preferably without the assistance of other powers. In the pursuit of perfect security in an imperfect world, we have always felt it desirable to act on our own—not isolating ourselves from other nations of the world, but walking a solitary path among them toward the kind of safety that might free us of any and all threats to our exceptional land, Herman Melville's "wilderness of untried things."

Our solitary way has led us from a determined defense of thirteen struggling colonies to a worldwide commitment to offer protection to all democratic—or at the very least, anticommunist —nations. This universalism has placed enormous economic and social strains on the United States (especially evident during the Vietnam War) which have prompted a reevaluation of America's concept of expansive security. But the retreat from Vietnam did

not finally produce any reasoned contraction of the perimeter of
U.S. security interests. Despite the fact that the development and
proliferation of nuclear arms have shown us that we will always
remain vulnerable to any enemy who can deliver the weapons of
destruction—whether atop intercontinental ballistic missiles or, in
the scenario of many other experts, smuggled across our borders
—American leaders have not abandoned their traditional quest for
absolute security. Every president since Harry Truman has tried
to escape the boundaries of nuclear deterrence, and each has been
finally forced to accept the uncomfortable conclusion that deterrence is, in the words of one nuclear analyst, "a fact of life and
almost beyond policy." Ronald Reagan, especially, has sought to
keep the goal of invulnerability alive, although he has come no
closer than any of his predecessors to achieving it. It is a dream,
apparently, that the nation cannot easily relinquish.

Security, as we approach the end of the second century of our
history, can never be more than relative. To say this is to do no
more than to admit a condition with which our country has always
lived, but which we have seldom been willing to acknowledge. In
the nuclear era, however, to do anything other than to accept our
lot would be dangerously quixotic. Relative security will mean that
despite our massive military and economic power and the blessings
of a liberal democracy, we will be required to live as other great
powers have lived in the past—with our safety, and the world's
peace, dependent on a judicious accommodation of often conflicting national interests.

Such an accommodation will no doubt be psychologically unsettling. Yet there have been signs that the Soviet Union—the latest
but by no means the only focus of our traditional concern for
national security—may be genuinely trying to move toward greater
nuclear stability based on the living reality of deterrence. If that is
so, America and Russia may thereafter hope to grapple jointly with
a whole range of problems that transcend national boundaries:
environmental devastation, the exploration of outer space and of
the earth's seabeds and the danger of international nuclear proliferation—to name only a few such issues.

But so long as the deceitful dream of absolute security is held up
before the American people as an attainable goal, no real progress
can be made. It is only by abandoning that fateful quest that America will finally be able to bring her commitments and her capabili-

ties into balance and learn to live within what even Thomas Jefferson, who was himself driven by a passion for security, once called the "safe measures of power," so that "our peace, commerce and friendship may be sought and cultivated by all."

NOTES

PROLOGUE

p. 11: Henry Adams: in his *History of the United States During the Administrations of Thomas Jefferson* (New York: Library of America, 1986), p. 120.

p. 13: Jefferson: from his first Inaugural Address, in James D. Richardson, ed., *Messages and Papers of the Presidents* (Washington, D.C.: GPO, 1899), 1:323.

p. 16: Hamilton, Benton, Lansing: see chaps. 1, 3, 5, below.

CHAPTER I: THE BURNING OF WASHINGTON: ABSOLUTE VULNERABILITY, 1811–1815

p. 17: The British expeditionary force is described in a firsthand account by Lieutenant G. R. Gleig in *The Campaigns of the British Army at Washington and New Orleans*. The 1847 edition was reprinted in 1972 by Roman and Littlefield.

p. 18: Ross's orders: Alan Lloyd, *The Scorching of Washington* (New York: Robert B. Luce, New York, 1974), p. 153; Walter Lord, *The Dawn's Early Light* (New York: Norton, 1972), p. 37.

p. 18: Cochrane: G. J. Marcus, *The Age of Nelson* (New York: Viking, 1971), p. 474.

p. 18: Theodore Roosevelt: see his *The Naval War of 1812* (New York: G. P. Putnam's Sons, 1882), p. 161.

p. 20: Armstrong: Lord, *Early Light*, p. 60; see also John Armstrong, *Notices of the War of 1812* (New York: George Dearborn, 1836).

p. 20: Jefferson: quoted in Richard B. Morris, *Witnesses at the Creation* (New York: Holt, Rinehart & Winston, 1985), pp. 104–5.

p. 20: Madison: Letter to John Armstrong, May 20, 1814, in the Madison Papers of the Library of Congress (hereafter: Madison LC).

p. 23: Monroe: Documents, Legislative and Executive, of the Congress of the United States, 13th Cong., 3rd sess., Doc. 137, *American State Papers*, Class 5, Military Affairs, 1:538. There is some confusion about this dispatch, as Armstrong (for reasons known only to himself but not difficult to divine) dated his copy of it "Tuesday, 9 o'clock," rather than Monday.

p. 23: Madison to Dolley: Gaillard Hunt, ed., *The Writings of James Madison* (New York: G. P. Putnam's Sons, 1908), 8:293–94.

p. 23: Armstrong: Lloyd, *Scorching of Washington*, p. 161; Lord, *Early Light*, p. 82.

p. 23: Madison: Presidential Memorandum of August 24, 1814, Madison LC.

p. 24: Dolley Madison: Merril D. Peterson, ed., *James Madison: A Biography in His Own Words* (New York: Harper and Row, 1974), pp. 344–345.

p. 24: Ross: Marcus, *Nelson*, p. 476.

p. 25: Cockburn: This quote is cited by different authors in different forms, quite probably because it became almost legendary and cannot be precisely verified. The form here is from Lord, *Early Light*, p. 176.

p. 25: Cockburn in the city: *National Intelligencer*, September 1, 1814.

p. 25: Ross: Lloyd, *Scorching of Washington*, p. 171.

p. 28: Frederick the Great: quoted by Hans Morgenthau in *Politics Among Nations* (New York: Knopf, 1968), p. 183.

p. 29: Jefferson: in Richardson, *Messages and Papers* 1:323.

p. 29: Adams: see Francis Wharton, ed., *The Revolutionary Diplomatic Correspondence of the United States* (Washington, 1889), 4:590.

p. 30: Hamilton: "The Federalist," no. 6, in *The Federalist Papers* (New York: New American Library, 1981), p. 59.

p. 31: Adams to Franklin: see Wharton, *Diplomatic Correspondence* 4:35.

p. 31: Jefferson on allying with England: quoted in Henry Adams, *History of the United States of America During the Administrations of Thomas Jefferson* (New York: Library of America, 1986), p. 277.

p. 31: Adams: *Administrations of Thomas Jefferson*, p. 304.

p. 31: Jefferson: quoted in Adams, ibid., p. 300.

p. 34: Josiah Quincy: quoted in Glenn Tucker, *Poltroons and Patriots* (New York: Bobbs-Merrill, 1954), p. 41.

p. 34: Lincoln: quoted in Clement Eaton, *Henry Clay and the Art of American Politics* (Boston: Little, Brown, 1957), p. 93.

p. 35: Clay: James F. Hopkins, ed., *The Papers of Henry Clay* (University of Kentucky Press, 1959), 1:606.

p. 35: Calhoun: Robert L. Meriwether, ed., *The Papers of John C. Calhoun* (Columbia: University of South Carolina Press, 1959), 1:90–91.

p. 36: Jackson: John Spencer Bassett, ed., *The Correspondence of Andrew Jackson* (Washington, D.C.: Carnegie Institution, 1927), 1:221–22.

p. 36: Richard Johnson: quoted in Henry Adams, *A History of the United States* (New York: Scribner's, 1930), 6:142.

p. 36: Felix Grundy: Henry Adams, ibid., p. 141.

p. 39: George M. Troup's speech: reprinted in the *National Intelligencer*, February 17, 1815, and the *Albany Argus*, February 21, 1815, among many other places.

ADDITIONAL SOURCES

Ingraham, Edward Duncan. *A Sketch of the Events Which Preceded the Capture of Washington by the British on the 24th of August, 1814*. Philadelphia: Carty & Hart, 1849.

Simmons, William. *A Letter to the House of Representatives of the United States, Shewing the Profligacy and Corruption of General John Armstrong in His Administration of the War Department*. Georgetown: Robert Alleson, 1814.

"Spectator." *An Enquiry Respecting the Capture of Washington by the British on the 24th of August, 1814*. Washington, 1816.

CHAPTER II: GENERAL JACKSON
AND MISTER ADAMS, 1816–1823

p. 41: Jackson and Florida, 1814: the best biographies of the general for this period remain James Parton, *The Life of Andrew Jackson* (New York: Mason Brothers, 1860), and John Spencer Bassett, *The Life of Andrew Jackson* (Archon, 1911). An example of Nicholls's inflated view of his own position was his famous letter to Colonel Hawkins, a U.S. Indian agent dealing with the Creeks, in which he stated, "I have, however, ordered them [the Indians] to stand on the defensive, and have sent them a large supply of arms and ammunition, and told them to put to death, without mercy, anyone molesting them." This can be found in the *American State Papers, Class 1, Foreign Affairs* (hereafter *ASPFA*), 4:549.

p. 42: Jackson: In John Spencer Bassett, ed., *The Correspondence of Andrew Jackson* (Washington, D.C.: Carnegie Institution, 1927), 2:28.

p. 43: An unusual and interesting treatment of the relationship between the blacks and the Seminoles and of the situation at the Negro Fort is given in Virginia Berman Peters, *The Florida Wars* (Hamden, Conn.: Archon, 1979).

p. 44: Jackson: *ASPFA* 4:495.

p. 44: Loomis and the attack: Loomis's own report to Commodore Daniel T. Patterson is included in *ASPFA* 4:559–60.

p. 46: John Quincy Adams to Abigail Adams, June 30, 1811: quoted in Samuel Flagg Bemis, *John Quincy Adams and the Foundations of American Foreign Policy* (New York: Knopf, 1949), p. 180.

p. 47: Adams's meeting with Castlereagh: see Charles Francis Adams, ed., *The Memoirs of John Quincy Adams, Comprising Portions of his Diary from 1795 to 1848* (Philadelphia: Lippincott, 1874), 3:560.

p. 48: Adams: quoted in Bemis, *John Quincy Adams*, p. 37.

p. 48: There are several other revealing anecdotes in *The Education of Henry Adams* (New York: Modern Library, 1931).

p. 49: Adams: also in the *Memoirs* account of the June 7 meeting.

p. 50: Report of Red Stick activities: contained in a letter from David B. Mitchell, an Indian agent (and future governor of Georgia) to acting Secretary of War George Graham, March 30, 1817. See the *American State Papers, Class 5, Military Affairs* (hereafter *ASPMA*), 1:683.

p. 51: Scott's party: see Gaines's dispatch of December 2, 1817, to the War Department, *ASPMA* 1:687–88.

p. 51: Gaines: ibid., p. 688.

p. 52: Jackson: ibid., p. 689.

p. 52: Gaines: ibid.

p. 52: Calhoun: ibid.

p. 53: Jackson: quoted in Richard Hofstadter, *The American Political Tradition* (New York: Vintage, 1973), p. 59.

p. 54: Adams to Onís: *Memoirs*, 4:42.

p. 54: Jackson to Monroe: Bassett, *Correspondence*, 2:345.

p. 56: The best examination of conflicting claims and evidence concerning the note is in Bassett's *Life*.

p. 56: Jackson to Calhoun: March 25, 1818, *ASPMA* 1:698.

p. 57: Jackson to Calhoun: April 8, 1818, ibid., pp. 699–700.

p. 58: Jackson to Calhoun: May 5, 1818, ibid., pp. 701–2.

p. 59: Onís to Adams: June 17, 1818, *ASPFA* 4:495.

p. 60: Adams: *Memoirs* 4:108–9.

p. 60: Onís to Adams: July 8, 1818, *ASPFA* 1:495.

p. 61: For the best examination of the evolution of Adams's ideas concerning the Pacific Coast (including the quoted conversation with Onís), see Bemis, *John Quincy Adams*, pp. 317–21.

p. 62: Adams in the cabinet, July 20: *Memoirs*, 4:112–14.

p. 62: Adams in the cabinet, July 21: ibid., p. 115.

p. 63: A complete text of the Instructions to Erving can be found in *ASPFA*, 4:539–45.

p. 65: Rush and John Adams Smith: Bemis, *John Quincy Adams*, p. 328.

p. 66: Adams: *Memoirs*, 4:274–75.

p. 67: Jackson to Monroe: June 20, 1820, Parton, *Life of Andrew Jackson* 2:584.

p. 67: Jefferson: quoted in Walter LaFeber, *Inevitable Revolutions* (New York: Norton, 1983), p. 22.

p. 67: Jefferson's expansionism: quoted in Frederick Merk, *Manifest Destiny and Mission in American History* (New York: Knopf, 1963), p. 9.

p. 68: Adams: *Memoirs*, 5:324–25.

p. 68: Clay: quoted in Ernest May, *The American Foreign Policy* (New York: Braziller, 1963), p. 63.

p. 69: Adams: *Memoirs*, 4:92.

p. 70: Adams to Clay: *Memoirs*, 5:324–25.

pp. 73, 74: Adams on Canning, and Canning on Latin America: quoted in Howard Jones, *The Course of American Diplomacy* (New York: Franklin Watts, 1985), p. 107.

CHAPTER III: MANIFEST DESTINY AS NATIONAL SECURITY, 1842–1849

p. 75: Jones: this and all subsequent quotes from the commodore can be found in the *House Executive Documents*, 27th Cong., 3d sess. (Serial 422, vol. 5), Doc. 166, "Taking Possession of Monterey." (Hereafter *HED* 422-5-166.) Jones's statements to his officers are on pp. 84–85. Document 166 contains the proceedings and evidence of a House investigation called for by none other than John Quincy Adams.

pp. 76, 77: Great Britain and the United States: the best general studies of this topic remain Kenneth Bourne's outstanding pair of works, *Britain and the Balance of Power in North America* (Berkeley: University of California Press, 1967), and *The Foreign Policy of Victorian England* (Oxford: Clarendon Press, 1970). The latter contains extensive documents that are particularly revealing on the subject of Oregon.

p. 77: French official: quoted in Neal Harlow, *California Conquered* (Berkeley: University of California Press, 1982), p. 35.

p. 78: Jones's orders: *HED* 422-5-166, p. 47.

p. 78: Jones's decisions: ibid., pp. 85–86.

p. 79: Jones's account: ibid., pp. 70–71.

p. 80: Jones's general order: ibid., pp. 41–42.

p. 80: Jones's proclamation: ibid., p. 31.

p. 81: Jones's account: ibid., p. 72.

p. 85: Governor James H. Hammond: to John C. Calhoun, May 10, 1844, in the *Annual Report of the American Historical Association for the Year 1899*, vol. 2 (Washington: GPO, 1900), pp. 953–54.

p. 87: Benton: in *The Congressional Globe*, 28th Cong., 1st sess., Appendix, pp. 474–86; also the *Washington Globe*, April 29, 1844.

p. 87: Benton: *Niles' Weekly Register* 66 (1844): 272, 295.

p. 88: Polk: the best political biographies of Polk are Charles Sellers, *James K. Polk, Jacksonian* (the first of two volumes), and *James K. Polk, Continentalist* (Princeton, N.J.: Princeton University Press, 1966); and Eugene Irving McCormac, *James K. Polk: A Political Biography* (New York: Russell & Russell, 1922).

p. 89: One of the most revealing—if rather biased—portraits of Polk is a typed manuscript that is contained in the New York Public Library's Bancroft Collection (hereafter Bancroft: NYPL). This quote is on pp. 14–15.

p. 90: Polk: Sellers, *Continentalist*, p. 67.

p. 91: Polk on Great Britain: Milo Milton Quaife, ed., *The Diary of James K. Polk During His Presidency* (Chicago: A. C. McClurg, 1910), 1:155.

p. 92: Polk's four great measures: Bancroft: NYPL, p. 25.

p. 93: The Inaugural Address: James D. Richardson, ed., *Compilation of the Messages and Papers of the Presidents: 1789–1897* (New York: Johnson Reprint, 1969), 4:381.

p. 93: Adams: *Memoirs* 12:173.

p. 94: Polk: *Diary* 4:261.

p. 94: The Sloat orders: in the *California Historical Society Quarterly* 2 (1923–24): 164.

p. 95: Frémont: see Allan Nevins, *Frémont: Pathfinder of the West* (New York: Ungar, 1955), and Ferol Egan, *Frémont: Explorer for a Restless Nation* (Garden City, N.Y.: Doubleday, 1977). Also John Charles Frémont, *Memoirs of My Life* (New York: Belford, Clarke, 1887). The latter, prepared by Frémont with—as always—the considerable assistance of his wife Jessie, contains many and severe inaccuracies, and is primarily of interest in determining Frémont's attitudes and motivations.

p. 95: Larkin's July 10 dispatch: in George P. Hammond, ed., *The Larkin Papers* (Berkeley: University of California Press, 1952), 3:265.

p. 96: Consul in Liverpool: Armstrong, to Polk, quoted in Sellers, *Polk, Continentalist*, p. 332.

p. 96: Jackson to Polk: McCormac, *Political Biography*, pp. 565–66.

pp. 96, 97: The Larkin orders: Hammond, *Larkin Papers* 3:44–47.

p. 97: An American agent (Duff Green, a close friend of Calhoun's): in *American Historical Association*, p. 979.

p. 98: The Slidell orders: in John Bassett Moore, ed., *The Works of James Buchanan* (New York: Antiquarian Press, 1960), 6:294–306.

p. 98: Larkin: Hammond, *Larkin Papers* 3:243–44.

p. 99: Larkin: ibid., p. 260.

p. 99: Manuel Castro, prefect of Monterey: in *Niles' Weekly Register* 71 (1846): 189.

p. 99: Larkin to Frémont: Hammond, *Larkin Papers* 3:240.

p. 99: Frémont to Larkin: ibid., p. 245.

p. 100: Kit Carson: quoted in Harlow, *California Conquered*, p. 75.

p. 100: Sloat's December 5 orders: in the *California Historical Society Quarterly* 2 (1923–24): 171.

p. 101: Sloat: Frederick Merk, *Manifest Destiny and Mission in American History* (New York: Knopf, 1963), p. 67.

p. 102: Frémont: J. C. Frémont, *Memoirs*, pp. 488–89.

p. 102: Gillespie's testimony: in *California Claims*, 30th Cong., 1st sess., S. Rept. 75 (Serial 512), 1:32–33.

p. 103: Polk on war: Sellers, *Polk, Continentalist*, p. 409.

p. 104: Sloat's account of his actions can be found in *California Claims* 2:70–75.

p. 105: Sloat: Harlow, *California Conquered*, p. 122.

p. 105: Larkin to Buchanan: Hammond, *Larkin Papers* 6:8.

p. 106: Jefferson on Cuba: Paul L. Ford, ed., *The Works of Jefferson* (New York, 1904–5), 12:318–21.

p. 107: Jefferson on defense: Andrew A. Lipscomb, ed., *The Writings of Thomas Jefferson* (Washington, 1903), 12:274–77.

p. 107: Adams on Cuba: Frederick Merk, *The Monroe Doctrine and American Expansionism* (New York: Knopf, 1966), p. 234.

ADDITIONAL SOURCES

Adams, Ephraim D. *British Interests and Activities in Texas, 1838–1846.* Baltimore: Johns Hopkins University Press, 1910.

Benton, Thomas Hart. *Thirty Years' View; or, A History of the Working of the American Government for Thirty Years, from 1820 to 1850.* New York: D. Appleton, 1856.

Cralle, Richard A., ed. *The Works, Reports and Public Letters of John C. Calhoun.* New York: Russell & Russell, 1851–56.

Engelson, Lester G. "Proposals for the Colonization of California by England in Connection with the Mexican Debt to British Bondholders, 1837–1846." *California Historical Society Quarterly* 18, no. 2 (June 1939).

Hittell, John S. *A History of the City of San Francisco, and Incidentally of the State of California.* San Francisco: A. L. Bancroft, 1878.

Hussey, John Adam. "The Origin of the Gillespie Mission." *California Historical Society Quarterly* 19, no. 1 (March 1940).

Smith, Elbert B. *Magnificent Missourian: The Life of Thomas Hart Benton.* Philadelphia: Lippincott, 1958.

CHAPTER IV: IMPERIALISM AND INSECURITY, 1890–1912

p. 109: Dewey: George Dewey, *Autobiography of George Dewey, Admiral of the Navy* (hereafter Dewey) (New York: Scribner's, 1913), p. 192.

p. 110: The Roosevelt cable: Theodore Roosevelt, *Theodore Roosevelt: An Autobiography* (hereafter Roosevelt) (New York: Macmillan, 1913), p. 234.

p. 110: Dewey: *Dewey*, pp. 5, 14.

p. 111: The Long orders: National Archives, Naval Records, Record Group 45: *Translations of Messages Sent in Cipher* 1:569.

p. 114: Dewey: *Dewey*, p. 205.

p. 114: Dewey takes the point: G. J. A. O'Toole, *The Spanish War: An American Epic, 1898* (New York: Norton, 1984), p. 181.

p. 114: One American seaman: E. G. Stovell, on board the collier *Nanshan*. His handwritten manuscript, "An Account of the Battle of May 1st, Seen From the U.S.S. Nanshan, Position NNW From Sangey Point, Dist.—4 Miles" can be found in the George Dewey Papers, Library of Congress. This quote is on p. 1.

p. 115: Dewey: *Dewey*, pp. 194, 214. The legendary remark to the *Olympia*'s captain has often been shortened and reemphasized to "You may fire when ready, Gridley!" But Dewey's own version fits far more closely 15ith his character.

p. 115: One American: Stovell, "An Account," p. 5.

p. 115: Dewey: *Dewey*, p. 221.

p. 116: Finley P. Dunne: *Mr. Dooley in Peace and War* (Boston: Small, Maynard, 1898), p. 43.

p. 116: Roosevelt: *Dewey*, p. 229.

p. 118: Jay Gould: quoted in Richard Hofstadter, *The American Political Tradition* (New York: Vintage, 1973), p. 215.

p. 119: The economy: the best study remains Walter LaFeber, *The New Empire* (Ithaca, N.Y.: Cornell University Press, 1963).

p. 120: Blaine's Waterville speech: *The New York Tribune*, August 30, 1890, p. 1, col. 6.

p. 121: The Olney note: *Papers Relating to the Foreign Relations of the United States, 1895* (Washington, D.C.: GPO, 1896), p. 558.

p. 123: Mahan: Margaret Tuttle Sprout, "Mahan: Evangelist of Sea Power," in Edward Mead Earle, ed., *Makers of Modern Strategy* (Princeton, N.J.: Princeton University Press, 1943), p. 417.

p. 123: Mahan on stations: Alfred Thayer Mahan, *The Influence of Sea Power Upon History, 1660–1783* (Boston: Little, Brown, 1890), pp. 27–28.

p. 124: Mahan on American weakness: Mahan, *Influence*, pp. 33, 39, 49, 88, 83.

p. 124: Mahan's article: "The United States Looking Outward," first published in the *Atlantic Monthly*, December 1890, reprinted in Captain

A. T. Mahan, *The Interest of America in Sea Power, Present and Future* (Boston: Little, Brown, 1897), p. 17.

p. 124: The secretary of the navy: Benjamin Tracy. See *Report of the Secretary of the Navy, 1889* (Washington, D.C.: GPO, 1890).

p. 124: The Naval Policy Board: Senate Executive Documents, 51st Cong., 1st sess., #43, "Report of the So-Called Policy Board" (Serial 2682), 5:4–6.

p. 126: Another senator: Pettigrew of South Dakota. His and Lodge's speeches can be found in the *Congressional Record*, 53d Cong., 3d sess., 27, pt. 4:3077–3108.

p. 127: Mahan: Mahan to Roosevelt, May 6, 1897, in the Library of Congress's Theodore Roosevelt papers.

p. 127: Roosevelt on other powers: to Mahan, May 3, 1897, in Elting E. Morison, ed., *The Letters of Theodore Roosevelt* (Cambridge, Mass.: Harvard University Press, 1951), 1:607–8.

p. 128: Lodge on the Kaiser: to Roosevelt, March 27, 1901, in *Selections From the Correspondence of Theodore Roosevelt and Henry Cabot Lodge, 1884–1918* (New York: Scribner's, 1925), 1:487.

p. 128: TR's desire for war: see, for instance, his letter to W. W. Kimball, November 19, 1897, in Morison, *Letters* 1:717.

p. 128: Mahan on Hawaii: to Roosevelt, May 1, 1897, in the Library of Congress's Roosevelt Papers.

p. 128: Roosevelt to Mahan: May 3, 1897, in Morison, *Letters* 1:607–8.

p. 128: Roosevelt on war with Spain: to Mahan, May 3, 1897, ibid.

p. 129: Kimball: quoted in Peter Karsten, *The Naval Aristocracy* (New York: Free Press, 1972), p. 235.

p. 130: Kimball's war plan: these and all quotes are from the original in the National Archives, Naval Division, Record Group 313, *Records of the Naval Operating Forces*, Entry 43, Box 11.

p. 131: Roosevelt's "intimate" contact with Kimball: quoted in Jeffrey M. Dorwart, *The Office of Naval Intelligence* (Annapolis: Naval Institute Press, 1979), p. 57.

p. 131: Roosevelt to Kimball: November 19 and December 17, 1897, in Morison, *Letters* 1:717, 743.

p. 132: McKinley: quoted in Honesto A. Villanueva, "Diplomacy of the Spanish-American War," chap. 5, *Philippine Social Sciences and Humanities Review* 15, no. 2 (June 1950): 116.

pp. 132, 133: William James and Mark Twain: quoted in Samuel Eliot Morison, Frederick Merk and Frank Freidel, *Dissent in Three American Wars* (Cambridge, Mass.: Harvard University Press, 1970), pp. 90, 95.

p. 133: Lodge: quoted in John Garraty, *Henry Cabot Lodge* (New York: Knopf, 1953), p. 197.

p. 134: Hippisley and Rockhill: see George Kennan, *American Diplomacy* (New York: New American Library, 1951), chap. 2.

p. 135: The Open Door notes: texts are in *Papers Relating to the Foreign Relations of the United States, 1899* (Washington, D.C.: GPO, 1900), pp. 128–41.

p. 135: Hay on response: to Conger, March 22, 1900, in *Papers Relating to the Foreign Relations of the United States, 1900* (Washington, D.C.: GPO, 1902), p. 111.

p. 135: Hay on alliances: to Conger, June 10, 1900, ibid., p. 143.

p. 135: Naval War Board on a China base: R.G. 45, *Naval War Board, Telegrams Recommended, Entry 372.* Sicard to Long, August 22, 1898, p. 5.

p. 135: Long on a China base: to Hay, December 2, 1901, Record Group 59, State Department Miscellaneous Letters (M179, 10-17-5, Roll 1119).

p. 136: Dewey on Manila: Dewey to Roosevelt, August 4, 1904, General Board File 425-2. This can be found in the Navy Department's Operational Archives.

p. 136: Rockhill: R.G. 59, to Adee, December 5, 1901.

p. 136: Roosevelt: to Frederic R. Coudert, July 3, 1901, Morison, *Letters* 3:105.

p. 137: Mark Hanna: quoted in Samuel Eliot Morison and Henry Steele Commager, *The Growth of the American Republic* (New York: Oxford University Press, 1940), 2:386.

p. 138: Sims: quoted in Edward L. Beach, *The United States Navy: 200 Years* (Boston: Houghton Mifflin, 1986), p. 393.

p. 138: Mahan: Beach, *Navy*, p. 386.

p. 138: Sims: quoted in Elting E. Morison, *Admiral Sims and the Modern American Navy* (Boston: Houghton Mifflin, 1942), p. 433.

p. 138: Roosevelt and Panama: quoted in Morison and Commager, *American Republic*, p. 404.

p. 139: Roosevelt on the Germans: O'Toole, *Spanish War*, p. 100.

p. 139: The General Board's coalition plans can be found both in the Library of Congress's Dewey Papers and in the General Board files of the Navy's Operational Archives, which have an index. This quote is from a memorandum in the Library of Congress's Dewey collection.

p. 140: Dewey expressing the board's opinions: this opinion is put forward in numerous board documents, including Dewey to Navy Secretary George von L. Meyer, November 16, 1910. *General Board Letterpress*, in the Navy's Operational Archives.

p. 140: Roosevelt on the Philippines: to Secretary of War William Howard Taft, August 21, 1907, Morison, *Letters* 5:761.

p. 141: Roosevelt and the World Cruise: in his *Autobiography*, p. 592.

p. 141: The decision to concentrate at Pearl: see William Reynolds Braisted, *The United States Navy in the Pacific, 1897–1909* (Austin: University of Texas Press, 1958), passim, and especially pp. 219–22.

p. 142: "Plan Orange": in the *War Portfolio No. 2—Orange War Plan,* dated April 1914 but approved by the General Board March 14, 1914, and revised in March 1915. This quote is taken from p. 14 of the *Strategic Section.* For comparison, see also *War Portfolio No. 1, Reference No. 5-Y, Germany War Plan—Black Plan.* Both are at the Navy's Operational Archives, as are numerous other board war plans of the period.

pp. 142, 143: Kitchin's speech: in the *Congressional Record,* August 15, 1916, 53:12697–98.

p. 144: Stimson: Beach, *Navy,* p. 421.

ADDITIONAL SOURCES

Perkins, Dexter. *The Monroe Doctrine, 1867–1907.* Gloucester, Mass.: Peter Smith, 1966.

Sargent, Nathan. *Admiral Dewey and the Manila Campaign.* Washington: Naval Historical Foundation, 1947.

Sprout, Harold and Margaret. *The Rise of American Naval Power.* Princeton, N.J.: Princeton University Press, 1939.

CHAPTER V: MR. WILSON INTERVENES, 1912–1921

p. 146: "blow him to perdition": William S. Graves, *America's Siberian Adventure* (New York: Jonathan Cape & Harrison Smith, 1931), p. 184.

p. 146: one American officer: Lieutenant Colonel H. H. Slaughter, who served as American military attaché to the Kolchak government in Omsk. After his return to the United States, Slaughter wrote an illuminating paper, "The American Expeditionary Force in Siberia as Part of Allied Intervention in 1918," which was read before the U.S. Army War College on March 29, 1934. It can be found in the archives of the U.S. Army Military History Institute at Carlisle Barracks, Carlisle, Pennsylvania. This quote is on p. 17 (hereafter Slaughter).

p. 146: one American diplomat: F. C. MacDonald, secretary to the U.S. ambassador to Japan. MacDonald accompanied the ambassador, Roland S. Morris, on a fact-finding trip to Omsk in 1919 and kept a diary of the trip, which can be found in the William J. Donovan Papers at the U.S. Army Military History Institute. This quote is on p. 10 (hereafter MacDonald).

p. 146: Graves: Graves, *Siberian Adventure,* p. 183.

p. 147: "a sort of bomb": Slaughter, p. 20.

p. 150: Graves: Graves, *Siberian Adventure,* p. 3.

p. 150: Graves: ibid., p. 4.

p. 151: The Aide-Memoire: *Papers Relating to the Foreign Relations of the United States* (hereafter *PRFRUS*) *Russia, 1918* (Washington, D.C.: GPO, 1932), 2:287–90.

p. 151: Graves: Graves, *Siberian Adventure*, p. 5.

p. 151: Graves: ibid., p. 10.

p. 152: "the forgotten men": one of the most revealing sources of first-hand information on the Siberian intervention was a survey conducted by the U.S. Army Military History Institute in 1978. Questionnaires were sent out to World War I veterans, and these included the men of the AEFS. Their comments can be found in the archives at Carlisle Barracks. This explanation of "the forgotten men" was given by Private First Class Otto H. Kern of the 27th Infantry, a native of Cotter, Arkansas (hereafter Kern).

p. 152: "Jews from the East Side . . . ": Graves, *Siberian Adventure*, p. 110.

p. 152: one American official: MacDonald, p. 29.

p. 152: Wilson's "incomparable father": Sigmund Freud and William C. Bullitt, *Thomas Woodrow Wilson: A Psychological Study* (Boston: Houghton Mifflin, 1967), passim. Despite the obvious prejudice of Bullitt and Freud's admitted dislike of Wilson, this book remains of great interest and use, as does Alexander and Juliette George's *Woodrow Wilson and Colonel House: A Personality Study* (Mineola, N.Y.: Dover, 1956), which also concentrates with great insight on the psychological motivations involved in Wilson's official behavior.

p. 153: "minor statesmanship": Freud and Bullitt, *Wilson*, p. 111.

p. 154: Wilson: taken from an early work, *The State*, as quoted in Richard Hofstadter, *The American Political Tradition* (New York: Vintage, 1973), pp. 313–14.

p. 154: Wilson on labor: Arthur S. Link, ed., *The Papers of Woodrow Wilson* (Princeton, N.J.: Princeton University Press, 1972) 17:82.

p. 155: House: quoted in Arthur D. Howden Smith, *Mr. House of Texas* (New York: Funk & Wagnalls, 1940), p. 11. Smith was a journalist and sometime intimate of House's, whose first treatment of the man in an article called "The *Real* Colonel House" did much to perpetuate House's mystique.

p. 156: Wilson on House: Freud and Bullitt, *Wilson*, p. 147.

p. 157: Wilson's New Freedom: Link, *Papers* 24:427.

pp. 157, 158: Wilson's Mobile address: *Senate Documents*, 64th Cong., 2d sess., Document #440 (Washington, D.C.: GPO, 1914), pp. 5–8.

p. 159: Wilson's new Latin policy: *PRFRUS, 1913* (Washington: GPO, 1920), p. 7.

p. 159: "I am going to teach . . .": Arthur S. Link, *The New Freedom* (Princeton, N.J.: Princeton University Press, 1956), p. 375.

p. 159: Wilson on Huerta: ibid., p. 367.

p. 159: Lodge on Mexico: quoted in John A. Garraty, *Henry Cabot Lodge: A Biography* (New York: Knopf, 1953), pp. 303–4.

p. 162: One contemporary magazine: *The World's Work* 30 (August 1915): 398.

p. 162: One friend and associate: quoted in "Robert Lansing as His Friends Know Him," *Collier's Magazine* 56 (November 13, 1915): 24.

p. 163: One of Wilson's advisers: George Creel, in his *Rebel at Large: Recollections of Fifty Crowded Years* (New York: G. P. Putnam's Sons, 1947), p. 160. It was Creel who later urged Wilson to publish the Sisson Documents that purported to show that Lenin and Trotsky were German agents.

p. 163: Josephus Daniels: in his *The Wilson Era: Years of Peace, 1910–1917* (Chapel Hill, N.C.: University of North Carolina Press, 1944), p. 441.

p. 163: House on Lansing: this comment is from the March 24, 1917, entry in the "Diary of Edward M. House," the manuscript of which can be seen at the Sterling Memorial Library at Yale University.

p. 163: Mrs. Wilson: in her *My Memoir* (New York: Bobbs-Merrill, 1939), p. 64.

p. 163: A piece of Washington humor: House, "Diary," March 3, 1917.

p. 163: Wilson on Lansing: as recalled by Agriculture Secretary David F. Houston in Daniels, *Wilson Era*, p. 436.

p. 164: House on Lansing: Charles Seymour, ed., *The Intimate Papers of Colonel House* (New York: Houghton Mifflin, 1926), 3:20–21.

p. 165: House and Lansing on Japanese aspirations: House, "Diary," July 25, 1915. Also in this entry, and in that of April 29, 1917, are discussions of House's and Lansing's similar views on the question of disposing of the Philippines.

p. 165: The Lansing-Ishii Agreement: *PRFRUS, 1917* (Washington: GPO, 1926), p. 264.

pp. 167, 168: Wilson's War Message: *PRFRUS, 1917, Supplement* (Washington: GPO, 1931–32), pp. 195–203.

p. 169: Lansing on Russia: "Memorandum on the Russian Situation," December 7, 1917. This and all Lansing's fascinating private memoranda—the only places in which he allowed his private feelings to surface—can be found in the Lansing Collection, Library of Congress, Container 66.

p. 169: The Fourteen Points: *House Documents*, 65th Cong., 2d sess. (Washington: GPO, 1918), Document 765.

p. 170: Lansing: "Memorandum on the Proposed Japanese Military Expedition into Siberia," March 18–19, 1918, Lansing Collection, Library of Congress.

p. 170: Wilson to Lansing: *PRFRUS, The Lansing Papers, 1914–20* (Washington: GPO, 1940), 2:360.

p. 171: Lansing on the Japanese: "Suspected Designs of the Japanese in Siberia," July 31, 1919, Lansing Collection, Library of Congress.

p. 171: Lansing to Wilson: December 4, 1919, Wilson Collection, Library of Congress, on microfilm: Series 2, Reel 99.

p. 172: Graves: to Secretary of War Newton Baker, November 22, 1918, Wilson Collection, Library of Congress, on microfilm: Series 2, Reel 102.

p. 172: Wilson's policies: quoted in Lloyd C. Gardner, *Safe for Democracy: The Anglo-American Response to Revolution, 1913–1923* (New York: Oxford University Press, 1984), p. 197.

p. 172: Hoover: in his *The Ordeal of Woodrow Wilson* (New York: McGraw-Hill, 1958), pp. 115–16.

p. 173: Wilson and the documents: House, "Diary," September 24, 1918.

p. 174: John Maynard Keynes: in his *Essays and Sketches in Biography* (New York: Meridian Books, 1956), pp. 265–67.

p. 174: Lansing on Wilson: "The Japanese Claims to Kiau Chau and Shantung Admitted," May 1, 1919, Lansing Collection, Library of Congress.

p. 174: Lansing on Shantung: "Japanese Claims and the League of Nations," April 28, 1919, Lansing Collection, Library of Congress.

p. 175: House on Bolshevism: quoted in N. Gordon Levin, *Woodrow Wilson and World Politics: America's Response to War and Revolution* (New York: Oxford University Press, 1968), p. 140.

p. 175: Wilson's Kansas City and Des Moines speeches: *PRFRUS, 1919, Russia* (Washington: GPO, 1937), pp. 119–20.

p. 176: Lansing on communism: "Tendency Toward Communistic Ideas," September 1, 1919, Lansing Collection, Library of Congress.

p. 176: Reports on Kolchak: Ambassador Morris to Acting Secretary of State Polk, July 22, 1919, *PRFRUS, 1919, Russia*, p. 395.

p. 176: Lansing: to George Kennan, quoted in N. Gordon Levin, *World Politics*, p. 229.

p. 176: One private: Kern.

p. 177: *San Francisco Examiner*, October 8, 1919.

p. 177: Graves: in his *Siberian Adventure*, p. 354.

p. 177: Wilson's "safe for democracy": in "The Road Away From Revolution," *Atlantic Monthly*, August 1923; can also be found in Ray Stannard Baker and William E. Dodd, eds., *The Public Papers of Woodrow Wilson* (New York: Harper & Bros., 1927), 2:537–39.

p. 178: Graves: in his *Siberian Adventure*, p. 356.

ADDITIONAL SOURCES

Beers, Burton F. *Vain Endeavor: Robert Lansing's Attempts to End the Japanese-American Rivalry.* Durham, N.C.: Duke University Press, 1962.

Haley, P. Edward. *Revolution and Intervention: The Diplomacy of Taft and Wilson with Mexico.* Cambridge, Mass.: MIT Press, 1970.

Kennan, George F. *The Decision to Intervene.* Princeton, N.J.: Princeton University Press, 1958.

Kennan, George F. *Russia Leaves the War.* Princeton, N.J.: Princeton University Press, 1956.

Lansing, Robert. *The Peace Negotiations: A Personal Narrative.* Boston: Houghton Mifflin, 1921.

————. *War Memoirs of Robert Lansing.* New York: Bobbs-Merrill, 1935.

Lasch, Christopher. *The American Liberals and the Russian Revolution.* New York: Columbia University Press, 1962.

Maddox, Robert J. *The Unknown War with Russia: Wilson's Siberian Intervention.* San Rafael, Calif.: Presidio Press, 1977.

Thompson, John M. *Russia, Bolshevism and the Versailles Peace.* Princeton, N.J.: Princeton University Press, 1966.

Ullman, Richard H. *Intervention and the War.* Princeton, N.J.: Princeton University Press, 1961.

Unterberger, Betty Miller. *America's Siberian Expedition: A Study of National Policy.* Durham, N.C.: Duke University Press, 1956.

CHAPTER VI: A RECKONING IN THE EAST, 1921–1941

p. 179: Lieutenant Okumiya: the only detailed study of the *Panay* bombing incident that has yet appeared is Hamilton Darby Perry's *The Panay Incident* (New York: Macmillan, 1969). Perry interviewed the *Panay* survivors as well as many Japanese officers involved in the attack. This account is taken from p. 71. Also useful in this connection is Manny Koginos's *The Panay Incident: Prelude to Pearl Harbor* (Lafayette, Ind.: Purdue University Studies, 1967), although this, like most discussions of the subject, tends to concentrate on the diplomatic repercussions rather than the actual incident.

p. 180: Captain Miki: Perry, *Panay Incident*, p. 248.

p. 180: Okumiya: ibid., p. 72.

p. 180: The Cherry Society: see Robert J. C. Butow, *Tojo and the Coming of War* (Princeton, N.J.: Princeton University Press, 1961), p. 33.

p. 184: Yamamoto: quoted in John Toland, *The Rising Sun: The Decline and Fall of the Japanese Empire* (New York: Random House, 1970), p. 55.

p. 184: Hirota: see *Papers Relating to the Foreign Relations of the United States* (hereafter *PRFRUS*), *Supplement: Japan, 1931–41* (Washington: GPO, 1943), p. 526.

p. 185: Hull: ibid., pp. 529–30.

p. 185: Ickes: Harold Ickes, *The Secret Diary of Harold L. Ickes* (New York: Simon and Schuster, 1954), 2:274–75.

p. 185: FDR: ibid., p. 275.

p. 186: *Christian Science Monitor:* December 13, 1937, p. 30.

p. 186: Morgenthau: John Morton Blum, ed., *From the Morgenthau Diaries* (Boston: Houghton Mifflin, 1959), pp. 487–88.

p. 193: Stimson: Elting E. Morison, *Turmoil and Tradition: A Study of the Life and Times of Henry L. Stimson* (Boston: Houghton Mifflin, 1960), p. 229.

p. 193: Stimson: Henry L. Stimson and McGeorge Bundy, *On Active Service in Peace and War* (New York: Harper, 1947), p. xv.

p. 195: Stimson on being a "loafer": This can be found in the Henry Stimson Diary, together with the rest of the Stimson Papers, at Yale University's Sterling Library. This is from the November 1, 1930, entry, which is in bound vol. 10 (hereafter Stimson Diary).

p. 196: Robert Olds: see James Chace, *Endless War* (New York: Vintage, 1984), p. 45.

p. 197: Stimson: in his *Active Service*, p. 127.

p. 201: Stimson: Stimson Diary, October 9, 1931, vol. 18.

p. 201: The Stimson note: in his *Active Service*, pp. 235–36.

p. 201: *The London Times:* January 11, 1932, p. 13.

p. 202: Stimson: Stimson Diary, January 26, 1932, vol. 20.

p. 202: Stimson's "mad dogs": Stimson Diary, November 19, 1931, vol. 10.

p. 203: Stimson: Stimson Diary, November 14, 1931, vol. 19.

p. 204: Stimson: the description of Roosevelt's home and of the circumstances of their meeting are in the *Diary* entry for January 9, 1933.

p. 205: Stimson: the comments on the meeting with Roosevelt are contained in a "Memorandum of Conversation with Franklin D. Roosevelt, January 9, at Hyde Park, New York," which, rather than being assembled with Stimson's other memoranda, is inserted in the Diary at January 9.

p. 206: Stimson and FDR: Stimson, *Active Service*, p. 293.

p. 207: Moley: Robert Dallek, *Franklin D. Roosevelt and American Foreign Policy, 1932–1945* (New York: Oxford University Press, 1979), p. 38.

p. 207: The Neutrality Act: see William Leuchtenberg, *Franklin Roosevelt and the New Deal, 1932–1940* (New York: Harper & Row, 1963), pp. 219–24.

p. 208: FDR's San Diego speech: Samuel I. Rosenman, ed., *The Public Papers and Addresses of Franklin D. Roosevelt* (New York: Random House, 1938), 4:410–11.

p. 208: Hopkins: Robert E. Sherwood, *Roosevelt and Hopkins: An Intimate History* (New York: Harper & Bros., 1948), p. 79.

p. 208: Hull: in his *The Memoirs of Cordell Hull* (New York: 1948), 1:482–84.

p. 210: Stimson: these comments were made in a brief assessment of an article by George Blakeslee in the July 1933 issue of *Foreign Affairs*, "The Japanese Monroe Doctrine." Stimson felt that the article was important enough to be "carefully kept at hand and used." The memorandum can be found in the Stimson Papers at Yale, on Roll 126 of microfilm.

p. 211: The Quarantine Speech: Rosenman, *Public Papers,* vol. 1937, pp. 406–11.

p. 211: The press conference: ibid., pp. 414–25.

p. 212: Roosevelt's "look over your shoulder": Samuel I. Rosenman, *Working with Roosevelt* (New York: Harper & Bros., 1952), p. 167.

p. 213: Plan Orange: see Louis Morton, "War Plan Orange: Evolution of a Strategy," *World Politics* 11, no. 2 (January 1959).

p. 214: The Rainbow Plans: see Stetson Conn and Byron Fairchild, *The U.S. Army in World War II: The Western Hemisphere: The Framework of Hemispheric Defense* (Washington, D.C.: Office of the Chief of Military History, Department of the Army, 1960).

p. 215: Grew: Joseph C. Grew, *Turbulent Era: A Diplomatic Record of Forty Years, 1904–45* (Boston: Houghton Mifflin, 1952), p. 1229.

p. 215: Ickes: this statement is in a letter to FDR that can be found in the President's Secretary File, Interior Department, Harold I. Ickes, 1940, File 17, letter dated October 17, 1940. It is in the FDR Library at Hyde Park, New York.

p. 216: Hull: in his *Memoirs* 1:602.

p. 216: Stark and Marshall: see *Hearings Before the Joint Committee on the Investigation of the Pearl Harbor Attack,* 79th Cong., 1st. sess., pt. 14, p. 1061.

p. 216: Stimson: in his *Active Service,* p. 323.

ADDITIONAL SOURCES

Borg, Dorothy. "The Meaning of the Quarantine Speech," on microfilm at the FDR Library at Hyde Park, Film 93, Group 1.

———. *The United States and the Far Eastern Crisis of 1933–1938.* Cambridge, Mass.: Harvard University Press, 1964.

Borg, Dorothy, and Okamoto, Shumpei, eds. *Pearl Harbor as History: Japanese-American Relations, 1931–1941.* New York: Columbia University Press, 1973.

Cantril, Hadley, and Strunk, Mildred, eds. *Public Opinion, 1935–1946.* Princeton, N.J.: Princeton University Press, 1951.

The Complete Press Conferences of Franklin D. Roosevelt. New York: Da Capo Press, 1972.

Current, Richard N. *Secretary Stimson: A Study in Statecraft.* Hamden, Conn.: Shoe String Press, Archon Books, 1970.

Feis, Herbert. *The Road to Pearl Harbor.* Princeton, N.J.: Princeton University Press, 1950.

Nixon, Edgar B., ed. *Franklin D. Roosevelt and Foreign Affairs*. Cambridge, Mass.: Harvard University Press, 1969.

Reischauer, Edwin O. *The United States and Japan*. Cambridge, Mass.: Harvard University Press, 1965.

Welles, Sumner. *Seven Decisions that Shaped History*. New York: Harper & Bros., 1950.

CHAPTER VII: DEFINING THE PERIMETER, 1945–1968

p. 218: Kennan: in his *Memoirs, 1925–1950* (Boston: Little, Brown, 1967), p. 484.

p. 219: Kennan: ibid., p. 485.

p. 219: Kennan: ibid.

p. 220: Acheson: in his *Present at the Creation* (New York: Norton, 1969), p. 402.

p. 220: Muccio's cable: in Harry S Truman, *Memoirs*, vol. 2: *Years of Trial and Hope* (Garden City, N.Y.: Doubleday, 1956), pp. 333–34.

pp. 220, 222: Acheson: in his *Present*, pp. 431–32.

p. 222: Rusk: "Memo to Paul Nitze," February 23, 1950, in *Foreign Relations of the United States* (hereafter *FRUS*), *1950* (Washington: GPO, 1977), 1:167.

p. 222: Trygve Lie: quoted in Gaddis Smith, *Dean Acheson* (New York: Cooper Square Publishers, 1972), p. 179.

p. 223: Acheson: Truman, *Memoirs* 2:332.

p. 223: Truman: ibid.

p. 223–24: Truman: ibid., pp. 332–33.

p. 224: Acheson: *Present*, p. 405.

p. 225: Acheson: ibid., pp. 412–13.

p. 226: Acheson's memo: *Department of State Bulletin*, July 31, 1950, pp. 173–78.

p. 227: Harriman: with Elie Abel, *Special Envoy to Churchill and Stalin, 1941–1946* (New York: Random House, 1975), p. 516.

pp. 228–29: Harriman: to the secretary of state, January 10, 1945, in *FRUS: The Conferences at Malta and Yalta, 1945* (Washington, GPO, 1955), p. 450.

p. 229: Churchill: ibid., pp. 678–79.

p. 229: Stalin: ibid., pp. 679–80.

p. 229: FDR: ibid., pp. 678, 718.

pp. 229–30: FDR's speech on Yalta: Samuel I. Rosenman, ed., *The Public Papers and Addresses of Franklin D. Roosevelt*, 1945 vol. (New York: Harper & Bros., 1950), pp. 570–86.

p. 230: FDR in private: quoted in Arthur M. Schlesinger, "Why the Cold War?" in *The Cycles of American History* (Boston: Houghton Mifflin, 1986), p. 167.

p. 230: FDR to Churchill: Warren F. Kimball, ed. *Churchill and Roosevelt: the Complete Correspondence* (Princeton, N.J.: Princeton University Press, 1984), Vol. 3, pp. 593–597.

p. 230: Hopkins: in Robert E. Sherwood, *Roosevelt and Hopkins: An Intimate History* (New York: Harper & Bros., 1948), p. 881.

p. 230: Truman: *The New York Times*, June 24, 1941, p. 7.

p. 231: Stimson: in Stimson Diary, April 16, 1945, with Henry Stimson Papers, Sterling Library, Yale University.

p. 231: Forrestal at the meeting: Stimson Diary, April 23, 1945.

p. 231: Harriman: ibid.

p. 231: Stimson: ibid.

p. 231: Leahy: Truman, *Memoirs*, vol. 1: *Year of Decisions*, p. 78.

p. 232: Truman and Molotov: ibid., p. 82.

p. 232: Stimson: Stimson Diary, April 26, 1945.

p. 234: Stalin's speech: *The New York Times*, February 10, 1946, p. 30.

p. 234: Douglas: quoted by Forrestal in Walter Millis, ed., *The Forrestal Diaries* (New York: Viking, 1951), p. 134.

p. 234: Kennan's Long Telegram: in his *Memoirs*, pp. 547–59.

p. 235: The Clifford Report: appended to Arthur Krock, *Memoirs: 60 Years on the Firing Line* (New York: Funk & Wagnalls, 1968), pp. 422–82.

p. 235: Acheson: in his *Morning and Noon* (Boston: Houghton Mifflin, 1965), pp. 1, 5.

p. 235: Acheson: ibid., pp. 26, 39.

p. 237: Acheson: ibid., p. 103.

p. 237: Acheson: ibid., p. 165.

p. 237: Acheson's Yale Speech: "An American Attitude Toward Foreign Affairs," November 28, 1939, in the Dean Acheson Personal Papers, Sterling Library, Yale University.

p. 238: Acheson on the UN: McGeorge Bundy, ed., *The Pattern of Responsibility: From the Record of Secretary of State Dean Acheson* (Boston: Houghton Mifflin, 1952), p. 17.

p. 238: Acheson on atomic energy: *FRUS, 1945* (Washington, D.C.: GPO, 1967), 2:48–49.

p. 239: Acheson on Truman: Acheson, *Present*, p. v.

p. 240: Stalin: in Milovan Djilas, *Conversations with Stalin* (New York: Harcourt, Brace & World, 1962), p. 182.

p. 241: Acheson: in his *Present*, p. 219.

p. 241: The Truman Doctrine: in *Public Papers of the Presidents: Harry S. Truman, 1947* (Washington: GPO, 1963), pp. 176–80.

p. 242: Acheson: Senate Committee on Foreign Relations, *Hearings Held in Executive Session on S. 938: A Bill to Provide Assistance for Greece and Turkey*, 80th Cong., 1st sess.; also known as *The Legislative Origins of the Truman Doctrine* (Washington: GPO, 1973), pp. 22, 95.

p. 242: Gaddis: in his *The United States and the Origins of the Cold War* (New York: Columbia University Press, 1972), p. 351.

p. 243: Kennan's "X" article: in his *American Diplomacy, 1900–1950* (New York: New American Library, 1951), pp. 89–106.

p. 243: The Rio Pact: Raymond Dennett and Robert K. Turner, *Documents on American Foreign Relations, 1947* (Princeton, N.J.: Princeton University Press, 1949), p. 536.

p. 244: Truman's speech: *Public Papers of the Presidents: Harry S. Truman, 1948* (Washington, D.C.: GPO, 1964), pp. 182–86.

p. 245: Marshall: ibid., p. 1178.

p. 245: Truman and Acheson: Acheson, *Present*, p. 249.

p. 246: Acheson on China: "Letter of Transmittal," the introduction to *The China White Paper* (Stanford, Calif.: Stanford University Press, 1967), pp. xvi–xvii.

p. 247: Acheson's Press Club speech: *Department of State Bulletin,* January 23, 1950, pp. 111–19.

p. 247: McCarthy: quoted in Eric F. Goldman, *The Crucial Decade: America, 1945–1955* (New York: Knopf, 1956), pp. 141–42.

p. 247: Truman: in Acheson, *Present*, p. 366.

p. 248: NSC-68: can be found in *FRUS, 1950* 1:235–92.

p. 249: A governor: quoted in Gaddis Smith, *Dean Acheson*, p. 171.

p. 249: Acheson: these remarks were made during a series of seminars given at Princeton in which Acheson participated. This session occurred on July 8–9, 1953. A transcript can be found in the Dean Acheson Papers at the Harry S Truman Library in Independence, Missouri.

p. 250: Chou En-lai: *The New York Times,* October 2, 1950, p. 3.

p. 250: Acheson's letter: to Richard Neustadt, May 9, 1960. It can be found in Box 23, Folder 295, of the Dean Acheson Personal Papers, at Yale.

p. 251: MacArthur: *Hearings Before the Committee on Armed Services and the Committee on Foreign Relations of the United States Senate, 82nd Congress, 1st Session* to "Conduct an Inquiry into the Military Situation in the Far East and the Facts Surrounding the Relief of General of the Army Douglas MacArthur from His Assignments in the Area," pp. 68, 81–83.

p. 251: Bradley: ibid., p. 732.

p. 251: Acheson: ibid., pp. 1816–18.

p. 252: Acheson: in his *Present*, p. 367.

p. 253: Dulles on moral distinctions: "The Relation of France to a Program of Reconstruction," an address before the Economic Club of New York, March 20, 1922. In Box 4 of the Dulles Papers, Mudd Library, Princeton University.

p. 253: Dulles on nature of Soviet state: *Hearings Before the Committee on*

Foreign Relations, United States Senate, 83d Cong., 1st sess., on "The Nomination of John Foster Dulles," pp. 5–6.

p. 254: Dulles: "The Evolution of Foreign Policy," *Department of State Bulletin,* January 25, 1954, p. 108.

p. 254: Dulles: in Sherman Adams, *Firsthand Report: The Story of the Eisenhower Administration* (New York: Harper & Bros., 1961), p. 124.

p. 255: Dulles: in Anthony Eden, *Full Circle* (Boston: Houghton Mifflin, 1960), p. 156.

p. 256: Dulles: Transcript of a "Face the Nation" interview, October 21, 1956, Dulles Papers, Princeton.

p. 258: Acheson on Dulles: quoted in Walter Isaacson and Evan Thomas, *The Wise Men* (New York: Simon and Schuster, 1986), p. 581.

p. 260: Acheson on Vietnam-Korea parallels: to John Cowles, August 21, 1967, in the Dean Acheson Personal Papers at Yale.

p. 260: Acheson on Truman and Johnson: to Anthony Eden, August 27, 1967, Acheson Personal Papers, Yale.

p. 260: Acheson on the bombing: to John Cowles, August 7, 1967, Acheson Personal Papers, Yale.

p. 261: Acheson to LBJ on Vietnam and the JCS: Isaacson and Thomas, *Wise Men,* p. 687.

p. 261: Acheson on relearning Vietnam: to John Cowles, March 14, 1968, Acheson Personal Papers, Yale.

p. 262: Acheson's "garden path": Isaacson and Thomas, *Wise Men,* p. 694.

p. 262: Acheson meeting with LBJ: ibid., p. 694.

p. 262: LBJ: in his *The Vantage Point: Perspectives on the Presidency, 1963–1969* (New York: Holt, Rinehart & Winston, 1971), p. 418.

p. 262: Acheson on the war: to John Cowles, March 27, 1971, Acheson Personal Papers, Yale.

CHAPTER VIII: SECURING THE HEMISPHERE, 1965–1986

p. 265: The task force: descriptions of its offshore patrols and interviews with its men can be found in Tad Szulc's *Dominican Diary* (New York: Delacorte, 1965).

p. 267: Mann's background: see his entry in the Lyndon Baines Johnson Oral History Collection at the LBJ Library in Austin, Texas.

p. 267: Mann: quoted in Theodore Draper, *The Dominican Revolt: A Case Study in American Policy* (New York: Commentary, 1968), p. 10.

p. 268: Fulbright: *The Congressional Record,* Senate, September 15, 1965, p. 23857.

p. 269: one official: quoted in Philip Geyelin, *Lyndon Johnson and the World* (New York: Praeger, 1966), p. 238.

p. 269: Johnson: Geyelin, *Lyndon Johnson,* pp. 237, 254.

p. 269: one aide: ibid., p. 251.

p. 270: Martin: his account of this meeting can be found in his entry in the LBJ Oral History Collection, pp. 23–25, at the LBJ Library in Austin, Texas.

p. 270: Martin's landing: this account is from his book, *Overtaken by Events* (Garden City, N.Y.: Doubleday, 1966), pp. 662–75.

p. 271: One longtime aide: George Reedy, quoted in Merle Miller, *Lyndon: An Oral Biography* (New York: G. P. Putnam's Sons, 1980), p. 298.

p. 271: Johnson's May 2 speech: in *American Foreign Policy: Current Documents, 1965* (Washington, D.C.: Department of State, 1968) (hereafter *AFPCD*), pp. 961–65.

p. 272: Dean Rusk: *The New York Times*, May 26, 1965, p. 14.

p. 272: The Selden Resolution: *The Congressional Record*, House, September 20, 1965, p. 24347.

p. 274: Franklin Pierce: quoted in Kenneth Bourne, *Britain and the Balance of Power in North America* (Berkeley, Calif.: University of California Press, 1967), p. 178.

p. 276: FDR: *Time*, November 15, 1948, p. 43.

p. 277: Kennan: quoted in Walter LaFeber's admirable study, *Inevitable Revolutions: The United States in Central America* (New York: Norton, 1983), p. 107.

p. 280: Khrushchev: *AFPCD, 1961*, p. 295.

p. 280: Kennedy: Theodore Sorensen, *Kennedy* (New York: Harper & Row, 1965), p. 309.

p. 280: Kennedy to Khrushchev: *AFPCD, 1961*, p. 297.

p. 281: Kennedy's doubts: Sorensen, *Kennedy*, p. 535.

p. 281: Kennedy on the Dominican Republic: Arthur Schlesinger, *A Thousand Days: John F. Kennedy in the White House* (Boston: Houghton Mifflin, 1965), p. 769.

p. 281: Castro: ibid., p. 794.

p. 282: The joint resolution: *AFPCD, 1962*, p. 389.

p. 282: A close adviser: Schlesinger, in *Thousand Days*, pp. 796–97.

pp. 283, 284: Kennedy's address: *AFPCD, 1962*, pp. 399–404.

p. 284: Khrushchev: a statement declassified in 1973 and published in the November 19 issue of the *Department of State Bulletin*, pp. 643–44.

p. 285: Kennedy: *AFPCD, 1963*, p. 355.

p. 285: Johnson: *Public Papers of the Presidents: Lyndon Johnson, 1966* (Washington, D.C.: GPO, 1966), book 2, pp. 1287–88.

p. 286: Kissinger's "dagger": this remark may well be apocryphal, or have been made in reference to all of Latin America; it has been quoted both ways, in its latter form by Walter LaFeber in his *America, Russia and the Cold War* (New York, Knopf, 1985), p. 285.

p. 286: Kissinger to the Chilean: quoted in Seymour Hersh, *The Price of*

Power: Kissinger in the Nixon White House (New York: Summit Books, 1983), p. 263.

p. 289: Reagan: an interview in *The Wall Street Journal,* June 3, 1980, p. 1.

p. 290: Reagan to Congress: see James Chace, *Endless War* (New York: Vintage, 1984), p. 81.

p. 291: The Kissinger Commission: see *The Report of the President's National Bipartisan Commission on Central America* (New York: Macmillan, 1984), passim.

CHAPTER IX: STAR WARS: THE SEARCH FOR ABSOLUTE SECURITY, 1967–1986

p. 294: Teller and Reagan: Dr. Teller gave this account of their meeting and of Reagan's visit to Lawrence Livermore in an interview he graciously granted the authors in February 1987. Dr. Teller wished to underline that these were the facts as best he could remember them.

p. 295: Teller at six: quoted in Stanley A. Blumberg and Gwinn Owens, *Energy and Conflict: The Life and Times of Edward Teller* (New York: G. P. Putnam's Sons, 1976), p. 9.

p. 296: A colleague: quoted in *The New York Times,* March 4, 1985, p. 8.

p. 298: Teller: in his *The Legacy of Hiroshima,* with Allen Brown (Garden City, N.Y.: Doubleday, 1962), pp. 233–35, 128.

pp. 298, 99: Teller: the first comment comes from a piece in *The New York Times,* March 4, 1985, p. 8, the second from the authors' interview.

p. 302: Winston Churchill: quoted in Daniel Yergin, *Shattered Peace: Origins of the Cold War and the National Security State* (Boston: Houghton Mifflin, 1977), p. 115.

p. 302: Byrnes and Molotov: ibid., p. 123. See Yergin also for Stalin's attitude toward the American bomb.

p. 303: Stimson's memo: the text of the memorandum and its covering letter (from which the quote concerning Russian liberty is taken) can be found in Stimson and McGeorge Bundy's *On Active Service in Peace and War* (New York: Harper & Bros., 1948), pp. 642–46.

p. 303: Stimson: ibid., p. 651.

p. 305: Dulles: in *Life* 40, no. 3 (January 16, 1956).

p. 305: Quarles: quoted in Samuel P. Huntington, *The Common Defense: Strategic Programs in National Politics* (New York: Columbia University Press, 1961), p. 101.

p. 306: Teller: in his *Legacy,* p. 124.

p. 306: Wohlstetter: in his "The Delicate Balance of Terror," *Foreign Affairs,* January 1959.

p. 308: Wiesner and York: in their "National Security and the Nuclear-Test Ban," *Scientific American* 211, no. 4 (October 1964).

p. 309: McNamara: his address, "The Dynamics of Nuclear Strategy," given before an annual convention of United Press editors and publishers, can be found in the October 9, 1967, *Department of State Bulletin,* pp. 443–51.

p. 310: Bundy: in his "To Cap the Volcano," *Foreign Affairs,* October 1969.

p. 312: Harrison Schmitt: *The New York Times,* March 4, 1985, p. 8.

p. 313: Reagan's speech: *The New York Times,* March 24, 1983, p. 20.

p. 314: Bundy et al.: in their "The President's Choice: Star Wars or Arms Control," *Foreign Affairs* 63, no. 2 (Winter, 1984/85).

p. 314: Haig: *The New York Times,* March 4, 1985, p. 8.

p. 314: Abrahamson: this theme is sounded by the general wherever he goes, this particular quote being taken from the text of a statement he submitted to the Senate Subcommittee on Appropriations, March 5, 1986.

p. 315: The Center for Defense Information: in their *Defense Monitor* 15, no. 2 (1986): p. 1.

p. 315: Weinberger: quoted in *The Fallacy of Star Wars* by the Union of Concerned Scientists (New York: Vintage, 1984), p. 28.

p. 316: Weinberger: *The Wall Street Journal,* February 10, 1983.

p. 316: Teller: in his *Legacy,* p. 129.

EPILOGUE

p. 320: one nuclear analyst: Lawrence Freedman, in his "The First Two Generations of Nuclear Strategists," in Peter Paret, ed., *Makers of Modern Strategy from Machiavelli to the Nuclear Age* (Princeton, N.J.: Princeton University Press, 1986), p. 773.

INDEX

ABOUT THE AUTHORS

James Chace grew up in Fall River, Massachusetts. He graduated from Harvard in 1953, Phi Beta Kappa, and then studied politics in Paris. During the 1960s he helped found *Interplay*, a magazine of politics, and then went to *Foreign Affairs* in 1970 where he worked as managing editor until 1983. During that period he published many, many articles on politics and foreign policy, as well as three books on foreign policy: *Endless War: How We Got Involved in Central America—And What Can Be Done* (Vintage, orig. paperback, 1984), *Solvency: The Price of Survival* (Random, 1981) and *A World Elsewhere: The New American Foreign Policy* (Scribners, 1973). He joined the staff of *The New York Times Book Review* as an editor for international affairs in 1983, and has recently left the *Times* to go to the Carnegie Endowment for International Peace to write on foreign policy. He was a Guggenheim fellow in 1986.

Caleb Carr was born in Manhattan, attended Kenyon College, and graduated from New York University where he took a degree in history, specializing in diplomatic and military history. He worked at the Council on Foreign Relations for four years and since 1980 has worked closely as a researcher with a number of authors on books and articles dealing with international relations and American history. He is the author of a novel, *Casing the Promised Land*.